Regression Models for Categorical and Limited Dependent Variables

Advanced Quantitative Techniques
in the Social Sciences

Regression Models for Categorical and Limited Dependent Variables

J. Scott Long

Advanced Quantitative Techniques
in the Social Sciences Series

7

SAGE Publications
International Educational and Professional Publisher
Thousand Oaks London New Delhi

For information address:

SAGE Publications, Inc.
2455 Teller Road
Thousand Oaks, California 91320
E-mail: order@sagepub.com

SAGE Publications Ltd.
6 Bonhill Street
London EC2A 4PU
United Kingdom

SAGE Publications India Pvt. Ltd.
M-32 Market
Greater Kailash I
New Delhi 110 048 India

Printed in the United States of America

Library of Congress Cataloging-in-Publication Data

Long, J. Scott
    Regression models for categorical and limited dependent variables
/ author, J. Scott Long.

        p.   cm. — (Advanced quantitative techniques in the social
sciences ; v. 7)
    Includes bibliographical references and index.
    ISBN 0-8039-7374-8 (cloth : alk. paper)
    1. Regression analysis.   I. Title.   II. Series: Advanced
quantitative techniques in the social sciences ; 7.
QA278.2.L65   1997   96-35710
519.5′36—dc20

05   10

Production Coordinator: Astrid Virding
Cover Design: Lesa Valdez
Book Design: Ravi Balasuriyia
Print Buyer: Anna Chin

To Valerie and Megan

Contents

List of Figures

List of Tables

Series Editor's Introduction

The tools broadly labeled as "regression" have expanded in number and power over the past two decades. In the "old days," researchers trying to link a set of explanatory variables to a single response variable were essentially limited to the general linear model: analysis of variance—analysis of covariance and multiple regression. These were useful tools when the response variable was measured on an equal interval scale. However, in the social and biomedical sciences, few of the response variables of interest come in equal interval metrics. Responses to survey questions are often, even typically, categorical (e.g., "employed," "unemployed") or ordinal (e.g., "agree," "uncertain," "disagree"). The same holds for the outcomes of people processing and medical institutions: sick or well, arrested or not, dropped out of school or not, lived or died, high school diploma or college degree or postgraduate degree, and so on. For these kinds of response variables, the general linear model is inappropriate and will often give misleading answers.

The solution within a regression framework is "regression-like" models, sometimes collected within the framework of the generalized linear model. The basic idea is still work with a linear combination of explanatory variables, but to allow them to be related to the response variables in a nonlinear way through a "link" function. Then the disturbance is given an appropriate distribution, usually not the normal. For example, in logistic regression the log of the odds of some binary outcome (e.g., lived or died) is regressed on the usual linear combination of explanatory variables with the underlying conditional distribution of the binary outcomes taken to be binomial.

In this volume, Scott Long addresses these and related kinds of statistical procedures. I am very pleased to add Scott Long's *Limited Dependent Variables* to the series. The topics are of both practical and theoretical importance, and Professor Long has done a excellent job of exposition. The book is well suited as a text for graduate students in the social and biomedical sciences. It will also serve as a wonderful reference for practitioners.

The core of Professor Long's approach is "statistical modeling." A "model" is a simplified rendering of the processes being studied and/or an algebraic representation of a scientific theory. A model is not merely a data reduction device. Given the emphasis on modeling, it is especially important that the techniques discussed be used judiciously and that Professor Long's caveats be taken to heart. Thus, even a state-of-the-art statistical analysis is unlikely to salvage much of use from a seriously flawed dataset. In addition, one must be able to make the case that the statistical model maps well onto the empirical phenomena being studied. Also, researchers use cause-and-effect language at their peril unless there has been real manipulation of the explanatory variables. Finally, when statistical inference is to be undertaken, the sources of uncertainty have to be articulated in a fashion that is consistent with what the model assumes about how the uncertainty operates.

There is really no argument about the validity of these principles, but there are strong disagreements about what these principles mean in practice. To put it a bit (but only a bit) too starkly, at one extreme there are those who never saw a model they did not like. At the opposite extreme are those who never saw a model they liked. Most researchers fall between these extremes where the issues often boil down to where the burden of proof lies—for some, a model is acceptable as long as there is no strong evidence to undermine it. For others, a model is unacceptable unless there is strong evidence to support it. I suspect that social and biomedical researchers tend to fall in the first camp and that statisticians tend to fall more in the second camp. However, from this tension in part has come a range of diagnostic tools that can help (but only help) to determine how sound a model is. Professor Long is to be commended for including a healthy dose of those diagnostics in this book. Practitioners should take them very seriously.

Finally, a word about software. For most of the procedures discussed in those book there exist statistical routines in all of the major statistical packages. This is both a blessing and a curse. The blessing is that minimal computer skills are required. The curse is that minimal computer skills are required. Right answers *and* wrong answers are easy to obtain. With this in mind, Professor Long discusses some of the most popular software. This too deserves serious study.

RICHARD BERK

Preface

This book is about regression models that are appropriate when the dependent variable is binary, ordinal, nominal, censored, truncated, or counted. I refer to these outcomes as categorical and limited dependent variables (CLDVs, for short). Within the last decade, advances in statistical software and increases in computing power have made it nearly as easy to estimate models for CLDVs as the linear regression model. This is reflected in the rapidly increasing use of these models. Nearly every issue of major journals in the social sciences contains examples of models such as logit, probit, or negative binomial regression. While computational problems have largely been eliminated, the models are more difficult to learn and to use. There are two quite different reasons for this. First, the models are nonlinear. As readers will learn well, the nonlinearity of many models for CLDVs makes interpretation of the results more difficult. With the linear regression model, most of the work is done when the estimates are obtained. With models for CLDVs, the task of interpretation is just beginning. Unfortunately, all too often when these models are used, the substantive meaning of the parameters is incompletely explained, incorrectly explained, or simply ignored. Sometimes only the statistical significance or possibly the sign is mentioned. A second reason that these models are difficult to learn is that while models for CLDVs are more complicated than the linear regression model, most books only discuss them briefly, if at all. While hundreds of pages may be devoted to the linear regression model, only a dozen or two pages are devoted to models for CLDVs.

My goal in writing this book is to provide a unified treatment of the most useful models for categorical and limited dependent variables. Throughout the book, the links among the models are made explicit, and common methods of derivation, interpretation, and testing are applied. Whenever possible, I relate these models to the more familiar linear regression model. While Chapter 2 is a brief review of this model, I assume that readers are familiar with the specification, estimation, and interpretation of the linear regression model.

The best way to learn these models is by seeing them applied to real data and by applying them as you read. To that end, I illustrate each model with data from a variety of applications ranging from attitudes toward working mothers to scientific productivity. You may find it useful to reproduce the results presented in the book using your statistical package. To that end, I have placed the data from the book along with sample programs on my homepage on the World Wide Web (http://www.indiana.edu/~jsl650) or access the Sage Website http://www.sagepub.com/sagepage/authors.HTM for information. While I used GAUSS-Markov for most of the computations, I will be adding sample programs written in Stata, SAS, and LIMDEP. And, a book on using Stata to estimate models for CLDVs is planned.

This book grew out of a course on categorical data analysis taught from 1978 to 1989 at Washington State University and at Indiana University since 1989. Teaching this course is a constant challenge and source of satisfaction. If you find the explanations that follow to be clear, it is largely the fault of those students who refused to accept unclear explanations. (A few refused to accept clear explanations, but that is a different issue.) Questions from students continually motivated me to find a way to make difficult topics accessible. And, indeed, some of the topics are difficult. While I have sought to present the models fully and clearly with the simplest mathematics possible, some readers will find the mathematics to be a challenge. I hope that these readers will persist, because I have yet to find an person who could not master these techniques and use them effectively to learn more about the social world.

J. Scott Long
Bloomington, IN
June 12, 1996

Acknowledgments

I am indebted to the many people who gave me comments on earlier drafts: Dick Berk, Ken Bollen, Brian Driscoll, Scott Eliason, Lowell Hargens, David James, Bob Kaufman, Herb Smith, Adrian Raftery, Ron Schoenberg, and Yu Xie. Members of the Workshop in Quantitative Methods at Indiana University—Clem Brooks, Bob Carini, Brian Driscoll, Laurie Ervin, David James, Patricia McManus, and Karl Schuessler—gave me feedback that substantially improved the book. Paul Allison, Laurie Ervin, Jacques Hagenaars, Scott Hershberger, and Pravin Trivedi gave me exceptionally detailed and useful advice. Technical Typesetting Inc. did an outstanding job typesetting the book. And, I want to thank C. Deborah Laughton, my editor at Sage, for all that she has done for me and this book. While the suggestions that these people made resulted in a much better book, I am responsible (as they say) for any errors that remain. Research support from the College of Arts and Sciences at Indiana University is gratefully acknowledged.

While planning and writing this book I encountered more than the usual number of problems, few of which were related to the book. My wife Valerie and my daughter Megan shared these challenges with me, and to them I dedicate this book.

Abbreviations and Notation

The following abbreviations and notation are used throughout the book. While I have tried to use consistent notation and to avoid using the same symbol for more than one purpose, there are a few exceptions, such as λ being used as the inverse Mills ratio and the logistic distribution.

Abbreviations

BRM:	binary response model.
cdf:	cumulative density function.
CLDVs:	categorical and limited dependent variables.
CLM:	conditional logit model.
IIA:	independence of irrelevant alternatives.
LM test:	Lagrange multiplier test.
LPM:	linear probability model.
LR test:	likelihood ratio test.
LRM:	linear regression model.
ML:	maximum likelihood.
MNLM:	multinomial logit model.
NB:	negative binomial.
NBRM:	negative binomial regression model.
OLS:	ordinary least squares.

ORM: ordinal regression model.
pdf: probability density function.
PRM: Poisson regression model.
ZINB model: zero-inflated negative binomial model.
ZIP model: zero-inflated Poisson model.

Notation

$\approx$: is approximately equal to (e.g., $\pi \approx 22/7$).
$D(M)$: the deviance of the model M.
e: the residual $y - \hat{y}$.
$\exp(x)$ or e^x: the exponential of x.
$E(y \mid \mathbf{x}, x_k)$: the expected value of y given $\mathbf{x}$ and noting the value of x_k.
$f(\cdot)$: either the logistic pdf $\lambda(\cdot)$ or the normal pdf $\phi(\cdot)$.
$F(\cdot)$: either the logistic cdf $\Lambda(\cdot)$ or the normal cdf $\Phi(\cdot)$.
$G^2(M_C \mid M_U)$: the likelihood ratio statistic comparing the constrained model M_C to the unconstrained model M_U.
$G^2(M_\beta)$: the likelihood ratio statistic comparing M_β to the model with just the intercept or intercepts.
$\mathbf{H}$: the Hessian matrix of second derivatives of the log likelihood function; also used for the hat matrix in Section 4.2.
i: the observation number (e.g., x_i).
J: the number of dependent categories in nominal and ordinal models.
k: the variable number (e.g., β_k).
K: the number of x's.
$L(a \mid b)$: the likelihood of parameters a given data b [e.g., $L(\boldsymbol{\beta} \mid \mathbf{X})$].
LRX^2: the likelihood ratio chi-square statistic; the same as G^2.
M_C: the constrained model (i.e., M_U with added constraints).
M_F: the full model with as many parameters as observations.
M_U: the unconstrained model.
M_α: the model with only the intercept or intercepts included.
M_β: the model with regressors and intercepts included.
N: the sample size.
$\mathcal{N}(\mu, \sigma^2)$: the normal distribution with mean μ and variance σ^2.
R^2: the coefficient of determination.
s^2: the sample variance of the residual e.
s_k: the sample standard deviation of x_k.
t: a t-statistic.
$\mathrm{Var}(\hat{\boldsymbol{\theta}})$: the variance-covariance matrix of $\hat{\boldsymbol{\theta}}$.
$\mathrm{Var}(\mathbf{x})$: the variance-covariance matrix of the x's.
W: the Wald chi-square test statistic; same as X^2.
X^2: the Wald chi-square test statistic; the same as W.

x:	the independent variable when there is a single independent variable (e.g., $y = \alpha + \beta x + \varepsilon$).
x_k:	the kth independent variable.
x_k^S:	the kth independent variable standardized to have a variance of 1.
$\overleftarrow{x_k}$:	the lower extreme of x_k; the minimum of x_k if β_k is positive; else the maximum.
$\overrightarrow{x_k}$:	the upper extreme of x_k; the maximum of x_k if β_k is positive; else the minimum.
$\mathbf{x}_i$:	a row vector of independent variables for the ith observation; the ith row of $\mathbf{X}$.
$\overline{\mathbf{x}}$:	a row vector containing the means of the independent variables.
$\mathbf{X}$:	a matrix of independent variables for the entire sample.
y:	the observed dependent variable; in Chapter 7, y is the observed censored variable.
y^*:	the latent dependent variable.
y^S:	y standardized to have a variance of 1.
$y \mid y > \tau$:	the truncated variable y given that y is greater than τ.
z:	a z-statistic.
$\mathbf{z}_{im}$:	a row vector of independent variables for ith observation for outcome m for the CLM in Chapter 7.
α and β:	the intercept and slope when there is a single independent variable (e.g., $y = \alpha + \beta x + \varepsilon$).
α:	the dispersion parameter for the NBRM.
$\boldsymbol{\beta}$:	a vector of coefficients; β_0 is the intercept; β_k is the coefficient for x_k.
β_k:	the unstandardized coefficient for x_k.
$\beta_{k, m\mid n}$:	in the MNLM, the coefficient for the effect of x_k on the odds of outcome m versus outcome n.
$\boldsymbol{\beta}_{m\mid n}$:	a vector of coefficients $\beta_{k, m\mid n}$ in the MNLM.
β_k^S:	the fully standardized coefficient for x_k; y and the x's are standardized.
$\beta_k^{S_x}$:	the x-standardized coefficient for x_k; y is not standardized but x_k is.
$\beta_k^{S_y}$:	the y-standardized coefficient for x_k; y is standardized but the x's are not.
δ:	an abbreviation for $(\mathbf{x}\boldsymbol{\beta} - \tau)/\sigma$ in Chapter 7.
δ_L:	an abbreviation for $(\tau_L - \mathbf{x}\boldsymbol{\beta})/\sigma$ in the two-limit tobit model of Chapter 7.
δ_U:	an abbreviation for $(\tau_U - \mathbf{x}\boldsymbol{\beta})/\sigma$ in the two-limit tobit model of Chapter 7.
$\overline{\Delta}$:	the average absolute discrete change.
$\Delta E(y \mid \mathbf{x})/\Delta x_k$:	the discrete change in y for a change in x_k holding other variables constant.

$\partial E(y \mid \mathbf{x})/\partial x_k$:   the partial change in y for an infinitesimal change in x_k holding other variables constant; also called the marginal effect.

ε: the error in equation (e.g., $y^* = \alpha + \beta x + \varepsilon$).

$\boldsymbol{\theta}$:   a vector of parameters [e.g., $\boldsymbol{\theta} = (\alpha\ \beta\ \sigma)'$].

$\lambda(\cdot)$, $\Lambda(\cdot)$:   the pdf and cdf for the standard logistic distribution with mean 0 and variance $\pi^2/3$.

$\lambda^S(\cdot)$, $\Lambda^S(\cdot)$:   the pdf and cdf for the standardized logistic distribution with mean 0 and variance 1.

$\lambda(\cdot)$:   the inverse Mills ratio defined as $\phi(\cdot)/\Phi(\cdot)$; used in Chapter 7.

λ_i: the inverse Mills ratio for the ith observation.

μ: the population mean.

$\prod_i y_i$:   the product $y_1 \times y_2 \times \cdots$.

σ: the standard deviation of ε given $\mathbf{x}$.

σ_k: the standard deviation of x_k.

σ_y: the standard deviation of y.

τ: the censoring threshold in the tobit, probit, and logit models.

τ_m: the threshold or cutpoint for the ORM.

τ_y: the value assigned to censored cases in tobit models.

τ_L: the lower threshold for the two-limit tobit model.

τ_U: the upper threshold for the two-limit tobit model.

$\phi(\cdot)$, $\Phi(\cdot)$:   the pdf and cdf for the standard normal distribution with mean 0 and variance 1.

ψ: the probability of being in a group where the count is always 0. Used with zero modified count models.

$\Omega(\mathbf{x})$:   the odds of outcome given $\mathbf{x}$.

$\Omega(\mathbf{x}, x_k)$:   the odds of outcome given $\mathbf{x}$ and noting specifically the value of x_k.

$\Omega_m(\mathbf{x})$:   the odds of outcomes less than or equal to m versus greater than m.

$\Omega_{m|n}(\mathbf{x})$:   the odds of outcome m versus n given $\mathbf{x}$ for the MNLM.

1 Introduction

The linear regression model is the most commonly used statistical method in the social sciences. Hundreds of books describe this model, and thousands of applications can be found. With few exceptions, the regression model assumes that the dependent variable is continuous and has been measured for all cases in the sample. Yet, many outcomes of fundamental interest to social scientists are not continuous or are not observed for all cases. This book considers regression models that are appropriate when the dependent variable is censored, truncated, binary, ordinal, nominal, or count. I refer to these variables as categorical and limited dependent variables (hereafter CLDVs).

A brief review of the literature in the social sciences shows how common CLDVs are. Indeed, continuous dependent variables may be the exception. Here are a few examples:

- *Binary variables* have two categories and are often used to indicate that an event has occurred or that some characteristic is present. Is an adult a member of the labor force? Did a citizen vote in the last election? Does a high school student decide to go to college? Is a consumer more likely to buy the same brand or to try a new brand? Did someone answer a given question on a survey?

- *Ordinal variables* have categories that can be ranked. Surveys often ask respondents to indicate their agreement to a statement using the choices

1

strongly agree, agree, disagree, and strongly disagree. Items asking the frequency of occurrence might use the categories often, occasionally, seldom, and never. Political orientation may be classified as radical, liberal, and conservative. Educational attainment can be measured in terms of the highest degree received, with the ordinal categories of less than high school, high school, college, and graduate school. Military rank and civil service grade are inherently ordinal.

- *Nominal variables* occur when there are multiple outcomes that cannot be ordered. Occupations can be grouped as manual, trade, blue collar, white collar, and professional. Marital status might be coded as single, married, divorced, and widowed. Political parties in European countries can be considered nominal classifications. Studies of brand preference may include choices among unordered alternatives.

- *Censored variables* occur when the value of a variable is unknown over some range of the variable. The classic example is expenditures for durable goods. Individuals with less disposable income than the price of the cheapest durable good will necessarily have zero expenditure. Measures of workers' hourly wages are restricted on the lower end by the minimum wage rate. Variables measuring percentage, such as the percentage of homes damaged in a natural disaster, are censored below at 0 and above at 100. Censoring can also occur for methodological reasons. In the 1990 Census, all salaries greater than $140,000 were recorded as $140,000 to ensure confidentiality.

- *Count variables* indicate the number of times that some event has occurred. How often did a person visit the doctor last year? How many jobs did someone have? How many strikes occurred? How many articles did a scientist publish? How many political demonstrations occurred? How many children did a family have? How many years of formal education were completed? How many newspapers were founded during a given period?

The level of measurement of a variable is not always clear or unambiguous. Indeed, you might disagree with some of the examples given above. Carter (1971, p. 12) notes that "...statements about levels of measurement of a [variable] cannot be sensibly made in isolation from the theoretical and substantive context in which the [variable] is to be used. Assumptions that a variable is somehow 'intrinsically' interval (ordinal, nominal) are analytically misleading." Education is a good example. Education can be measured as a binary variable that distinguishes those with a high school education or less from others. Or, it could be ordinal indicating the highest degree received: junior high, high school, college, or graduate. Or, it can be a count variable indicating the number of years of school completed. Each of these is reasonable and appropriate depending on the substantive purpose of the analysis.

Once the level of the dependent variable is determined, it is important to match the model used to the level of measurement. If the model chosen assumes the wrong level of measurement, the estimator could be biased, inefficient, or simply inappropriate. Fortunately, there are a large number of models specifically designed for CLDVs. Binary logit and probit are appropriate for binary outcomes. The ordered logit and probit models explicitly deal with the ordered nature of the dependent variable. Multinomial logit is appropriate for nominal outcomes. The tobit model is designed for censored outcomes. Furthermore, a variety of models such as Poisson and negative binomial regression can be used for count outcomes. These and related models are the subject of this book.

Until recently, the greatest obstacle in using models for CLDVs was the lack of software that was flexible, stable, and easy to use. This limitation no longer applies since these models can be estimated routinely with standard software. Now, the greatest impediment is the complexity of the models and the difficulty in interpreting the results. The difficulties arise because most models for CLDVs are nonlinear.

1.1. Linear and Nonlinear Models

The linear regression model is linear, while most models for CLDVs are nonlinear. This difference is so basic for understanding the materials in later chapters that I begin with a general overview of the implications of nonlinearity for interpreting the effects of independent variables. Just as the nonlinearities introduced by relativity theory made physical models substantially more complicated than their Newtonian counterparts, the use of nonlinear statistical models has added new complications for the data analyst.

Figure 1.1 shows a linear and a nonlinear model predicting the dependent variable y. Each model has two independent variables: x is continuous and d is dichotomous with values 0 and 1. To keep the example simple, I assume that there is no random error. Panel A plots the linear model

$$y = \alpha + \beta x + \delta d \qquad [1.1]$$

The solid line beginning at α plots y as x changes when $d = 0$: $y = \alpha + \beta x$. The dashed line beginning at $\alpha + \delta$ plots y as x changes when

Panel A: Linear Model

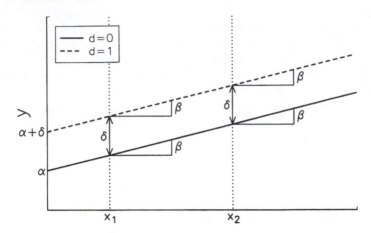

Panel B: Nonlinear Model

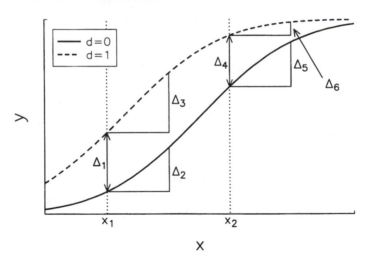

X

Figure 1.1. Effects of Continuous and Dummy Variables in Linear and Nonlinear Models

$d = 1$: $y = \alpha + \beta x + 1\delta = (\alpha + \delta) + \beta x$. The effect of x on y can be computed by taking the partial derivative with respect to x:

$$\frac{\partial y}{\partial x} = \frac{\partial (\alpha + \beta x + \delta d)}{\partial x} = \beta$$

The partial derivative, often called the *marginal effect*, is the ratio of the change in y to the change in x, when the change in x is infinitely small, holding d constant. In a linear model, the partial derivative is the same at *all* values of x and d. Consequently, when x increases by one unit, y increases by β units regardless of the current level of x or d. This is shown in panel A by the four small triangles with bases of length 1 and heights of length β.

The effect of d cannot be computed by taking the partial derivative since d is not continuous. Instead, we measure the *discrete change* in y as d changes from 0 to 1, holding x constant:

$$\frac{\Delta y}{\Delta d} = (\alpha + \beta x + \delta 1) - (\alpha + \beta x + \delta 0) = \delta$$

When d changes from 0 to 1, y changes by δ units regardless of the level of x. This is shown in panel A by the two arrows marking the distance between the solid and dashed lines.

Panel B plots the model

$$y = g(\alpha^* + \beta^* x + \delta^* d) \qquad [1.2]$$

where g is a nonlinear function. For example, for the logit model of Chapter 3, Equation 1.2 becomes

$$y = \frac{\exp(\alpha^* + \beta^* x + \delta^* d)}{1 + \exp(\alpha^* + \beta^* x + \delta^* d)} \qquad [1.3]$$

Interpretation of the effects of x and d is now more complicated. The solid curve for $d = 0$ and the dashed curve for $d = 1$ are no longer parallel: $\Delta_1 \neq \Delta_4$. The effect of a unit change in x differs according to the level of both d and x: $\Delta_2 \neq \Delta_3 \neq \Delta_5 \neq \Delta_6$. The partial derivative of y with respect to x is a function of both x and d. In general, the effect of a unit change in a variable depends on the values of all variables in the model and is no longer simply equal to a parameter of the model.

While Equation 1.2 is nonlinear in y, it is often possible to find some function h that transforms the nonlinear model into a linear model:

$$h(y) = \alpha^* + \beta^* x + \delta^* d$$

For example, we can rewrite Equation 1.3 as

$$\ln\left(\frac{y}{1-y}\right) = \alpha^* + \beta^* x + \delta^* d$$

(*Show this.*[1]) The dependent variable is now $\ln y/(1 - y)$, a quantity known as the *logit*. The logit increases by β^* units for every unit increase in x, holding d constant. As with Equation 1.1, this is true regardless of the level of x or d. The problem is that it is often unclear what a unit increase in $h(y)$ means. For example, an increase of β^* in the logit is meaningless to most people.

One of the greatest difficulties in effectively using models for CLDVs is interpreting the nonlinear effects of the independent variables. An all too common, albeit unnecessary, solution is to talk only about the statistical significance of coefficients without indicating how these parameters correspond to meaningful changes in the outcome of interest. A key objective of this book is to show how models for CLDVs can be effectively interpreted.

Throughout the book, I use the term "effect" to refer to a change in an outcome for a change in an independent variable, holding all other variables constant. For example, in the probit model the effect of education on labor force participation might be described as: for an additional year of education the probability of being in the labor force increases by .05, holding all other variables at their means. Or, for count models we might conclude: for each increase in income of $1000, the expected number of children in the family decreases by 5%, holding all other variables constant. The interpretation of an "effect" as causal depends on the nature of the problem being analyzed and the assumptions that a researcher is willing to make. For a detailed discussion of the issues involved in making causal inferences, see Sobel (1995) and the literature cited therein.

1.2. Organization

Chapter 2 reviews the linear regression model to highlight issues that are important for the models in later chapters. Maximum likelihood estimation is introduced within this familiar context to make it is easier to understand how to apply this method to the models in later chapters. Chapter 3 develops models for binary outcomes. I begin with regression of a binary variable to illustrate how CLDVs can cause violations of the assumptions of the linear regression model. Binary probit and logit are first derived using an unobserved or latent dependent variable. I then

---

[1] Exercises for the reader are given in italics. Solutions are found in the Appendix.

show how the same model can be understood as a nonlinear probability model without appealing to a latent variable. Issues of identification are introduced to explain the apparent differences in results from the logit and probit models. Since numerical methods are often necessary for estimating these models, as well as later models, these methods are discussed in some detail. I also introduce a variety of approaches for interpreting the results from nonlinear models. These techniques are the basis for interpreting all of the models in later chapters. Chapter 4 reviews standard statistical tests associated with maximum likelihood estimation, and considers a variety of measures for assessing the fit of a model. Chapter 5 extends the binary logit and probit models to ordered outcomes. While the resulting ordered logit and probit models are simple extensions of their binary counterparts, having additional outcome categories makes interpretation more complex. Chapter 6 presents the multinomial and conditional logit models for nominal outcomes. The greatest difficulty in using these models is the large number of parameters required and the corresponding problems of interpretation. Chapter 7 considers models with censored and truncated dependent variables, with a focus on the tobit model. The tobit model is developed in terms of a latent variable that is mapped to the observed, censored outcome. The chapter ends by considering a number of related models, including models for sample selection bias. Chapter 8 presents models for count outcomes, beginning with the Poisson regression model. Negative binomial regression and zero modified models are considered as alternatives that allow for overdispersion or heteroscedasticity in the data. Chapter 9 compares and contrasts the models from earlier chapters, and discusses the links between these models and models not discussed in the book, such as log-linear and event history models.

The material in this book can be learned most effectively by reading the chapters in order, but it is possible to skip some chapters or to change the order in which others are read. Everyone should read Chapter 2 to learn the basic terminology and notation. Chapter 3 is essential for all that follows since it introduces key concepts, such as latent variables, and methods of interpretation, such as discrete change. Those who are familiar with Wald and likelihood ratio tests can skip that section of Chapter 4. The discussion of assessing fit in Chapter 4 is not needed for later chapters. Chapter 5 on ordinal outcomes can be read after Chapter 6 on nominal outcomes. Chapter 8 on count models builds on the results for truncated distributions in Chapter 7 to develop the zero modified models. However, most of Chapter 8 is accessible without reading Chapter 7.

While each model studied has unique characteristics, there are important similarities among the models that are exploited. First, each model has the same *systematic component* (McCullagh and Nelder, 1989, pp. 26–27). Specifically, each model enters the independent variables as a linear combination: $\beta_0 + \beta_1 x_1 + \cdots + \beta_K x_K$. Consequently, in specifying your model you can use all of the "tricks" that you know for entering variables in the linear regression model: nominal variables can be coded as a set of dummy variables; nonlinearities can be introduced by transforming the independent variables; the effects of an independent variable can differ by group by adding interaction variables; and so on. Second, each model is estimated by maximum likelihood. Once the general characteristics of maximum likelihood are understood and the associated statistical tests are learned, these can be applied to all of the models. Third, the same general ideas are used for interpreting each model. Expected values, marginal effects, and discrete changes are computed at interesting values of the independent variables and are presented in plots or tables. Fourth, whenever possible the mathematical tools used for one model are carried over in the presentation of later models.

Many of these models can be derived in different ways. For example, the binary logit model can be developed as a latent variable model in which the observed binary variable is an imperfect measurement of an underlying latent variable. Or, the model can be derived as a discrete choice model in which an individual chooses the outcome that provides the maximum utility. Finally, the model can be viewed as a probability model with the characteristic S-shaped relationship between independent variables and the probability of an event. Each of these approaches results in the same formula relating the independent variables to the expected probability. I show alternative derivations of some models in order to highlight different characteristics of the models. This also serves to link my presentation to the diverse literature in which these models were developed.

Models for CLDVs were often developed independently in different fields, such as biometrics, engineering, statistics, and econometrics, with very little contact across the fields. Consequently, there is no universally accepted notation or terminology. For example, the ordered logit model of Chapter 5 is also known as the ordinal logit model, the proportional odds model, the parallel regression model, and the grouped continuous model. I have tried to use what appears to be emerging as standard terminology within the social sciences. Every effort has been made to keep the notation consistent across chapters. On rare occasions, this has resulted in notation that is different from that commonly used in the literature. To help you keep the notation clear, a table of notation is given on pages xxvii to xxx.

1.3. Orientation

Before ending this chapter, a few words about the general orientation of this book are in order. This is a book about data analysis rather than about statistical theory. The mathematics has been kept as simple as possible without oversimplifying the models in ways that could result in misuse or misunderstanding. The mathematics that is used, however, is essential for understanding the correct *application* of these models. To master the methods, it is important to work with the equations and to try some derivations on your own. To help you do this, I have included exercises in italics at various points. In the long run, it will be worth your while to think about each of these questions before proceeding. Brief answers to the exercises are given in the Appendix.

Seeing how these models can be applied in substantive research is also important for understanding the models. Accordingly, each chapter includes a substantive example that is used to illustrate the interpretation of each model. You are also encouraged to apply these models to your own data while you are reading. To this end, comments are given about four statistical packages for estimating models for CLDVs: LIMDEP Version 7 (Greene, 1995), Markov Version 2 (Long, 1993), SAS Version 6 (SAS Institute, 1990a), and Stata Version 5 (Stata Corporation, 1997). These comments are not designed to teach you how to use these packages, but rather are general comments about difficulties that might be encountered with any statistical package. While nearly all of the analyses in the book were done with my program Markov (Long, 1993) written in GAUSS (Aptech Systems Inc., 1996), any of these four packages could have been used for most analyses. To help you use these methods, I have placed the data sets, programs, and output for the examples on my homepage (http://www.indiana.edu/˜jsl650) or access the Sage Website http://www.sagepub.com/sagepage/authors.HTM for information.

While this book contains what I believe are the most basic and useful methods for the analysis of CLDVs, a number of important topics were excluded due to limitations of space. Topics that have not been discussed include: robust and nonparametric methods of estimation, specification tests (Davidson & MacKinnon, 1993, pp. 522–528; Greene, 1993, pp. 648–650), complex sampling, multiple equation systems (see Browne & Arminger, 1995, for a review), and hierarchical models (Longford,

1995, pp. 551–556). Additional citations are given in later chapters. While these are extremely important topics, they presuppose the models considered here and are beyond the scope of this book. I chose a fuller treatment of a smaller number of models rather than less detailed discussion of more methods. Hopefully, this will provide a firm foundation for further reading from the vast and growing literature on limited and categorical dependent variables.

1.4. Bibliographic Notes

Each chapter ends with "Bibliographic Notes." These notes present a brief history of the models in that chapter and provide a list of basic sources.

There are several alternative sources that deal with some of the models presented in this book. Maddala (1983) considers dozens of models for CLDVs. Amemiya (1985) reviews extensions to the tobit model, including sample selection models. McCullagh and Nelder (1989) discuss some of the same models from the standpoint of the generalized linear model. King (1989a) presents many of these models with particular application to political science. Agresti (1990) is particularly useful if all of your variables are nominal or ordinal. Liao (1994) considers the interpretation of probability models within the context of the generalized linear model. Arminger (1995) provides a comprehensive review of many related topics. Finally, Stokes et al. (1995) discuss models for categorical variables in terms of the SAS system.

2 Continuous Outcomes: The Linear Regression Model

This chapter briefly reviews the linear regression model (LRM). While I assume that you are familiar with regression, you should read this chapter carefully since the model is described in a way that facilitates the development of models for categorical and limited dependent variables. Moreover, while the LRM is usually estimated by ordinary least squares, I focus on maximum likelihood estimation since this method is used extensively in later chapters. My discussion of the LRM is by no means comprehensive; for further details, see the references in Section 2.8.

2.1. The Linear Regression Model

The linear regression model can be written as

$$y_i = \beta_0 + \beta_1 x_{i1} + \cdots + \beta_k x_{ik} + \cdots + \beta_K x_{iK} + \varepsilon_i \qquad [2.1]$$

where y is the dependent variable, the x's are independent variables, and ε is a stochastic error. The subscript i is the observation number from N random observations. β_1 through β_K are parameters that indicate the effect of a given x on y. β_0 is the intercept which indicates the expected value of y when all of the x's are 0. The model can be written in matrix notation for all observations as

$$y = X\beta + \varepsilon$$

where

$$y = \begin{pmatrix} y_1 \\ \vdots \\ y_N \end{pmatrix} \quad X = \begin{pmatrix} 1 & x_{11} & \cdots & x_{1K} \\ \vdots & \vdots & \ddots & \vdots \\ 1 & x_{N1} & \cdots & x_{NK} \end{pmatrix} \quad \beta = \begin{pmatrix} \beta_0 \\ \beta_1 \\ \vdots \\ \beta_K \end{pmatrix} \quad \varepsilon = \begin{pmatrix} \varepsilon_1 \\ \vdots \\ \varepsilon_N \end{pmatrix}$$

If we define x_i as the ith *row* of X, Equation 2.1 can be written as

$$y_i = x_i\beta + \varepsilon_i$$

The Assumptions of the LRM

A number of assumptions are added to complete the specification of the model. The first set of assumptions concerns the independent variables.

Linearity. According to Equation 2.1, y is linearly related to the x's through the β parameters. Nonlinear relationships between the x's and y are possible through the inclusion of transformed variables. For example, $y = \beta_0 + \beta_1\sqrt{x_1} + \beta_2 x_1 + \varepsilon$ or $y = \beta_0 + \beta_1 x_1 + \beta_2 x_1^2 + \varepsilon$. This assumption is considered further in Section 2.4.

Collinearity. The x's are linearly independent. This means that none of the x's is a linear combination of the remaining x's. More formally, this requires that X is of full rank.

A second set of assumptions concerns the distribution of the error ε, which can be thought of as an intrinsically random, unobservable influence on y. Alternatively, ε can be viewed as the effect of a large number of excluded variables that individually have small effects on y.

Zero Conditional Mean of ε. The conditional expectation of the error is 0:

$$E(\varepsilon_i \,|\, x_i) = 0$$

This means that for a given set of values for the x's, the error is expected to be 0. This assumption implies that the conditional expectation of y

given **x** is a linear combination of the *x*'s:

$$E(y_i \mid \mathbf{x}_i) = E(\mathbf{x}_i\boldsymbol{\beta} + \varepsilon_i \mid \mathbf{x}_i) = \mathbf{x}_i\boldsymbol{\beta} + E(\varepsilon_i \mid \mathbf{x}_i) = \mathbf{x}_i\boldsymbol{\beta}$$

This is shown in Figure 2.1 for the simple regression model: $y = \alpha + \beta x + \varepsilon$. Notice that I use α and β for the parameters in the simple regression model rather than the more cumbersome: $y = \beta_0 + \beta_1 x_1 + \varepsilon$. The expected value of *y* given *x* is drawn as a thick line starting at α and moving up and to the right with slope β.

Homoscedastic and Uncorrelated Errors. The errors are assumed to be *homoscedastic*, which means that for a given **x**, the errors have a constant variance. Formally,

$$\text{Var}(\varepsilon_i \mid \mathbf{x}_i) = \sigma^2 \quad \text{for all } i$$

When the variance differs across observations, the errors are *heteroscedastic* and $\text{Var}(\varepsilon_i \mid \mathbf{x}_i) = \sigma_i^2$. The errors are also assumed to be uncorrelated across observations, so that for two observations *i* and *j*, the covariance between ε_i and ε_j is 0.

In Figure 2.1, the distribution of ε is represented by a dotted curve that should be thought of as coming out of the page into a third dimension.

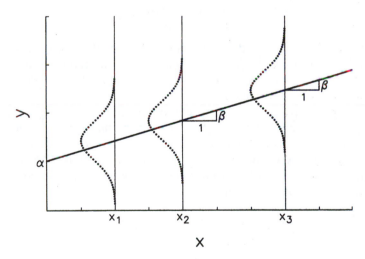

Figure 2.1. Simple Linear Regression Model With the Distribution of *y* Given *x*

The higher the curve, the more likely it is to have an error of that value. The errors are homoscedastic since the variance of the error distribution is the same for each x. While the curves are drawn as normal, normality is not required for the errors to be homoscedastic.

Normality. When the errors are thought of as the combined effects of many small factors, it is reasonable to assume that they are normally distributed when conditioned on the x's. With this assumption, the curves in Figure 2.1 should be thought of as normal.

See the references in Section 2.8 for a more detailed discussion of the assumptions.

2.2. Interpreting Regression Coefficients

In Chapter 1, partial derivatives and discrete change were used to describe the effects of an independent variable on the dependent outcome. Even though these two measures of change give identical answers for the LRM, I consider both in order to introduce ideas that are critical in later chapters. The subscript i is dropped to simplify the notation.

The *partial derivative* of y with respect to x_k is

$$\frac{\partial E(y\,|\,\mathbf{x})}{\partial x_k} = \frac{\partial \mathbf{x}\boldsymbol{\beta}}{\partial x_k} = \beta_k$$

In the LRM, the partial derivative is the slope of the line relating y and x_k, holding all other variables constant. Since the model is linear, the value of the partial is a constant β_k that does *not* depend on the level of any of the x's in the model.

The second approach to interpretation involves computing the *discrete change* in the expected value of y for a given change in x_k, holding all other variables constant. The notation $E(y\,|\,\mathbf{x}, x_k)$ indicates the expected value of y given $\mathbf{x}$, explicitly noting the value of x_k. Thus, $E(y\,|\,\mathbf{x}, x_k + 1)$ is the expected value of y given $\mathbf{x}$ when the kth variable equals $x_k + 1$. The discrete change in y for a unit change in x_k equals

$$\frac{\Delta E(y\,|\,\mathbf{x})}{\Delta x_k} = E(y\,|\,\mathbf{x}, x_k + 1) - E(y\,|\,\mathbf{x}, x_k)$$

$$= [\beta_0 + \beta_1 x_1 + \cdots + \beta_k(x_k + 1) + \cdots + \beta_K x_K + \varepsilon]$$
$$\quad - [\beta_0 + \beta_1 x_1 + \cdots + \beta_k x_k + \cdots + \beta_K x_K + \varepsilon]$$
$$= \beta_k$$

This means that when x_k increases by one unit, y is expected to change by β_k units, holding other x's constant.

In the LRM,

$$\frac{\partial E(y \mid \mathbf{x})}{\partial x_k} = \frac{\Delta E(y \mid \mathbf{x})}{\Delta x_k} = \beta_k$$

which allows a simple interpretation of the β's:

- For a unit increase in x_k, the expected change in y equals β_k, holding all other variables constant.

Since dummy variables are coded as 1 if an observation has some characteristic and else 0, the coefficient for a dummy variable can be interpreted in the same way:

- Having characteristic x_k (as opposed to not having the characteristic) results in an expected change of β_k in y, holding all other variables constant.

The slope coefficient is represented in Figure 2.1 by small triangles. The base of each triangle is one unit long, with the rise in the triangle equal to β. Thus, for a unit increase in x, whether starting at x_2, x_3, or any other value of x, y is expected to increase by β units.

2.2.1. Standardized and Semi-Standardized Coefficients

The β coefficients are defined in terms of the original metric of the variables, and are sometimes called *metric coefficients* or *unstandardized coefficients*. It is often useful to compute coefficients after some or all of the variables have been standardized to have a unit variance. This is particularly useful for the models introduced in later chapters where the scale of the dependent variable is arbitrary. This section considers coefficients that are standardized for y, standardized for the x's, and fully standardized for both y and the x's.

y-Standardized Coefficients

Let σ_y be the standard deviation of y. We can standardize y to a variance of 1 by dividing Equation 2.1 by σ_y:

$$\frac{y}{\sigma_y} = \frac{\beta_0}{\sigma_y} + \frac{\beta_1}{\sigma_y} x_1 + \cdots + \frac{\beta_k}{\sigma_y} x_k + \cdots + \frac{\beta_K}{\sigma_y} x_K + \frac{\varepsilon}{\sigma_y}$$

Adding new notation,

$$y^S = \beta_0^{S_y} + \beta_1^{S_y} x_1 + \cdots + \beta_k^{S_y} x_k + \cdots + \beta_K^{S_y} x_K + \varepsilon^{S_y}$$

where y^S is y standardized to have a unit variance. $\beta_k^{S_y} = \beta_k / \sigma_y$ is a *semi-standardized coefficient with respect to* y or simply a *y-standardized coefficient*. It is still the case that

$$\frac{\partial E(y^S \mid \mathbf{x})}{\partial x_k} = \frac{\Delta E(y^S \mid \mathbf{x})}{\Delta x_k} = \beta_k^{S_y}.$$

For a continuous variable, $\beta_k^{S_y}$ can be interpreted as:

- For a unit increase in x_k, y is expected to change by $\beta_k^{S_y}$ standard deviations, holding all other variables constant.

For a dummy variable,

- Having characteristic x_k (as opposed to not having the characteristic) results in an expected change in y of $\beta_k^{S_y}$ standard deviations, holding all other variables constant.

x-Standardized Coefficients

Let σ_k be the standard deviation of x_k. Then, dividing each x_k by σ_k and multiplying the corresponding β_k by σ_k,

$$y = \beta_0 + (\sigma_1 \beta_1) \frac{x_1}{\sigma_1} + \cdots + (\sigma_k \beta_k) \frac{x_k}{\sigma_k} + \cdots + (\sigma_K \beta_K) \frac{x_K}{\sigma_K} + \varepsilon$$

and, adding new notation,

$$y = \beta_0 + \beta_1^{S_x} x_1^S + \cdots + \beta_k^{S_x} x_k^S + \cdots + \beta_K^{S_x} x_K^S + \varepsilon$$

where x_k^S is x_k standardized to have a unit variance, and $\beta_k^{S_x} = \sigma_k \beta_k$ is a *semi-standardized coefficient with respect to* x or simply an *x-standardized coefficient*. For a continuous variable, $\beta_k^{S_x}$ can be interpreted as:

- For a standard deviation increase in x_k, y is expected to change by $\beta_k^{S_x}$ units, holding all other variables constant.

Fully Standardized Coefficients

It is also possible to standardize both y and the x's:

$$\frac{y}{\sigma_y} = \frac{\beta_0}{\sigma_y} + \left(\frac{\sigma_1 \beta_1}{\sigma_y}\right)\frac{x_1}{\sigma_1} + \cdots + \left(\frac{\sigma_k \beta_k}{\sigma_y}\right)\frac{x_k}{\sigma_k} + \cdots + \left(\frac{\sigma_K \beta_K}{\sigma_y}\right)\frac{x_K}{\sigma_K} + \frac{\varepsilon}{\sigma_y}$$

and, adding new notation,

$$y^S = \beta_0^S + \beta_1^S x_1^S + \cdots + \beta_k^S x_k^S + \cdots + \beta_K^S x_K^S + \varepsilon^{S_y}$$

$\beta_k^S = (\sigma_k \beta_k)/\sigma_y$ is a *fully standardized coefficient* or a *path coefficient*. Since

$$\frac{\partial E(y^S \mid \mathbf{x}^S)}{\partial x_k^S} = \frac{\Delta E(y^S \mid \mathbf{x}^S)}{\Delta x_k^S} = \beta_k^S$$

the following interpretation applies:

- For a standard deviation increase in x_k, y is expected to change by β_k^S standard deviations, holding all other variables constant.

Standardized Coefficients for Dummy Variables

For a dummy variable, the meaning of a standard deviation change is unclear. For example, consider the variable *MALE* defined as 1 for men and 0 for women. Assume that the regression coefficient for *MALE* equals .5. The effect of *MALE* changing from 0 to 1 is quite clear: being male increases the dependent variable by .5, holding all other variables constant. Now consider the x-standardized coefficient. Suppose that the standard deviation of *MALE* is .25. Then the x-standardized coefficient would equal .125 ($= .5 \times .25$). To say that a standard deviation change in a person's gender increases the dependent variable by .125 does not make substantive sense. While fully standardized and x-standardized coefficients for dummy variables are sometimes used to compare the magnitudes of the effects of variables, I do not find such comparisons useful. Consequently, x-standardized and fully standardized coefficients for dummy variables are not used in later chapters.

Comparison to Nonlinear Models

The interpretation of the coefficients in the LRM differs in two important respects from the nonlinear models in later chapters. First, in nonlinear models, $\partial E(\cdot)/\partial x_k$ depends on the value of x_k and on the values of the other x's in the model. Second, in nonlinear models, $\partial E(\cdot)/\partial x_k$ does not necessarily equal $\Delta E(\cdot)/\Delta x_k$. *It is extremely important to avoid generalizing the simple interpretation of the LRM to the models in later chapters.*

2.3. Estimation by Ordinary Least Squares

Ordinary least squares (OLS) is the most frequently used method of estimation for the LRM. The OLS estimator of $\boldsymbol{\beta}$ is that value $\widehat{\boldsymbol{\beta}}$ that minimizes the sum of the squared residuals: $\sum_{i=1}^{N}(y_i - \mathbf{x}_i\widehat{\boldsymbol{\beta}})^2$. The resulting estimator is

$$\widehat{\boldsymbol{\beta}} = (\mathbf{X}'\mathbf{X})^{-1}\mathbf{X}'\mathbf{y}$$

with the covariance matrix:

$$\text{Var}(\widehat{\boldsymbol{\beta}}) = \sigma^2(\mathbf{X}'\mathbf{X})^{-1}$$

$$= \begin{pmatrix} \text{Var}(\widehat{\beta}_0) & \text{Cov}(\widehat{\beta}_0, \widehat{\beta}_1) & \cdots & \text{Cov}(\widehat{\beta}_0, \widehat{\beta}_K) \\ \text{Cov}(\widehat{\beta}_1, \widehat{\beta}_0) & \text{Var}(\widehat{\beta}_1) & \cdots & \text{Cov}(\widehat{\beta}_1, \widehat{\beta}_K) \\ \vdots & \vdots & \ddots & \vdots \\ \text{Cov}(\widehat{\beta}_K, \widehat{\beta}_0) & \text{Cov}(\widehat{\beta}_K, \widehat{\beta}_1) & \cdots & \text{Var}(\widehat{\beta}_K) \end{pmatrix}$$

When the assumptions of the model hold, the OLS estimator is the best linear unbiased estimator. This means that if the assumptions hold, the OLS estimator $\widehat{\boldsymbol{\beta}}$ is an unbiased estimator [i.e., $E(\widehat{\boldsymbol{\beta}}) = \boldsymbol{\beta}$] that has the minimum variance among all linear estimators.

To estimate $\text{Var}(\widehat{\boldsymbol{\beta}})$, we need an estimate of the variance of the errors, σ^2. Defining the residual as $e_i = y_i - \mathbf{x}_i\widehat{\boldsymbol{\beta}}$, we can use the unbiased estimator:

$$s^2 = \frac{1}{N-K-1}\sum_{i=1}^{N} e_i^2$$

where K is the number of independent variables. This allows us to estimate the covariance matrix as $\widehat{\text{Var}}(\widehat{\boldsymbol{\beta}}) = s^2(\mathbf{X}'\mathbf{X})^{-1}$. If the errors are normal and $\beta_k = \beta^*$, then

$$t_k = \frac{\widehat{\beta}_k - \beta^*}{\sqrt{\widehat{\text{Var}}(\widehat{\beta}_k)}}$$

has a *t*-distribution with $N - K - 1$ degrees of freedom and can be used to test the hypothesis that H_0: $\beta_k = \beta^*$. Without assuming normality, t_k has a *t*-distribution as the sample becomes infinitely large (Greene, 1993, pp. 299–301). Issues involved in testing hypotheses are discussed in Chapter 4.

Example of the LRM: Prestige of the First Job

Long et al. (1980) examined factors that affect the prestige of a scientist's first academic job for a sample of male biochemists. Their primary interest was whether characteristics associated with scientific productivity were more important than characteristics associated with educational background. Here I extend those analyses to include information on female scientists.

The dependent variable is the prestige of the first job (*JOB*). Prestige is rated on a continuous scale from 1.00 to 5.00, with schools from 1.00 to 1.99 classified as adequate, those from 2.00 to 2.99 as good, 3.00 to 3.99 as strong, and those above 3.99 as distinguished. Graduate programs rated below adequate or departments without graduate programs were coded as 1.00. The implications of this decision are considered in Chapter 7 when this example is used to illustrate the tobit model. The independent variables are described in Table 2.1. Our regression model is

$$JOB = \beta_0 + \beta_1 FEM + \beta_2 PHD + \beta_3 MENT + \beta_4 FEL + \beta_5 ART + \beta_6 CIT + \varepsilon$$

Table 2.2 presents the estimates of the unstandardized and standardized coefficients. *t*-values are also presented, but are not discussed until

TABLE 2.1 Descriptive Statistics for the First Academic Job Example

Name	Mean	Standard Deviation	Minimum	Maximum	Description
JOB	2.23	0.97	1.00	4.80	Prestige of job (from 1 to 5)
FEM	0.39	0.49	0.00	1.00	1 if female; 0 if male
PHD	3.20	0.95	1.00	4.80	Prestige of Ph.D. department
MENT	45.47	65.53	0.00	532.00	Citations received by mentor
FEL	0.62	0.49	0.00	1.00	1 if held fellowship; else 0
ART	2.28	2.26	0.00	18.00	Number of articles published
CIT	21.72	33.06	0.00	203.00	Number of citations received

NOTE: $N = 408$.

TABLE 2.2 Linear Regression of the Prestige of the First Academic Job

Name	β	β^{S_x}	β^{S_y}	β^{S}	t
Constant	1.067	—	—	—	6.42
FEM	−0.139	—	−0.143	—	−1.54
PHD	0.273	0.260	0.280	0.267	5.53
MENT	0.001	0.078	0.001	0.080	1.69
FEL	0.234	—	0.240	—	2.47
ART	0.023	0.051	0.023	0.053	0.79
CIT	0.004	0.148	0.005	0.153	2.28

NOTE: $N = 408$. β is an unstandardized coefficient; β^{S_x} is an x-standardized coefficient; β^{S_y} is a y-standardized coefficient; β^{S} is a fully standardized coefficient; t is a t-test of β.

Chapter 4. The variables *FEM* and *CIT* can be used to illustrate the interpretation of coefficients.

- *Unstandardized coefficients.* Being a female scientist decreases the expected prestige of the first job by .14 points on a five-point scale, holding all other variables constant. For every additional citation, the prestige of the first job is expected to increase by .004 units, holding all other variables constant. (This effect is small due to the large standard deviation in *CIT*.)

- *x-standardized coefficients.* For every standard deviation increase in citations, the prestige of the first job is expected to increase by .15 units, holding all other variables constant.

- *y-standardized coefficients.* Being a woman decreases the expected prestige of the first job by .14 standard deviations, holding all other variables constant. For every additional citation, the prestige of the first job is expected to increase by .005 standard deviations, holding all other variables constant. (The unstandardized and *y*-standardized coefficients are nearly identical since the variance of *y* is about 1.)

- *Fully standardized coefficients.* For every standard deviation increase in citations, the prestige of the first job is expected to increase by .15 standard deviations, holding all other variables constant.

Both fully standardized and *y*-standardized coefficients are used to interpret many of the models in later chapters.

2.4. Nonlinear Linear Regression Models

While the LRM is a linear model, nonlinear relationships between the independent variables and the dependent variable can be incorporated by transforming the variables. For example, consider the nonlinear model:

$$z = \exp(\beta_0 + \beta_1 x_1 + \beta_2 x_2 + \varepsilon) \qquad [2.2]$$

If we take the log of both sides,

$$\ln(z) = \beta_0 + \beta_1 x_1 + \beta_2 x_2 + \varepsilon$$

the resulting equation is linear in $\ln(z)$ even though it is nonlinear in z. Accordingly, the slope β_1 can be interpreted as discussed above: for a unit increase in x_1, $\ln(z)$ is expected to increase by β_1 units, holding x_2 constant. Note, however, that a β_1 unit increase in $\ln(z)$ from 1 to $1 + \beta_1$ involves a different change in z than a change in $\ln(z)$ from, say, 2 to $2 + \beta_1$. This can be seen by taking the derivative of z with respect to x:[1]

$$\frac{\partial z}{\partial x_1} = \frac{\partial \exp(\beta_0 + \beta_1 x_1 + \beta_2 x_2 + \varepsilon)}{\partial x_1}$$

$$= \exp(\beta_0 + \beta_1 x_1 + \beta_2 x_2 + \varepsilon) \frac{\partial(\beta_0 + \beta_1 x_1 + \beta_2 x_2 + \varepsilon)}{\partial x_1}$$

$$= \exp(\beta_0 + \beta_1 x_1 + \beta_2 x_2 + \varepsilon)\beta_1$$

$$= z\beta_1$$

Thus, even though the expected change in $y = \ln(z)$ is the same regardless of the current levels of x_1 and x_2, the change in z [not $\ln(z)$] depends on the level of z.

Equation 2.2 is an example of a class of nonlinear models known as *log-linear models:* while z is nonlinearly related to the x's, the log of z is linearly related to the x's. Since the logit models of Chapters 3, 4, and 6 and the count models of Chapter 8 are log-linear models, it is worth considering a simple method of interpretation that can be used for any log-linear model.

Since $\exp(a + b) = \exp(a)\exp(b)$, Equation 2.2 can be written as

$$z(x_1) = \exp(\beta_0)\exp(\beta_1 x_1)\exp(\beta_2 x_2)\exp(\varepsilon)$$

---

[1] This requires the chain rule:

$$\frac{\partial f(g(x))}{\partial x} = \frac{\partial f(g(x))}{\partial g(x)}\frac{\partial g(x)}{\partial x} \quad \text{and} \quad \frac{\partial \exp(x)}{\partial x} = \exp(x).$$

where $z(x_1)$ indicates the value of z when x_1 has a given value. Consider increasing x_1 by 1 to $x_1 + 1$:

$$z(x_1 + 1) = \exp(\beta_0)\exp[\beta_1(x_1 + 1)]\exp(\beta_2 x_2)\exp(\varepsilon)$$
$$= \exp(\beta_0)\exp(\beta_1 x_1)\exp(\beta_1)\exp(\beta_2 x_2)\exp(\varepsilon)$$

The ratio of $z(x + 1)$ and $z(x)$ is the multiplicative factor change in z for a unit change in x_1:

$$\frac{z(x_1 + 1)}{z(x_1)} = \frac{\exp(\beta_0)\exp(\beta_1 x_1)\exp(\beta_1)\exp(\beta_2 x_2)\exp(\varepsilon)}{\exp(\beta_0)\exp(\beta_1 x_1)\exp(\beta_2 x_2)\exp(\varepsilon)} = \exp(\beta_1)$$

This leads to the following interpretation:

- For a unit increase in x_1, z is expected to change by the factor $\exp(\beta_1)$, holding all other variables constant.

Or, the percentage change in z for a unit change in x_1 can be computed as

$$100\,\frac{z(x_1 + 1) - z(x_1)}{z(x_1)} = 100\left[\frac{z(x_1 + 1)}{z(x_1)} - \frac{z(x_1)}{z(x_1)}\right] = 100[\exp(\beta_1) - 1]$$

This can be interpreted as:

- For a unit increase in x_1, z is expected to change by $100[\exp(\beta_1) - 1]\%$, holding all other variables constant.

Note that other nonlinear models do not have this simple interpretation in terms of a factor or a percentage change.

2.5. Violations of the Assumptions

While a complete discussion of the consequences of violating the assumptions of the LRM is beyond the scope of my review, I consider two violations that are particularly useful for understanding the models in later chapters.

2.5.1. The Nonzero Conditional Mean of ε

In the LRM,

$$y = \beta_0 + \beta_1 x_1 + \cdots + \beta_K x_K + \varepsilon \qquad [2.3]$$

we assume that $E(\varepsilon \,|\, \mathbf{x}) = 0$. Consider a simple modification where we now assume that $E(\varepsilon \,|\, \mathbf{x}) = \delta$. Here δ is an unknown, *nonzero* constant. We can modify Equation 2.3 so that the new error will have a zero mean:

$$y = (\beta_0 + \delta) + \beta_1 x_1 + \cdots + \beta_K x_K + (\varepsilon - \delta)$$
$$= \beta_0^* + \beta_1 x_1 + \cdots + \beta_K x_K + \varepsilon^*$$

We have subtracted the mean of ε $(= \delta)$ from ε to create a new error ε^* with a zero mean. (*Show that the mean of ε^* is 0.*) To maintain the equality, we also added δ which is combined with β_0 and relabeled as β_0^*. The resulting equation has all of the properties of the LRM, including a mean of 0 for the error ε^*. Consequently, we can use OLS to obtain best, linear, unbiased estimates of β_0^* (not β_0) and the β_k's. The expected value of $\widehat{\beta_0^*}$ is a combination of the intercept β_0 and the mean of ε: $E(\widehat{\beta_0^*}) = \beta_0 + \delta$. No matter how large the sample, it is impossible to disentangle estimates of β_0 and δ. More formally, β_0 and δ are not identified individually, although their sum $\beta_0 + \delta$ is identified.

Since the idea of *identification* is essential for understanding models for CLDVs, it is worth reinforcing the key ideas with Figure 2.2. Assume that the sample data, which are indicated by the dots, are generated by the model $y = \alpha + \beta x + \varepsilon$, where ε is normally distributed with mean δ. The solid line represents $E(y \,|\, x) = \alpha + \beta x$. As would be expected, the

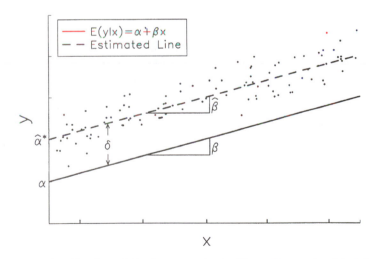

Figure 2.2. Identification of the Intercept in the Linear Regression Model

observed data are located approximately $\delta = E(\varepsilon \mid x)$ units above the regression line. The OLS *estimate* of the regression line is the dashed line that runs through the observations, with intercept $\widehat{\alpha}^*$ and slope $\widehat{\beta}$. The sample estimate of the slope appears unaffected by the nonzero mean of the errors, and is approximately equal to β. Consistent with our algebraic argument, the estimated intercept is about δ units above the population intercept α as a consequence of the nonzero mean of the errors. While neither α nor δ is identified, the sum $\alpha + \delta$ is identified and can be estimated by $\widehat{\alpha}^*$.

This simple example illustrates a number of critical ideas related to the concept of identification. First, a parameter is unidentified when it is impossible to estimate a parameter regardless of the data available. Identification is a limitation of the model that cannot be remedied by increasing the sample size. Second, models become identified by adding assumptions. The intercept β_0 is identified if we assume that $E(\varepsilon \mid x) = 0$; without this assumption it is unidentified. Third, it is possible for some parameters to be identified while others are not. Thus, while β_0 is not identified unless the value of $E(\varepsilon \mid x)$ is assumed, β_1 through β_K are identified without this assumption. Finally, while individual parameters may not be identified, combinations of those parameters may be identified. Thus, while neither δ nor β_0 is identified, the sum $\beta_0 + \delta$ is identified. These ideas are important for understanding how we identify the models in later chapters.

2.5.2. The x's and ε Are Correlated

The assumption $E(\varepsilon \mid x) = 0$ implies that the x's and ε are uncorrelated. In practice, there are several reasons why the x's might be correlated with the errors, including reciprocal effects among variables, measurement error, incorrect functional form, and β's that differ across observations (Kmenta, 1986, pp. 334–350). Here I consider the effect of excluding a variable since this will help us understand the tobit model in Chapter 7.

If we estimate a model that excludes an independent variable which is correlated with included independent variables, the OLS estimates are biased and inconsistent. Kmenta (1986, pp. 443–446) shows that this is due to the correlation between the error and the independent variables in the misspecified model. To see why they are correlated, assume that the data are generated by the model:

$$y = \beta_0 + \beta_1 x_1 + \beta_2 x_2 + \varepsilon \qquad [2.4]$$

but that we have estimated the model:

$$y = \beta_0 + \beta_1 x_1 + \nu \qquad [2.5]$$

The error ν absorbs the excluded variable x_2 and the original ε:

$$\nu = \beta_2 x_2 + \varepsilon$$

If x_1 and x_2 are correlated, then ν and x_1 must be correlated. (*Why must this be the case?*) Consequently, the OLS estimate of β_1 in Equation 2.5 is a biased and inconsistent estimate of β_1 in Equation 2.4.

2.6. Maximum Likelihood Estimation

If we assume that the errors are normally distributed, the LRM can be estimated by maximum likelihood (ML). While the OLS and ML estimators of β are identical for the LRM, I introduce ML estimation within the familiar context of regression to make it easier to understand the application of ML to the models in later chapters.

2.6.1. Introduction to ML Estimation

Consider the problem of estimating the probability of having a given number of men in your sample. The binomial formula computes the probability of having s men in a sample of size N with the population parameter π indicating the probability of being male:

$$\Pr(s \mid \pi, N) = \frac{N!}{s!(N-s)!} \, \pi^s (1-\pi)^{N-s} \qquad [2.6]$$

where $k! = k \cdot (k-1) \cdots 2 \cdot 1$. For example, the probability of having three men in a sample of 10 with the probability of being a male equal to .5 is

$$\Pr(s = 3 \mid \pi = .5, \ N = 10) = \frac{10!}{3!7!} \, .5^3 (1 - .5)^7 = 0.117$$

This is a typical problem in probability. We know the formula for the probability distribution and the values of the parameters π and N. We want to know the probability of a particular outcome s. In statistics, we know s and N, but want to estimate π from the sample information. *The ML estimate is that value of the parameter that makes the observed data most likely.*

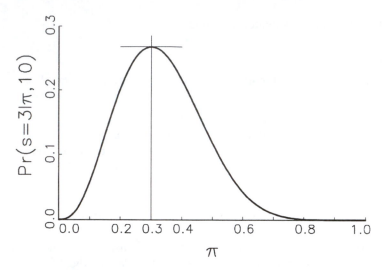

Figure 2.3. Probability of $s = 3$ for Different Values of π

To continue our example, assume that we know that $s = 3$ and $N = 10$, but that we do not know π. What value of π is most likely to have generated the observed $s = 3$? Figure 2.3 plots the probability of observing three successes out of 10 tries for all possible values of π. The tangent on the top of the curve shows that the highest probability occurs at .3. Thus, $\hat{\pi} = .3$ is our ML estimate.

2.6.2. The Likelihood Function

When Equation 2.6 is thought of as computing the probability of s events as a function of the parameters N and π, it is referred to as a probability function: the values of N and π are held constant while s varies. When we think of the same equation as a function of π, we refer to it as a *likelihood function*: the values of N and s are held constant while π varies. The likelihood function for our example is

$$L(\pi \mid s = 3, \ N = 10) = \frac{10!}{3!7!}\, \pi^3 (1 - \pi)^7$$

The maximum likelihood estimate is that value $\hat{\pi}$ that maximizes the likelihood of observing the sample data that were actually observed. The maximum occurs when the derivative of the likelihood function, called the *gradient* or *score*, equals 0:

$$\frac{\partial L(\pi \mid s = 3, N = 10)}{\partial \pi} = 0$$

This is represented in Figure 2.3 by the tangent line with slope 0 located at $\pi = .3$.

The value that maximizes the likelihood function also maximizes the log of the likelihood. Since it is generally easier to solve the gradient of the log likelihood than the likelihood itself, the ML estimate is usually computed by solving the equation:

$$\frac{\partial \ln L(\pi \mid s = 3, \ N = 10)}{\partial \pi} = 0$$

For our example,[2]

$$
\begin{aligned}
\frac{\partial \ln L(\pi \mid s = 3, \ N = 10)}{\partial \pi} &= \frac{\partial \ln[(10!/3!7!)\pi^3(1 - \pi)^7]}{\partial \pi} \\
&= \frac{\partial \ln(10!/3!7!)}{\partial \pi} + \frac{\partial 3 \ln \pi}{\partial \pi} + \frac{\partial 7 \ln(1 - \pi)}{\partial \pi} \\
&= 0 + \frac{\partial 3 \ln \pi}{\partial \pi} + \frac{\partial 7 \ln(1 - \pi)}{\partial (1 - \pi)} \frac{\partial (1 - \pi)}{\partial \pi} \\
&= \frac{3}{\pi} - \frac{7}{1 - \pi}
\end{aligned}
$$

Setting $\partial \ln L(\pi \mid s = 3, N = 10)/\partial \pi = 0$ and solving for π results in $\hat{\pi} = .3 = s/N$.

2.6.3. ML Estimation of the Sample Mean

Before estimating the regression model with ML, it is useful to consider the similar but simpler problem of estimating the mean of a standard normal distribution. If y is drawn from a normal distribution with a standard deviation of 1, then the probability density function (pdf) for y is

$$f(y_i \mid \mu, \sigma = 1) = \frac{1}{\sqrt{2\pi}} \exp\left(\frac{-(y_i - \mu)^2}{2}\right)$$

---

[2] We use the chain rule:

$$\frac{\partial f(g(x))}{\partial x} = \frac{\partial f(g(x))}{\partial g(x)} \frac{\partial g(x)}{\partial x} \quad \text{and} \quad \frac{\partial \ln x}{\partial x} = \frac{1}{x}$$

Since μ is unknown, we write the likelihood function as

$$L(\mu \mid y_i, \ \sigma = 1) = f(y_i \mid \mu, \ \sigma = 1)$$

For three independent observations, the likelihood is the product of the individual likelihoods:

$$L(\mu \mid \mathbf{y}, \ \sigma = 1) = \prod_{i=1}^{3} L(\mu \mid y_i, \ \sigma = 1) = \prod_{i=1}^{3} f(y_i \mid \mu, \ \sigma = 1)$$

and the log likelihood is

$$\ln L(\mu \mid \mathbf{y}, \ \sigma = 1) = \sum_{i=1}^{3} \ln L(\mu \mid y_i, \ \sigma = 1) = \sum_{i=1}^{3} \ln f(y_i \mid \mu, \ \sigma = 1)$$

The ML estimate is the value $\widehat{\mu}$ that maximizes this equation.

To get a better sense of how the ML estimate is determined, consider Figure 2.4. Suppose that there are three observations with values

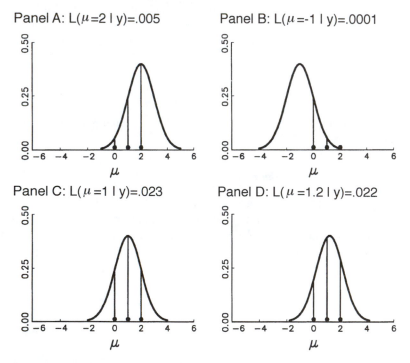

Figure 2.4. Maximum Likelihood Estimation of μ From a Normal Distribution

0, 1, and 2. These are represented in the figure as solid circles. The four panels correspond to a sequence of guesses for the value of μ that maximizes the likelihood. In panel A, the normal curve is centered on $\mu = 2$. The likelihood of each point is indicated by a vertical line, with the overall likelihood equal to the product of the lengths of the lines: $L(\mu = 2 \,|\, \mathbf{y}) = .005$. Panel B computes the likelihood for $\mu = -1$, resulting in $L(\mu = -1 \,|\, \mathbf{y}) = .0001$. To increase the likelihood, we need a value of μ somewhere between 2 and -1. Panel C shows $\mu = 1$, resulting in $L(\mu = 1 \,|\, \mathbf{y}) = .023$. When we increase the mean slightly to 1.2 in panel D, the likelihood is reduced to .022. Of our four tries, $\mu = 1$ produces the largest likelihood. Tentatively, we conclude that $\widehat{\mu}_{\text{ML}} = 1$.

In practice, ML is more complicated. First, we would usually have more observations. Second, we would often be estimating more than one parameter (e.g., μ and σ). Finally, we would have to consider all possible values of the parameters being estimated, not just the four values in our figure. Still, the general ideas are the same.

2.6.4. ML Estimation for Regression

Maximum likelihood for the LRM is a direct extension of fitting a normal distribution to a set of points. Consider estimating the simple regression $y = \alpha + \beta x + \varepsilon$ using three observations: (x_1, y_1), (x_2, y_2), and (x_3, y_3). Panels A and B of Figure 2.5 compare the likelihoods for two sets of possible estimates. The observed data are indicated by circles. The assumed distribution of y conditional on x is represented by the normal curves which should be visualized as coming out of the page into a third dimension. The likelihood of an observation for a given pair α and β is indicated by the length of the line from an observation, indicated by a circle, to the normal curve. In panel A for α^a and β^a, we find that (x_3, y_3) is very unlikely, while (x_1, y_1) is quite likely. The likelihood of α^a and β^a is the product of the three lines in panel A. Clearly, α^a and β^a are not the ML estimates since it is easy to find other estimates that increase the likelihood, such as α^b and β^b in panel B. The ML estimates are those values $\widehat{\alpha}$ and $\widehat{\beta}$ that make the likelihood as large as possible.

Mathematically, we can develop the ML estimator for the LRM as follows. Since y conditional on x is distributed normally with mean $\alpha + \beta x$ and variance σ^2, the pdf for an observation is

$$f(y_i \,|\, \alpha + \beta x_i, \sigma) = \frac{1}{\sigma\sqrt{2\pi}} \exp\left(-\frac{1}{2}\frac{[y_i - (\alpha + \beta x_i)]^2}{\sigma^2}\right) \qquad [2.7]$$

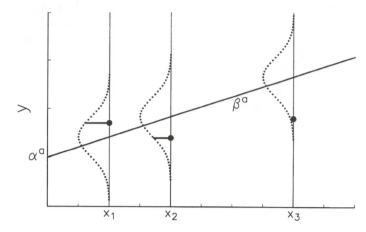

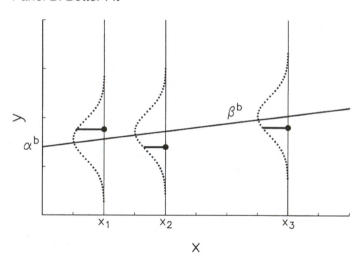

Figure 2.5. Maximum Likelihood Estimation for the Linear Regression Model

The pdf of a normal variable with mean μ and variance σ^2 is often expressed in terms of the pdf of a standardized normal variable ϕ with mean 0 and variance 1:

$$\phi(z) = \frac{1}{\sqrt{2\pi}} \exp\left(-\frac{z^2}{2}\right)$$

Using this definition, Equation 2.7 becomes

$$f(y_i \mid \alpha + \beta x_i, \sigma) = \frac{1}{\sigma} \left[\frac{1}{\sqrt{2\pi}} \exp\left(-\frac{\left(\frac{y_i - [\alpha + \beta x_i]}{\sigma}\right)^2}{2} \right) \right]$$

$$= \frac{1}{\sigma} \phi\left(\frac{y_i - [\alpha + \beta x_i]}{\sigma} \right)$$

and the likelihood equation can be written as

$$L(\alpha, \beta, \sigma \mid \mathbf{y}, \mathbf{X}) = \prod_{i=1}^{N} \frac{1}{\sigma} \phi\left(\frac{y_i - [\alpha + \beta x_i]}{\sigma} \right)$$

Taking logs,

$$\ln L(\alpha, \beta, \sigma \mid \mathbf{y}, \mathbf{X}) = \sum_{i=1}^{N} \ln \frac{1}{\sigma} \phi\left(\frac{y_i - [\alpha + \beta x_i]}{\sigma} \right) \qquad [2.8]$$

ML estimates $\widehat{\alpha}$, $\widehat{\beta}$, and $\widehat{\sigma}$ are obtained by maximizing this equation. For multiple regression, $y = \mathbf{x}\boldsymbol{\beta} + \varepsilon$ and

$$\ln L(\boldsymbol{\beta}, \sigma \mid \mathbf{y}, \mathbf{X}) = \sum_{i=1}^{N} \ln \frac{1}{\sigma} \phi\left(\frac{y_i - \mathbf{x}_i \boldsymbol{\beta}}{\sigma} \right)$$

The likelihood function is maximized when $\widehat{\boldsymbol{\beta}} = (\mathbf{X}'\mathbf{X})^{-1}\mathbf{X}'\mathbf{y}$, which is the same as the OLS estimator. Maximum likelihood for the LRM is unusual since a *closed-form* solution is available. This means that the estimates can be obtained by algebraically solving the gradient of the log likelihood equation for the unknown parameters. Closed-form solutions are not possible for most of the models considered in later chapters and, consequently, iterative methods must be used. This topic is discussed in Chapter 3.

2.6.5. The Variance of ML Estimators

Maximum likelihood can also estimate the variance of the estimators. While the technical details are beyond the scope of our discussion (see Cramer, 1986, pp. 27–28; Davidson & MacKinnon, 1993, pp. 260–267; Eliason, 1993, pp. 40–41), we need a few definitions and results that are used in later chapters.

Let $\boldsymbol{\theta}$ be a vector containing the parameters being estimated. For example, in the simple regression $y = \alpha + \beta x + \varepsilon$ with $\text{Var}(\varepsilon \,|\, \mathbf{x}) = \sigma$, $\boldsymbol{\theta}$ will contain α, β, and σ. The *Hessian* is a matrix of second derivatives defined as

$$\mathbf{H}(\boldsymbol{\theta}) = \frac{\partial^2 \ln L(\boldsymbol{\theta})}{\partial \boldsymbol{\theta} \, \partial \boldsymbol{\theta}'}$$

This is a square, symmetric matrix. For our example,

$$\mathbf{H}(\boldsymbol{\theta}) = \begin{pmatrix} \dfrac{\partial^2 \ln L(\boldsymbol{\theta})}{\partial \alpha \partial \alpha} & \dfrac{\partial^2 \ln L(\boldsymbol{\theta})}{\partial \alpha \partial \beta} & \dfrac{\partial^2 \ln L(\boldsymbol{\theta})}{\partial \alpha \partial \sigma} \\[2ex] \dfrac{\partial^2 \ln L(\boldsymbol{\theta})}{\partial \beta \partial \alpha} & \dfrac{\partial^2 \ln L(\boldsymbol{\theta})}{\partial \beta \partial \beta} & \dfrac{\partial^2 \ln L(\boldsymbol{\theta})}{\partial \beta \partial \sigma} \\[2ex] \dfrac{\partial^2 \ln L(\boldsymbol{\theta})}{\partial \sigma \partial \alpha} & \dfrac{\partial^2 \ln L(\boldsymbol{\theta})}{\partial \sigma \partial \beta} & \dfrac{\partial^2 \ln L(\boldsymbol{\theta})}{\partial \sigma \partial \sigma} \end{pmatrix}$$

The second derivative indicates the rate at which the slope of the function is changing. For example, if $\partial^2 \ln L(\boldsymbol{\theta})/\partial \beta \partial \beta$ is small, then the log likelihood is changing slowly as β changes. That is, $\ln L$ is nearly flat. Intuitively, it makes sense that if $\ln L$ is flat, then it will be difficult to choose the value $\widehat{\beta}$ that maximizes the log likelihood. This should be reflected in the variance of $\widehat{\beta}$, since the variance reflects our certainty about the estimate. Indeed, the Hessian is related to the variance of the estimates through the information matrix.

The *information matrix* is defined as the negative of the expected value of the Hessian: $-E[\mathbf{H}(\boldsymbol{\theta})]$. Under very general conditions, the covariance matrix for the ML estimator is the inverse of the information matrix:

$$\text{Var}(\widehat{\boldsymbol{\theta}}) = -E[\mathbf{H}(\boldsymbol{\theta})]^{-1}$$

For our example,

$$\text{Var}(\widehat{\boldsymbol{\theta}}) = \begin{pmatrix} -E\left(\dfrac{\partial^2 \ln L(\boldsymbol{\theta})}{\partial \alpha \partial \alpha}\right) & -E\left(\dfrac{\partial^2 \ln L(\boldsymbol{\theta})}{\partial \alpha \partial \beta}\right) & -E\left(\dfrac{\partial^2 \ln L(\boldsymbol{\theta})}{\partial \alpha \partial \sigma}\right) \\[2ex] -E\left(\dfrac{\partial^2 \ln L(\boldsymbol{\theta})}{\partial \beta \partial \alpha}\right) & -E\left(\dfrac{\partial^2 \ln L(\boldsymbol{\theta})}{\partial \beta \partial \beta}\right) & -E\left(\dfrac{\partial^2 \ln L(\boldsymbol{\theta})}{\partial \beta \partial \sigma}\right) \\[2ex] -E\left(\dfrac{\partial^2 \ln L(\boldsymbol{\theta})}{\partial \sigma \partial \alpha}\right) & -E\left(\dfrac{\partial^2 \ln L(\boldsymbol{\theta})}{\partial \sigma \partial \beta}\right) & -E\left(\dfrac{\partial^2 \ln L(\boldsymbol{\theta})}{\partial \sigma \partial \sigma}\right) \end{pmatrix}^{-1}$$

Various methods for estimating $\text{Var}(\widehat{\boldsymbol{\theta}})$ are considered in Chapter 3.

2.6.6. The Properties of ML Estimators

Under very general conditions, the ML estimator has a number of desirable properties. First, the ML estimator is *consistent*. This means roughly that as the sample size grows large, the probability that the ML estimator differs from the true parameter by an arbitrarily small amount tends toward 0. Second, the ML estimator is *asymptotically efficient*, which means that the variance of the ML estimator is the smallest possible among consistent estimators. Finally, the ML esimator is *asymptotically normally distributed*, which justifies the statistical tests that are discussed in Chapter 4. Notice that these are asymptotic properties, which means that they describe the ML estimator as the sample size approaches ∞. The degree to which they apply in finite samples is discussed in Section 3.5.

2.7. Conclusions

The linear regression model is our point of departure for presenting the models in later chapters. The next chapter begins by showing the problems inherent in using the LRM with a binary dependent variable. These problems lead to a latent regression model that generates the binary logit and probit models.

2.8. Bibliographic Notes

There are hundreds of texts dealing with the linear regression model. In order of increasing difficulty, I recommend Griffiths et al. (1993) for an introductory text; Kmenta (1986), Greene (1993), and Theil (1971) as intermediate texts; and Amemiya (1985) for an advanced treatment. Manski (1995) provides a detailed discussion of the identification problem. Four recommended sources on maximum likelihood, in order of increasing difficulty, are: Eliason (1993), Cramer (1986), Greene (1993, Chapter 12), and Davidson and MacKinnon (1993, Chapter 8).

3 Binary Outcomes: The Linear Probability, Probit, and Logit Models

Binary dependent variables are extremely common in the social sciences. Maddala and Trost (1982) studied the decisions by a bank to accept loan applications. Domencich and McFadden (1975) analyzed factors affecting the use of public versus private transportation for commuting. Aldrich and Cnudde (1975) considered the decision to vote for McGovern in the 1972 presidential election; Allen (1991) examined contributions by the corporate elite to the Democratic Party; while Ragsdale (1984) studied the president's decision to make a discretionary speech to the nation. Other outcomes include whether fraud was committed by a savings and loan institution (Tillman & Pantell, 1995); if a trainee decided to remain with the sponsoring employer (Gunderson, 1974); and whether a student collaborated with his or her mentor during graduate study (Long, 1990). Even a cursory glance at recent journals in the social sciences turns up dozens of additional examples, ranging from having intercourse before marriage, dropping out of high school, joining a union, to enlisting in the military.

In this chapter, I present four models for the analysis of binary outcomes: the linear probability model (LPM), the binary probit model, the binary logit model, and, briefly, the complementary log-log model. The LPM is the linear regression model applied to a binary dependent variable. While I do not recommend the LPM, the model illustrates the problems resulting from a binary dependent variable, and motivates our discussion of the logit and probit models. The probit and logit models are developed first in terms of the regression of a latent variable. The latent variable is related to the observed, binary variable in a simple way: if the latent variable is greater than some value, the observed variable is 1; otherwise it is 0. This model is linear in the latent variable, but results in a nonlinear, S-shaped model relating the independent variables to the probability that an event has occurred. Given the great similarity between the logit and probit models, I refer to them jointly as the *binary response model*, abbreviated as BRM. The BRM is also developed as a nonlinear probability model. Within this context, the complementary log-log model is introduced as an asymmetric alternative to the logit and probit models.

3.1. The Linear Probability Model

The *linear probability model* is the regression model applied to a binary dependent variable. The structural model is

$$y_i = \mathbf{x}_i \boldsymbol{\beta} + \varepsilon_i$$

where $\mathbf{x}_i$ is a vector of values for the ith observation, $\boldsymbol{\beta}$ is a vector of parameters, and ε is the error term. $y = 1$ when some event occurs, and $y = 0$ if the event does not occur. For example, $y = 1$ if a woman is in the paid labor force, and $y = 0$ if she is not. If we have a single independent variable, the model can be written as

$$y_i = \alpha + \beta x_i + \varepsilon_i$$

which is plotted in Figure 3.1. The conditional expectation of y given x, $E(y \mid x) = \alpha + \beta x$, is shown as a solid line. Observations are plotted as circles at $y = 0$ and $y = 1$.

To understand the LPM, we must consider the meaning of $E(y \mid \mathbf{x})$. When y is a binary random variable, the unconditional expectation of y is the probability that the event occurs:

$$E(y_i) = [1 \times \Pr(y_i = 1)] + [0 \times \Pr(y_i = 0)] = \Pr(y_i = 1)$$

For the regression model, we are taking conditional expectations:

$$E(y_i \mid \mathbf{x}_i) = [1 \times \Pr(y_i = 1 \mid \mathbf{x}_i)] + [0 \times \Pr(y_i = 0 \mid \mathbf{x}_i)] = \Pr(y_i = 1 \mid \mathbf{x}_i)$$

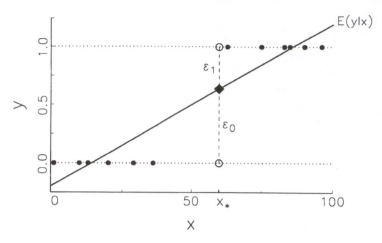

Figure 3.1. Linear Probability Model for a Single Independent Variable

Therefore, the expected value of y given $\mathbf{x}$ is the probability that $y = 1$ given $\mathbf{x}$. This allows us to rewrite the LPM as

$$\Pr(y_i = 1 \mid \mathbf{x}_i) = \mathbf{x}_i\boldsymbol{\beta}$$

Having a binary outcome does not affect the interpretation of the parameters that was presented in Chapter 2: for a unit increase in x_k, the expected change in the probability of an event occurring is β_k, holding all other variables constant. Since the model is linear, a unit change in x_k always results in the same change in the probability. That is, the model is linear in the probability, and hence the name *linear probability model*.

Example of the LPM: Labor Force Participation

Many authors have presented models in which the dependent variable is whether a married woman was in the paid labor force. For example, Gunderson (1974) compares the use of logit, probit, and LPM models. Nakamura and Nakamura (1981, pp. 464–468) use a probit model to compare labor force participation in the United States and Canada. While Mroz (1987) focuses on models for a woman's hours of paid labor, he uses a probit model to correct for sample selection bias. Berndt (1991, pp. 618–619) reviews the research in this area.

TABLE 3.1 Descriptive Statistics for the Labor Force Participation Example

Name	Mean	Standard Deviation	Minimum	Maximum	Description
LFP	0.57	0.50	0.00	1.00	1 if wife is in the paid labor force; else 0
K5	0.24	0.52	0.00	3.00	Number of children ages 5 and younger
K618	1.35	1.32	0.00	8.00	Number of children ages 6 to 18
AGE	42.54	8.07	30.00	60.00	Wife's age in years
WC	0.28	0.45	0.00	1.00	1 if wife attended college; else 0
HC	0.39	0.49	0.00	1.00	1 if husband attended college; else 0
LWG	1.10	0.59	−2.05	3.22	Log of wife's estimated wage rate
INC	20.13	11.63	−0.03	96.00	Family income excluding wife's wages

NOTE: $N = 753$.

Our analysis is based on data extracted by Mroz (1987) from the 1976 Panel Study of Income Dynamics.[1] The sample consists of 753 white, married women between the ages of 30 and 60. The dependent variable *LFP* is 1 if a woman is employed and is 0 otherwise. The independent variables, which are similar to those used by Nakamura and Nakamura (1981), Mroz (1987), and Berndt (1991), are listed in Table 3.1. Our measures of educational attainment are dummy variables indicating whether the husband or wife spent at least one year in college, rather than the more commonly used measures of the number of years of education. This was done to illustrate the interpretation of dummy independent variables.

The model being estimated is

$$LFP = \beta_0 + \beta_1 K5 + \beta_2 K618 + \beta_3 AGE + \beta_4 WC + \beta_5 HC + \beta_6 LWG + \beta_7 INC + \varepsilon$$

with estimates presented in Table 3.2. Interpretation is straightforward. For example:

- *Unstandardized coefficients for continuous variables.* For every additional child under 6, the predicted probability of a woman being employed decreases by .30, holding all other variables constant.

- *x-standardized coefficients for continuous variables.* For a standard deviation increase in family income, the predicted probability of being employed decreases by .08, holding all other variables constant.

- *Unstandardized coefficients for dummy variables.* If the wife attended college, the predicted probability of being in the labor force increases by .16, holding all other variables constant.

---

[1] These data were generously made available by Thomas Mroz.

TABLE 3.2 Linear Probability Model of Labor Force
Participation

Variable	β	β^{S_x}	t
Constant	1.144	—	9.00
K5	−0.295	−0.154	−8.21
K618	−0.011	−0.015	−0.80
AGE	−0.013	−0.103	−5.02
WC	0.164	—	3.57
HC	0.019	—	0.45
LWG	0.123	0.072	4.07
INC	−0.007	−0.079	−4.30

NOTE: $N = 753$. β is an unstandardized coefficient; β^{S_x} is an x-standardized coefficient; t is a t-test of β.

There are several things to note about these interpretations. First, the effect of a variable is the same regardless of the values of the other variables. Second, the effect of a unit change for a variable is the same regardless of the current value of that variable. For example, if a woman has four young children compared to no young children, her predicted probability of employment decreases by 1.18 ($= 4 \times -.295$), which is obviously unrealistic. This problem is considered in the next section. Finally, fully standardized and y-standardized coefficients are inappropriate given the binary outcome, and x-standardized coefficients are inappropriate for binary independent variables.

3.1.1. Problems With the LPM

While the interpretation of the parameters is unaffected by having a binary outcome, several assumptions of the LRM are necessarily violated.

Heteroscedasticity. If a binary random variable has mean μ, then its variance is $\mu(1 - \mu)$. (*Prove this.*) Since the expected value of y given $\mathbf{x}$ is $\mathbf{x\beta}$, the conditional variance of y depends on $\mathbf{x}$ according to the equation:

$$\text{Var}(y \mid \mathbf{x}) = \Pr(y = 1 \mid \mathbf{x})[1 - \Pr(y = 1 \mid \mathbf{x})] = \mathbf{x\beta}(1 - \mathbf{x\beta})$$

which implies that the variance of the errors depends on the x's and is not constant. (*Plot the* $\text{Var}(y \mid \mathbf{x})$ *as* $\mathbf{x\beta}$ *ranges from* $-.2$ *to* 1.2.) Since the LPM is heteroscedastic, the OLS estimator of $\mathbf{\beta}$ is inefficient and the standard errors are biased, resulting in incorrect test statistics.

Goldberger (1964, pp. 248–250) suggested that the LPM could be corrected for heteroscedasticity with a two-step estimator. In the first step, $\widehat{y}$ is estimated by OLS. In the second step, the model is estimated with generalized least squares using $\widehat{\text{Var}}(\widehat{\varepsilon}) = \widehat{y}(1 - \widehat{y})$ to correct for heteroscedasticity. While this approach increases the efficiency of the estimates, it does not correct for other problems with the LPM. Further, for $\widehat{y} < 0$ or $\widehat{y} > 1$, the estimated variance is negative and ad hoc adjustments are required.

Normality. Consider a specific value of x, say x_*. In Figure 3.1, $E(y \mid x_*)$ is represented by a diamond on the regression line. ε is the distance from $E(y \mid x)$ to the observed value. Since y can only have the values 0 and 1, which are indicated by the open circles, the error must equal either $\varepsilon_1 = 1 - E(y \mid x_*)$ or $\varepsilon_0 = 0 - E(y \mid x_*)$. Clearly, the errors cannot be normally distributed. Recall that normality is not required for the OLS estimates to be unbiased.

Nonsensical Predictions. The LPM predicts values of y that are negative or greater than 1. Given our interpretation of $E(y \mid x)$ as $\Pr(y = 1 \mid x)$, this leads to nonsensical predictions for the probabilities. For example, using the means in Table 3.1 and the LPM estimates in Table 3.2, we find that a 35-year-old woman with four young children, who did not attend college nor did her husband, and who is average on other variables, has a predicted probability of being employed of $-.48$. (*Verify this result.*) While unreasonable predictions are sometimes used to dismiss the LPM, such predications at extreme values of the independent variables are also common in regressions with continuous outcomes.

Functional Form. Since the model is linear, a unit increase in x_k results in a constant change of β_k in the probability of an event, holding all other variables constant. The increase is the same regardless of the current value of $\mathbf{x}$. In many applications, this is unrealistic. For example, with the LPM each additional young child decreases the probability of being employed by .295, which implies that a woman with four young children has a probability that is 1.18 less than that of a woman without young children, all other variables being held constant. More realistically, each additional child would have a diminishing effect on the probability. While the first child might decrease the probability by .3, the second child might only decrease the probability an additional .2, and so on. That is to say, the model should be nonlinear. In general, when the outcome is a probability, it is often *substantively* reasonable that the effects of independent variables will have diminishing returns as the predicted probability approaches 0 or 1. In my opinion, the most serious problem with the LPM is its functional form.

The binary response model has an S-shaped relationship between the independent variables and the probability of an event, which addresses the problem with the functional form in the LPM. In the following section I develop this model in terms of a latent dependent variable. Section 3.4 shows how the logit and probit models can also be thought of as nonlinear probability models without appealing to a latent variable. And, in Chapter 6, the models are derived as *discrete choice models* in which an individual chooses the option that maximizes her utility.

3.2. A Latent Variable Model for Binary Variables

As with the LPM, we have an observed binary variable y. Suppose that there is an unobserved or *latent* variable y^* ranging from $-\infty$ to ∞ that generates the observed y's. Those who have larger values of y^* are observed as $y = 1$, while those with smaller values of y^* are observed as $y = 0$.

Since the notion of a latent variable is central to this approach to deriving the BRM, it is important to understand what is meant by a latent variable. Consider a woman's labor force participation as the observed y. The variable y can only be observed in two states: a woman is in the labor force, or she is not. However, not all women in the labor force are there with the same certainty. One woman might be very close to the decision of leaving the labor force, while another woman could be very firm in her decision. In both cases, we observe the same $y = 1$. The idea of a latent y^* is that there is an underlying propensity to work that generates the observed state. While we cannot directly observe y^*, at some point a change in y^* results in a change in what we observe, namely, whether a woman is in the labor force. For example, as the number of young children in the family increases, it is reasonable that a woman's propensity to be in the labor force (as opposed to working at home) would decrease. At some point, the propensity would cross a threshold that would result in a decision to leave the labor force.

Can *all* binary outcomes be viewed as manifestations of a latent variable? Some researchers argue that invoking a latent variable is usually inappropriate, others believe that an underlying latent variable is perfectly reasonable in all cases, while most seem to take a middle ground. Regardless of your assessment of the use of a latent variable, it is important to realize that the derivation and application of the BRM is not dependent on your acceptance of the notion of a latent variable. Section 3.4 shows that the same BRM can be derived as a nonlinear probability model, without invoking the idea of a latent variable.

The latent y^* is assumed to be linearly related to the observed x's through the structural model:

$$y_i^* = \mathbf{x}_i \boldsymbol{\beta} + \varepsilon_i$$

The latent variable y^* is linked to the observed binary variable y by the measurement equation:

$$y_i = \begin{cases} 1 & \text{if } y_i^* > \tau \\ 0 & \text{if } y_i^* \leq \tau \end{cases} \qquad [3.1]$$

where τ is the *threshold* or *cutpoint*. If $y^* \leq \tau$, then $y = 0$. If y^* crosses the threshold τ (i.e., $y^* > \tau$), then $y = 1$. For now, we assume that $\tau = 0$. Section 5.2 (p. 122) discusses this identifying assumption in detail.

The link between the latent y^* and the observed y is illustrated in Figure 3.2 for the model $y^* = \alpha + \beta x + \varepsilon$. In this figure, y^* is on the vertical axis, with the threshold τ indicated by a horizontal dashed line. The distribution of y^* is shown by the bell-shaped curves which should be thought of as coming out of the figure into a third dimension. When y^* is larger than τ, indicated by the shaded region, we observe $y = 1$.

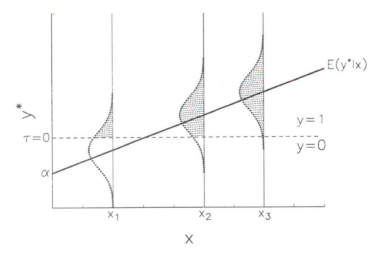

Figure 3.2. The Distribution of y^* Given x in the Binary Response Model

For example, at x_1 about 25% of the y's equal 1, at x_2 nearly 90% are 1's, and at x_3 nearly all cases are 1's.

Since y^* is continuous, the model avoids the problems encountered with the LPM. However, since the dependent variable is unobserved, the model cannot be estimated with OLS. Instead, we use ML estimation, which requires assumptions about the distribution of the errors. Most often, the choice is between normal errors which result in the *probit* model, and logistic errors which result in the *logit* model. As with the LRM, we assume that $E(\varepsilon \mid \mathbf{x}) = 0$.

Since y^* is unobserved, we cannot estimate the variance of the errors as we did with the LRM. In the probit model, we assume that $\mathrm{Var}(\varepsilon \mid \mathbf{x}) = 1$ and in the logit model that $\mathrm{Var}(\varepsilon \mid \mathbf{x}) = \pi^2/3 \approx 3.29$. (The symbol "$\approx$" means "is approximately equal to.") The specific value assumed for the variance is arbitrary in the sense that it cannot be disconfirmed by the data. We choose a value that results in the simplest formula for the distribution of ε.

The logistic and normal distributions are used so frequently for models with CLDVs that it is worth examining these distributions in detail. The probability density functions and cumulative distribution functions for the normal and logistic distributions are shown in Figure 3.3. The normal distribution is drawn with a solid line. When ε is normal with $E(\varepsilon \mid \mathbf{x}) = 0$ and $\mathrm{Var}(\varepsilon \mid \mathbf{x}) = 1$, the pdf is

$$\phi(\varepsilon) = \frac{1}{\sqrt{2\pi}} \exp\left(-\frac{\varepsilon^2}{2}\right)$$

and the cumulative distribution function (hereafter, cdf) is

$$\Phi(\varepsilon) = \int_{-\infty}^{\varepsilon} \frac{1}{\sqrt{2\pi}} \exp\left(-\frac{t^2}{2}\right) dt$$

The cdf indicates the probability that a random variable is less than or equal to a given value. For example, $\Phi(0) = \mathrm{Pr}(\varepsilon \leq 0) = .5$. (*Find this point in panel B of Figure 3.3.*)

In the logit model, the errors are assumed to have a *standard logistic distribution* with mean 0 and variance $\pi^2/3$. This unusual variance is chosen because it results in a particularly simple equation for the pdf:

$$\lambda(\varepsilon) = \frac{\exp(\varepsilon)}{[1 + \exp(\varepsilon)]^2}$$

and an even simpler equation for the cdf:

$$\Lambda(\varepsilon) = \frac{\exp(\varepsilon)}{1 + \exp(\varepsilon)}$$

Panel A: pdf's for logistic and normal distributions

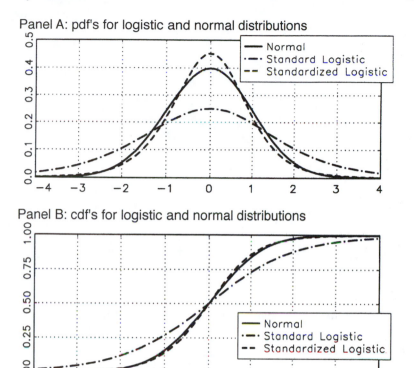

Panel B: cdf's for logistic and normal distributions

Figure 3.3. Normal and Logistic Distributions

These distributions are drawn with long dot-dashes in Figure 3.3. The standard logistic pdf is flatter than the normal distribution since it has a larger variance.

If we rescale the logistic distribution to have a unit variance, known as the *standardized* (not standard) logistic distribution, the logistic and normal cdf's are nearly identical, as shown in panel B of Figure 3.3. However, the pdf and cdf for the standardized logistic distribution with a unit variance are more complicated:

$$\lambda^S(\varepsilon) = \frac{\gamma \exp(\gamma \varepsilon)}{[1 + \exp(\gamma \varepsilon)]^2} \quad \text{and} \quad \Lambda^S(\varepsilon) = \frac{\exp(\gamma \varepsilon)}{1 + \exp(\gamma \varepsilon)} \qquad [3.2]$$

where $\gamma = \pi/\sqrt{3}$. Because of the simpler equations for the standard (not standard*ized*) logistic distribution, it is generally used for deriving

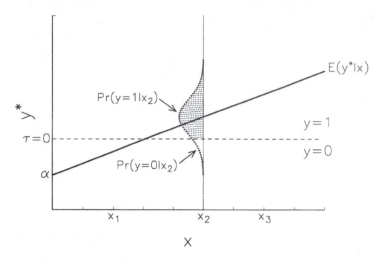

Figure 3.4. Probability of Observed Values in the Binary Response Model

the logit model. The consequences of assuming different variances for the probit and logit models are considered in Section 3.3.

By assuming a specific form for the distribution of ε, it is possible to compute the probability of $y = 1$ for a given $\mathbf{x}$. To see this, consider Figure 3.4, where ε is distributed either logistically or normally around $E(y^* \mid x) = \alpha + \beta x$. Values of $y = 1$ are observed for the shaded portion of the error distribution above τ. Even if $E(y^* \mid x)$ is in the shaded region where $y = 1$ (e.g., at x_2), it is possible to observe a 0 if ε is large and negative. The negative error moves y^* into the unshaded region of the curve.

Figure 3.5 illustrates the translation of these ideas into a formula for computing $\Pr(y = 1 \mid \mathbf{x})$. Panel A takes the error distribution from Figure

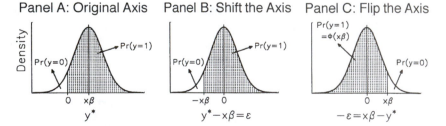

Figure 3.5. Computing $\Pr(y = 1 \mid x)$ in the Binary Response Model

3.4 and places it on its side. Since $y = 1$ when $y^* > 0$,

$$\Pr(y = 1 \mid \mathbf{x}) = \Pr(y^* > 0 \mid \mathbf{x})$$

Substituting $y^* = \mathbf{x}\boldsymbol{\beta} + \varepsilon$, it follows that

$$\Pr(y = 1 \mid \mathbf{x}) = \Pr(\mathbf{x}\boldsymbol{\beta} + \varepsilon > 0 \mid \mathbf{x})$$

Subtracting $\mathbf{x}\boldsymbol{\beta}$ from each side of the inequality corresponds to shifting the x-axis as shown in panel B. Then

$$\Pr(y = 1 \mid \mathbf{x}) = \Pr(\varepsilon > -\mathbf{x}\boldsymbol{\beta} \mid \mathbf{x})$$

Since cdf's express the probability of a variable being less than some value, we must change the direction of the inequality. The normal and logistic distributions are symmetric, which means that the shaded area of the distribution greater than $-\mathbf{x}\boldsymbol{\beta}$ in panel B equals the shaded area less than $\mathbf{x}\boldsymbol{\beta}$ in panel C. Consequently,

$$\Pr(y = 1 \mid \mathbf{x}) = \Pr(\varepsilon \leq \mathbf{x}\boldsymbol{\beta} \mid \mathbf{x})$$

This is simply the cdf of the error distribution evaluated at $\mathbf{x}\boldsymbol{\beta}$. Accordingly,

$$\Pr(y = 1 \mid \mathbf{x}) = F(\mathbf{x}\boldsymbol{\beta}) \qquad\qquad [3.3]$$

where F is the normal cdf Φ for the probit model and the logistic cdf Λ for the logit model. The probability of observing an event given $\mathbf{x}$ is the cumulative density evaluated at $\mathbf{x}\boldsymbol{\beta}$.

To understand the functional form of the resulting model, consider the BRM for a single independent variable:

$$\Pr(y = 1 \mid x) = F(\alpha + \beta x) \qquad\qquad [3.4]$$

As x increases by one unit, the argument of F increases by β units. Plotting Equation 3.4 corresponds to plotting the cdf of either the normal or the logistic distribution as its argument increases. This is shown in Figure 3.6. Panel A illustrates the error distribution for nine values of x. The region of the distribution where $y^* > \tau$ corresponds to $\Pr(y = 1 \mid x)$ and has been shaded. Panel B plots $\Pr(y = 1 \mid x)$. At x_1, only a small portion of the tail of the curve crosses the threshold in panel A, resulting in a small value of $\Pr(y = 1 \mid x)$ in panel B. As we move to x_2, the error distribution shifts up slightly. (*This shift is exactly* $\beta(x_2 - x_1)$. *Why?*

Panel A: Plot of y*

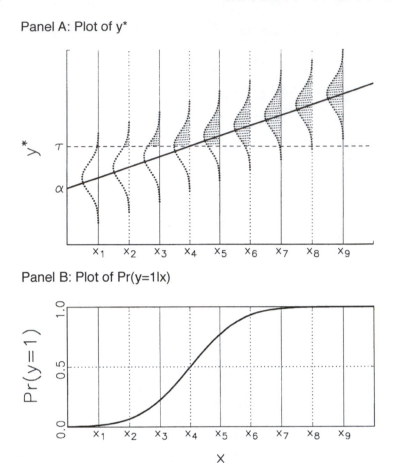

Panel B: Plot of Pr(y=1|x)

Figure 3.6. Plot of y^* and $\Pr(y = 1 \mid \mathbf{x})$ in the Binary Response Model

What is the amount of the change in the probability?) Since only a small portion of the thin tail moves over the threshold, $\Pr(y = 1 \mid x)$ increases only slightly as shown in panel B. As we continue to move to the right, from x_2 to x_3 to x_4, thicker regions of the error distribution slide over the threshold and the increase in $\Pr(y = 1 \mid x)$ becomes larger. After x_4, increasingly thinner sections of the distribution cross the threshold and the value of $\Pr(y = 1 \mid x)$ increases increasingly more slowly as it approaches 1. The resulting curve is the well-known S-curve associated with the BRM.

Before considering the interpretation of the parameters and how they are related to the predicted probability of an event, we must consider the issue of identification.

3.3. Identification

In specifying the BRM, we made three identifying assumptions: (1) the threshold is 0: $\tau = 0$; (2) the conditional mean of ε is 0: $E(\varepsilon \mid \mathbf{x}) = 0$; and (3) the conditional variance of ε is a constant: $\text{Var}(\varepsilon \mid \mathbf{x}) = 1$ in the probit model and $\text{Var}(\varepsilon \mid \mathbf{x}) = \pi^2/3$ in the logit model. These assumptions are *arbitrary* in the sense that they cannot be tested, but they are *necessary* to identify the model. Identification is an issue that is essential for understanding models with latent variables. Since a latent variable is unobserved, its mean and variance cannot be estimated. For example, in the covariance structure model, commonly referred to as the LISREL model, the variance of a latent variable is unidentified. Assumptions are required to fix the variance to a constant or to link the latent variable to an observed variable (Bollen, 1989, pp. 238–246; Long, 1983, pp. 49–52). In the BRM, the model is not identified until we impose assumptions that determine the mean and variance of y^*.

To see the relationship between the variance of the dependent variable and the identification of the β's in a regression model, consider the model $y = \mathbf{x}\boldsymbol{\beta}_y + \varepsilon_y$, where y is observed. Construct a new dependent variable $w = \delta y$, where δ is any nonzero constant. The variance of w equals:

$$\text{Var}(w) = \text{Var}(\delta y) = \delta^2 \text{Var}(y)$$

For example, if $\delta = 1/\sqrt{\text{Var}(y)}$, then $\text{Var}(w) = 1$. Since $w = \delta y$ and $y = \mathbf{x}\boldsymbol{\beta}_y + \varepsilon_y$, it follows that

$$w = \delta(\mathbf{x}\boldsymbol{\beta}_y + \varepsilon_y) = \mathbf{x}(\delta\boldsymbol{\beta}_y) + \delta\varepsilon_y$$

Therefore, the β's in a regression of w on $\mathbf{x}$ are δ times the β's in the regression of y on $\mathbf{x}$. That is,

$$\boldsymbol{\beta}_w = \delta\boldsymbol{\beta}_y \qquad [3.5]$$

Since the magnitude of the slope depends on the scale of the dependent variable, if we do not know the variance of the dependent variable, then the slope coefficients are not identified.

To apply this result to the BRM and to understand the relationship between the magnitudes of the logit compared to the probit coefficients, we need to distinguish between the structural models for logit and probit. Let

$$y_L^* = \mathbf{x}\boldsymbol{\beta}_L + \varepsilon_L \quad \text{and} \quad y_P^* = \mathbf{x}\boldsymbol{\beta}_P + \varepsilon_P$$

where L indicates the logit model and P the probit model. Since y_L^* and y_P^* are latent, it is impossible to determine their variances from the observed data, and, consequently, $\boldsymbol{\beta}_L$ and $\boldsymbol{\beta}_P$ are unidentified. For both models, the variance of y^* is determined by assuming the variance of ε. Since $\text{Var}(\varepsilon_L \,|\, \mathbf{x}) = (\pi^2/3)\,\text{Var}(\varepsilon_P \,|\, \mathbf{x})$ (*Why?*), it follows that $\varepsilon_L \approx (\pi/\sqrt{3})\varepsilon_P$. The errors are not identical since the logistic and normal distributions with unit variance are only approximately equal (see Figure 3.3). From Equation 3.5,

$$\boldsymbol{\beta}_L \approx \sqrt{\text{Var}(\varepsilon_L \,|\, \mathbf{x})}\,\boldsymbol{\beta}_P \approx \sqrt{\pi^2/3}\,\boldsymbol{\beta}_P \approx 1.81\boldsymbol{\beta}_P$$

where $\sqrt{\pi^2/3} \approx 1.81$. This transformation can be used to compare coefficients from a published logit analysis to comparable coefficients from a probit analysis and vice versa.

The approximation $\boldsymbol{\beta}_L \approx 1.8\,\boldsymbol{\beta}_P$ is based on equating the variances of the logistic and normal distributions. Amemiya (1981) suggested making the cdf's of the logistic and normal distributions as close as possible, not just making their variances equal. He proposed that the cdf's were most similar when $\varepsilon_L \approx 1.6\varepsilon_P$, which led to his approximation: $\boldsymbol{\beta}_L \approx 1.6\,\boldsymbol{\beta}_P$. My own calculations indicate that the cdf's are closest when $\varepsilon_L \approx 1.7\varepsilon_P$, which, conveniently, corresponds to the results in the example I now present.

Example of Logit and Probit: Labor Force Participation

Even though we have not considered estimation, it is useful to examine the logit and probit estimates from our model of labor force participation. The model is

$$\Pr(LFP = 1) = F(\beta_0 + \beta_1 K5 + \beta_2 K618 + \beta_3 AGE$$
$$+ \beta_4 WC + \beta_5 HC + \beta_6 LWG + \beta_7 INC)$$

Estimates are given in Table 3.3. The first thing to notice is that the log likelihood and z-tests are nearly identical. This reflects the basic similarity, except for scaling, in the structure of the logit and probit models, and the fact that these statistics are unaffected by the assumed variance

TABLE 3.3 Logit and Probit Analyses of Labor Force Participation

	Logit		Probit		Ratio	
Variable	β	z	β	z	β	z
Constant	3.182	4.94	1.918	5.04	1.66	0.98
K5	−1.463	−7.43	−0.875	−7.70	1.67	0.96
K618	−0.065	−0.95	−0.039	−0.95	1.67	1.00
AGE	−0.063	−4.92	−0.038	−4.97	1.66	0.99
WC	0.807	3.51	0.488	3.60	1.65	0.97
HC	0.112	0.54	0.057	0.46	1.95	1.18
LWG	0.605	4.01	0.366	4.17	1.65	0.96
INC	−0.034	−4.20	−0.021	−4.30	1.68	0.98
−2 ln L	905.27		905.39		1.00	

NOTE: $N = 753$. β is an unstandardized coefficient; z is the z-test for β. "Ratio" is the ratio of a logit to a probit coefficient.

of the error. The effects of the identifying assumptions about Var(ε) are seen by taking the ratio of the logit coefficients to the probit coefficients, contained in the column labeled "Ratio." The logit coefficients are about 1.7 times larger than the corresponding probit coefficients, with the exception of the coefficient for *HC* which is the least statistically significant parameter. Clearly, interpretation of the β's must take the effects of the identifying assumptions into account. This issue is now considered.

3.3.1. The Identification of Probabilities

Since the β's are unidentified without assumptions about the mean and variance of ε, the β's are arbitrary in this sense: if we change the identifying assumption regarding Var($\varepsilon | \mathbf{x}$), the β's also change. *Accordingly, the β's cannot be interpreted directly since they reflect both*: (1) *the relationship between the x's and y***; and* (2) *the identifying assumptions.* While the identifying assumptions affect the β's, they do not affect Pr($y = 1 | \mathbf{x}$). More technically, Pr($y = 1 | \mathbf{x}$) is an *estimable function.* An estimable function is a function of the parameters that is invariant to the identifying assumptions (Searle, 1971, pp. 180–188).

Consider the logit model where

$$\Pr(y_i = 1 | \mathbf{x}_i) = \frac{\exp(\mathbf{x}_i\boldsymbol{\beta})}{1 + \exp(\mathbf{x}_i\boldsymbol{\beta})} = \frac{1}{1 + \exp(-\mathbf{x}_i\boldsymbol{\beta})}$$

(*Prove the last equality.*) The right-hand side is the cdf for the logistic distribution with variance $\sigma^2 = \pi^2/3$. We can standardize ε to have a unit variance by dividing the structural model by σ:

$$\frac{y_i^*}{\sigma} = \frac{\mathbf{x}_i \boldsymbol{\beta}}{\sigma} + \frac{\varepsilon_i}{\sigma}$$

ε/σ has a standardized logistic distribution with cdf (see Equation 3.2):

$$\Lambda^S \left(\frac{\varepsilon_i}{\sigma} \right) = \frac{\exp\left(\dfrac{\pi}{\sqrt{3}} \dfrac{\varepsilon_i}{\sigma} \right)}{1 + \exp\left(\dfrac{\pi}{\sqrt{3}} \dfrac{\varepsilon_i}{\sigma} \right)}$$

Since $\sigma = \pi/\sqrt{3}$,

$$\Lambda^S \left(\frac{\varepsilon_i}{\sigma} \right) = \frac{\exp(\varepsilon_i)}{1 + \exp(\varepsilon_i)} = \Lambda(\varepsilon_i)$$

Consequently, *the probability of an event is unaffected by the identifying assumption regarding* $\text{Var}(\varepsilon \,|\, \mathbf{x})$. While the specific value assumed for $\text{Var}(\varepsilon \,|\, \mathbf{x})$ is arbitrary and affects the β's, it does not affect the quantity that is of fundamental interest, namely, the probability that an event occurred. The same result holds for the probit model.

The critical point is that while the β's are affected by the arbitrary scale assumed for ε, the probabilities are not affected. Consequently, the probabilities can be interpreted without concern about the arbitrary assumption that is made to identify the model. That is to say, the probabilities are estimable functions. Further, any function of the probabilities is also estimable. Importantly, we can interpret changes in probabilities and odds, which are ratios of probabilities. This is done in Section 3.7, but first we consider an alternative method of deriving the logit and probit models.

3.4. A Nonlinear Probability Model

The BRM can also be derived without appealing to an underlying latent variable. This is done by specifying a nonlinear model relating the x's to the probability of an event. For example, Aldrich and Nelson (1984, pp. 31–32) derive the logit model by starting with the problem that the LPM can predict values of $\Pr(y = 1 \,|\, \mathbf{x})$ that are greater than 1 or less than 0. To eliminate this problem, they transform $\Pr(y = 1 \,|\, \mathbf{x})$ into a function that ranges from $-\infty$ to ∞. First, the probability is transformed into the *odds*:

$$\frac{\Pr(y=1\,|\,\mathbf{x})}{\Pr(y=0\,|\,\mathbf{x})} = \frac{\Pr(y=1\,|\,\mathbf{x})}{1 - \Pr(y=1\,|\,\mathbf{x})}$$

The odds indicate how often something (e.g., $y = 1$) happens relative to how often it does not happen (e.g., $y = 0$), and range from 0 when $\Pr(y = 1\,|\,\mathbf{x}) = 0$ to ∞ when $\Pr(y = 1\,|\,\mathbf{x}) = 1$. The log of the odds, known as the *logit*, ranges from $-\infty$ to ∞. This suggests a model that is linear in the logit:

$$\ln\left[\frac{\Pr(y=1\,|\,\mathbf{x})}{1 - \Pr(y=1\,|\,\mathbf{x})}\right] = \mathbf{x}\boldsymbol{\beta} \qquad [3.6]$$

This is equivalent to the logit model derived above (*Show this.*):

$$\Pr(y=1\,|\,\mathbf{x}) = \frac{\exp(\mathbf{x}\boldsymbol{\beta})}{1 + \exp(\mathbf{x}\boldsymbol{\beta})} \qquad [3.7]$$

Other probability models can be constructed by choosing functions of $\mathbf{x}\boldsymbol{\beta}$ that range from 0 to 1. Cumulative distribution functions have this property and readily provide a number of examples. The cdf for the standard normal distribution results in the probit model:

$$\Pr(y=1\,|\,\mathbf{x}) = \int_{-\infty}^{\mathbf{x}\boldsymbol{\beta}} \frac{1}{\sqrt{2\pi}} \exp\left(-\frac{t^2}{2}\right) dt = \Phi(\mathbf{x}\boldsymbol{\beta})$$

Another example is the complementary log-log model (Agresti, 1990, pp. 104–107; McCullagh & Nelder, 1989, p. 108), defined by

$$\ln(-\ln[1 - \Pr(y=1\,|\,\mathbf{x})]) = \mathbf{x}\boldsymbol{\beta}$$

or, equivalently,

$$\Pr(y=1\,|\,\mathbf{x}) = 1 - \exp[-\exp(\mathbf{x}\boldsymbol{\beta})]$$

Unlike the logit and probit models, the complementary log-log model is asymmetric. In the logit and probit models, if you are at that point on the probability curve where $\Pr(y = 1\,|\,x) = .5$, increasing x by a given amount δ changes the probability by the same amount as if x is decreased by δ. This is not the case for the complementary log-log model as shown in Figure 3.7. As x increases, the probability increases slowly at the left until it reaches about .2; the change from .8 toward 1 occurs much more rapidly. The log-log model, which is defined as

$$\Pr(y=1\,|\,\mathbf{x}) = \exp[-\exp(-\mathbf{x}\boldsymbol{\beta})]$$

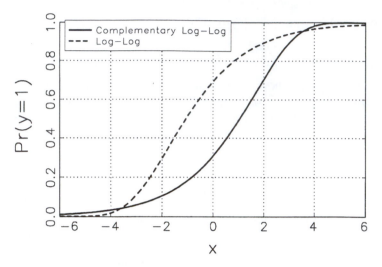

Figure 3.7. Complementary Log-Log and Log-Log Models

has the opposite pattern. These models can be estimated with GLIM, Stata, and SAS, and have links to the proportional hazards model (see Allison, 1995, pp. 216–217, or Petersen, 1995, p. 499, for details).

3.5. ML Estimation[2]

To specify the likelihood equation, define p as the probability of observing whatever value of y was actually observed for a given observation:

$$p_i = \begin{cases} \Pr(y_i = 1 \,|\, \mathbf{x}_i) & \text{if } y_i = 1 \text{ is observed} \\ 1 - \Pr(y_i = 1 \,|\, \mathbf{x}_i) & \text{if } y_i = 0 \text{ is observed} \end{cases} \qquad [3.8]$$

$\Pr(y_i = 1 \,|\, \mathbf{x}_i)$ is defined by Equation 3.3. If the observations are independent, the likelihood equation is

$$L(\boldsymbol{\beta} \,|\, \mathbf{y}, \mathbf{X}) = \prod_{i=1}^{N} p_i \qquad [3.9]$$

---

[2] When there is more than one observation for each combination of values of independent variables, Berkson's minimum chi-square estimation can be used. Since the requirement of many observations per cell is rarely satisfied in social science research, I do not consider this method. See Hanushek and Jackson (1977, pp. 190–200) or Maddala (1983, pp. 28–34).

Combining Equations 3.8 and 3.9,

$$L(\boldsymbol{\beta} \mid \mathbf{y}, \mathbf{X}) = \prod_{y=1} \Pr(y_i = 1 \mid \mathbf{x}_i) \prod_{y=0} [1 - \Pr(y_i = 1 \mid \mathbf{x}_i)]$$

where the index for multiplication indicates that the product is taken over only those cases where $y = 1$ and $y = 0$, respectively.

The β's are incorporated into the likelihood equation by substituting the right-hand side of Equation 3.3:

$$L(\boldsymbol{\beta} \mid \mathbf{y}, \mathbf{X}) = \prod_{y=1} F(\mathbf{x}_i\boldsymbol{\beta}) \prod_{y=0} [1 - F(\mathbf{x}_i\boldsymbol{\beta})]$$

Taking logs, we obtain the log likelihood equation:

$$\ln L(\boldsymbol{\beta} \mid \mathbf{y}, \mathbf{X}) = \sum_{y=1} \ln F(\mathbf{x}_i\boldsymbol{\beta}) + \sum_{y=0} \ln[1 - F(\mathbf{x}_i\boldsymbol{\beta})]$$

Amemiya (1985, pp. 273–274) proves that under conditions that are likely to apply in practice, the likelihood function is globally concave which ensures the uniqueness of the ML estimates. These estimates are consistent, asymptotically normal, and asymptotically efficient.

3.5.1. Maximum Likelihood and Sample Size

For ML estimation, the desirable properties of consistency, normality, and efficiency are asymptotic. This means that these properties have been proven to hold as the sample size approaches ∞. While ML estimators are not necessarily bad estimators in small samples, indeed OLS for the linear regression model is an ML estimator that works quite well in small-samples, the small-sample behavior of ML estimators for the models in this book is largely unknown. Since alternative estimators with known small sample properties are generally not available for the models we consider, the practical question is: *When is the sample large enough to use the ML estimates and the resulting significance tests?* While I am reluctant to give advice without firm evidence to justify the advice, it seems necessary to add a cautionary note since it is easy to get the impression that ML estimation works well with any sample size. For example, the 32 observations from a study by Spector and Mazzeo (1980) are used frequently to illustrate the logit and probit models, yet 32 is too small of a sample to justify the use of ML. The following guidelines are not hard and fast. They are based on my experience of when the models seem to produce reasonable and robust results and my discussions with other researchers who use these methods.

It is risky to use ML with samples smaller than 100, while samples over 500 seem adequate. These values should be raised depending on characteristics of the model and the data. First, if there are a lot of parameters in the model, more observations are needed. In the literature on the covariance structure model, the rule of at least five observations per parameter is often given. A rule of at least 10 observations per parameter seems reasonable for the models in this book. This rule does not imply that a minimum of 100 is not needed if you have only two parameters. Second, if the data are ill conditioned (e.g., independent variables are highly collinear) or if there is little variation in the dependent variable (e.g., nearly all of the outcomes are 1), a larger sample is required. Third, some models seem to require more observations. The ordinal regression model of Chapter 5 is an example. In discussing the use of ML for small samples, Allison (1995, p. 80) makes a useful point. While the standard advice is that with small samples you should accept larger p-values as evidence against the null hypothesis, given that the degree to which ML estimates are normally distributed in small samples is unknown, it is more reasonable to require smaller p-values in small samples.

3.6. Numerical Methods for ML Estimation

For the LRM, ML estimates are obtained by setting the gradient of the log likelihood to 0 and solving for the parameters using algebra. Algebraic solutions are rarely possible with nonlinear models. Consequently, *numerical methods* are used to find the estimates that maximize the log likelihood function. Numerical methods start with a guess of the values of the parameters and iterate to improve on that guess. While you may be tempted to dismiss numerical methods as an esoteric topic of little practical concern, programs using numerical methods for estimation can produce incorrect estimates or fail to provide any estimates. To recognize and correct such problems, an elementary understanding of numerical methods is useful. I begin with an introduction to numerical methods, followed by practical advice on using these methods.

3.6.1. Iterative Solutions

Assume that we are trying to estimate the vector of parameters $\boldsymbol{\theta}$. We begin with an initial guess $\boldsymbol{\theta}_0$, called *start values*, and attempt to improve on this guess by adding a vector ζ_0 of adjustments:

$$\theta_1 = \theta_0 + \zeta_0$$

We proceed by updating the previous iteration according to the equation:

$$\theta_{n+1} = \theta_n + \zeta_n$$

Iterations continue until there is *convergence*. Roughly, convergence occurs when the gradient of the log likelihood is close to 0 or the estimates do not change from one step to the next. Convergence must occur to obtain the ML estimator $\widehat{\theta}$.

The problem is to find a ζ_n that moves the process rapidly toward a solution. It is useful to think of ζ_n as consisting of two parts: $\zeta_n = \mathbf{D}_n \gamma_n$. γ_n is the *gradient* vector defined as $\partial \ln L / \partial \theta_n$, which indicates the direction of the change in the log likelihood for a change in the parameters. $\mathbf{D}_n$ is a *direction matrix* that reflects the curvature of the log likelihood function; that is, it indicates how rapidly the gradient is changing. A clearer understanding of these components is gained by examining the simplest methods of maximization.

The Method of Steepest Ascent. The method of steepest ascent lets $\mathbf{D} = \mathbf{I}$:

$$\theta_{n+1} = \theta_n + \frac{\partial \ln L}{\partial \theta_n}$$

An estimate increases if the gradient is positive, and it decreases if the gradient is negative. Iterations stop when the derivative becomes nearly 0. The problem with this approach is that it considers the slope of $\ln L$, but not how quickly the slope is changing. To see why this is a problem, consider two log likelihood functions with the same gradient at a given point but with one function changing shape more quickly than the other. (*Sketch these functions.*) You should move more gradually for the function that is changing quickly, in order to avoid moving too far. Steepest descent tends to work poorly since it treats both functions in the same way.

The next three commonly used methods address this problem by adding a direction matrix that assesses how quickly the log likelihood function is changing. They differ in their choice of a direction matrix. In all cases, it takes longer to compute the direction matrix than the identity matrix used with the method of steepest ascent. Usually, the additional computational costs are made up for by the fewer iterations that are required to reach convergence.

No one method works best all of the time. An algorithm applied to one set of data may not converge, while another algorithm applied to the same data may converge rapidly. For a different set of data, the opposite may occur. In general, the algorithm used in commercial software depends on the preferences of the programmer and the ease with which an algorithm can be programmed for a given model.

The Newton-Raphson Method. The rate of change in the slope of $\ln L$ is indicated by the second derivatives, which are contained in the *Hessian matrix* $\partial^2 \ln L / \partial \theta \partial \theta'$. For example, with two parameters $\theta = (\alpha \ \beta)'$, the Hessian is

$$\frac{\partial^2 \ln L}{\partial \theta \partial \theta'} = \begin{pmatrix} \dfrac{\partial^2 \ln L}{\partial \alpha \partial \alpha} & \dfrac{\partial^2 \ln L}{\partial \alpha \partial \beta} \\[2ex] \dfrac{\partial^2 \ln L}{\partial \beta \partial \alpha} & \dfrac{\partial^2 \ln L}{\partial \beta \partial \beta} \end{pmatrix}$$

If $\partial^2 \ln L / \partial \alpha \partial \alpha$ is large relative to $\partial^2 \ln L / \partial \beta \partial \beta$, the gradient is changing more rapidly as α changes than as β changes. Thus, smaller a djustments to the estimate of α would be indicated. The Newton-Raphson algorithm proceeds according to the equation:

$$\theta_{n+1} = \theta_n - \left(\frac{\partial^2 \ln L}{\partial \theta_n \partial \theta'_n} \right)^{-1} \frac{\partial \ln L}{\partial \theta_n}$$

(*Why are we taking the inverse of the Hessian?*)

The Method of Scoring. In some cases, the expectation of the Hessian, known as the *information matrix*, can be easier to compute than the Hessian. The method of scoring uses the information matrix as the direction matrix, which results in

$$\theta_{n+1} = \theta_n + \left(E\left[\frac{\partial^2 \ln L}{\partial \theta_n \partial \theta'_n} \right] \right)^{-1} \frac{\partial \ln L}{\partial \theta_n}$$

The BHHH Method. When the Hessian and the information matrix are difficult to compute, Berndt et al. (1974) propose using an outer product of the gradient approximation to the information matrix:

$$\sum_{i=1}^{N} \frac{\partial \ln L_i}{\partial \theta_n} \frac{\partial \ln L_i}{\partial \theta_n}'$$

where $\ln L_i$ is the value of the likelihood function evaluated for the ith observation. This approximation is often simpler to compute since only the gradient needs to be evaluated. Iterations proceed according to

$$\boldsymbol{\theta}_{n+1} = \boldsymbol{\theta}_n + \left(\sum_{i=1}^{N} \frac{\partial \ln L_i}{\partial \boldsymbol{\theta}_n} \frac{\partial \ln L_i}{\partial \boldsymbol{\theta}_n}' \right)^{-1} \frac{\partial \ln L}{\partial \boldsymbol{\theta}_n}$$

which is known as the BHHH (pronounced "B-triple-H") algorithm or the modified method of scoring.

Numerical Derivatives. If you cannot obtain an algebraic solution for the gradient or the Hessian, numerical methods can be used to estimate them. For example, consider a log likelihood based on a single parameter θ. The gradient is approximated by computing the slope of the change in $\ln L$ when θ changes by a small amount. If Δ is a small number relative to θ,

$$\frac{\partial \ln L}{\partial \theta} \approx \frac{\ln L(\theta + \Delta) - \ln L(\theta)}{\Delta}$$

Using numerical estimates can greatly increase the time and number of iterations needed, and results can be sensitive to the choice of Δ. Further, different start values can result in different estimates of the Hessian at convergence, which translates into different estimates of the standard errors. Programs that use numerical methods for computing derivatives should only be used if no alternatives are available. When they must be used, you should experiment with different starting values to make sure that the estimates that you obtain are stable.

3.6.2. The Variance of the ML Estimator

In addition to estimating the parameters $\boldsymbol{\theta}$, numerical methods provide estimates of the asymptotic covariance matrix $\mathrm{Var}(\widehat{\boldsymbol{\theta}})$, which are used for the statistical tests in Chapter 4. The theory of maximum likelihood shows that if the assumptions justifying ML estimation hold, then the asymptotic covariance matrix equals

$$\mathrm{Var}(\widehat{\boldsymbol{\theta}}) = \left(-E\left[\frac{\partial^2 \ln L}{\partial \boldsymbol{\theta} \partial \boldsymbol{\theta}'} \right] \right)^{-1} \qquad [3.10]$$

In words, the asymptotic covariance equals the inverse of the negative of the expected value of the Hessian, known as the *information matrix*.

The covariance matrix is often written in an equivalent form using the outer product of the gradient:

$$\text{Var}(\widehat{\theta}) = \left(E\left[\frac{\partial \ln L}{\partial \theta} \frac{\partial \ln L'}{\partial \theta} \right] \right)^{-1} \qquad [3.11]$$

In both cases, the expression is evaluated at θ. Since we only have an estimate of θ, the covariance matrix must be estimated. Three consistent estimators of $\text{Var}(\widehat{\theta})$ are commonly used.

The first estimator evaluates Equation 3.10 using the ML estimates $\widehat{\theta}$:

$$\widehat{\text{Var}}_1(\widehat{\theta}) = -\left(E\left[\frac{\partial^2 \ln L}{\partial \widehat{\theta} \partial \widehat{\theta}'} \right] \right)^{-1}$$

This estimator is generally used with the method of scoring since that method requires evaluating the information matrix at each iteration.

A second estimator is obtained by evaluating the negative of the Hessian, sometimes referred to as the observed information matrix, rather than the information matrix itself:

$$\widehat{\text{Var}}_2(\widehat{\theta}) = -\left(\sum_{i=1}^{N} \frac{\partial^2 \ln L_i}{\partial \widehat{\theta} \partial \widehat{\theta}'} \right)^{-1} \qquad [3.12]$$

$\widehat{\text{Var}}_2(\widehat{\theta})$ is generally used with the Newton-Raphson algorithm. Equation 3.12 shows the relationship between the curvature of the likelihood function and the variance of the estimator. The size of the variance is inversely related to the second derivative: the smaller the second derivative, the larger the variance. When the second derivative is smaller, the likelihood function is flatter. If the likelihood equation is very flat, the variance will be large. This should match your intuition that the flatter the likelihood function, the harder it will be to find the maximum of the function, and the less confidence (i.e., the more variance) you should have in the solution you obtain.

A third estimator, which is related to the BHHH algorithm, is simple to compute since it does not require evaluation of the second derivatives:

$$\widehat{\text{Var}}_3(\widehat{\theta}) = \left(\sum_{i=1}^{N} \frac{\partial \ln L_i}{\partial \widehat{\theta}} \frac{\partial \ln L_i}{\partial \widehat{\theta}'} \right)^{-1}$$

While these estimators of the covariance matrix are asymptotically equivalent, in practice they sometimes provide very different estimates, especially when the sample is small or the data are ill conditioned. Consequently, if you estimate the same model with the same data using two programs that use different estimators, you can get different results.

3.6.3. Problems With Numerical Methods and Possible Solutions

While numerical methods generally work well, there can be problems. First, it may be difficult or impossible to reach convergence. You might get an error such as "Convergence not obtained after 250 iterations." Or, it might not be possible to invert the Hessian when $\ln L$ is nearly flat. This generates a message such as "Singularity encountered," "Hessian could not be inverted," or "Hessian was not of full rank." The message might refer to the covariance matrix or the information matrix. Second, sometimes convergence occurs, but the wrong solution is obtained. This occurs when $\ln L$ has more than one location where the gradient is 0. The iterative process might locate a saddle point or local maximum, where the gradient is also 0, rather than the global maximum. (Think of a two-humped Bactrian camel. The top of the smaller hump is a local maximum; the low spot between the two humps is a saddle point.) In such cases, the covariance matrix which should be positive definite is negative definite. When $\ln L$ is globally concave, there is only one solution, and that is a maximum. This is the case for most of the models considered in this book. However, even when the log likelihood is globally concave, it is possible to have false convergence. This can occur when the function is very flat and the precision of the estimates of the gradient is insufficient. This is common when numerical gradients are used and can also be caused by problems with scaling (discussed below). Finally, in some cases, ML estimates do not exist for a particular pattern of data. For example, with a binary outcome and a single binary independent variable, ML estimates are not possible if there is no variation in the independent variable for one of the outcomes. You can try estimating a probit model using: $\mathbf{y}' = (0\ 0\ 1\ 1\ 1)$ and $\mathbf{x}' = (1\ 0\ 1\ 1\ 0)$. This works fine, since there are x's equal to 0 and 1 for both $y = 1$ and $y = 0$. However, now try to estimate the model for: $\mathbf{y}' = (0\ 0\ 1\ 1)$ and $\mathbf{x}' = (1\ 0\ 1\ 1)$. Your program will "crash" since whenever $y = 1$, all x's are 1's.

When you cannot get a solution or appear to get the wrong solution, the first thing to check is that the software is estimating the model that you want to estimate. It is easy to make an error in specifying the commands to estimate your model. If the model and commands are correct, there may be problems with the data.

Incorrect variables. Most simply, you may have constructed a variable incorrectly. Be sure to check the descriptive statistics for all variables. My experience suggests that most problems with numerical methods are due to data that have not been "cleaned."

Number of observations. Convergence generally occurs more rapidly when there are more observations, and when the ratio of the number of observations to the number of variables is larger. While there is generally little you can do about sample size, it can explain why you are having problems getting your models to converge.

Scaling of variables. Scaling is a very common cause of problems with numerical methods. The larger the ratio between the largest standard deviation and the smallest standard deviation, the more problems you will have with numerical methods. For example, if you have income measured in dollars, it may have a very large standard deviation relative to other variables. Recoding income to thousands of dollars, may solve the problem. My experience suggests that problems are much more likely when the ratio between the largest and smallest standard deviation exceeds 10.

Distribution of the outcome. If a large proportion of cases are censored in the tobit model or if one of the categories of a categorical variable has very few cases, convergence may be difficult. There is little that can be done with such data limitations.

Numerical methods for ML estimation tend to work well when your model is appropriate for your data. In such cases, convergence generally occurs quite rapidly, often within five iterations. If you have too few cases, too many variables, or a poor model, convergence may be a problem. In such cases, rescaling your data can solve the problem. If that does not work, you can try using a program that uses a different numerical algorithm. A problem that may be very difficult for one algorithm may work quite well for another.

While numerical methods generally work well, I heartily endorse Cramer's (1986, p. 10) advice: "Check the data, check their transfer into the computer, check the actual computations (preferably by repeating at least a sample by a rival program), and always remain suspicious of the results, regardless of the appeal."

3.6.4. Software Issues

There are several issues related to software for logit and probit that should be considered.

The Method of Numerical Maximization. Different programs use different methods of numerical maximization. In most cases, estimates of the parameters from the different programs are identical to at least four decimal digits. Estimates of the standard errors and the z-values may differ at the first decimal digit as a result of the different methods used to estimate $\text{Var}(\widehat{\boldsymbol{\beta}})$.

Parameterizations of the Model. A more basic difference is found in the outcome being modeled. While most programs model the probability of a 1, some programs (e.g., SAS) model the probability of a 0. This is a trivial difference *if* you are aware of what the program is doing. For the BRM,

$$\text{Pr}(y_i = 0 \mid x_i) = 1 - \text{Pr}(y_i = 1 \mid x_i) = 1 - F(x_i'\boldsymbol{\beta}) = F(-x_i'\boldsymbol{\beta})$$

where the last equality follows from the symmetry of the pdf for the logit and probit models. Thus, all coefficients will have the opposite sign. Note that this will *not* be the case for the complementary log-log model since it is asymmetric.

With estimates in hand, we can consider the interpretation of the binary response model.

3.7. Interpretation

In this section, I present four methods of interpretation, each of which is generalized to other models in later chapters. First, I show how to present predicted probabilities using graphs and tables. Second, I examine the partial change in y^* and in the probability. Third, I use discrete change in the probability to summarize the effects of each variable. Finally, for the logit model, I derive a simple transformation of the parameters that indicates the effect of a variable on the odds that the event occurred.

Since the BRM is nonlinear, no single approach to interpretation can fully describe the relationship between a variable and the outcome probability. You should search for an elegant and concise way to summarize the results that does justice to the complexities of the nonlinear model. For any given application, you may need to try each method before a final approach is determined. For example, you might have to construct a plot of the predicted probabilities before realizing that a single measure of discrete change is sufficient to summarize the effect of a variable. I illustrate these methods with the data on the labor force participation of women. You should be able to replicate many of the results using Tables 3.1 and 3.3, although your answers may differ slightly due to rounding error.

I begin by showing how the intercept and the slope affect the curve relating an independent variable to the probability of an event. Understanding how the parameters affect the probability curves is fundamental to applying each method of interpretation.

3.7.1. The Effects of the Parameters

Consider the BRM with a single x:

$$\Pr(y = 1 \mid x) = F(\alpha + \beta x)$$

Panel A of Figure 3.8 shows the effect of the intercept on the probability curve. When $\alpha = 0$, shown by the short dashed line, the curve passes through the point $(0, .5)$. As α gets larger, the curve shifts to the left; as α gets smaller, the curve shifts to the right. (*Why does the curve shift to the left when α increases?*) When the curve shifts, the slope at a given value of $\Pr(y = 1 \mid x)$ does not change. This idea of shifting, "parallel" curves is used to explain several of the methods presented below. It is also fundamental to understanding the ordinal regression model in Chapter 5.

Panel B of Figure 3.8 shows the effects of changing the slope. Since $\alpha = 0$, the curves go through point $(0, .5)$. The smaller the β, the more stretched out the curve. At $\beta = .25$, shown by the solid line, the curve increases steadily as it moves from -20 to 20. When β increases to $.5$, shown by the long dashed line, the curve initially increases more slowly. As x approaches 0, the increase is more rapid. In general, as β increases, the curve increases more rapidly as x approaches 0. While I have not drawn the curves, when the slope is negative, the curve is rotated $180°$ around $x = 0$. For example, if $\beta = -.25$, the curve would be near 1 at $x = -20$, and would gradually decrease toward 0 at $x = 20$.

It is also important to understand how the probability curve generalizes to more than one variable. Figure 3.9 plots the probit model:

$$\Pr(y = 1 \mid x, z) = \Phi(1 + 1x + .75z)$$

Similar results apply for the logit model. The surface begins near zero when $x = -4$ and $z = -8$. If we fix $z = -8$, then

$$\Pr(y = 1 \mid x, z = -8) = \Phi(1 + 1x + [.75 \times -8]) = \Phi(-5.0 + 1x)$$

which is the first S-shaped curve along the x-axis. If we increase z by 1, which corresponds to the next curve back along the z-axis, then

$$\Pr(y = 1 \mid x, z = -7) = \Phi(1 + 1x + [.75 \times -7]) = \Phi(-4.25 + 1x)$$

Panel A: Effects of Changing α

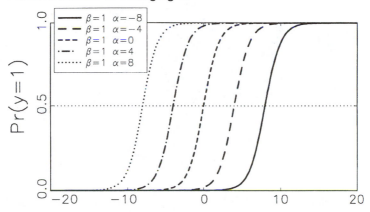

Panel B: Effects of Changing β

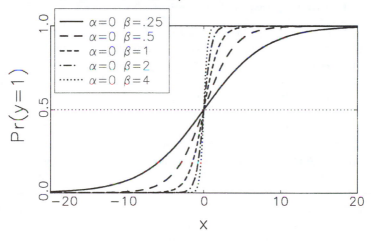

X

Figure 3.8. Effects of Changing the Slope and Intercept on the Binary Response Model: $\Pr(y = 1 \mid x) = F(\alpha + \beta x)$

Only the intercept has changed, which causes the curve to shift to the left (see panel A of Figure 3.8). The level of z affects the intercept of the curve, but does not affect the slope. Conversely, controlling for x affects the intercept of the curve for z, but not the slope.

With these ideas in mind, we can consider several methods for interpreting the binary response model.

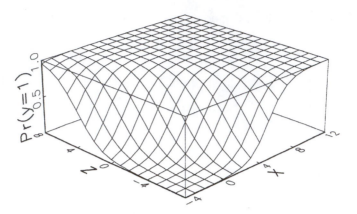

Figure 3.9. Plot of Probit Model: $\Pr(y = 1 \mid x, z) = \Phi(1.0 + 1.0x + 0.75z)$

3.7.2. Interpretation Using Predicted Probabilities

The most direct approach for interpretation is to examine the predicted probabilities of an event for different values of the independent
variables. When there are more than two variables, it is no longer possible to plot the entire probability surface and a decision must be made
regarding which probabilities to compute and how to present them. A
useful first step is to examine the range of predicted probabilities within
the sample, and the degree to which each variable affects the probabilities. If the range of probabilities is between .2 and .8 (or, more con-
servatively, between .3 and .7), the relationship between the x's and the
predicted probability is nearly linear, and simple measures can be used
to summarize the results. Or, if the range of the probability is small,
the relationship between the x's and the probability will also be approximately linear. For example, the segment of the probability curve between
.05 and .10 is nearly linear. These points are illustrated below.

Determining the Range of Probabilities

The predicted probability of an event given **x** for the ith individual is

$$\widehat{\Pr}(y_i = 1 \mid \mathbf{x}_i) = F(\mathbf{x}_i\widehat{\boldsymbol{\beta}})$$

The minimum and maximum probabilities in the sample are defined as

$$\min \widehat{\Pr}(y = 1 \mid \mathbf{x}) = \min_i F(\mathbf{x}_i\widehat{\boldsymbol{\beta}})$$

$$\max \widehat{\Pr}(y = 1 \mid \mathbf{x}) = \max_i F(\mathbf{x}_i\widehat{\boldsymbol{\beta}})$$

where min$_i$ indicates taking the minimum value over all observations, and similarly for max$_i$. In our example, the predicted probabilities from the probit model range from .01 to .97, which indicates that the nonlinearities that occur below .2 and above .8 need to be taken into account. If the coefficients from the logit model are used, the predicted probabilities range from .01 to .96. This illustrates the great similarity between the predictions of the logit and probit models, even for observations that fall in the tail of the distribution. Consequently, in the remainder of this section, only the results from the probit analysis are shown.

Computing the minimum and maximum predicted probabilities requires your software to save each observation's predicted probability for further analysis. If this is not possible, or if you are doing a meta-analysis, the minimum and maximum can be approximated by using the estimated β's and the descriptive statistics. The *lower extreme* of the variables is defined by setting each variable associated with a positive β to its minimum and each variable associated with a negative β to its maximum. In our example, this involves taking the maximum number of young children (since *K6* has a negative effect), the minimum anticipated wage (since *LWG* has a positive effect), and so on. Formally, let

$$\overleftarrow{x}_k = \begin{cases} \min\limits_i x_{ik} & \text{if } \beta_k \geq 0 \\ \max\limits_i x_{ik} & \text{if } \beta_k < 0 \end{cases}$$

and let $\overleftarrow{\mathbf{x}}$ be the vector whose kth element is $\overleftarrow{x}_k$. The *upper extreme* can be defined in a corresponding way, with the values contained in $\overrightarrow{\mathbf{x}}$. The minimum and maximum probabilities are computed as

$$\widehat{\Pr}(y = 1 \mid \overleftarrow{\mathbf{x}}) = F(\overleftarrow{\mathbf{x}}\widehat{\boldsymbol{\beta}}) \quad \text{and} \quad \widehat{\Pr}(y = 1 \mid \overrightarrow{\mathbf{x}}) = F(\overrightarrow{\mathbf{x}}\widehat{\boldsymbol{\beta}})$$

In our example, the computed probability at the lower extreme is less than .01 and at the upper extreme is .99. While these values are quite close to the minimum and maximum predicted probabilities for the sample, $\overleftarrow{\mathbf{x}}$ and $\overrightarrow{\mathbf{x}}$ are constructs that do not necessarily approximate any member of the sample. If they differ substantially from any $\mathbf{x}_i$ in the sample, then $\widehat{\Pr}(y = 1 \mid \overleftarrow{\mathbf{x}})$ and $\widehat{\Pr}(y = 1 \mid \overrightarrow{\mathbf{x}})$ will be poor approximations of the probabilities $\min \widehat{\Pr}(y = 1 \mid \mathbf{x})$ and $\max \widehat{\Pr}(y = 1 \mid \mathbf{x})$.

Warning on the Use of Minimums and Maximums. The use of the minimum or maximum value of a variable can be misleading if there are extreme values in the sample. For example, if our sample includes an extremely wealthy person, the change in the probability when we move from the minimum to the maximum income would be unrealistically large. Before using the minimum and maximum, you should examine the frequency distribution of each variable. If extreme values are present, you should consider using the 5th percentile and the 95th percentile, for example, rather than the minimum and maximum.

The Effect of Each Variable on the Predicted Probability

The next step is to determine the extent to which change in a variable affects the predicted probability. One way to do this is to allow one variable to vary from its minimum to its maximum, while all other variables are fixed at their means. Let $\Pr(y = 1 \mid \bar{x}, x_k)$ be the probability computed when all variables except x_k are set equal to their means, and x_k equals some specified value. For example, $\Pr(y = 1 \mid \bar{x}, \min x_k)$ is the probability when x_k equals its minimum. The predicted change in the probability as x_k changes from its minimum to its maximum equals

$$\Pr(y = 1 \mid \bar{x}, \max x_k) - \Pr(y = 1 \mid \bar{x}, \min x_k)$$

For our example, the results are given in Table 3.4. The range of predicted probabilities can be used to guide further analysis. For example, there is little to be learned by analyzing variables whose range of probabilities is small, such as *HC*. For variables that have a larger range, the end points of the range affect how interpretation should proceed. For example, the predicted probabilities for *AGE* range from .75 when age is 30 to .32 when age is 60, which is a region where the probability curve is nearly linear. The range for *INC*, however, is from .09 to .73, where nonlinearities are present. The implications of these differences are shown in the next section.

TABLE 3.4 Probabilities of Labor Force Participation Over the Range of Each Independent Variable for the Probit Model

Variable	At Maximum	At Minimum	Range of $\hat{Pr}$
K5	0.01	0.66	0.64
K618	0.48	0.60	0.12
AGE	0.32	0.75	0.43
WC	0.71	0.52	0.18
HC	0.59	0.57	0.02
LWG	0.83	0.17	0.66
INC	0.09	0.73	0.64

Plotting Probabilities Over the Range of a Variable

When there are more than two independent variables, we must examine the effects of one or two variables while the remaining variables are held constant. For example, consider the effects of age and the wife attending college on labor force participation. The effects of both variables can be plotted by holding all other variables at their means and allowing age and college status to vary. To do this, let x_0 contain the mean of all variables, except let $WC = 0$ and allow AGE to vary. x_1 is defined similarly for $WC = 1$. Then

$$\widehat{\Pr}(LFP = 1 | AGE, WC = 0) = \Phi(x_0 \widehat{\beta})$$

is the predicted probability of being in the labor force for women of a given age who did not attend college and who are average on all other characteristics. $\widehat{\Pr}(LFP = 1 | AGE, WC = 1)$ can be computed similarly. These probabilities are plotted in Figure 3.10. As suggested by Table 3.4, the relationship between age and the probability of being employed is approximately linear. This allows a very simple interpretation:

- Attending college increases the probability of being employed by about .18 for women of all ages, holding all other variables at their means.

- For each additional 10 years of age, the probability of being employed decreases by about .13, holding all other variables at their means.

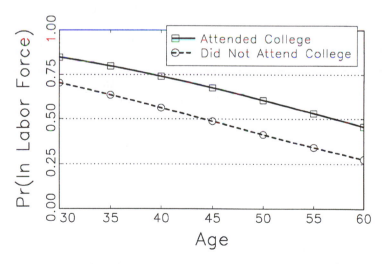

Figure 3.10. Probability of Labor Force Participation by Age and Wife's Education

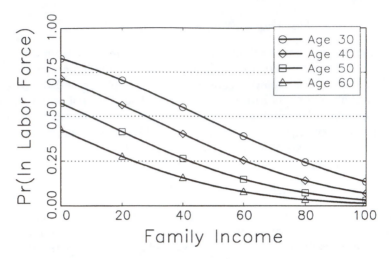

Figure 3.11. Probability of Labor Force Participation by Age and Family Income for Women Without Some College Education

The effect of age was computed by subtracting the predicted probability at age 30 (= .85) from that at age 60 (= .46) and dividing by 3 (for three periods of ten years). It would also be appropriate to use the marginal effect computed at the mean, which is discussed in Section 3.7.4.

The relationship between age and the probability of working was nearly linear and the plot was superfluous. In other cases, plotting is very useful. Consider the effects of income and age. While we could hold all other variables at their means and draw a three-dimensional plot, it is often more informative to divide one of the variables into groups and plot the results in two dimensions. Figure 3.11 shows the probability of employment as income changes for women aged 30, 40, 50, and 60. The nonlinearities are apparent, with the effect of income decreasing with age. When relationships are nonlinear, plots are often useful for uncovering relationships, even if they are not used to present the findings.

Tables of Predicted Probabilities at Selected Values

You can also use tables to present predicted probabilities. For example, the effects of young children and the wife's education on the probability of employment are shown in Table 3.5. The strong, nonlinear effect of having young children is clearly evident. It also shows that the effect

TABLE 3.5 Probability of Employment by College Attendence and the Number of Young Children for the Probit Model

Number of Young Children	Predicted Probability		
	Did Not Attend	*Attended College*	*Difference*
0	0.61	0.78	0.17
1	0.27	0.45	0.18
2	0.07	0.16	0.09
3	0.01	0.03	0.02

of attending college decreases as the number of children increases. (*The difference in the probability for those attending and not attending college increases and then decreases. Draw the probability curves that produce this result.*)

Another strategy for presenting probabilities is to define combinations of characteristics that correspond to ideal types in the population. For example, in his study of factors that affected the retention of workers by their employer after training programs, Gunderson (1974) defined five "hypothetical trainees" based on combinations of the independent variables: typical, disadvantaged, advantaged, housewife, and teenage entrant. Predicted probabilities of being retained were computed for each hypothetical person. In some situations, this can quickly and convincingly summarize the effects of key variables.

3.7.3. The Partial Change in y^*

Measures of partial change can also be used to summarize the effects of each independent variable on the probability of an event occurring. Recall that the logit and probit models are linear in the latent variable:

$$y^* = \mathbf{x}\boldsymbol{\beta} + \varepsilon$$

Taking the partial derivative with respect to x_k,

$$\frac{\partial y^*}{\partial x_k} = \beta_k$$

Since the model is linear in y^*, the partial derivative can be interpreted as:

- For a unit change in x_k, y^* is expected to change by β_k units, holding all other variables constant.

The problem with this interpretation is that the variance of y^* is unknown, so the meaning of a change of β_k in y^* is unclear. This issue was discussed by Winship and Mare (1984, p. 517) and McKelvey and Zavoina (1975, pp. 114–116) regarding the ordinal regression model, but their concerns apply equally to the BRM. Since the variance of y^* changes when new variables are added to the model, the magnitudes of all β's will change even if the added variable is uncorrelated with the original variables. This makes it misleading to compare coefficients from different specifications of the independent variables. (*Why is this not a problem with the LRM?*) To compare coefficients across equations, McKelvey and Zavoina proposed fully standardized coefficients, while Winship and Mare suggested y^*-standardized coefficients.

If σ_{y^*} is the unconditional standard deviation of y^*, then the y^*-*standardized coefficient* for x_k is

$$\beta_k^{Sy^*} = \frac{\beta_k}{\sigma_{y^*}}$$

which can be interpreted as:

- For a unit increase in x_k, y^* is expected to increase by $\beta_k^{Sy^*}$ standard deviations, holding all other variables constant.

y^*-standardized coefficients indicate the effect of an independent variable in its original unit of measurement. This is sometimes preferable for substantive reasons and is necessary for binary independent variables.

Fully standardized coefficients also standardize the independent variable. If σ_k is the standard deviation of x_k, then the *fully standardized coefficient* for x_k is

$$\beta_k^S = \frac{\sigma_k \beta_k}{\sigma_{y^*}} = \sigma_k \beta_k^{Sy^*}$$

which can be interpreted as:

- For a standard deviation increase in x_k, y^* is expected to increase by β_k^S standard deviations, holding all other variables constant.

To compute $\widehat{\beta}_k^{Sy}$ and $\widehat{\beta}_k^S$, we need estimates of β_k, σ_k, and σ_{y^*}. The standard deviations of the x's can be computed directly from the observed data. Since $y^* = \mathbf{x}\boldsymbol{\beta} + \varepsilon$, and $\mathbf{x}$ and ε are uncorrelated, $\sigma_{y^*}^2$ can be estimated by the quadratic form:

$$\widehat{\mathrm{Var}}(y^*) = \widehat{\boldsymbol{\beta}}'\widehat{\mathrm{Var}}(\mathbf{x})\widehat{\boldsymbol{\beta}} + \mathrm{Var}(\varepsilon)$$

TABLE 3.6 Standardized and Unstandardized Probit Coefficients for Labor Force Participation

Variable	β	β^{Sy^*}	β^S	z
K5	−0.875	−0.759	−0.398	−7.70
K618	−0.039	−0.033	−0.044	−0.95
AGE	−0.038	−0.033	−0.265	−4.97
WC	0.488	0.424	0.191	3.60
HC	0.057	0.050	0.024	0.46
LWG	0.366	0.317	0.186	4.17
INC	−0.021	−0.018	−0.207	−4.30
$\widehat{\mathrm{Var}}(y^*)$	1.328			

NOTE: $N = 753$. β is an unstandardized coefficient β^{Sy^*} is a y^*-standardized coefficient; β^S is a fully standardized coefficient. z is the z-test.

$\widehat{\mathrm{Var}}(\mathbf{x})$ is the covariance matrix for the x's computed from the observed data; $\widehat{\boldsymbol{\beta}}$ contains ML estimates; and $\mathrm{Var}(\varepsilon) = 1$ in the probit model and $\mathrm{Var}(\varepsilon) = \pi^2/3$ in the logit model.

If you accept the notion that it is meaningful to discuss the latent propensity to work, the fully standardized and y^*-standardized coefficients in Table 3.6 can be interpreted just as their counterparts for the LRM.[3] For example,

- Each additional young child decreases the mother's propensity to enter the labor market by .76 standard deviations, holding all other variables constant.

- A standard deviation increase in age decreases a woman's propensity to enter the labor market by .27 standard deviations, holding all other variables constant.

3.7.4. The Partial Change in $\Pr(y = 1 \,|\, \mathbf{x})$

The β's can also be used to compute the partial change in the probability of an event. Let

$$\Pr(y = 1 \,|\, \mathbf{x}) = F(\mathbf{x}\boldsymbol{\beta}) \qquad [3.13]$$

where F is either the cdf Φ for the normal distribution or the cdf Λ for the logistic distribution. The corresponding pdf is indicated as f. The *partial change in the probability*, also called the *marginal effect*, is

---

[3] If you try to reproduce the standardized coefficients in Table 3.6 using the descriptive statistics from Table 3.1, your answers will only match to the first decimal digit due to rounding.

computed by taking the partial derivative of Equation 3.13 with respect to x_k:[4]

$$\frac{\partial \Pr(y=1\,|\,\mathbf{x})}{\partial x_k} = \frac{\partial F(\mathbf{x}\boldsymbol{\beta})}{\partial x_k} = \frac{dF(\mathbf{x}\boldsymbol{\beta})}{d\,\mathbf{x}\boldsymbol{\beta}}\frac{\partial\,\mathbf{x}\boldsymbol{\beta}}{\partial x_k} = f(\mathbf{x}\boldsymbol{\beta})\beta_k \qquad [3.14]$$

For the probit model,

$$\frac{\partial \Pr(y=1\,|\,\mathbf{x})}{\partial x_k} = \phi(\mathbf{x}\boldsymbol{\beta})\beta_k$$

and for the logit model,

$$\frac{\partial \Pr(y=1\,|\,\mathbf{x})}{\partial x_k} = \lambda(\mathbf{x}\boldsymbol{\beta})\beta_k = \frac{\exp(\mathbf{x}\boldsymbol{\beta})}{[1+\exp(\mathbf{x}\boldsymbol{\beta})]^2}\beta_k$$
$$= \Pr(y=1\,|\,\mathbf{x})[1-\Pr(y=1\,|\,\mathbf{x})]\beta_k$$

(*Prove the last equality.*)

The marginal effect is the slope of the probability curve relating x_k to $\Pr(y = 1\,|\,\mathbf{x})$, holding all other variables constant. The *sign* of the marginal effect is determined by β_k, since $f(\mathbf{x}\boldsymbol{\beta})$ is always positive. The *magnitude* of the change depends on the magnitude of β_k and the value of $\mathbf{x}\boldsymbol{\beta}$. This is shown in Figure 3.12, where the solid line graphs $\Pr(y = 1\,|\,x)$ and the dashed line graphs the marginal effect. The marginal is largest at $x = x_2$, which corresponds to $\Pr(y = 1\,|\,x) = .5$. The marginal is symmetric around x_2, reflecting the symmetry of f. Therefore,

$$\frac{\partial \Pr(y=1\,|\,x=x_1)}{\partial x} = \frac{\Pr(y=1\,|\,x=x_3)}{\partial x}.$$

The magnitude of the marginal effect depends on the values of the other variables and their coefficients, since f is computed at $\mathbf{x}\boldsymbol{\beta}$. Consequently, the marginal depends on the β's for all variables and the levels of all x's. To understand how the value of the marginal effect of x_k depends on the level of other variables, consider Figure 3.9 which plots the probability surface for variables x and z. Pick a point (x, z), which

---

[4] We use the chain rule:

$$\frac{\partial f(g(x))}{\partial x} = \frac{\partial f(g(x))}{\partial g(x)}\frac{\partial g(x)}{\partial x}$$

and the derivative:

$$\frac{\partial F(x)}{\partial x} = f(x)$$

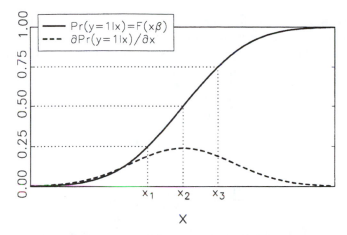

Figure 3.12. Marginal Effect in the Binary Response Model

corresponds to the intersection of lines within the figure. The partial $\partial \Pr(y = 1 \mid x, z)/\partial x$ is the slope of the line parallel to the x-axis at the point (x, z); $\partial \Pr(y = 1 \mid x, z)/\partial z$ is the slope of the line parallel to the z axis at the point (x, z). For example, at $(-4, -8)$, the slope with respect to x is nearly 0. As z increases, the slope with respect to x increases steadily. At $(-4, 0)$, where $\Pr(y = 1 \mid x, z)$ is about .5, the slope is near its maximum. As z continues to increase, the slope gradually decreases. Hanushek and Jackson (1977, p. 189) show this relationship by taking the second derivative:

$$\frac{\partial^2 \Pr(y = 1 \mid \mathbf{x})}{\partial x_k \partial x_\ell}$$

$$= \beta_k \beta_\ell \Pr(y = 1 \mid \mathbf{x})[1 - \Pr(y = 1 \mid \mathbf{x})][1 - 2\Pr(y = 1 \mid \mathbf{x})]$$

The β's can also be used to assess the relative magnitudes of the marginal effect for two variables. From Equation 3.14, the ratio of marginal effects for x_k and x_ℓ is

$$\frac{\dfrac{\partial \Pr(y = 1 \mid \mathbf{x})}{\partial x_k}}{\dfrac{\partial \Pr(y = 1 \mid \mathbf{x})}{\partial x_\ell}} = \frac{f(\mathbf{x}\boldsymbol{\beta})\beta_k}{f(\mathbf{x}\boldsymbol{\beta})\beta_\ell} = \frac{\beta_k}{\beta_\ell}$$

Thus, while the β's are only identified up to a scale factor, their ratio is identified and can be used to compare the effects of independent variables.

Since the value of the marginal effect depends on the levels of all variables, we must decide on which values of the variables to use when computing the effect. One method is to compute the average over all observations:

$$\text{mean } \frac{\partial \Pr(y = 1 \mid \mathbf{x})}{\partial x_k} = \frac{1}{N} \sum_{i=1}^{N} f(\mathbf{x}_i \boldsymbol{\beta}) \beta_k$$

Another method is to compute the marginal effect at the mean of the independent variables:

$$\frac{\partial \Pr(y = 1 \mid \bar{\mathbf{x}})}{\partial x_k} = f(\bar{\mathbf{x}} \boldsymbol{\beta}) \beta_k$$

The *marginal effect at the mean* is a popular summary measure for models with categorical dependent variables. It is frequently included in tables presenting results, and is automatically computed by programs such as LIMDEP. However, the measure is limited. First, given the nonlinearity of the model, it is difficult to translate the marginal effect into the change in the predicted probability that will occur if there is a discrete change in x_k. Second, since $\bar{\mathbf{x}}$ might not correspond to any observed values in the population, averaging over observations might be preferred. Finally, the measure is inappropriate for binary independent variables. For these reasons, I much prefer the measures of discrete change that are discussed in Section 3.7.5.

Table 3.7 contains marginal effects for our example of labor force participation. Several things should be noted. First, the marginal effects averaged over all observations are close to the marginals computed when all variables are held at their means. They are close since the predicted probability overall is approximately .5 in the sample. In general, these

TABLE 3.7 Marginal Effects on the Probability of Being Employed for the Probit Model

Variable	Average	At Mean
K5	−0.300	−0.342
K618	−0.013	−0.015
AGE	−0.013	−0.015
WC	0.167	0.191
HC	0.020	0.022
LWG	0.125	0.143
INC	−0.007	−0.008

two measures of change can be quite different. Second, the marginal effect at the mean for AGE approximates the slope of the lines in Figure 3.10. If an independent variable varies over a region of the probability curve that is nearly linear, the marginal effect can be used to summarize the effect of a unit change in the variable on the probability of an event. However, if the range of an independent variable corresponds to a region of the probability curve that is nonlinear, the marginal cannot be used to assess the overall effect of the variable.

3.7.5. Discrete Change in $\Pr(y = 1 \mid \mathbf{x})$

The change in the predicted probabilities for a discrete change in an independent variable is an alternative to the marginal effect that I find more effective for interpreting the BRM (as well as other models for categorical outcomes). Let $\Pr(y = 1 \mid \mathbf{x}, x_k)$ be the probability of an event given $\mathbf{x}$, noting, in particular, the value of x_k. Thus, $\Pr(y = 1 \mid \mathbf{x}, x_k + \delta)$ is the probability with x_k increased by δ, while the other variables are unchanged. The *discrete change* in the probability for a change of δ in x_k equals

$$\frac{\Delta \Pr(y = 1 \mid \mathbf{x})}{\Delta x_k} = \Pr(y = 1 \mid \mathbf{x}, x_k + \delta) - \Pr(y = 1 \mid \mathbf{x}, x_k)$$

The discrete change can be interpreted as:

- For a change in the variable x_k from x_k to $x_k + \delta$, the predicted probability of an event changes by $\Delta \Pr(y = 1 \mid \mathbf{x})/\Delta x_k$, holding all other variables constant.

When interpreting the results of the BRM, it is essential to understand that the partial change does not equal the discrete change:

$$\frac{\partial \Pr(y = 1 \mid \mathbf{x})}{\partial x_k} \neq \frac{\Delta \Pr(y = 1 \mid \mathbf{x})}{\Delta x_k}$$

except in the limit as δ becomes infinitely small (which is, by definition, the partial change). The difference between these two measures is shown in Figure 3.13 which plots a segment of the probability curve. The partial change is the tangent at x_1, and its value corresponds to the solid triangle. For simplicity, assume that $\delta = 1$. The discrete change measures the change in the probability computed at x_1 and $x_1 + 1$. This is represented by a triangle formed of dashed lines. The discrete and partial changes are not equal since the rate of change in the curve changes

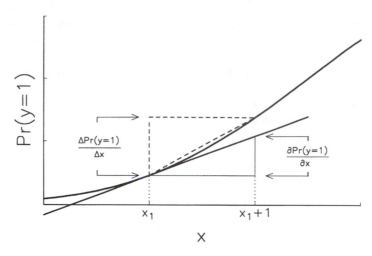

Figure 3.13. Partial Change Versus Discrete Change in Nonlinear Models

as x_k changes. While the measures are not equal, if the change in x_k occurs over a region of the probability curve that is roughly linear, the two measures will be close. This is the case for the example in Figure 3.10.

The amount of discrete change in the probability for a change in x_k depends on: (1) the amount of change in x_k; (2) the starting value of x_k; and (3) the values of all other variables. For example, if we have independent variables x_1 and x_2, the change in $\Pr(y = 1 \mid \mathbf{x})$ when x_1 changes from 1 to 2 does not necessarily equal the change when x goes from 2 to 3. (*Why would they be equal if* $\Pr(y = 1 \mid \mathbf{x}) = .5?$) Moreover, the change in $\Pr(y = 1 \mid \mathbf{x})$ when x_1 changes from 1 to 2 with $x_2 = 1$ does not necessarily equal the change when $x_2 = 2$. Thus, the practical problem is choosing which values of the variables to consider and how much to let them change.

Choosing Values of the Independent Variables

Since the change in the probability for a given change in x_k depends on the levels of all independent variables, we must decide at which values of the x's to compute the discrete change. A common approach is to assess the probability for an "average" member of the sample. For example, we could hold all values at their means. If the independent variables are highly skewed, assessing change relative to the mean may be misleading and changes relative to the median would be more useful.

Dummy variables require special consideration. If x_d is a dummy variable, $\bar{x}_d$ is the proportion of the sample with $x_d = 1$. The predicted probability at $\bar{x}_d$ is between the predicted probability at $x_d = 1$ and $x_d = 0$. Alternatively, you could compute the predicted probability for each combination of the dummy variables, with the other variables held at their means. In our labor force example, this would require four base probabilities: husband and wife attending college; only the husband attending; only the wife attending; and neither attending. Alternatively, dummy variables could be held at the modal value for each variable.

If there is a combination of the independent variables that is of particular substantive interest, those values could be used as a baseline. For example, if you were interested in the effects of education on labor force participation for young women without children, you could hold *AGE* at 30, *K5* at 0, *K618* at 0, and all other variables at their means. In the following examples, I hold all variables at their means.

Amounts of Change in the Independent Variables

Discrete change can be computed for any amount of change in an independent variable, holding all other variables at some fixed value. The amount of change that you allow for an independent variable depends on the type of variable and your purpose. Here are some useful options.

A Unit Change in x_k. If x_k increases from $\bar{x}_k$ to $\bar{x}_k + 1$,

$$\frac{\Delta \Pr(y = 1 \mid \bar{x})}{\Delta x_k} = \Pr(y = 1 \mid \bar{x}, \bar{x}_k + 1) - \Pr(y = 1 \mid \bar{x}, \bar{x}_k)$$

By examining the probability curves (see Figure 3.8), it is clear that a unit *increase* in x_k from its mean will only have the same effect as a unit *decrease* in x_k from its mean when $\Pr(y = 1 \mid \bar{x}) = .5$. This implies that if you have two variables such that $\beta_k = -\beta_\ell$, the effect of a unit increase in x_k will not equal the effect of a unit decrease in x_ℓ. For these reasons, Kaufman (1996) suggested examining a unit increase that is centered around $\bar{x}_k$. That is,

$$\frac{\Delta \Pr(y = 1 \mid \bar{x})}{\Delta x_k} = \Pr\left(y = 1 \mid \bar{x}, \bar{x}_k + \frac{1}{2}\right) - \Pr\left(y = 1 \mid \bar{x}, \bar{x}_k - \frac{1}{2}\right)$$

The *centered discrete change* can be interpreted as:

- A unit change in x_k that is centered around $\bar{x}_k$ results in a change of $\Delta \Pr(y = 1 \mid \bar{x})/\Delta x_k$ in the predicted probability, holding all other variables at their means.

A Standard Deviation Change in x_k. This idea can be extended to examine the effect of a standard deviation change:

$$\frac{\Delta \Pr(y = 1 \mid \bar{\mathbf{x}})}{\Delta x_k} = \Pr\left(y = 1 \mid \bar{\mathbf{x}}, \bar{x}_k + \frac{s_k}{2}\right) - \Pr\left(y = 1 \mid \bar{\mathbf{x}}, \bar{x}_k - \frac{s_k}{2}\right)$$

where s_k is the standard deviation of x_k.

A Change From 0 to 1 for Dummy Variables. When computing a discrete change in probability, you must make certain that the change in the variable does not result in values that exceed the variable's range. For example, if x_k is a dummy variable, either $\bar{x}_k + 1/2$ will exceed 1 or $\bar{x}_k - 1/2$ will be negative (unless $\bar{x}_k = 1/2$). Consequently, a preferred measure of discrete change for dummy variables is

$$\frac{\Delta \Pr(y = 1 \mid \bar{\mathbf{x}})}{\Delta x_k} = \Pr(y = 1 \mid \bar{\mathbf{x}}, \; x_k = 1) - \Pr(y = 1 \mid \bar{\mathbf{x}}, \; x_k = 0)$$

This is the change as x_k goes from 0 to 1, holding all other variables at their means.

Other Choices. The idea of discrete change can be extended in many ways depending on the application. If a change of a specific amount is substantively important, such as the addition of four years of schooling, changes other than 1 or s_k can be used.

Example of Discrete Change: Labor Force Participation

Table 3.8 contains measures of discrete change for the probit model of women's labor force participation. Some of the effects can be inter-

TABLE 3.8 Discrete Change in the Probability of Employment for the Probit Model

Variable	Centered Unit Change	Centered Standard Deviation Change	Change From 0 to 1
K5	−0.33	−0.18	—
K618	−0.02	−0.02	—
AGE	−0.01	−0.12	—
WC	—	—	0.18
HC	—	—	0.02
LWG	0.14	0.08	—
INC	−0.01	−0.09	—

NOTE: Changes are computed with other variables held at their means.

preted as:

- For a woman who is average on all characteristics, an additional young child decreases the probability of employment by .33.

- A standard deviation change in age centered around the mean will decrease the probability of working by .12, holding all other variables at their means.

- If a woman attends college, her probability of being in the labor force is .18 greater than a woman who does not attend college, holding all other variables at their means.

Notice that the discrete change from 0 to 1 for *WC* and *HC* is nearly identical to the effect of a unit change. This is a consequence of the near linearity of the probability curve over the range of these variables, and will not necessarily be true in other examples.

3.8. Interpretation Using Odds Ratios

Our final method of interpretation takes advantage of the tractable form of the logit model. A simple transformation of the β's in the logit model indicates the factor change in the odds of an event occurring. There is no corresponding transformation of the parameters of the probit model.

From Equation 3.6, the logit model can be written as the log-linear model:

$$\ln \Omega(\mathbf{x}) = \mathbf{x}\boldsymbol{\beta} \qquad [3.15]$$

where

$$\Omega(\mathbf{x}) = \frac{\Pr(y=1\,|\,\mathbf{x})}{\Pr(y=0\,|\,\mathbf{x})} = \frac{\Pr(y=1\,|\,\mathbf{x})}{1 - \Pr(y=1\,|\,\mathbf{x})} \qquad [3.16]$$

is the odds of the event given $\mathbf{x}$. $\ln \Omega(\mathbf{x})$ is the log of the odds, known as the *logit*. Equation 3.15 shows that the logit model is linear in the logit. Consequently,

$$\frac{\partial \ln \Omega(\mathbf{x})}{\partial x_k} = \beta_k$$

Since the model is linear, β_k can be interpreted as:

- For a unit change in x_k, we expect the logit to change by β_k, holding all other variables constant.

This interpretation is simple since the effect of a unit change in x_k on the logit does not depend on the level of x_k or on the level of any other variable. Unfortunately, most of us do not have an intuitive understanding of what a change in the logit means. This requires another transformation.

Taking the exponential of Equation 3.15,

$$\Omega(\mathbf{x}) = \exp(\mathbf{x}\boldsymbol{\beta})$$

$$= \exp(\beta_0 + \beta_1 x_1 + \cdots + \beta_k x_k + \cdots + \beta_K x_K)$$

$$= \exp(\beta_0)\exp(\beta_1 x_1)\cdots\exp(\beta_k x_k)\cdots\exp(\beta_K x_K) = \Omega(\mathbf{x}, x_k)$$

The last equality introduces notation that makes explicit the value of x_k. To assess the effect of x_k, we want to see how Ω changes when x_k changes by some quantity δ. Most often, we consider $\delta = 1$ or $\delta = s_k$. If we change x_k by δ, the odds become

$$\Omega(\mathbf{x}, x_k + \delta)$$

$$= \exp(\beta_0)\exp(\beta_1 x_1)\cdots\exp(\beta_k(x_k + \delta))\cdots\exp(\beta_K x_K)$$

$$= \exp(\beta_0)\exp(\beta_1 x_1)\cdots\exp(\beta_k x_k)\exp(\beta_k \delta)\cdots\exp(\beta_K x_K)$$

To compare the odds before and after adding δ to x_k, we take the *odds ratio*:

$$\frac{\Omega(\mathbf{x}, x_k + \delta)}{\Omega(\mathbf{x}, x_k)}$$

$$= \frac{\exp(\beta_0)\exp(\beta_1 x_1)\cdots\exp(\beta_k x_k)\exp(\beta_k \delta)\cdots\exp(\beta_K x_K)}{\exp(\beta_0)\exp(\beta_1 x_1)\cdots\exp(\beta_k x_k)\cdots\exp(\beta_K x_K)}$$

$$= \exp(\beta_k \delta)$$

Therefore, the parameters can be interpreted in terms of odds ratios:

- For a change of δ in x_k, the odds are expected to change by a factor of $\exp(\beta_k \times \delta)$, holding all other variables constant.

For $\delta = 1$, we have:

- *Factor change.* For a unit change in x_k, the odds are expected to change by a factor of $\exp(\beta_k)$, holding all other variables constant.

If $\exp(\beta_k)$ is greater than 1, you could say that the odds are "$\exp(\beta_k)$ times larger." If $\exp(\beta_k)$ is less than 1, you could say that the odds are

"$\exp(\beta_k)$ times smaller." For $\delta = s_k$, we have:

- *Standardized factor change.* For a standard deviation change in x_k, the odds are expected to change by a factor of $\exp(\beta_k \times s_k)$, holding all other variables constant.

Notice that the effect of a change in x_k does not depend on the level of x_k or on the level of any other variable.

We can also compute the percentage change in the odds:

$$100 \frac{\Omega(\mathbf{x}, x_k + \delta) - \Omega(\mathbf{x}, x_k)}{\Omega(\mathbf{x}, x_k)} = 100[\exp(\beta_k \times \delta) - 1]$$

This quantity can be interpreted as the percentage change in the odds for a δ unit change in x_k, holding all other variables constant.

The factor change and standardized factor change coefficients for the logit model analyzing labor force participation are presented in Table 3.9. Here is how some of the coefficients can be interpreted using factor and percentage changes:

- For each additional young child, the odds of being employed are decreased by a factor of .23, holding all other variables constant. Or, equivalently, for each additional young child, the odds of working are decreased 77%, holding all other variables constant.

- For a standard deviation increase in anticipated wages, the odds of being employed are 1.43 times greater, holding all other variables constant. Or, for a standard deviation increase in anticipated wages, the odds of working are 43% greater, holding all other variables constant.

- Being 10 years older decreases the odds by a factor of .52 ($= e^{-.063 \times 10}$), holding all other variables constant.

TABLE 3.9 Factor Change Coefficients for Labor Force Participation for the Logit Model

Variable	Logit Coefficient	Factor Change	Standard Factor Change	z-value
Constant	3.182	—	—	4.94
K5	−1.463	0.232	0.465	−7.43
K618	−0.065	0.937	0.918	−0.95
AGE	−0.063	0.939	0.602	−4.92
WCOL	0.807	2.242	—	3.51
HCOL	0.112	1.118	—	0.54
WAGE	0.605	1.831	1.427	4.01
INC	−0.034	0.966	0.670	−4.20

The odds ratio is a multiplicative coefficient, which means that "positive" effects are greater than 1, while "negative" effects are between 0 and 1. *Magnitudes of positive and negative effects should be compared by taking the inverse of the negative effect (or vice versa).* For example, a positive factor change of 2 has the same magnitude as a negative factor change of .5 = 1/2. Thus, a coefficient of .1 = 1/10 indicates a stronger effect than a coefficient of 2. Another consequence of the multiplicative scale is that to determine the effect on the odds of the event not occurring, you simply take the inverse of the effect on the odds of the event occurring. For example,

- Being 10 years older makes the odds of not being in the labor force 1.9 (= 1/.52) times greater, holding all other variables constant.

When interpreting the odds ratio, it is essential to keep the following in mind: *A constant factor change in the odds does not correspond to a constant change or constant factor change in the probability.* This can be seen in Table 3.10. While the odds are being changed by a constant factor of 2, the probabilities do not change by a constant factor or a constant amount. When the odds are very small, the factor change in the probability is approximately equal to the factor change in the odds. When the odds are large, the probability remains essentially unchanged. Consequently, when interpreting a factor change in the odds, it is *essential* to know what the current level of the odds is. This can be done using the methods in Section 3.7.2 to compute the predicted probability, and then computing the odds according to Equation 3.16.

TABLE 3.10 Factor Change of Two in the Odds With the Corresponding Factor Change and Change in the Probability

| Original | | Changed | | Factor Change | | Change |
Odds	Probability	Odds	Probability	Odds	Probability	in Probability
1/1000	0.001	2/1000	0.002	2.000	1.998	0.001
1/100	0.010	2/100	0.020	2.000	1.980	0.010
1/10	0.091	2/10	0.167	2.000	1.833	0.076
1/2	0.333	2/2	0.500	2.000	1.500	0.167
1/1	0.500	2/1	0.667	2.000	1.333	0.167
2/1	0.667	4/1	0.800	2.000	1.200	0.133
10/1	0.909	20/1	0.952	2.000	1.048	0.043
100/1	0.990	200/1	0.995	2.000	1.005	0.005
1000/1	0.999	2000/1	0.999	2.000	1.000	0.000

3.9. Conclusions

The choice between the logit and probit models is largely one of convenience and convention, since the substantive results are generally indistinguishable. Chambers and Cox (1967) show that extremely large samples are necessary to distinguish whether observations were generated from the logit or the probit model. The availability of software is no longer an issue in choosing which model to use. Often the choice is a matter of convention. Some research areas tend to use logit, while others favor probit. For some users, the simple interpretation of logit coefficients as odds ratios is the deciding factor. In other cases, the need to generalize a model may be an issue. For example, multiple-equation systems involving qualitative dependent variables are based on the probit model, as discussed in Chapter 9. Or, if an analysis also includes equations with a nominal dependent variable, the logit model may be preferred since the probit model for nominal dependent variables is computationally too demanding. Or, in case-control studies where sampling is stratified by the binary outcome, the logit model is required (see Hosmer & Lemeshow, 1989, Chapter 6, for details).

Many of the ideas presented in this chapter are used to develop and interpret models for ordinal and nominal variables in Chapters 5 and 6. First, however, Chapter 4 considers hypothesis testing, methods for detecting outliers and influential observations, and measures of fit.

3.10. Bibliographic Notes

The very early history of these models begins in the 1860s and is discussed by Finney (1971, pp. 38–41). The more recent history of the probit model involves attempts to model the effects of toxins on insects. Work by Gaddum (1933) and Bliss (1934) was codified in Finney's influential *Probit Analysis* (1971), whose first edition appeared in 1947. The logit model was championed by Berkson (1944, 1951) in the 1940s as an alternative to the probit model. Cox's (1970) *The Analysis of Binary Data* was highly influential in the acceptance of the logit model. Applications of the logit and probit models appeared in economics in the 1950s (Cramer, 1991, p. 41). Goldberger's (1964, pp. 248–251) *Econometric Theory* was important in establishing these models as standard tools in economics, while Hanushek and Jackson's (1977) *Statistical Methods for Social Scientists* was important in disseminating these models to areas outside of economics.

McCullagh and Nelder (1989, Chapter 4) develop the logit and probit models, along with several alternatives, within the framework of the
generalized linear model. Pudney (1989, Chapter 3) derives these models from behavioral assumptions associated with utility maximization.
Agresti (1990, Chapter 4) presents both models with special attention
to the links between logit analysis and log-linear models for categorical
data. While the interpretation of the results of these models has often
been neglected, each of the methods of interpretation considered in this
chapter can be found in one form or another in earlier work. Recent
treatments that focus on interpretation include Hanushek and Jackson
(1977, pp. 187–207), King (1989a, pp. 97–117), Liao (1994), Long (1987),
and Petersen (1985).

For a more advanced discussion of numerical methods, see Judge et
al. (1985, pp. 951–979) and Greene (1993, pp. 343–357). For details on
estimates of the covariance matrix, see Cramer (1986, pp. 27–29), Greene
(1993, pp. 115–116), and Davidson and MacKinnon (1993, pp. 263–267).

4 Hypothesis Testing and Goodness of Fit

This chapter begins by reviewing tests of hypothesis that can be used with any model estimated by maximum likelihood. Next, methods for detecting outliers and influential observations for the binary logit and probit models are examined; comparable methods for ordinal and nominal outcomes are not available. The chapter ends with a review of scalar measures for assessing the overall goodness of fit of a model. While some of these measures apply only to the binary response model, most can be adapted to the models in later chapters.

4.1. Hypothesis Testing

ML estimators are distributed asymptotically normally. This means that as the sample size increases, the sampling distribution of an ML estimator becomes approximately normal. For an individual parameter,

$$\widehat{\beta}_k \overset{a}{\sim} \mathcal{N}(\beta_k, \mathrm{Var}(\widehat{\beta}_k))$$

where "$\overset{a}{\sim}$" reads "is distributed asymptotically as." For a vector of parameters,

$$\widehat{\boldsymbol{\beta}} \overset{a}{\sim} \mathcal{N}(\boldsymbol{\beta}, \mathrm{Var}(\widehat{\boldsymbol{\beta}}))$$

where $\text{Var}(\widehat{\boldsymbol{\beta}})$ is the covariance matrix for $\widehat{\boldsymbol{\beta}}$. For example, with three coefficients:

$$\text{Var}\begin{pmatrix} \widehat{\beta}_0 \\ \widehat{\beta}_1 \\ \widehat{\beta}_2 \end{pmatrix} = \begin{pmatrix} \sigma^2_{\widehat{\beta}_0} & \sigma_{\widehat{\beta}_0, \widehat{\beta}_1} & \sigma_{\widehat{\beta}_0, \widehat{\beta}_2} \\ \sigma_{\widehat{\beta}_1, \widehat{\beta}_0} & \sigma^2_{\widehat{\beta}_1} & \sigma_{\widehat{\beta}_1, \widehat{\beta}_2} \\ \sigma_{\widehat{\beta}_2, \widehat{\beta}_0} & \sigma_{\widehat{\beta}_2, \widehat{\beta}_1} & \sigma^2_{\widehat{\beta}_2} \end{pmatrix}$$

The off-diagonal elements are the covariances between the estimates of two parameters.

Consider the simple hypothesis $H_0: \beta_k = \beta^*$, where β^* is the hypothesized value, often equal to 0. Since $\sigma_{\widehat{\beta}_k}$ is unknown, it must be estimated, which results in the test:

$$z = \frac{\widehat{\beta}_k - \beta^*}{\widehat{\sigma}_{\widehat{\beta}_k}} \qquad [4.1]$$

Under the assumptions justifying ML, if H_0 is true, then z is distributed approximately normally with a mean of 0 and a variance of 1 for large samples. The sampling distribution for z, drawn in Figure 4.1, shows the probability of various values of z when H_0 is true. For example, the shaded region for $z > 1.96$ indicates that values of z greater than 1.96 will occur due to sampling variation 2.5% of the time. Similarly, the shaded region on the left indicates how frequently values less than -1.96 will occur. For a two-tailed test, H_0 is rejected at the .05 level when z falls in the shaded region of either tail. If past research or theory suggests the sign of the coefficient, a one-tailed test is used and the null hypothesis would only be rejected when z is in the expected tail.

The test statistic in Equation 4.1 is sometimes considered to have an asymptotic t-distribution, and the test is referred to as a t-test or a quasi-t-test. When N is large, which is required for the asymptotic justification of the test, it makes little difference whether a t-distribution or a normal

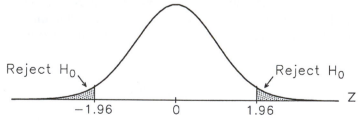

Figure 4.1. Sampling Distribution for a z-Statistic

distribution is used. Accordingly, some programs label this statistic a z-test, while other programs label it a *t*-test.

Example of the z-Test: Labor Force Participation

To test the hypothesis that having young children affects a woman's probability of working, we can use the z-statistic in Table 3.3 for the logit model. Since prior research suggests that the effect is negative, a one-tailed test is used. We conclude that:

- Having young children has a significant effect on the probability of working ($z = -7.43$, $p < .01$ for a one-tailed test).

4.1.1. Wald, Likelihood Ratio, and Lagrange Multiplier Tests

It is often useful to test complex hypotheses. For example, you might want to test that several coefficients are simultaneously equal to 0, or that two coefficients are equal. Such hypotheses can be tested with Wald, likelihood ratio (LR), or Lagrange multiplier (LM) tests. These tests can be thought of as a comparison between the estimates obtained after the constraints implied by the hypothesis have been imposed to the estimates obtained without the constraints. This is illustrated in panel A of Figure 4.2, which is based on a figure from Buse (1982).

The log likelihood function for estimating β is drawn as a solid curve. The *unconstrained* estimator $\widehat{\beta}_U$ maximizes the log likelihood function, with the log likelihood equal to $\ln L(\widehat{\beta}_U)$. The hypothesis H_0: $\beta = \beta^*$ imposes the constraint $\beta = \beta^*$, so that the *constrained* estimate $\widehat{\beta}_C$ equals β^*. Unless $\widehat{\beta}_U$ is *exactly* equal to β^*, $\ln L(\widehat{\beta}_C)$ is smaller than $\ln L(\widehat{\beta}_U)$, as shown in the figure. The LR test assesses the constraint by comparing the log likelihood of the unconstrained model, $\ln L(\widehat{\beta}_U)$, to the log likelihood of the constrained model, $\ln L(\widehat{\beta}_C)$. If the constraint significantly reduces the likelihood, then the null hypothesis is rejected.

The Wald test estimates the model without constraints, and assesses the constraint by considering two things. First, it measures the distance between the unconstrained and the constrained estimates. In our example, this quantity is $\widehat{\beta}_U - \widehat{\beta}_C = \widehat{\beta}_U - \beta^*$. The larger the distance, the less likely it is that the constraint is true. Second, this distance $\widehat{\beta}_U - \widehat{\beta}_C$ is weighted by the curvature of the log likelihood function, which is indicated by the second derivative $\partial^2 \ln L / \partial \beta^2$. The larger the second derivative, the faster the curve is changing. (*What does it mean if the second derivative is 0?*) The importance of the shape of the function is illustrated in panel B. The log likelihood drawn with a dashed line is nearly

Panel A: Wald, LR, and LM Tests

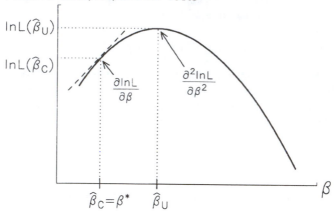

Panel B: Shape of the Likelihood Function

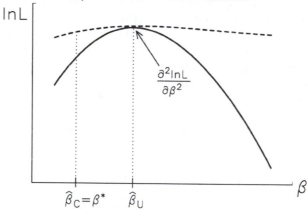

Figure 4.2. Wald, Likelihood Ratio, and Lagrange Multiplier Tests

flat, so the second derivative evaluated at $\widehat{\beta}_U$ is relatively small. When the second derivative is small, the distance between $\widehat{\beta}_U$ and $\widehat{\beta}_C$ is minor relative to the sampling variation. The second function, drawn with a solid line, has a larger second derivative, indicating a more rapidly changing likelihood function. With a larger second derivative, the same distance between $\widehat{\beta}_U$ and $\widehat{\beta}_C$ might be significant. (*How would increasing the sample size affect the curvature of the log likelihood function?*)

The Lagrange multiplier (LM) test, also known as the score test, only estimates the constrained model, and assesses the slope of the log

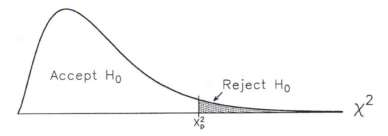

Figure 4.3. Sampling Distribution of a Chi-Square Statistic with 5 Degrees of Freedom

likelihood function at the constraint. If the hypothesis is true, the slope (known as the score) at the constraint should be close to 0. In panel A of Figure 4.2, the slope is represented by the tangent to the curve drawn with a dashed line, which is labeled $\partial \ln L/\partial \beta$. As with the Wald test, the curvature of the log likelihood function at the constraint is used to assess the significance of a nonzero slope.

When H_0 is true, the Wald, LR, and LM tests are *asymptotically* equivalent. As N increases, the sampling distributions of the three tests converge to the same chi-square distribution with degrees of freedom equal to the number of constraints being tested. Figure 4.3 shows the sampling distribution for a chi-square statistic with 5 degrees of freedom. The area to the right of X_p^2 is equal to p, and indicates the probability of observing a value of the test statistic greater than X_p^2 if H_0 is true. The null hypothesis is rejected at the p level of significance if the test statistic is larger than X_p^2.

It is important to remember that the Wald, LR, and LM tests only have asymptotic justifications. The degree to which these tests approximate a chi-square distribution in small samples is largely unknown. See Section 3.5.1 (p. 53) for guidelines on the sample size needed for using these tests.

With these ideas in mind, we are ready for formal definitions of the Wald and LR tests. The LM test is discussed further in Chapter 7.

4.1.2. The Wald Test

While in its most general form the Wald test can be used to test nonlinear constraints, here we consider only linear constraints of the form:

$$\mathbf{Q\beta} = \mathbf{r} \qquad [4.2]$$

where $\boldsymbol{\beta}$ is the vector of parameters being tested, $\mathbf{Q}$ is a matrix of constants, and $\mathbf{r}$ is a vector of constants. While we are usually interested only in the intercepts and slopes of a model, $\boldsymbol{\beta}$ could contain other parameters such as σ in the LRM. By specifying $\mathbf{Q}$ and $\mathbf{r}$, a variety of linear constraints can be imposed. For example, consider the probit model $\Pr(y = 1 \mid \mathbf{x}) = \Phi(\beta_0 + \beta_1 x_1 + \beta_2 x_2)$. To test that $\beta_1 = 0$, Equation 4.2 becomes

$$(0\ 1\ 0) \begin{pmatrix} \beta_0 \\ \beta_1 \\ \beta_2 \end{pmatrix} = (0)$$

Or, to test the constraint that $\beta_1 = \beta_2 = 0$,

$$\begin{pmatrix} 0 & 1 & 0 \\ 0 & 0 & 1 \end{pmatrix} \begin{pmatrix} \beta_0 \\ \beta_1 \\ \beta_2 \end{pmatrix} = \begin{pmatrix} 0 \\ 0 \end{pmatrix}$$

The hypothesis H_0: $\mathbf{Q}\boldsymbol{\beta} = \mathbf{r}$ can be tested with the Wald statistic:

$$W = [\mathbf{Q}\widehat{\boldsymbol{\beta}} - \mathbf{r}]'[\mathbf{Q}\widehat{\mathrm{Var}}(\widehat{\boldsymbol{\beta}})\mathbf{Q}']^{-1}[\mathbf{Q}\widehat{\boldsymbol{\beta}} - \mathbf{r}] \qquad [4.3]$$

W is distributed as chi-square with degrees of freedom equal to the number of constraints (i.e., the number of rows of $\mathbf{Q}$). The Wald statistic consists of two components. First, $\mathbf{Q}\widehat{\boldsymbol{\beta}} - \mathbf{r}$ at each end of the formula measures the distance between the estimated and hypothesized values. Second, $[\mathbf{Q}\widehat{\mathrm{Var}}(\widehat{\boldsymbol{\beta}})\mathbf{Q}']^{-1}$ reflects the variability in the estimator, or, alternatively, the curvature of the likelihood function. To see this more clearly, consider a simple example.

For the model $\Pr(y = 1 \mid \mathbf{x}) = \Phi(\beta_0 + \beta_1 x_1 + \beta_2 x_2)$ with H_0: $\beta_1 = \beta^*$, $\mathbf{Q}\widehat{\boldsymbol{\beta}} - \mathbf{r}$ can be written as

$$(0\ 1\ 0) \begin{pmatrix} \widehat{\beta}_0 \\ \widehat{\beta}_1 \\ \widehat{\beta}_2 \end{pmatrix} - (\beta^*) = \widehat{\beta}_1 - \beta^*$$

$\mathbf{Q}\widehat{\boldsymbol{\beta}} - \mathbf{r}$ is repeated at the end of the formula, which squares the distance between the hypothesized value and the estimate. Therefore, negative and positive distances have the same effect on the test statistic. The middle portion of the Wald statistic is

$$[\mathbf{Q}\widehat{\mathrm{Var}}(\widehat{\boldsymbol{\beta}})\mathbf{Q}']^{-1} = \left[(0\ 1\ 0)\ \widehat{\mathrm{Var}}(\widehat{\boldsymbol{\beta}}) \begin{pmatrix} 0 \\ 1 \\ 0 \end{pmatrix} \right]^{-1} = \frac{1}{\widehat{\sigma}^2_{\widehat{\beta}_1}}$$

which is simply the inverse of the variance. The larger the variance, the smaller the weight given to the distance between the hypothesized and estimated value. Equivalently, the faster the likelihood function is changing in the region around $\hat{\beta}_1$, the more significant the difference $\hat{\beta}_1 - \beta^*$. (*Why should we give less weight when the variance is larger?*) Combining these results,

$$W = \frac{(\hat{\beta}_1 - \beta^*)^2}{\hat{\sigma}_{\hat{\beta}_1}^2} = \left(\frac{\hat{\beta}_1 - \beta^*}{\hat{\sigma}_{\hat{\beta}_1}}\right)^2$$

which is distributed as chi-square with 1 degree of freedom if H_0 is true. Notice that W is the square of the z-statistic in Equation 4.1, which corresponds to a chi-square variable with 1 degree of freedom being equal to the square of a normal variable. Some programs, such as SAS, present a single degree of freedom chi-square statistic for individual coefficients, rather than the z-statistic.

The same ideas apply to more complex hypotheses. Consider H_0: $\beta_1 = \beta_2 = 0$, which can be written as

$$H_0: \begin{pmatrix} 0 & 1 & 0 \\ 0 & 0 & 1 \end{pmatrix} \begin{pmatrix} \beta_0 \\ \beta_1 \\ \beta_2 \end{pmatrix} = \begin{pmatrix} 0 \\ 0 \end{pmatrix}$$

$\mathbf{Q}\hat{\boldsymbol{\beta}} - \mathbf{r}$ is simply $(\hat{\beta}_1 \ \hat{\beta}_2)'$. The middle portion of the Wald formula is

$$[\mathbf{Q}\widehat{\text{Var}}(\hat{\boldsymbol{\beta}})\mathbf{Q}']^{-1} = \left[\begin{pmatrix} 0 & 1 & 0 \\ 0 & 0 & 1 \end{pmatrix} \widehat{\text{Var}}(\hat{\boldsymbol{\beta}}) \begin{pmatrix} 0 & 0 \\ 1 & 0 \\ 0 & 1 \end{pmatrix}\right]^{-1}$$

To keep the example simple, assume that the estimates are uncorrelated. (In practice, the estimates will be correlated.) Then

$$[\mathbf{Q}\widehat{\text{Var}}(\hat{\boldsymbol{\beta}})\mathbf{Q}']^{-1} = \begin{pmatrix} \hat{\sigma}_{\hat{\beta}_1}^2 & 0 \\ 0 & \hat{\sigma}_{\hat{\beta}_2}^2 \end{pmatrix}^{-1} = \begin{pmatrix} 1/\hat{\sigma}_{\hat{\beta}_1}^2 & 0 \\ 0 & 1/\hat{\sigma}_{\hat{\beta}_2}^2 \end{pmatrix} \qquad [4.4]$$

The larger the variance, the less weight is given to the distance between the hypothesized and estimated parameter. Carrying out the algebra, we obtain

$$W = \sum_{k=1}^{2} \frac{\hat{\beta}_k^2}{\hat{\sigma}_{\hat{\beta}_k}^2} = \sum_{k=1}^{2} \left(\frac{\hat{\beta}_k}{\hat{\sigma}_{\hat{\beta}_k}}\right)^2 = \sum_{k=1}^{2} z_{\hat{\beta}_k}^2$$

With uncorrelated parameters, the Wald statistic is the sum of squared z's. Recall that a chi-square distribution with J degrees of freedom is defined as the sum of J independent, squared normal random variables. When the estimates are correlated, which is normally the case, the resulting formula is more complicated, but the general ideas are the same.

Examples of the Wald Test: Labor Force Participation

To illustrate the Wald test, consider the logit model:

$$\Pr(LFP = 1) = \Lambda(\beta_0 + \beta_1 K5 + \beta_2 K618 + \beta_3 AGE \qquad [4.5]$$
$$+ \beta_4 WC + \beta_5 HC + \beta_6 LWG + \beta_7 INC)$$

Wald Test of a Single Coefficient. To test H_0: $\beta_1 = 0$, let

$$\mathbf{Q} = (0\ 1\ 0\ 0\ 0\ 0\ 0\ 0) \qquad \text{and} \qquad \mathbf{r} = (0)$$

Then $W = 55.14$, which is the square of the z-statistic for $K5$ in Table 3.3. We describe the result as:

- The effect of having young children on the probability of entering the labor force is significant at the .01 level ($X^2 = 55.14$, $df = 1$, $p < .01$).

The symbol X^2 is often used rather than W since the Wald statistic has a chi-square distribution.

Wald Test That Two Coefficients Are 0. The hypothesis that the effects of the husband's and wife's education are simultaneously 0 can be written as: H_0: $\beta_4 = \beta_5 = 0$. To test this hypothesis, let

$$\mathbf{Q} = \begin{pmatrix} 0\ 0\ 0\ 0\ 1\ 0\ 0\ 0 \\ 0\ 0\ 0\ 0\ 0\ 1\ 0\ 0 \end{pmatrix} \qquad \text{and} \qquad \mathbf{r} = \begin{pmatrix} 0 \\ 0 \end{pmatrix}$$

Then $W = 17.66$ with 2 degrees of freedom. We conclude:

- The hypothesis that the effects of the husband's and wife's education are simultaneously equal to 0 can be rejected at the .01 level ($X^2 = 17.66$, $df = 2$, $p < .01$).

(*Specify* $\mathbf{Q}$ *and* $\mathbf{r}$ *to test the hypothesis that all of the coefficients except the intercept are simultaneously* 0.)

Wald Test That Two Coefficients Are Equal. To test that the effect of the husband's education equals the effect of the wife's education, define

$$\mathbf{Q} = (0\ 0\ 0\ 0\ 1{-}1\ 0\ 0) \qquad \text{and} \qquad \mathbf{r} = (0)$$

Substituting these matrices into Equation 4.3 and simplifying results in the usual formula:

$$W = \frac{(\widehat{\beta}_4 - \widehat{\beta}_5)^2}{\widehat{\text{Var}}(\widehat{\beta}_4) + \widehat{\text{Var}}(\widehat{\beta}_5) - 2\widehat{\text{Cov}}(\widehat{\beta}_4, \widehat{\beta}_5)}$$

Then $W = 3.54$ with 1 degree of freedom. There is 1 degree of freedom since there is a single restriction, even though that restriction involves two parameters. We conclude:

- The hypothesis that the effects of the husband's and wife's education are equal is marginally significant at the .05 level ($X^2 = 3.54$, $df = 1$, $p = .06$).

4.1.3. The Likelihood Ratio Test

The LR test can also be used to test constraints on a model. While in its most general form these constraints can be complex and nonlinear, I only consider constraints that involve eliminating one or more regressors from the model. For example, consider the logit models:

$$M_1: \quad \Pr(y = 1 \,|\, \mathbf{x}) = \Lambda(\beta_0 + \beta_1 x_1 + \beta_2 x_2)$$
$$M_2: \quad \Pr(y = 1 \,|\, \mathbf{x}) = \Lambda(\beta_0 + \beta_1 x_1 + \beta_2 x_2 + \beta_3 x_3)$$
$$M_3: \quad \Pr(y = 1 \,|\, \mathbf{x}) = \Lambda(\beta_0 + \beta_1 x_1 + \beta_2 x_2 \qquad\quad + \beta_4 x_4)$$
$$M_4: \quad \Pr(y = 1 \,|\, \mathbf{x}) = \Lambda(\beta_0 + \beta_1 x_1 + \beta_2 x_2 + \beta_3 x_3 + \beta_4 x_4)$$

Model M_1 is formed from M_2 by imposing the constraint $\beta_3 = 0$, and M_1 is formed from M_3 by imposing the constraint $\beta_4 = 0$. When one model can be obtained from another model by imposing constraints, the *constrained* model is said to be *nested* in the *unconstrained* model. Thus, M_1 is nested in M_2 and in M_3 . However, M_2 is not nested in M_3, nor is M_3 nested in M_2. (*Which models are nested in M_4?*)

The LR test is defined as follows. The constrained model M_C with parameters $\boldsymbol{\beta}_C$ is nested in the unconstrained model M_U with parameters $\boldsymbol{\beta}_U$. The null hypothesis is that the constraints imposed to create M_C are true. Let $L(M_U)$ be the value of the likelihood function evaluated at the ML estimates for the unconstrained model, and let $L(M_C)$ be the value at the constrained estimates. The *likelihood ratio statistic*, hereafter the LR statistic, equals

$$G^2(M_C \mid M_U) = 2 \ln L(M_U) - 2 \ln L(M_C)$$

Under very general conditions, if H_0 is true, then G^2 is asymptotically distributed as chi-square with degrees of freedom equal to the number of independent constraints. While the LR statistic can be used to compare any pair of nested models, there are two tests that are commonly computed by standard software and are often included in tables presenting the results of models estimated by ML.

The first test compares a given model to the constrained model in which all slope coefficients are equal to 0. This test is frequently referred to as the *likelihood ratio chi-square* or the *LR chi-square*. To define the test, let model M_β be the unconstrained model that includes an intercept, slope coefficients, and any other parameters in the model (e.g., σ in the LRM). Let M_α be the constrained model that excludes all regressors from the model (e.g., only parameters β_0 and σ would be included for the LRM). To test the hypothesis that all of the slope coefficients are simultaneously equal to 0, we use the test statistic:

$$G^2(M_\beta) = 2 \ln L(M_\beta) - 2 \ln L(M_\alpha) \qquad [4.6]$$

The simpler notation $G^2(M_\beta)$ replaces the more cumbersome $G^2(M_\alpha \mid M_\beta)$. If the null hypothesis that all slopes are 0 is true, then $G^2(M_\beta)$ is distributed as chi-square with degrees of freedom equal to the number of regressors.

The second test, known as the *scaled deviance* or simply the *deviance*, is used extensively within the framework known as the generalized linear model (McCullagh & Nelder, 1989, pp. 33–34). The deviance compares a given model to the *full model M_F*. The full model has one parameter for each observation, and can reproduce perfectly the observed data. Since the observed data are perfectly predicted, the likelihood of M_F is 1, and the log likelihood is 0. To test that M_F significantly improves the fit over M_β, the deviance is defined as

$$D(M_\beta) = 2 \ln L(M_F) - 2 \ln L(M_\beta)$$
$$= -2 \ln L(M_\beta)$$
$$= G^2(M_\beta \mid M_F)$$

Since the deviance is -2 times the log likelihood of the given model, its value can be computed readily from any program that provides the log likelihood of the model being estimated.

While $D(M_\beta)$ is sometimes reported as having a chi-square distribution, McCullagh (1986) shows that $D(M_\beta)$ has an asymptotic normal distribution as a consequence of the number of parameters in the full model increasing directly with the number of observations. McCullagh and Nelder (1989, pp. 120–122) suggest that when the data are *sparse* (i.e., when each combination of values of the independent variables occurs only once in the sample), $D(M_\beta)$ should not be used as a measure of fit in the model. See Hosmer and Lemeshow (1989, pp. 137–145) for further details.

$G^2(M_\beta)$ and $D(M_\beta)$ can be used to compare nested models. Consider the unconstrained model M_U and the constrained model M_C. If the values of the likelihood function are known, we could test the constraints on M_U with $G^2(M_C \mid M_U) = 2 \ln L(M_U) - 2 \ln L(M_C)$. This statistic could also be computed using the LR chi-squares:

$$G^2(M_U) = 2 \ln L(M_U) - 2 \ln L(M_\alpha)$$
$$G^2(M_C) = 2 \ln L(M_C) - 2 \ln L(M_\alpha)$$

Since M_α is the same for both models,

$$G^2(M_C \mid M_U) = G^2(M_U) - G^2(M_C)$$
$$= 2 \ln L(M_U) - 2 \ln L(M_C)$$

This is why $G^2(M_C \mid M_U)$ is often referred to as a *difference of chi-square test*. Similarly, the deviance can be used to compute the test. If

$$D(M_U) = -2 \ln L(M_U) \qquad \text{and} \qquad D(M_C) = -2 \ln L(M_C)$$

then

$$G^2(M_C \mid M_U) = D(M_C) - D(M_U)$$
$$= -2 \ln L(M_C) - -2 \ln L(M_U)$$
$$= 2 \ln L(M_U) - 2 \ln L(M_C)$$

Examples of the LR Test: Labor Force Participation

For the unconstrained model in Equation 4.5, the LR chi-square $G^2(M_U) = 124.48$ and the deviance $D(M_U) = 905.27$. These statistics are used for computing the following tests.

LR Test of a Single Coefficient. To test H_0: $\beta_1 = 0$, the model $M_{[K5]}$ is estimated, where the bracketed subscript indicates that $K5$ is excluded from the unconstrained model. The LR chi-square and deviance for the constrained model are

$$G^2(M_{[K5]}) = 58.00 \qquad \text{and} \qquad D(M_{[K5]}) = 971.75$$

Then,

$$G^2(M_{[K5]} \mid M_U) = G^2(M_U) - G^2(M_{[K5]}) = 66.48$$
$$= D(M_{[K5]}) - D(M_U) = 66.48$$

We conclude:

- The effect of having young children is significant at the .01 level ($LRX^2 = 66.5$, $df = 1$, $p < .01$).

Notice that I have used LRX^2 rather than G^2 in presenting the result. This makes it explicit that a likelihood ratio test is being reported.

LR Test of Multiple Coefficients. To test the hypothesis that the effects of the husband's and wife's education are simultaneously 0, H_0: $\beta_4 = \beta_5 = 0$, the model $M_{[WC,HC]}$ is estimated, resulting in

$$G^2(M_{[WC,HC]}) = 105.98 \qquad \text{and} \qquad D(M_{[WC,HC]}) = 923.76$$

The test statistic is

$$G^2(M_{[WC,HC]} \mid M_U) = G^2(M_U) - G^2(M_{[WC,HC]}) = 18.50$$
$$= D(M_{[WC,HC]}) - D(M_U) = 18.50$$

We conclude:

- The hypothesis that the effects of the husband's and wife's education are simultaneously equal to 0 can be rejected at the .01 level ($LRX^2 = 18.5$, $df = 2$, $p < .01$).

LR Test That All Coefficients Are 0. $G^2(M_U) = G^2(M_\alpha \mid M_U)$ can be used to test the hypothesis that none of the regressors affects the probability of entering the labor force. Formally, H_0: $\beta_1 = \beta_2 = \beta_3 = \beta_4 = \beta_5 = \beta_6 = \beta_7 = 0$. We conclude:

- We can reject the hypothesis that all coefficients except the intercept are 0 at the .01 level ($LRX^2 = 124.5$, $df = 7$, $p < .01$).

While a Wald test could be used to test this hypothesis, the LR test is more commonly used.

TABLE 4.1 Comparing Results From the LR and Wald Tests

Hypothesis	df	LR Test		Wald Test	
		G^2	p	W	p
$\beta_1 = 0$	1	66.5	< 0.01	55.1	< 0.01
$\beta_4 = \beta_5 = 0$	2	18.5	< 0.01	17.7	< 0.01
All slopes $= 0$	7	124.5	< 0.01	95.0	< 0.01

4.1.4. Comparing the LR and Wald Tests

Even though the LR and Wald tests are asymptotically equivalent, in finite samples they give different answers, particularly for small samples. In general, it is unclear whether one test is to be preferred to the other. Rothenberg (1984) suggests that neither test is uniformly superior, while Hauck and Donner (1977) suggest that the Wald test is less powerful than the LR test. In practice, the choice of which test to use is often determined by convenience. While the LR test requires the estimation of two models, the computation of the test only involves subtraction. The Wald test only requires estimation of a single model, but the computation of the test involves matrix manipulations. Which test is more convenient depends on the software being used.

Table 4.1 compares the results of the LR and Wald tests for our example based on a sample of 753. For all hypotheses, the conclusions from both tests are the same. Note, however, that the values of the LR statistics are larger than the corresponding Wald statistics.

4.1.5. Computational Issues

There are two important computational considerations that must be taken into account when computing Wald and LR tests. If they are not, you run the risk of drawing the wrong conclusions from your tests.

Computing the LR Test

The LR test requires using the same sample for all models being compared. Since ML estimation excludes cases with missing data, it is common for the sample size to change when a variable has been excluded. For example, if x_1 has three missing observations that are not missing for any other variables, the usable sample increases by 3 when x_1 is excluded from the model. To ensure that the sample size does not change, you should construct a data set that excludes every observation that has missing values for any of the variables used in any of the models being tested. Alternatively, missing values can be imputed using methods discussed in Little and Rubin (1987).

Computing the Wald Test

The matrix computations for the Wald test can accumulate appreciable rounding error if you do not use the full precision of the estimated coefficients and covariance matrix. Practically speaking, this means that you should use a program in which the estimates can be stored and then analyzed. Using the rounded values listed in the output can result in incorrect values for the test statistic.

4.2. Residuals and Influence

When assessing a model, it is useful to consider how well the model fits each case and how much influence each case has on the estimates of the parameters. *Residuals* measure the difference between the model's prediction for a given case and the observed value for that case, with observations that fit poorly thought of as *outliers*. *Influence* is the effect of an observation on estimates of the model's parameters or measures of fit. The analysis of residuals and influence is well developed for the LRM, and I assume that you have some familiarity with this material (see Fox, 1991, and Weisberg, 1980, Chapter 5, for good introductions). This section considers Pregibon's (1981) extensions of these methods to the BRM.

For a binary model, define $\pi_i = E(y_i \mid \mathbf{x}_i) = \Pr(y_i = 1 \mid \mathbf{x}_i)$. Since y is a binary variable, the deviations $y_i - \pi_i$ are heteroscedastic, with $\text{Var}(y_i \mid \mathbf{x}_i) = \pi_i(1 - \pi_i)$. This suggests the *Pearson residual*:

$$r_i = \frac{y_i - \widehat{\pi}_i}{\sqrt{\widehat{\pi}_i(1 - \widehat{\pi}_i)}}$$

Large values of r_i suggest a failure of the model to fit a given observation. Pearson residuals can be used to construct a summary measure of fit, known as a *Pearson statistic*:

$$X^2 = \sum_{i=1}^{N} r_i^2$$

While X^2 is sometimes reported as having a chi-square distribution, Mc-Cullagh (1986) demonstrated that when the data are sparse (e.g., when there are continuous independent variables), X^2 has an asymptotic normal distribution with a mean and variance that are difficult to compute. McCullagh and Nelder (1989, pp. 112–122) recommended that X^2 not be used as an absolute measure of fit. Hosmer and Lemeshow (1989, pp. 140–145) propose an alternative test constructed by grouping data that can be used with sparse data.

While $\text{Var}(y_i - \pi_i) = \pi_i(1 - \pi_i)$, $\text{Var}(y_i - \hat{\pi}_i) \neq \hat{\pi}_i(1 - \hat{\pi}_i)$. Consequently, the variance of r_i is not 1. To compute the variance of the estimated residuals, we need what is known as the *hat matrix*, so named because it transforms the observed y into $\hat{y}$ in the LRM. For the BRM, Pregibon (1981) derived the hat matrix:

$$\mathbf{H} = \hat{\mathbf{V}}\mathbf{X}(\mathbf{X}'\hat{\mathbf{V}}\mathbf{X})^{-1}\mathbf{X}'\hat{\mathbf{V}}$$

where $\hat{\mathbf{V}}$ is a diagonal matrix with $\sqrt{\hat{\pi}_i(1 - \hat{\pi}_i)}$ on the diagonal. Since only the diagonal of $\mathbf{H}$ is needed, we can use the computationally simpler formula:

$$h_{ii} = \hat{\pi}_i(1 - \hat{\pi}_i)\mathbf{x}_i \widehat{\text{Var}(\hat{\boldsymbol{\beta}})}\mathbf{x}_i'$$

where $\mathbf{x}_i$ is a row vector with values of the independent variables for the ith observation and $\widehat{\text{Var}(\hat{\boldsymbol{\beta}})}$ is the estimated covariance of the ML estimator $\hat{\boldsymbol{\beta}}$. Using $1 - h_{ii}$ to estimate the variance of r_i, the *standardized Pearson residual* is

$$r_i^{\text{Std}} = \frac{r_i}{\sqrt{1 - h_{ii}}}$$

While r^{Std} is preferred to r, the two residuals are often similar in practice.

An *index plot* of the standardized residuals against the observation number can be used to search for outliers. Figure 4.4 is an index plot of the standardized residual for the labor force data. Only half of the observations are shown in order to make the figure clearer. Two observations stand out as extreme and are marked with boxes. Observation 142 has a residual of 3.2; observation 512 has a residual of -2.7. Further analyses of these cases might reveal either incorrectly coded data or some inadequacy in the specification of the model. Cases with large positive or negative residuals should *not* simply be discarded from the analysis, but rather should be examined to determine why they were fit so poorly.

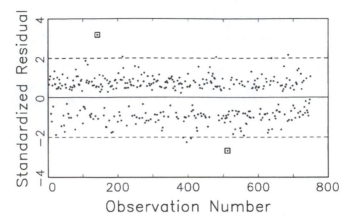

Figure 4.4. Index Plot of Standardized Pearson Residuals

While large residuals indicate that an observation is not fit well, they do not indicate whether an observation has a large influence on the estimated β's or the overall fit. For example, a large residual for the ith observation will not have a large influence on the estimates of β (i.e., removing that observation will not change the estimates very much) if $\mathbf{x}_i$ is near the center of the data. Being near the center of the data means that an observation's values for each independent variable are close to that variable's mean in the sample. On the other hand, extreme observations can influence the estimates, even when they do not have large residuals. A useful way to detect such observations, known as *high leverage* points, is to compute the change in $\widehat{\boldsymbol{\beta}}$ that occurs when the ith observation is deleted. Since it is computationally impractical to estimate the model N times, once with each observation removed, Pregibon (1981) derived an approximation that only requires estimating the model once. The expected change in $\widehat{\boldsymbol{\beta}}$ if the ith observation is removed is approximately equal to

$$\Delta_i \widehat{\boldsymbol{\beta}} = \widehat{\mathrm{Var}}(\widehat{\boldsymbol{\beta}})\mathbf{x}_i' \frac{y_i - \widehat{\pi}_i}{1 - h_{ii}}$$

The standardized change in β_k due to the deletion of $\mathbf{x}_i$, known as the *DFBETA*, equals

$$DFBETA_{ik} = \frac{\Delta_i \widehat{\beta}_k}{\sqrt{\widehat{\mathrm{Var}}(\widehat{\beta}_k)}}$$

A large value of $DFBETA_{ik}$ indicates that the ith observation has a large influence on the estimate of β_k.

A second measure summarizes the effect of removing the ith observation on the entire vector $\widehat{\beta}$, which is the counterpart to Cook's distance for the LRM:

$$C_i = (\Delta_i\widehat{\beta})'\widehat{\mathrm{Var}}(\widehat{\beta})(\Delta_i\widehat{\beta}) = \frac{r_i^2 h_{ii}}{(1 - h_{ii})^2}$$

Another measure of the impact of a single observation is the change in X^2 when the ith observation is removed:

$$\Delta_i X^2 = \frac{r_i^2}{1 - h_{ii}}$$

Figure 4.5 shows an index plot of C. Comparing this figure to Figure 4.4 illustrates the difference between an outlier and an influential observation. In both figures, observation 142 stands out. However, while observation 554 has a large residual, it has a C of only .06. Analysis of the $DFBETA_{ik}$'s for observation 142 would indicate which coefficients are being affected.

Methods for plotting residuals and outliers can be extended in many ways, including plots of different diagnostics against one another. Details of these plots are found in Landwehr et al. (1984) and Hosmer and Lemeshow (1989, pp. 149–170). While Lesaffre and Albert (1989) have proposed extensions of these diagnostics to the multinomial logit model, these extensions have not been added to standard software. Diagnostics for logit and probit are included in SAS and Stata.

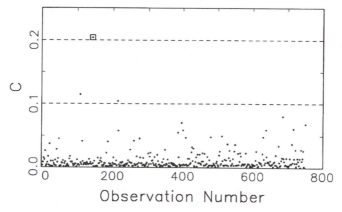

Figure 4.5. Index Plot of Cook's Influence Statistics

4.3. Scalar Measures of Fit

In addition to assessing the fit of each observation, it is sometimes useful to have a single number to summarize the overall goodness of fit of a model. Such a measure might aid in comparing competing models and, ultimately, in selecting a final model. Within a substantive area of research, measures of fit can provide a *rough* index of whether a model is adequate. For example, if prior models of labor force participation routinely have values of .4 for a given measure of fit, you would expect that new analyses with a different sample and perhaps with revised measures of the independent variables would result in a similar value for that measure of fit. Much larger or smaller values would suggest the need to reassess the changes made in the new study.

While the desirability of a scalar measure of fit is clear, in practice their use is problematic. First, I am unaware of convincing evidence that selecting a model that maximizes the value of a given measure of fit results in a model that is optimal in any sense other than the model having a larger value of that measure. While measures of fit provide some information, it is only partial information that must be assessed within the context of the theory motivating the analysis, past research, and the estimated parameters of the model being considered. Second, while in the LRM the coefficient of determination R^2 is the standard measure of fit, there is no clear choice for models with categorical outcomes. There have been numerous attempts to construct a counterpart to R^2 in the LRM, but no one measure is clearly superior and none has the advantages of a clear interpretation in terms of explained variation. Other measures have been constructed based on the ability of a model to predict the observed outcome. Finally, the Bayesian measures AIC and BIC, which are useful for comparing nonnested models, are increasingly popular. Overall, while I approach scalar measures of fit with some skepticism, their popularity and proliferation makes a review useful.

4.3.1. R^2 in the LRM

Many scalar measures of fit for models with CLDVs are constructed to approximate the coefficient of determination R^2 in the LRM. Most commonly, R^2 is defined as the proportion of the variation in y that can be explained by the x's in the model. However, R^2 can be defined in other ways, each of which produces an identical value for R^2 in the LRM. However, when these equivalent formulas are applied to models for CLDVs, they often produce different values and thus provide different measures of fit. [1]

Let the structural model be $y = \mathbf{x}\boldsymbol{\beta} + \varepsilon$, with K regressors, an intercept, and N observations. The expected value of y is $\widehat{y} = \mathbf{x}\widehat{\boldsymbol{\beta}}$, where $\widehat{\boldsymbol{\beta}}$ is the OLS estimator. The coefficient of determination can be defined in each of the following ways. Derivations of these formulas can be found in Judge et al. (1985, pp. 29–31), Goldberger (1991, pp. 176–179), and Pindyck and Rubinfeld (1991, pp. 61, 76–78, 98–99).

The Percentage of Explained Variation. Let $RSS = \sum_{i=1}^{N}(y_i - \widehat{y}_i)^2$ be the sum of squared residuals, and let $TSS = \sum_{i=1}^{N}(y_i - \bar{y})^2$ be the total sum of squares. Then R^2 is the percentage of TSS explained by the x's:

$$R^2 = \frac{TSS - RSS}{TSS} = 1 - \frac{RSS}{TSS} = 1 - \frac{\sum_{i=1}^{N}(y_i - \widehat{y}_i)^2}{\sum_{i=1}^{N}(y_i - \bar{y})^2} \qquad [4.7]$$

The Ratio of $\mathrm{Var}(y)$ *and* $\mathrm{Var}(\widehat{y})$ The ratio of the variances of $\widehat{y}$ and y is another definition:

$$R^2 = \frac{\widehat{\mathrm{Var}}(\widehat{y})}{\widehat{\mathrm{Var}}(y)} = \frac{\widehat{\mathrm{Var}}(\widehat{y})}{\widehat{\mathrm{Var}}(\widehat{y}) + \widehat{\mathrm{Var}}(\varepsilon)} \qquad [4.8]$$

A Transformation of the Likelihood Ratio. If the errors are assumed to be normal, then R^2 can be written as

$$R^2 = 1 - \left[\frac{L(M_\alpha)}{L(M_\beta)}\right]^{2/N} \qquad [4.9]$$

where $L(M_\alpha)$ is the likelihood for the model with just the intercept, and $L(M_\beta)$ is the likelihood for the model including the regressors.

A Transformation of the F-Test. The hypothesis $H_0: \beta_1 = \cdots = \beta_K = 0$ can be tested using an F-test, with the test statistic F. R^2 can be written in terms of F as

$$R^2 = \frac{FK}{FK + (N - K - 1)}$$

where K is the number of independent variables.

---

[1] This is similar to the case in the LRM when there is no intercept. See Judge et al. (1985, pp. 30–31).

4.3.2. Pseudo-R^2's Based on R^2 in the LRM

Several pseudo-R^2's for models with CLDVs have been defined by analogy to the formula given in the last section. These formulas produce different values in models with categorical outcomes, and, consequently, are thought of as distinct measures.

The Percentage of Explained "Variation." For binary outcomes, Efron's (1978) pseudo-R^2 defines $\hat{y}$ as $\hat{\pi} = \widehat{\text{Pr}}(y \mid \mathbf{x})$ and applies Equation 4.7:

$$R^2_{\text{Efron}} = 1 - \frac{\sum_{i=1}^{N}(y_i - \hat{\pi}_i)^2}{\sum_{i=1}^{N}(y_i - \bar{y})^2}$$

(Show that in the case of a binary outcome, $\sum_{i=1}^{N}(y_i - \bar{y})^2 = (n_0 n_1)/N$, where n_0 is the number of 0's and n_1 is the number of 1's in the sample.)

McFadden (1973) suggested a different analogy to explained variation in the LRM that can be applied to any model estimated with ML. This popular measure is also referred to as the "likelihood ratio index." In this measure, the log likelihood for model M_α without regressors is thought of as the total sum of squares, while the log likelihood of model M_β with regressors is thought of as the residual sum of squares. By analogy to Equation 4.7,

$$R^2_{\text{McF}} = 1 - \frac{\ln \widehat{L}(M_\beta)}{\ln \widehat{L}(M_\alpha)}$$

If model $M_\alpha = M_\beta$ (i.e., the slopes are all 0), R^2_{McF} equals 0, but R^2_{McF} can never exactly equal 1.

Like R^2 for the LRM, R^2_{McF} increases as new variables are added to the model. To compensate, Ben-Akiva and Lerman (1985, p. 167) suggest adjusting R^2_{McF} for the number of parameters in the model (just as the adjusted $\bar{R}^2$ in the LRM):

$$\bar{R}^2_{\text{McF}} = 1 - \frac{\ln \widehat{L}(M_\beta) - K}{\ln \widehat{L}(M_\alpha)}$$

$\bar{R}^2_{\text{McF}}$ will only increase if $\ln \widehat{L}(M_\beta)$ increases by more than 1 for each parameter added to the model.

Ben-Akiva and Lerman (1985, p. 167) discuss the logic behind and limitations of these measures. All else being equal, models with a larger value of the log likelihood are preferred, and R^2_{McF} provides a convenient way to compare log likelihoods across different models. Unfortunately, there is no clear interpretation of values other than 0 and 1, nor is there any standard by which to judge if the value is "large enough."

The Ratio of $\text{Var}(y^*)$ *and* $\text{Var}(\hat{y}^*)$. For models defined in terms of a latent outcome according to $y^* = \mathbf{x}\boldsymbol{\beta} + \varepsilon$, McKelvey and Zavoina (1975, pp. 111–112) proposed a pseudo-R^2 by analogy to Equation 4.8:

$$R^2_{\text{M\&Z}} = \frac{\widehat{\text{Var}}(\hat{y}^*)}{\widehat{\text{Var}}(y^*)} = \frac{\widehat{\text{Var}}(\hat{y}^*)}{\widehat{\text{Var}}(\hat{y}^*) + \text{Var}(\varepsilon)}$$

This formula differs from that for the LRM in two respects. First, we are using the estimated variance of the latent variable y^* rather than the observed y. Second, the variance of ε is fixed by assumption, rather than being estimated. For the logit model, $\text{Var}(\varepsilon) = \pi^2/3$, and for the probit model, $\text{Var}(\varepsilon) = 1$. The variance of $\hat{y}^*$ can be computed as

$$\widehat{\text{Var}}(\hat{y}^*) = \hat{\boldsymbol{\beta}}' \widehat{\text{Var}}(\mathbf{x}) \hat{\boldsymbol{\beta}}$$

where $\widehat{\text{Var}}(\mathbf{x})$ is the estimated covariance matrix among the x's.

$R^2_{\text{M\&Z}}$ was suggested by McKelvey and Zavoina (1975, pp. 111–112) for ordinal outcomes, but can also be applied to binary and censored outcomes (Laitila, 1993). In simulation studies, Hagle and Mitchell (1992) and Windmeijer (1995) find that $R^2_{\text{M\&Z}}$ most closely approximates the R^2 obtained from regressions on the underlying latent variable.

A Transformation of the Likelihood Ratio. If we define M_α as the model with just the intercept, and M_β as the model with the regressors included, by analogy to Equation 4.9 a pseudo-R^2 can be defined as

$$R^2_{\text{ML}} = 1 - \left[\frac{L(M_\alpha)}{L(M_\beta)}\right]^{2/N} \tag{4.10}$$

Maddala (1983, p. 39) shows that R^2_{ML} can be expressed as a transformation of the likelihood ratio chi-square $G^2 = -2\ln[L(M_\alpha)/L(M_\beta)]$:

$$R^2_{\text{ML}} = 1 - \exp(-G^2/N)$$

which illustrates that measures of fit such as R^2 and the various pseudo-R^2's are often closely related to tests of hypothesis. See Magee (1990) for other measures of fit based on the Wald and score tests.

TABLE 4.2 R^2-Type Measures of Fit for the Logit and LPM Models

Measure	LPM		Logit	
	M_1	M_2	M_1	M_2
$\ln L_\beta$	−478.086	−486.426	−452.633	−461.653
$\ln L_\alpha$	−539.410	−539.410	−514.873	−514.873
R^2_{Efron}	0.150	0.131	0.155	0.135
R^2_{McF}	0.114	0.098	0.121	0.103
$R^2_{\text{M\&Z}}$	0.150	0.131	0.217	0.182
R^2_{ML}	0.150	0.131	0.152	0.132
$R^2_{\text{C\&U}}$	0.197	0.172	0.205	0.177

NOTE: $N = 753$. $\ln L_\beta$ is the log likelihood for the full model; $\ln L_\alpha$ is the log likelihood for the model with no regressors; see the text for definitions of other measures.

As the fit of M_β approaches the fit of M_α [i.e., as $L(M_\beta) \to L(M_\alpha)$], R^2_{ML} approaches 0. However, Maddala (1983, pp. 39–40) shows that R^2_{ML} only reaches a maximum of $1 - L(M_\alpha)^{2/N}$. This led Cragg and Uhler (1970) to suggest the normed measure:

$$R^2_{\text{C\&U}} = \frac{R^2_{\text{ML}}}{\max R^2_{\text{ML}}} = \frac{1 - [L(M_\alpha)/L(M_\beta)]^{2/N}}{1 - L(M_\alpha)^{2/N}}$$

Since both R^2_{ML} and $R^2_{\text{C\&U}}$ are defined in terms of the likelihood function, they can be applied to any model estimated by ML.

Examples of Pseudo-R^2's: Labor Force Participation

To illustrate scalar measures of fit, consider two models. Model M_1 has the original specification of independent variables: *K5, K618, AGE, WC, HC, LWG,* and *INC.* Model M_2 adds a squared age term *AGE2* and drops the variables *K618, HC,* and *LWG.* The resulting measures of fit for the LPM and logit models are given in Table 4.2. Notice that for a given model many of the measures are identical for the LPM, but not for the logit model. You should try to reproduce these measures using the log likelihoods for the full and restricted models.

4.3.3. Pseudo-R^2's Using Observed Versus Predicted Values

Another approach to assessing goodness of fit in models with categorical outcomes is to compare the observed values to the predicted values. While I develop this idea for models with two outcomes, it can be easily generalized to models with J ordinal or nominal outcomes.

Let the observed y equal 0 or 1. The predicted probability that $y = 1$ is

$$\widehat{\pi}_i = \widehat{\Pr}(y = 1 \mid \mathbf{x}_i) = F(\mathbf{x}_i\widehat{\boldsymbol{\beta}}) \qquad [4.11]$$

where F is the cdf for the normal distribution for probit and for the logistic distribution for logit. Define the expected outcome $\widehat{y}$ as

$$\widehat{y}_i = \begin{cases} 0 & \text{if } \widehat{\pi}_i \leq 0.5 \\ 1 & \text{if } \widehat{\pi}_i > 0.5 \end{cases}$$

which Cramer (1991, p. 90) calls the "maximum probability rule." This allows us to construct a table of observed and predicted values, such as Table 4.3, which is sometimes called a *classification table*.

The Count R^2. A simple and *seemingly* appealing measure based on the table of observed and expected counts is the proportion of correct predictions, which Maddala (1992, p. 334) refers to as the *count R^2*:

$$R^2_{\text{Count}} = \frac{1}{N} \sum_j n_{jj}$$

where the n_{jj}'s are the number of correct predictions for outcome j, which are located on the diagonal cells in Table 4.3.

The Adjusted Count R^2. The count R^2 can give the faulty impression that the model is predicting very well, when, in fact, it is not. In a binary model without knowledge about the independent variables, it is possible to correctly predict at least 50% of the cases by choosing the outcome category with the largest percentage of observed cases. For example, 57% of our sample were in the paid labor force. If we predict that all women are working, we would be correct 57% of the time. Accordingly,

TABLE 4.3 Classification Table of Observed and Predicted Outcomes for a Binary Response Model

Observed Outcome	Predicted Outcome		Row Total
	$\widehat{y} = 1$	$\widehat{y} = 0$	
$y = 1$	n_{11} :: correct	n_{12} :: incorrect	n_{1+}
$y = 0$	n_{21} :: incorrect	n_{22} :: correct	n_{2+}
Column Total	n_{+1}	n_{+2}	N

R^2_{Count} needs to be adjusted to account for the largest row marginal. This can be done by

$$R^2_{AdjCount} = \frac{\sum_j n_{jj} - max_r(n_{r+})}{N - max_r(n_{r+})}$$

n_{r+} is the marginal for row r, so that $max_r(n_{r+})$ is the maximum row marginal (i.e., the number of cases in the outcome with the most observations). The *adjusted count* R^2 is the proportion of correct guesses beyond the number that would be correctly guessed by choosing the largest marginal, and can be interpreted as:

- Knowledge of the independent variables, compared to basing our prediction only on the marginal distributions, reduces the error in prediction by $100 \times R^2_{AdjCount}\%$.

$R^2_{AdjCount}$ is equal to Goodman and Kruskal's λ (Bishop et al. 1975, p. 388) applied to the classification table. Other measures of association could also be applied to the classification table (Menard, 1995 pp. 24–36).

Examples of Count Measures: Labor Force Participation

Table 4.4 shows the observed and predicted values from the logit model with independent variables: *K5, K618, AGE, WC, HC, LWG*, and *INC*. The row percentages indicate the percentage of a given outcome that were predicted to be either 1's or 0's. They show that the model is more effective at predicting 1's (80% are predicted correctly) than 0's (55% are predicted correctly). In this example, the count R^2 is

$$R^2_{Count} = \frac{180 + 342}{753} = .69$$

which can be compared to 57% of the cases that were observed as 1's. On the other hand, the adjusted R^2 is

$$R^2_{AdjCount} = \frac{(180 + 342) - 428}{753 - 428} = .29$$

shows that the models reduces the errors in prediction by 29%.

TABLE 4.4 Observed and Predicted Outcomes for the Logit Model of Labor Force Participation

Observed Outcome	Predicted Outcome		Row Total
	$\hat{y} = 0$	$\hat{y} = 1$	
$y = 0$	180	145	325
Row %	55.4	44.6	
$y = 1$	86	342	428
Row %	20.1	79.9	
Column Total	266	487	753
Row %	35.3	64.7	

4.3.4. Information Measures

A different approach to assessing the fit of a model and for comparing competing models is based on measures of information. Akaike's information criterion (AIC) is a well-known measure, while the Bayesian information criterion (BIC) is a measure that is gaining increasing popularity. For a general discussion of information-based measures, see Judge et al. (1985, pp. 870–875).

Akaike's Information Criterion (AIC)

Akaike's (1973) information criterion is defined as

$$\text{AIC} = \frac{-2\ln\widehat{L}(M_\beta) + 2P}{N}$$ [4.12]

where $\widehat{L}(M_\beta)$ is the likelihood of the model and P is the number of parameters in the model (e.g., $K + 1$ in the binary regression model where K is the number of regressors). While Akaike (1973) formally derives AIC through the comparison of a given model to a set of inferior alternative models, here I only provide a heuristic motivation for the reasonableness of the formula.

$\widehat{L}(M_\beta)$ indicates the likelihood of the data for the model, with larger values indicating a better fit. $-2\ln\widehat{L}(M_\beta)$ ranges from 0 to $+\infty$ with smaller values indicating a better fit. As the number of parameters in the model becomes larger, $-2\ln\widehat{L}(M_\beta)$ becomes smaller since more parameters make what is observed more likely. $2P$ is added to $-2\ln\widehat{L}(M_\beta)$ as a penalty for increasing the number of parameters. Since the number of observations affects $-2\ln\widehat{L}(M_\beta)$, we divide by N to obtain the per observation contribution to the adjusted $-2\ln\widehat{L}(M_\beta)$. All else being equal, smaller values suggest a better fitting model.

AIC is often used to compare models across different samples or to compare nonnested models that cannot be compared with the LR test. All else being equal, the model with the smaller AIC is considered the better fitting model.

The Bayesian Information Criterion (BIC)

The Bayesian information criterion has been proposed by Raftery (1996, and the literature cited therein) as a measure to assess the overall fit of a model and to allow the comparison of both nested and nonnested models. This section summarizes Raftery (1996), which derives the formulas given below.

BIC is based on a Bayesian comparison of models. Consider models M_1 andM_2. The *posterior odds* of M_2 relative to M_1 equal

$$\frac{\Pr(M_2\,|\,\text{Observed Data})}{\Pr(M_1\,|\,\text{Observed Data})}$$

If the probability of M_2 given the observed data is greater than the probability of M_1 given the observed data, M_2 would be preferred. Under the assumption that the prior odds $Pr(M_2)/Pr(M_1)$ of the two models are 1 (i.e., we have no prior preference for one model over the other), the Bayes theorem can be used to show that the posterior odds equal the *Bayes factor*:

$$\frac{\Pr(\text{Observed Data}\,|\,M_2)}{\Pr(\text{Observed Data}\,|\,M_1)}$$

Model M_2 would be chosen if the probability of the observed data given that M_2 generated the data is greater than the probability of the observed data given M_1. Even if neither M_2 nor M_1 is the "true" model, the Bayes factor "is designed to choose the model that will, on average, give better out-of-sample predictions" (Raftery, 1996, p. 14).

The BIC statistic is a computationally convenient approximation to the Bayes factor. Given N observations, consider model M_k with deviance $D(M_k)$ comparing M_k to the saturated model M_S with df_k equal to the sample size minus the number of parameters in M_k.[2] The first

---

[2] In Section 4.1.3, I used the term "full model" to refer to what Raftery calls the saturated model.

BIC measure equals

$$\text{BIC}_k = D(M_k) - df_k \ln N \qquad [4.13]$$

Since BIC_S for the saturated model equals 0 (*Why must this be the case?*), the saturated model is preferred when $\text{BIC}_k > 0$. When $\text{BIC}_k < 0$, M_k is preferred with the more negative the BIC_k the better the fit.

A second version of BIC is based on the LR chi-square in Equation 4.6 with df_k' equal to the number of regressors (not parameters) in the model:

$$\text{BIC}_k' = -G^2(M_k) + df_k' \ln N \qquad [4.14]$$

If M_α is the null model without any regressors, then BIC_α' is 0. The null model is preferred when $\text{BIC}_k' > 0$, suggesting that M_k includes too many parameters or variables. When $\text{BIC}_k' < 0$, then M_k is preferred with the more negative the BIC_k' the better the fit. Basically, BIC_k' assesses whether M_k fits the data sufficiently well to justify the number of parameters that are used.

Either BIC_k or BIC_k' can be used to compare models, whether or not they are nested. Raftery (1996) shows that

$$2\ln\left[\frac{\Pr(\text{Observed Data} \mid M_2)}{\Pr(\text{Observed Data} \mid M_1)}\right] \approx \text{BIC}_1 - \text{BIC}_2 \qquad [4.15]$$

Thus, the difference in the BICs from two models indicates which model is more likely to have generated the observed data. Further, it can be shown that

$$\text{BIC}_1 - \text{BIC}_2 = \text{BIC}_1' - \text{BIC}_2'$$

so that the choice of which BIC measure to use is a matter of convenience.

Based on Equation 4.15, the model with the smaller BIC or BIC' is preferred. How strong the preference is depends on the magnitude of the difference. Raftery, based on Jeffreys (1961), suggested guidelines for the strength of evidence favoring M_2 against M_1 based on a difference in BIC or BIC'. These are listed in Table 4.5. Since the model with the more negative BIC or BIC' is preferred, if $\text{BIC}_1 - \text{BIC}_2 < 0$, then the first model is preferred. If $\text{BIC}_1 - \text{BIC}_2 > 0$, then the second model is preferred.

TABLE 4.5 Strength of Evidence Based on the
Absolute Value of the Difference in
BIC or BIC′

Absolute Difference	Evidence
0–2	Weak
2–6	Positive
6–10	Strong
> 10	Very Strong

Finally, to see the link between BIC and other measures of fit, consider the formula that Raftery (1996, p. 19) provides for computing BIC′ in the LRM:

$$\text{BIC}'_k = N \ln(1 - R^2_k) + df_k \ln N$$

This convenient computational formula for BIC′ in the LRM can also be used for models with CLDVs by replacing R^2_k by R^2_{ML} from Equation 4.10.

Example of Information Measures: Labor Force Participation

To illustrate the AIC and BIC measures, the logit model M_1 with the original specification of independent variables: *K5, K618, AGE, WC, HC, LWG,* and *INC*; and M_2 which adds a squared age term *AGE2* and drops the variables *K618, HC,* and *LWG* were estimated. Table 4.6 contains the test statistics, along with the components that are used to compute them. Since many programs do not compute the AIC and BIC, it is important to verify that you can obtain the listed statistics using the formula in Equations 4.12 through 4.14.

Based on the values of AIC, BIC, and BIC′, model M_1 is favored by all measures. Using the difference in BIC,

$$\text{BIC}_1 - \text{BIC}_2 = -4{,}029.66 - -4{,}024.87 = -4.79$$
$$\text{BIC}'_1 - \text{BIC}'_2 = - \quad 78.11 - - \quad 73.32 = -4.79$$

According to Table 4.5, the evidence favoring M_1 over M_2 is positive but not strong.

4.4. Conclusions

The methods for hypothesis testing are quite general and can be used with all models considered in this book. Pregibon's methods for detecting

TABLE 4.6 AIC and BIC for the Logit Model

Measure	M_1	M_2
$\ln L_\beta$	−452.633	−461.653
$\ln L_\alpha$	−514.873	−514.873
G^2	124.481	106.441
D	905.266	923.306
df	745	747
df'	7	5
P	8	6
AIC	1.223	1.242
BIC	−4029.663	−4024.871
BIC$'$	−78.112	−73.321

NOTE: $\ln L_\beta$ is the log likelihood for the full model; $\ln L_\alpha$ is the log likelihood for the model with no regressors. $N = 753$.

outliers and influential observations apply only to models with binary outcomes. While some of the scalar measures of goodness of fit are only appropriate for models with binary outcomes, others apply with minor adjustments to any model estimated with ML.

4.5. Bibliographic Notes

The tests presented in this chapter have a long history. R. A. Fisher introduced the LR test in the 1920s, and A. Wald proposed the Wald test in the 1940s. Further details on these tests can be found in most econometrics texts. Godfrey (1988, pp. 8–20) and Cramer (1986, pp. 30–42) contain thorough discussions of the foundations of these tests. Buse (1982) provides an informative geometric interpretation. Maddala (1992, pp. 118–124) presents an interesting discussion within the context of the linear regression model. Regression diagnostics for the binary response model were developed by Pregibon (1981). Amemiya (1981) and Windmeijer (1995) have reviews of measures of fit. Hosmer and Lemeshow (1989, Chapter 5) provide further details on diagnostics and tests of fit. The AIC was proposed by Akaike (1973). The BIC has been advocated by Raftery in a series of papers summarized in Raftery (1996). His work developed from Schwarz (1978) and Jeffreys (1961). See Judge et al. (1985, pp. 870–875) for a discussion of these and related measures.

5 Ordinal Outcomes: Ordered Logit and Ordered Probit Analysis

When a variable is ordinal, its categories can be ranked from low to high, but the distances between adjacent categories are unknown. Ordinal outcomes are common in the social sciences. McKelvey and Zavoina (1975) studied votes for the 1965 Medicare bill where each member of Congress was rated as against, weakly for, or strongly for the bill. Marcus and Greene (1985) analyzed factors affecting the assignment of Navy recruits into jobs that were ordered as medium skilled, highly skilled, and nuclear qualified. Winship and Mare (1984) modeled educational attainment with education classified as less than 8 years of school, 8 to 11 years, 12 years, or 13 or more. Many studies have considered ordinal measures of occupational status. Hartog et al. (1994) analyzed the job levels that workers desired; Meng and Miller (1995) studied occupational attainment in China where workers were ranked as shift leader, middle level, and ordinary staff; Hedström (1994) studied organizational rank in Sweden where workers were classified as having low organizational responsibilities, first-line supervisory responsibilities, middle management, and top management. Many surveys have respondents indicate their income within ordered groupings, such as less than $15,000, between $15,000 and $30,000, and so on. Likert scales on surveys ask respondents whether they strongly agree, agree, have no opinion, disagree, or strongly disagree with a statement.

Researchers often, and perhaps usually, treat ordinal dependent variables as if they were interval. The dependent categories are numbered sequentially and the LRM is used. This involves the implicit assumption that the intervals between adjacent categories are equal. For example, the distance between strongly agreeing and agreeing is assumed to be the same as the distance between agreeing and being neutral on a Likert scale. Winship and Mare (1984) review the debate between those who argue that the ease of use, simple interpretation, and flexibility of the LRM justify its use with ordinal outcomes versus those who argue that the bias introduced by regression of an ordinal variable makes this practice unacceptable. Both McKelvey and Zavoina (1975, p. 117) and Winship and Mare (1984, pp. 521–523) give examples where regression of an ordinal outcome provides misleading results. Given this risk, prudent researchers should use models specifically designed for ordinal variables.

Before considering methods for ordinal outcomes, it is important to note that simply because the values of a variable *can* be ordered does not imply that the variable *should* be analyzed as ordinal. A variable might be ordered when considered for one purpose, but be unordered or ordered differently when used for another purpose. McCullagh and Nelder (1989, p. 151) make this point with the example of colors. While colors can be arranged according to the electromagnetic spectrum, this does not imply that this ordering is appropriate for all purposes. When consumers buy a car, there is no reason to believe that they prefer colors in an order that moves around the color wheel from red, to orange, to yellow, and so on. Miller and Volker (1985) illustrate this point in their analysis of occupational attainment. Occupational groupings were ordered both by the status of the occupations and by the income of the occupations. The alternative rankings resulted in different conclusions when analyzed with the ordered regression model. Another example is Likert scales which might reflect two dimensions, intensity and opinion, rather than a single dimension. While in one sense the categories strongly agree, agree, neutral, disagree, and strongly disagree are ordered, if a researcher is interested in the intensity of opinion, then the ordering should be strongly agree or strongly disagree, agree or disagree, followed by neutral. When the proper ordering of a variable is ambiguous, the models for nominal variables in Chapter 6 should be considered in addition to models for ordinal variables.

In this chapter, I focus on the ordered logit and the ordered probit models. Since these models are so closely related, I refer to them together as the *ordered regression model*, abbreviated as ORM. Within the social sciences, this model was introduced by McKelvey and Zavoina

(1975) in terms of an underlying latent variable with observed, ordered categories. At about the same time, the model was developed in bio-statistics (McCullagh, 1980), where it is referred to as the *proportional odds model*, the *parallel regression model*, or the *grouped continuous model*. The name "proportional odds model" emphasizes an interpretation in terms of odds ratios, which is considered in Section 5.4.5. This approach to the model is similar to the presentation in Chapter 3 of the binary response model as a nonlinear probability model. The name "parallel regression model" emphasizes an implicit assumption about the structure of the probability curves that are generated by the model, which is considered in Section 5.5. The name "grouped continuous model" emphasizes the relationship between an underlying continuous variable and the observed, grouped variable. I begin with this view of the model.

5.1. A Latent Variable Model for Ordinal Variables

The ORM can be derived from a measurement model in which a latent variable y^* ranging from $-\infty$ to ∞ is mapped to an observed variable y. The variable y is thought of as providing incomplete information about an underlying y^* according to the measurement equation:

$$y_i = m \quad \text{if } \tau_{m-1} \le y_i^* < \tau_m \quad \text{for } m = 1 \text{ to } J \qquad [5.1]$$

The τ's are called *thresholds* or *cutpoints*. The extreme categories 1 and J are defined by open-ended intervals with $\tau_0 = -\infty$ and $\tau_J = \infty$. When $J = 2$, Equation 5.1 is identical to the measurement equation for the BRM of Chapter 3 (see Equation 3.1).

To illustrate the measurement equation, consider the dependent variable used as an example throughout the chapter. People are asked to respond to the statement: "A working mother can establish just as warm and secure a relationship with her children as a mother who does not work." Response categories are "Strongly Disagree" (SD), "Disagree" (D), "Agree" (A), and "Strongly Agree" (SA). Assume that this ordinal variable is related to a continuous, latent variable y^* that indicates an individual's degree of support for the statement about working mothers. The observed y is related to y^* according to the measurement model:

$$y_i = \begin{cases} 1 \Rightarrow \text{SD} & \text{if } \tau_0 = -\infty \le y_i^* < \tau_1 \\ 2 \Rightarrow \text{D} & \text{if } \tau_1 \le y_i^* < \tau_2 \\ 3 \Rightarrow \text{A} & \text{if } \tau_2 \le y_i^* < \tau_3 \\ 4 \Rightarrow \text{SA} & \text{if } \tau_3 \le y_i^* < \tau_4 = \infty \end{cases}$$

This mapping from the latent variable to the observed categories is illustrated in the following figure:

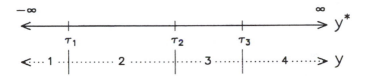

The solid line represents the latent variable y^*. The cutpoints are indicated by the horizontal lines marked τ_1, τ_2, and τ_3. The values of the observed variable y over the range of y^* are marked below with a dotted line.

As with the binary response model, the structural model is

$$y_i^* = \mathbf{x}_i\boldsymbol{\beta} + \varepsilon_i$$

$\mathbf{x}_i$ is a row vector with a 1 in the first column for the intercept and the ith observation for x_k in column $k + 1$. $\boldsymbol{\beta}$ is a column vector of structural coefficients with the first element being the intercept β_0. For reasons that will become clear when I discuss identification, the intercept is always included.

For a single independent variable, the structural model is

$$y_i^* = \alpha + \beta x_i + \varepsilon_i$$

This is plotted in panel A of Figure 5.1. The latent y^* is on the vertical axis. The values 15, 0, and −5 are labeled to give you a sense of the scale of y^*. The thresholds τ_1, τ_2, and τ_3 are indicated by dashed lines that divide y^* into four values of the observed y. $\tau_0 = -\infty$ is located below and $\tau_4 = \infty$ is located above. The values of the observed y's are shown at the right. The regression $E(y^* \mid x) = \alpha + \beta x$ for $\alpha = 1$ and $\beta = .1$ is shown with a thick line. Since y^* is unobserved, α and β cannot be estimated by regressing y^* on x.

Panel B plots the observed y against x. The y's are constructed from the y^*'s in panel A by assigning all cases with y^* above τ_3 to 4, cases with y^* between τ_2 and τ_3 to 3, and so on. The OLS estimate of the regression of y on x is indicated by the dashed line with an estimated slope of .026. Regressing y on x does not reasonably approximate the regression of y^* on x, which has a slope that is four times larger. The regression lines in panels A and B only look similar because the scales

Panel A: Regression of Latent y*

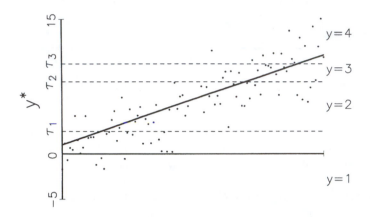

Panel B: Regression of Observed y

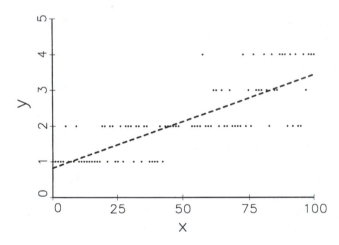

Figure 5.1. Regression of a Latent Variable y^* Compared to the Regression of the Corresponding Observed Variable y

of the vertical axes are different. If the y-axis in panel B were drawn with the same scale as the y^*-axis in panel A, the regression line for y on x would be nearly horizontal. Another problem with the regression of y on x is that the errors are heteroscedastic and are not normal. In general, the results of the LRM only correspond to those of the ORM *if* the thresholds are all about the same distance apart. When this is not the case, the LRM can give very misleading results.

Figure 5.1 also illustrates an important characteristic of the ORM. In panel A, you could add (or delete) another cutpoint without changing the structural model. Imagine placing a horizontal line between τ_1 and τ_2. This would correspond to adding another category to the ordinal scale, such as the category "Neutral" between "Disagree" and "Agree." The regression line for y^* on x would not be affected. In panel B, the new category would correspond to adding a new horizontal row of observations, which would affect the results of the regression of y on x.

5.1.1. Distributional Assumptions

As with the BRM, ML estimation can be used to estimate the regression of y^* on $\mathbf{x}$. To use ML, we must assume a specific form of the error distribution. Once again, we consider normal and logistic errors. Other distributions for the errors have been considered, but are not used often (see McCullagh, 1980, p. 115, for details).

For the ordered probit model, ε is distributed normally with mean 0 and variance 1. The pdf is

$$\phi(\varepsilon) = \frac{1}{\sqrt{2\pi}} \exp\left(-\frac{\varepsilon^2}{2}\right)$$

and the cdf is

$$\Phi(\varepsilon) = \int_{-\infty}^{\varepsilon} \frac{1}{\sqrt{2\pi}} \exp\left(-\frac{t^2}{2}\right) dt$$

For the ordered logit model, ε has a logistic distribution with a mean of 0 and a variance of $\pi^2/3$. The pdf is

$$\lambda(\varepsilon) = \frac{\exp(\varepsilon)}{[1 + \exp(\varepsilon)]^2}$$

and the cdf is

$$\Lambda(\varepsilon) = \frac{\exp(\varepsilon)}{1 + \exp(\varepsilon)} \qquad [5.2]$$

For the rest of this chapter, F represents either Φ or Λ, and f represents either ϕ or λ.

As with the binary logit and probit models, the choice between the ordered logit and probit models is largely one of convenience. However, certain extensions of the model to multiple equation systems assume a normally distributed error and hence use the ordered probit model (see Chapter 9 for further discussion). On the other hand, interpretation of the parameters in terms of odds in Section 5.4.5 requires the ordered logit model. For most purposes, however, the choice is likely to depend on which software is available and which model is most common in your area of research.

5.1.2. The Probabilities of Observed Values

Once the distribution of the errors is specified, we can compute the probabilities of observing values of y given $\mathbf{x}$. To see this, consider Figure 5.2 which illustrates the distribution of y^* for three values of x. The errors are distributed either logistically or normally around the regression line $E(y^* \mid x) = \alpha + \beta x$. The probability of outcome m corresponds to the area of the error distribution between the cutpoints τ_{m-1} and τ_m. This area is computed as follows.

First, consider the formula for the probability that $y = 1$. We observe $y = 1$ when y^* falls between $\tau_0 = -\infty$ and τ_1. This implies that

$$\Pr(y_i = 1 \mid \mathbf{x}_i) = \Pr(\tau_0 \le y_i^* < \tau_1 \mid \mathbf{x}_i)$$

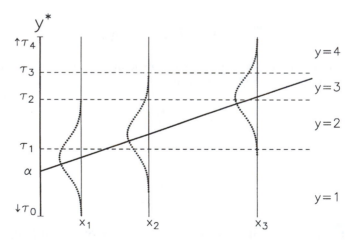

Figure 5.2. Distribution of y^* Given x for the Ordered Regression Model

Substituting $y^* = \mathbf{x\beta} + \varepsilon$,

$$Pr(y_i = 1 \mid \mathbf{x}_i) = Pr(\tau_0 \le \mathbf{x}_i\mathbf{\beta} + \varepsilon_i < \tau_1 \mid \mathbf{x}_i)$$

Then, subtracting $\mathbf{x\beta}$ within the inequality,

$$Pr(y_i = 1 \mid \mathbf{x}_i) = Pr(\tau_0 - \mathbf{x}_i\mathbf{\beta} \le \varepsilon_i < \tau_1 - \mathbf{x}_i\mathbf{\beta} \mid \mathbf{x}_i)$$

The probability that a random variable is between two values is the difference between the cdf evaluated at these values. Therefore,

$$Pr(y_i = 1 \mid \mathbf{x}_i) = Pr(\varepsilon_i < \tau_1 - \mathbf{x}_i\mathbf{\beta} \mid \mathbf{x}_i) - Pr(\varepsilon_i \le \tau_0 - \mathbf{x}_i\mathbf{\beta} \mid \mathbf{x}_i)$$
$$= F(\tau_1 - \mathbf{x}_i\mathbf{\beta}) - F(\tau_0 - \mathbf{x}_i\mathbf{\beta})$$

These steps can be generalized to compute the probability of any observed outcome $y = m$ given $\mathbf{x}$:

$$Pr(y_i = m \mid \mathbf{x}_i) = F(\tau_m - \mathbf{x}_i\mathbf{\beta}) - F(\tau_{m-1} - \mathbf{x}_i\mathbf{\beta}) \qquad [5.3]$$

When computing $Pr(y = 1 \mid \mathbf{x})$, the second term on the right-hand side drops out since $F(\tau_0 - \mathbf{x\beta}) = F(-\infty - \mathbf{x\beta}) = 0$; when computing $Pr(y = J \mid \mathbf{x})$, the first term equals 1 since $F(\tau_J - \mathbf{x\beta}) = F(\infty - \mathbf{x\beta}) = 1$. Thus, for a model with four observed outcomes, such as shown in Figure 5.2, the formulas for the ordered probit model are

$$Pr(y_i = 1 \mid x_i) = \Phi(\tau_1 - \alpha - \beta x_i)$$
$$Pr(y_i = 2 \mid x_i) = \Phi(\tau_2 - \alpha - \beta x_i) - \Phi(\tau_1 - \alpha - \beta x_i)$$
$$Pr(y_i = 3 \mid x_i) = \Phi(\tau_3 - \alpha - \beta x_i) - \Phi(\tau_2 - \alpha - \beta x_i)$$
$$Pr(y_i = 4 \mid x_i) = 1 - \Phi(\tau_3 - \alpha - \beta x_i)$$

For example, if $\alpha = -.50$, $\beta = .052$, $\tau_1 = .75$, $\tau_2 = 3.5$, and $\tau_3 = 5.0$, then for $x = 15$, 40, and 80, the following probabilities are obtained (*Reproduce this table.*):

Predicted Probability	$x = 15$	$x = 40$	$x = 80$
$Pr(y = 1 \mid x)$	0.68	0.20	0.00
$Pr(y = 2 \mid x)$	0.32	0.77	0.44
$Pr(y = 3 \mid x)$	0.00	0.03	0.47
$Pr(y = 4 \mid x)$	0.00	0.00	0.09

Equation 5.3 was derived from the assumption that there is an underlying, latent variable. While this is a useful way to develop the model, sometimes the idea of a latent variable is untenable. For example, academic rank is ordinal, but it is hard to imagine an underlying variable that would generate the rankings of assistant, associate, and full professor. [1] In such cases, it is possible to think of Equation 5.3 as a probability model of the relationship between the x's and the outcome probabilities. The only cost of forgoing the assumption of the latent variable is that interpretation in terms of partial change in y^* (discussed in Section 5.4) cannot be used.

5.2. Identification

Since y^* is latent, its mean and variance cannot be estimated. The variance is identified by assuming that $\text{Var } \varepsilon \mid x) = \pi^2/3$ in the ordered logit model and $\text{Var}(\varepsilon \mid x) = 1$ in the ordered probit model. While these assumptions identify the variance, the mean of y^* is still unidentified. The consequences of this can be seen by considering the model $y^* = \alpha + \beta x + \varepsilon$ with cutpoints τ_m. Think of α and the τ's as the "true" parameters in the sense that they were used to generate the observed data. Define an alternative set of parameters:

$$\alpha^* = \alpha - \delta \quad \text{and} \quad \tau_m^* = \tau_m - \delta \qquad [5.4]$$

where δ is an arbitrary constant. The probability that $y = m$ is identical, whether the true or alternative parameters are used:

$$\Pr(y = m \mid x) = F(\tau_m - \alpha - \beta x) - F(\tau_{m-1} - \alpha - \beta x) \qquad [5.5]$$
$$= F([\tau_m - \delta] - [\alpha - \delta] - \beta x)$$
$$\quad - F([\tau_{m-1} - \delta] - [\alpha - \delta] - \beta x)$$
$$= F(\tau_m^* - \alpha^* - \beta x) - F(\tau_{m-1}^* - \alpha^* - \beta x)$$

Since both sets of parameters generate the same value for the probability of an observed outcome, there is no way to choose between the two

---

[1] There is a longstanding debate, beginning at least with G. U. Yule and K. Pearson in the early 1900s, on whether ordinal variables are intrinsically ordinal rather than being imperfect measures of a continuous latent variable (see Agresti, 1996, Chapter 10, for an interesting history of this and related topics). The debate continues as one reviewer praised this example of an intrinsically ordinal variable, while another chastised me for choosing a variable that clearly has an underlying latent variable behind it.

sets of parameters using the observed data: a change in the intercept in the structural model can always be compensated for by a corresponding change in the thresholds. That is to say, the model is unidentified.

While there is an infinite number of assumptions that could be made to identify the model, only two are commonly used:

1. Assume that $\tau_1 = 0$. This involves setting $\delta = \tau_1$ in Equation 5.4. This is the identifying assumption used for the BRM in Chapter 3.
2. Assume that $\alpha = 0$. This involves setting $\delta = \alpha$ in Equation 5.4.

Both assumptions identify the model by imposing a constraint on one of the parameters. (*Are there other assumptions that would identify the model?*) The different identifying assumptions lead to what are known as different *parameterizations* of the model. The choice of which parameterization to use is arbitrary and does not affect the β's (except for β_0) or associated significance tests. Further, as shown by Equation 5.5, the probabilities are not affected by the identifying assumption. However, understanding the different parameterizations is important since different software uses different parameterizations (see Section 5.3.1).

5.3. Estimation

Let $\boldsymbol{\beta}$ be the vector with parameters from the structural model, with the intercept β_0 in the first row, and let $\boldsymbol{\tau}$ be the vector containing the threshold parameters. Either β_0 or τ_1 is constrained to 0 to identify the model. From Equation 5.3,

$$\Pr(y_i = m \mid \mathbf{x}_i, \boldsymbol{\beta}, \boldsymbol{\tau}) = F(\tau_m - \mathbf{x}_i\boldsymbol{\beta}) - F(\tau_{m-1} - \mathbf{x}_i\boldsymbol{\beta}) \qquad [5.6]$$

The probability of observing whatever value of y was actually observed for the ith observation is

$$p_i = \begin{cases} \Pr(y_i = 1 \mid \mathbf{x}_i, \boldsymbol{\beta}, \boldsymbol{\tau}) & \text{if } y = 1 \\ \quad \vdots & \quad \vdots \\ \Pr(y_i = m \mid \mathbf{x}_i, \boldsymbol{\beta}, \boldsymbol{\tau}) & \text{if } y = m \\ \quad \vdots & \quad \vdots \\ \Pr(y_i = J \mid \mathbf{x}_i, \boldsymbol{\beta}, \boldsymbol{\tau}) & \text{if } y = J \end{cases} \qquad [5.7]$$

If the observations are independent, the likelihood equation is

$$L(\boldsymbol{\beta}, \boldsymbol{\tau} \,|\, \mathbf{y}, \mathbf{X}) = \prod_{i=1}^{N} p_i \qquad\qquad [5.8]$$

Combining Equations 5.6 through 5.8,

$$L(\boldsymbol{\beta}, \boldsymbol{\tau} \,|\, \mathbf{y}, \mathbf{X}) = \prod_{j=1}^{J} \prod_{y_i=j} \Pr(y_i = j \,|\, \mathbf{x}_i, \boldsymbol{\beta}, \boldsymbol{\tau})$$

$$= \prod_{j=1}^{J} \prod_{y_i=j} \left[F(\tau_j - \mathbf{x}_i\boldsymbol{\beta}) - F(\tau_{j-1} - \mathbf{x}_i\boldsymbol{\beta}) \right]$$

$\prod_{y_i=j}$ indicates multiplying over all cases where y is observed to equal j. Taking logs, the log likelihood is

$$\ln L(\boldsymbol{\beta}, \boldsymbol{\tau} \,|\, \mathbf{y}, \mathbf{X}) = \sum_{j=1}^{J} \sum_{y_i=j} \ln \left[F(\tau_j - \mathbf{x}_i\boldsymbol{\beta}) - F(\tau_{j-1} - \mathbf{x}_i\boldsymbol{\beta}) \right]$$

This equation can be maximized with numerical methods to estimate the τ's and the β's. Maddala (1983, pp. 48–49) presents the gradient and Hessian for Newton-Raphson estimation and reviews Pratt's (1981) results demonstrating that Newton-Raphson will converge to a global maximum. The resulting estimates are consistent, asymptotically normal, and asymptotically efficient.

5.3.1. Software Issues

There are several issues related to software that should be considered when estimating the ORM.

Parameterizations of the Model. The most important issue is knowing which parameterization your program uses. Programs such as LIMDEP assume that $\tau_1 = 0$ and estimate β_0, while programs such as Markov, SAS's LOGISTIC, and Stata assume that $\beta_0 = 0$ and estimate τ_1. The choice of parameterization does not affect estimates of the slopes, but does affect the estimates of β_0 and the τ's. In SAS's LOGISTIC, you must use the DESCENDING option in order for the estimates of the slopes to have the same sign as those presented here. Without this option, LOGISTIC is estimating the model $y^* = -\mathbf{x}\boldsymbol{\beta} + \varepsilon$.

Methods of Numerical Maximization. Different programs use different methods of numerical maximization. Regardless of the method used, programs should produce the same estimates of the parameters up to five significant digits, but the standard errors and test statistics can differ substantially, especially with small samples or with ill-conditioned data.

Failure to Converge. In my experience, the ORM takes longer to converge than other models considered in this book; between five and ten iterations is typical. If the number of cases in a response category is small, the model may fail to converge. When this occurs, estimation can proceed by merging the outcome category with a small number of cases into an adjacent category. The only effect of combining adjacent categories is a loss of efficiency (McCullagh, 1980). This property is a consequence of the parallel regression assumption, which is discussed in Section 5.5.

Binary Outcome. With $J = 2$ and the constraint $\tau_1 = 0$, the ORM is identical to the BRM after a change in notation. However, some programs for the ORM have been optimized for $J > 2$ and do not work for $J = 2$.

5.3.2. Example of the ORM and the LRM: Attitudes Toward Working Mothers

In 1977 and 1989, the General Social Survey asked respondents to evaluate the following statement: "A working mother can establish just as warm and secure a relationship with her children as a mother who does not work." Responses were coded in the variable *WARM* as: $1 =$ Strongly Disagree (SD); $2 =$ Disagree (D); $3 =$ Agree (A); and $4 =$ Strongly Agree (SA). With a sample of 2,293, the marginal percentages are 13, 32, 37, and 18, respectively. The variables used in our analysis are described in Table 5.1. See Clogg and Shihadeh (1994, pp. 158–162) for an alternative analysis of the same data.

Table 5.2 contains the estimates from four models. Column 1 contains OLS estimates for the LRM:

$$WARM = \beta_0 + \beta_1 YR89 + \beta_2 MALE + \beta_3 WHITE$$
$$+ \beta_4 AGE + \beta_5 ED + \beta_6 PRST + \varepsilon$$

Column 2 contains estimates from the ordered probit model with the constraint that $\tau_1 = 0$; column 3 contains estimates from the ordered probit model with the constraint that $\beta_0 = 0$; and column 4 contains estimates from the ordered logit model with $\beta_0 = 0$.

TABLE 5.1 Descriptive Statistics for the Attitudes Toward Working Mothers Example

Name	Mean	Standard Deviation	Minimum	Maximum	Description
WARM	2.61	0.93	1.00	4.00	1 = SD; 2 = D; 3 = A; 4 = SA
YR89	0.40	0.49	0.00	1.00	Survey year: 1 = 1989; 0 = 1977
MALE	0.47	0.50	0.00	1.00	1 = male; 0 = female
WHITE	0.88	0.33	0.00	1.00	1 = white; 0 = nonwhite
AGE	44.94	16.78	18.00	89.00	Age in years
ED	12.22	3.16	0.00	20.00	Years of education
PRST	39.59	14.49	12.00	82.00	Occupational prestige

NOTE: $N = 2293$.

There are several things to notice before we consider how these results should be interpreted.

1. The significance levels of the β's for the LRM are similar to those for the ORM. The relative magnitudes of the LRM estimates are very similar to those for the ordered logit model, and the LRM estimates themselves are very similar to those for the ordered probit model. To see why the results are so close, look at the estimates of the τ's. The distances between the cutpoints are nearly identical, and for the ordered probit model they are almost equal to 1. While in this example the implicit assumption of the LRM that the ordinal categories are equally spaced appears to hold, you should not assume that this will generally be the case.

2. The magnitudes of the estimates of the slopes from the ordered logit and ordered probit models differ since the two models assume different variances of the errors. The relative magnitudes of the coefficients are quite similar, since relative magnitudes are not affected by the assumed variance of the errors.

3. The slope coefficients and z-values for the two parameterizations of the ordered probit model are identical, while the intercept and thresholds differ. This illustrates that the identifying constraints on the intercept and thresholds do not affect the other coefficients in the model.

The next section shows how these coefficients can be interpreted in terms of the latent variable and how they can be used to compute the effects on the probabilities of observed outcomes.

TABLE 5.2 Comparison of the Linear Regression Model and Different Parameterizations of the Ordered Regression Model

Variable		LRM	Ordered Probit $\tau_1 = 0$	Ordered Probit $\beta_0 = 0$	Ordered Logit $\beta_0 = 0$
YR89	β	0.262	0.319	0.319	0.524
	z	6.94	6.56	6.56	6.33
MALE	β	−0.336	−0.417	−0.417	−0.733
	z	−9.17	−9.06	−9.06	−9.23
WHITE	β	−0.177	−0.227	−0.227	−0.391
	z	−3.17	−3.23	−3.23	−3.27
AGE	β	−0.010	−0.012	−0.012	−0.022
	z	−8.70	−8.27	−8.27	−8.52
ED	β	0.031	0.039	0.039	0.067
	z	4.14	4.17	4.17	4.20
PRST	β	0.003	0.003	0.003	0.006
	z	1.73	1.71	1.71	1.84
	β_0	2.780	1.429	—	—
	z	25.26	10.26	—	—
	τ_1		—	−1.429	−2.465
	z		—	−10.26	−10.26
	τ_2		1.068	−0.361	−0.631
	z		30.70	−2.60	−2.66
	τ_3		2.197	0.768	1.262
	z		50.54	5.55	5.32
	$-2\ln L$		5697.2	5697.2	5689.8
	G^2		294.3	294.3	301.7
	df		6	6	6
	p		< 0.001	< 0.001	< 0.001

NOTE: $N = 2293$. β is an unstandardized coefficient; z is the z-test of β.

5.4. Interpretation

If the idea of a continuous, latent variable makes substantive sense, simple interpretations are possible by rescaling the latent variable to a unit variance and computing y^*-standardized and fully standardized coefficients. When concern is with the observed categories, regardless of whether a latent variable is reasonable, methods from Chapter 3 can be extended to the case of multiple outcomes: predicted probabilities of the observed outcomes can be presented in tables or plots, partial and discrete change in probabilities can be examined, and the ordered logit model can be interpreted in terms of odds ratios. Since the ORM is non-linear in the outcome probabilities, no single approach can fully describe the relationship between a variable and the outcome probabilities. Consequently, you should consider each of these methods before deciding which approach is most effective in a given application.

5.4.1. The Partial Change in y^*

In the ordered regression model,

$$y^* = \mathbf{x}\boldsymbol{\beta} + \varepsilon$$

and the partial change in y^* with respect to x_k is

$$\frac{\partial y^*}{\partial x_k} = \beta_k$$

Since the model is linear in y^*, the partial change can be interpreted as:

- For a unit increase in x_k, y^* is expected to change by β_k units, holding all other variables constant.

Since the variance of y^* cannot be estimated from the observed data, the meaning of a change of β_k units in y^* is unclear. As discussed by McKelvey and Zavoina (1975, pp. 114–116) and Winship and Mare (1984, p. 517), interpretations should be based on fully standardized coefficients or y^*-standardized coefficients.

If σ_{y^*} is the unconditional standard deviation of the latent y^*, then the *y^*-standardized coefficient* for x_k is

$$\beta_k^{Sy^*} = \frac{\beta_k}{\sigma_{y^*}}$$

which can be interpreted as:

- For a unit increase in x_k, y^* is expected to increase by $\beta_k^{Sy^*}$ standard deviations, holding all other variables constant.

y^*-standardized coefficients indicate the effect of an independent variable in its original unit of measurement. This is sometimes preferable for substantive reasons and is necessary for binary independent variables.

Fully standardized coefficients also standardize the independent variables. If σ_k is the standard deviation of x_k, then the *fully standardized coefficient* is

$$\beta_k^S = \frac{\sigma_k \beta_k}{\sigma_{y^*}} = \sigma_k \beta_k^{Sy^*}$$

The fully standardized coefficient can be interpreted as:

- For a standard deviation increase in x_k, y^* is expected to increase by β_k^S standard deviations, holding all other variables constant.

As with the BRM, the variance of y^* can be estimated by the quadratic form:

$$\hat{\sigma}_{y^*}^2 = \hat{\beta}'\widehat{\text{Var}}(\mathbf{x})\hat{\beta} + \text{Var}(\varepsilon) \qquad [5.9]$$

where $\widehat{\text{Var}}(\mathbf{x})$ is the covariance matrix for the x's computed from the observed data; $\hat{\beta}$ contains ML estimates; and $\text{Var}(\varepsilon) = 1$ in the ordered probit model and $\text{Var}(\varepsilon) = \pi^2/3$ in the ordered logit model. The coefficients in Table 5.3 were computed from the slope coefficients in Table 5.2 and the descriptive statistics from Table 5.1. The variance of y^* was estimated using Equation 5.9, resulting in $\hat{\sigma}_{y_L^*}^2 = 3.77$ for the ordered logit model and $\hat{\sigma}_{y_P^*}^2 = 1.16$ for the ordered probit model. Notice that $\hat{\sigma}_{y_P^*}^2/\hat{\sigma}_{y_L^*}^2 = 3.25$, which is close to the ratio of the assumed variances: $\text{Var}(\varepsilon_P)/\text{Var}(\varepsilon_L) = \pi^2/3 \approx 3.29$. The difference in the variance of y^* for the two models is reflected in the magnitudes of the unstandardized β's, where the coefficients from the ordered logit model are 1.6 to 1.8 times larger than those for the ordered probit model. The fully standardized and y^*-standardized coefficients are nearly identical across models since the scale of y^* has been eliminated by dividing by $\hat{\sigma}_{y^*}$. (*Why are they not exactly equal?*)

If you are willing to consider the four ordinal categories as reflecting an underlying measure of the respondent's support, then the fully

TABLE 5.3 Standardized Coefficients for the Ordered Regression Model

	Ordered Logit			*Ordered Probit*		
Variable	β	β^{Sy^*}	β^S	β	β^{Sy^*}	β^S
YR89	0.524	0.270	—	0.319	0.296	—
MALE	−0.733	−0.378	—	−0.417	−0.388	—
WHITE	−0.391	−0.202	—	−0.227	−0.210	—
AGE	−0.022	−0.011	−0.187	−0.012	−0.011	−0.191
ED	0.067	0.035	0.109	0.039	0.036	0.114
PRST	0.006	0.003	0.045	0.003	0.003	0.044

NOTE: β is an unstandardized coefficient; β^{Sy^*} is a y^*-standardized coefficient; β^S is a fully standardized coefficient.

standardized and y^*-standardized logit coefficients can be interpreted as follows:

- In 1989, support was .27 standard deviations higher than in 1977, holding all other variables constant.

- Each additional year of age decreases support by .01 standard deviations, holding all other variables constant. Alternatively, each additional 10 years of age decreases support by .11 standard deviations, holding all other variables constant.

- Each standard deviation increase in education increases support by .109 standard deviations, holding all other variables constant.

If the idea of a latent variable is inappropriate or if interest is in the specific category of the response (e.g., the probability of strongly agreeing), then methods based on probabilities of observed outcomes can be used.

5.4.2. Predicted Probabilities

The predicted probability that $y = m$ given $\mathbf{x}$ is

$$\widehat{\Pr}(y = m \mid \mathbf{x}) = F(\widehat{\tau}_m - \mathbf{x}\widehat{\boldsymbol{\beta}}) - F(\widehat{\tau}_{m-1} - \mathbf{x}\widehat{\boldsymbol{\beta}})$$

These probabilities can be used in a variety of ways to show the relationships between the independent variables and the dependent categories.

Determining the Mean and Range of Predicted Probabilities

It is useful to begin by examining the mean, minimum, and maximum predicted probabilities over the sample:

$$\text{mean } \widehat{\Pr}(y = m \mid \mathbf{x}) = \frac{1}{N} \sum_{i=1}^{N} \widehat{\Pr}(y_i = m \mid \mathbf{x}_i)$$

$$\min \widehat{\Pr}(y = m \mid \mathbf{x}) = \min_i \widehat{\Pr}(y_i = m \mid \mathbf{x}_i)$$

$$\max \widehat{\Pr}(y = m \mid \mathbf{x}) = \max_i \widehat{\Pr}(y_i = m \mid \mathbf{x}_i)$$

where $\min_i$ indicates taking the minimum predicted probability over all observations, and similarly for $\max_i$. These values are presented in Table 5.4. Consider the outcome SD. Within the sample, the minimum

TABLE 5.4 Predicted Probabilities of Outcomes Within the Sample for the Ordered Logit Model

	Probability of Outcome			
	SD	D	A	SA
Minimum	0.02	0.07	0.13	0.03
Mean	0.13	0.32	0.37	0.18
Maximum	0.47	0.43	0.44	0.61
Range	0.45	0.36	0.31	0.58

probability of strongly disagreeing is .02 and the maximum probability is .47, resulting in a range of .45. Similar results are listed for the other categories. In our example, there is sufficient variation in each category to justify further analysis. When the range is too small to be of substantive interest, further analysis is unnecessary.

Plotting Predicted Probabilities

With a single independent variable, the entire probability curve can be plotted. When there are more variables, the effect of a single variable can be examined while the remaining variables are held constant. For example, the effect of age on the probability of ordinal outcomes can be plotted by holding all other variables constant and allowing age to vary. To do this, let x_* contain a 1 in the first column for the intercept, a 1 in the second column to specify the survey year 1989, a 0 in the third column to select women, and the means for the variables except for age in the remaining columns. Then

$$\widehat{\Pr}(WARM = m \mid x_*) = F(\widehat{\tau}_m - x_*\widehat{\beta}) - F(\widehat{\tau}_{m-1} - x_*\widehat{\beta})$$

is the predicted probability of outcome m for women in 1989 for a given age who are average on all other characteristics.

These probabilities are plotted in panel A of Figure 5.3. Consider the probability of strongly agreeing, which is indicated by the line with circles. At age 20, the probability is .39. As age increases, the predicted probability decreases to .25 at age 50 and .15 at age 80. The probability of disagreeing, indicated by the triangles, is nearly the mirror image. It begins at .16 at age 20 and ends at .34 at age 80. There is a smaller change in the probability of strongly disagreeing, indicated by diamonds, that starts at .04 and ends at .12. The probability of agreeing, shown

Panel A: Predicted Probability

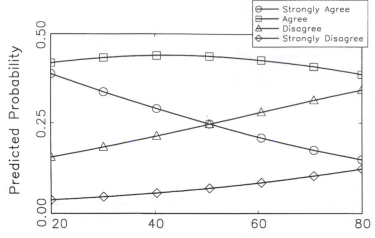

Panel B: Cumulative Probability

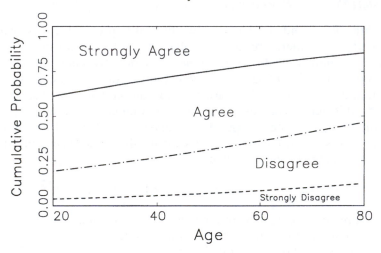

Age

Figure 5.3. Predicted and Cumulative Probabilities for Women in 1989

by squares, illustrates an unusual characteristic of the ORM (which also applies to nominal models in Chapter 6). The probability begins at .42, increases to .44, and then decreases to .38. The effect of age on agreeing is initially positive and is then negative. This occurs because as age increases from 20, more cases from category SA move into category A than move from A into D; consequently, the probability of A increases. When age is larger, more cases leave A for D than enter A from SA, resulting in a smaller probability. (*Study Figure 5.3 until you are convinced of this explanation.*)

Plotting Cumulative Probabilities

The cumulative probability is the probability that the outcome is less than or equal to some value. Formally, the cumulative probability of being less than or equal to m is

$$\Pr(y \leq m \mid \mathbf{x}) = \sum_{j=1}^{m} \Pr(y = j \mid \mathbf{x}) = F(\tau_m - \mathbf{x}\boldsymbol{\beta}) \qquad [5.10]$$

(*Prove this equality.*) In our example, the cumulative probabilities would be the probability of strongly disagreeing, $\Pr(y \leq 1 \mid \mathbf{x})$, the probability of strongly disagreeing or disagreeing, $\Pr(y \leq 2 \mid \mathbf{x})$, and so on. These probabilities can be plotted to uncover overall trends. The cumulative probabilities from our example are plotted in panel B of Figure 5.3. Notice that the cumulative probabilities "stack" the corresponding probabilities from the top panel, and show the overall increase with age in negative attitudes toward the statement that a working mother can establish just as warm and secure a relationship with her child as a mother who does not work.

Tables of Predicted Probabilities

Tables can also be used to present probabilities. Table 5.5 contains the predicted probabilities for men and women by the year of the survey, along with differences by gender in the probabilities within year and across years. The first thing to notice is that men are more likely than women to disagree and strongly disagree that a working mother can establish just as warm and secure a relationship with her child as a mother who does not work; and men are less likely to agree and strongly agree. Second, between 1977 and 1989, there was a movement for both men and women toward more positive attitudes.

5.4.3. Partial Change in Predicted Probabilities

A third method for interpreting the ORM is to compute the partial change in the probabilities. Recall that

$$\Pr(y = m \mid \mathbf{x}) = F(\tau_m - \mathbf{x}\boldsymbol{\beta}) - F(\tau_{m-1} - \mathbf{x}\boldsymbol{\beta})$$

TABLE 5.5 Predicted Probabilities by Sex and Year for the Ordered Logit Model

1977	SD	D	A	SA
Men	0.19	0.40	0.32	0.10
Women	0.10	0.31	0.41	0.18
Men-Women	0.09	0.09	−0.09	−0.08
1989	SD	D	A	SA
Men	0.12	0.34	0.39	0.15
Women	0.06	0.23	0.44	0.27
Men-Women	0.06	0.11	−0.05	−0.12
Change from 1977 to 1989	SD	D	A	SA
Men	−0.07	−0.06	0.07	0.05
Women	−0.04	−0.08	0.03	0.09

Taking the partial derivative with respect to x_k,

$$\frac{\partial \Pr(y=m \mid \mathbf{x})}{\partial x_k} = \frac{\partial F(\tau_m - \mathbf{x}\boldsymbol{\beta})}{\partial x_k} - \frac{\partial F(\tau_{m-1} - \mathbf{x}\boldsymbol{\beta})}{\partial x_k}$$

$$= \beta_k f(\tau_{m-1} - \mathbf{x}\boldsymbol{\beta}) - \beta_k f(\tau_m - \mathbf{x}\boldsymbol{\beta})$$

$$= \beta_k \left[f(\tau_{m-1} - \mathbf{x}\boldsymbol{\beta}) - f(\tau_m - \mathbf{x}\boldsymbol{\beta}) \right]$$

The partial change or marginal effect is the slope of the curve relating x_k to $\Pr(y = m \mid \mathbf{x})$, holding all other variables constant. The sign of the marginal effect is not necessarily the same as the sign of β, since $f(\tau_{m-1} - \mathbf{x}\boldsymbol{\beta}) - f(\tau_m - \mathbf{x}\boldsymbol{\beta})$ can be negative. Indeed, it is possible for the marginal effect of x_k to change signs as x_k changes. This is seen in panel A of Figure 5.3 for the probability of agreeing (shown with small squares). Initially, the slope of the probability curve is positive, indicating a positive marginal effect of age. Around age 40, the marginal turns negative, showing that increasing age decreases the probability of agreeing.

Since the marginal effect depends on the levels of all variables, we must decide on which values of the variables to use when computing the effect. One method is to compute the average over all observations:

$$\text{mean} \frac{\partial \Pr(y=m \mid \mathbf{x})}{\partial x_k} = \frac{1}{N} \sum_{i=1}^{N} \beta_k \left[f(\tau_{m-1} - \mathbf{x}\boldsymbol{\beta}) -, f(\tau_m - \mathbf{x}\boldsymbol{\beta}) \right]$$

TABLE 5.6 Marginal Effects on Probabilities for Women in 1989, Computed at the Means of Other Variables, for the Ordered Logit Model

Variable	SD	D	A	SA
AGE	0.00124	0.00321	−0.00018	−0.00427
ED	−0.00385	−0.00996	0.00056	0.01325
PRST	−0.00035	−0.00090	0.00005	0.00120

More commonly, the marginal effect is computed at the mean values of all variables:

$$\frac{\partial \Pr(y = m \mid \bar{\mathbf{x}})}{\partial x_k} = \beta_k \left[f(\tau_{m-1} - \bar{\mathbf{x}}\boldsymbol{\beta}) - f(\tau_m - \bar{\mathbf{x}}\boldsymbol{\beta}) \right]$$

Or, the marginal can be evaluated at other values. For example, Table 5.6 contains the partial changes in probabilities for women in 1989. These are computed by fixing *MALE* at 0 and *YR89* at 1 with the other variables at their means.

In general, the marginal effect does *not* indicate the change in the probability that would be observed for a unit change in x_k. However, if an independent variable varies over a region of the probability curve that is nearly linear, the marginal effect can be used to summarize the effect of a unit change in the variable on the probability of an outcome. For example, given the nearly linear relationship between age and the probability of disagreeing shown in panel A of Figure 5.3, we conclude:

- For women in 1989, each additional 10 years of age increases the probability of disagreeing that a working mother can establish just as warm and secure a relationship with her child as a mother who does not work by .032.

The value .032 is 10 times (for the effect of 10 years) the marginal effect of age for outcome D. Beware that this interpretation of the marginal effect is only possible when the probability curve is nearly linear.

5.4.4. Discrete Change

Interpretation using marginal effects can be misleading when the probability curve is changing rapidly or when an independent variable is a dummy variable. For the ORM, I find that measures of discrete change are much more informative.

Discrete change is the change in the predicted probability for a change in x_k from the start value x_S to the end value x_E (e.g., a change from 0 to 1):

$$\frac{\Delta \Pr(y = m \mid \mathbf{x})}{\Delta x_k} = \Pr(y = m \mid \mathbf{x}, x_k = x_E) - \Pr(y = m \mid \mathbf{x}, x_k = x_S)$$

where the notation $\Pr(y = m \mid \mathbf{x}, x_k)$ indicates the probability that $y = m$ given $\mathbf{x}$, noting a specific value for x_k. The change is interpreted as:

- When x_k changes from x_S to x_E, the predicted probability of outcome m changes by $\Delta \Pr(y = m \mid \mathbf{x})/\Delta x_k$, holding all other variables at $\mathbf{x}$.

Since the model is nonlinear, the value of the discrete change depends on three factors: (1) the level of all of the variables that are not changing; (2) the value at which x_k starts; and (3) the amount of change in x_k. Most frequently, each continuous variable except x_k is held at its mean. For dummy independent variables, the change might be computed for both values of the variable. For example, we could compute the discrete change for age for men and women separately.

The start value of x_k and the amount of change depend on the purpose of the analysis. Useful choices include:

1. The total possible effect of x_k is found by letting x_k change from its minimum to its maximum.
2. The effect of a binary variable is obtained by letting x_k change from 0 to 1.
3. The effect of a unit change in x_k is computed by changing from $\bar{x}_k$ to $\bar{x}_k + 1$, while the centered discrete change can be computed by changing from $(\bar{x}_k - 1/2)$ to $(\bar{x}_k + 1/2)$.
4. The effect of a standard deviation change in x_k is computed by changing from $\bar{x}_k$ to $\bar{x}_k + s_k$, while the centered change is computed by changing from $(\bar{x}_k - s_k/2)$ to $(\bar{x}_k + s_k/2)$.

Table 5.7 contains measures of discrete change for our example using the ordered logit model. For binary variables, I present the change in the predicted probability when the variable changes from 0 to 1. For example,

- The probability of strongly disagreeing is .08 higher for men than women, holding all other variables at their means.

For variables that are not binary, you should examine the change in the predicted probability for a unit change centered around the mean, the change for a standard deviation change centered around the mean, and

TABLE 5.7 Discrete Change in the Probability of Attitudes About Working Mothers for the Ordered Logit Model

Variable	Change	$\overline{\Delta}$	SD	D	A	SA
Overall	Probability	—	0.11	0.33	0.40	0.16
YR89	$0 \to 1$	0.06	−0.05	−0.08	0.05	0.07
MALE	$0 \to 1$	0.09	0.07	0.10	−0.08	−0.10
WHITE	$0 \to 1$	0.05	0.03	0.06	−0.04	−0.06
AGE	$\Delta 1$	0.00	0.00	0.00	−0.00	−0.00
	$\Delta\sigma$	0.04	0.04	0.05	−0.04	−0.05
	ΔRange	0.18	0.18	0.19	−0.18	−0.19
ED	$\Delta 1$	0.01	−0.01	−0.01	0.01	0.01
	$\Delta\sigma$	0.03	−0.02	−0.03	0.02	0.03
	ΔRange	0.16	−0.15	−0.17	0.16	0.17
PRST	$\Delta 1$	0.00	−0.00	−0.00	0.00	0.00
	$\Delta\sigma$	0.01	−0.01	−0.01	0.01	0.01
	ΔRange	0.05	−0.04	−0.06	0.04	0.06

NOTE: $0 \to 1$ is change from 0 to 1; $\Delta 1$ is centered change of 1 around the mean; $\Delta\sigma$ is centered change of 1 standard deviation around the mean; ΔRange is change from the minimum to the maximum. $\overline{\Delta}$ is the average absolute discrete change.

the change when the variable goes from its minimum to its maximum value. For example,

- For each additional year of education, the probability of strongly agreeing increases by .01, holding all other variables constant at their means.

- For a standard deviation increase in age, the probability of disagreeing increases by .05, holding all other variables constant at their means.

- Moving from the minimum prestige to the maximum prestige changes the predicted probability of strongly agreeing by .06, holding all other variables constant at their means.

The effects of a variable can be summarized by computing the average of the absolute values of the changes across all of the outcome categories. The absolute value is taken since the sum of the changes without taking the absolute value is necessarily 0. The *average absolute discrete change* equals

$$\overline{\Delta} = \frac{1}{J} \sum_{j=1}^{J} \left| \frac{\Delta \Pr(y = j \mid \overline{\mathbf{x}})}{\Delta x_k} \right|$$

These values are listed in the column labeled $\overline{\Delta}$ in the table. Clearly, the respondent's sex, education, and age have the strongest effects on attitudes toward whether a working mother can have as warm a relationship with her child as a mother who does not work.

The idea of discrete change can be extended in many ways depending on the application. If the independent variables are highly skewed, assessing change relative to the mean can be misleading and changes relative to the median might be more useful. If a change of a specific amount is substantively important, such as the addition of four years of schooling, a change in an amount other than 1 or a standard deviation can be used. When several independent variables are binary, you may want to compute discrete changes for each of the groups defined by the binary variables.

5.4.5. Modeling Odds in the Ordered Logit Model

Within the biometrics literature, where the model is referred to as the *proportional odds model* (Agresti, 1990, p. 322; McCullagh & Nelder, 1989, pp. 151–155), the ordered logit model is often interpreted in terms of odds ratios for cumulative probabilities. The *cumulative probability* that the outcome is less than or equal to m equals

$$\Pr(y \leq m \,|\, \mathbf{x}) = \sum_{j=1}^{m} \Pr(y = j \,|\, \mathbf{x}) \quad \text{for } m = 1, J - 1$$

The odds that an outcome is m or less versus greater than m given $\mathbf{x}$ are

$$\Omega_m(\mathbf{x}) = \frac{\Pr(y \leq m \,|\, \mathbf{x})}{1 - \Pr(y \leq m \,|\, \mathbf{x})} = \frac{\Pr(y \leq m \,|\, \mathbf{x})}{\Pr(y > m \,|\, \mathbf{x})}$$

For example, we could compute the odds of disagreeing or strongly disagreeing (i.e., $m \leq 2$) versus agreeing or strongly agreeing.

For the ordered logit model, the odds of an outcome being less than or equal to m versus being greater than m have the simple equation (*Derive this result using Equations 5.2 and 5.10.*):

$$\Omega_m(\mathbf{x}) = \frac{\Pr(y \leq m \,|\, \mathbf{x})}{\Pr(y > m \,|\, \mathbf{x})} = \exp(\tau_m - \mathbf{x}\boldsymbol{\beta})$$

Taking the log results in the logit equation:

$$\ln \Omega_m(\mathbf{x}) = \tau_m - \mathbf{x}\boldsymbol{\beta}$$

Discussions of the ordered logit model that do not use a latent variable to generate the model often begin with this equation. In such cases, the model is referred to as the *cumulative logit model*.

To determine the effect of a change in $\mathbf{x}$, consider two values of $\mathbf{x}$: $\mathbf{x} = \mathbf{x}_i$ and $\mathbf{x} = \mathbf{x}_\ell$. The odds ratio at $\mathbf{x}_i$ versus $\mathbf{x}_\ell$ equals

$$\frac{\Omega_m(\mathbf{x}_i)}{\Omega_m(\mathbf{x}_\ell)} = \frac{\exp(\tau_m - \mathbf{x}_i\boldsymbol{\beta})}{\exp(\tau_m - \mathbf{x}_\ell\boldsymbol{\beta})} = \exp([\,\mathbf{x}_\ell - \mathbf{x}_i\,]\boldsymbol{\beta})$$

This equation is most useful when only a single variable changes. For example, if x_k changes by δ, then

$$\frac{\Omega_m(\mathbf{x}, x_k + \delta)}{\Omega_m(\mathbf{x}, x_k)} = \exp(-\delta \times \beta_k) = \frac{1}{\exp(\delta \times \beta_k)}$$

which is interpreted as:

- For an increase of δ in x_k, the odds of an outcome being less than or equal to m are changed by the factor $\exp(-\delta \times \beta_k)$, holding all other variables constant.

If x_k changes by 1, the odds ratio equals

$$\frac{\Omega_m(\mathbf{x}, x_k + 1)}{\Omega_m(\mathbf{x}, x_k)} = \exp(-\beta_k) \qquad\qquad [5.11]$$

Notice that the factor change equals $\exp(-\beta_k)$, compared to $\exp(\beta_k)$ in Chapter 3 for the binary logit model. This is because the ordered logit model is parameterized as $\ln \Omega_m(\mathbf{x}) = \tau_m - \mathbf{x}\boldsymbol{\beta}$, compared to $\ln \Omega(\mathbf{x}) = \mathbf{x}\boldsymbol{\beta}$ for the binary model.

To illustrate the interpretation using odds ratios, consider the coefficient for gender from Table 5.3: $\beta_2 = -.73$, so that $\exp(-\beta_2) = 2.1$. This can be interpreted as:

- The odds of SD versus the combined outcomes D, A, and SA are 2.1 times greater for men than women, holding all other variables constant. Similarly, the odds of SD and D versus A and SA are 2.1 times greater for men than women; and the odds of SD, D, and A versus SA are 2.1 times greater.

The coefficient for age is $\beta_4 = -.02$ with a standard deviation $s_4 = 16.8$. Thus, $100[\,\exp(-s_4 \times \beta_4) - 1] = 44$, which can be interpreted as:

- For a standard deviation increase in age, the odds of SD versus D, A, and SA are increased by 44%, holding all other variables constant. Similarly, the odds of SD and D versus A and SA are 44% greater for every standard deviation increase in age; and the odds of SD, D, and A versus SA are 44% greater.

These examples show that Equation 5.11 implies that the odds ratio $\Omega_m(\mathbf{x}, x_k + 1)/\Omega_m(\mathbf{x}, x_k)$ is the same for *all* values of m. This is known as the *proportional odds assumption*. In terms of our example, we must ask whether it makes sense that a change in age has the same effect on the odds of answering SD versus other categories, as for answering SD, D or A versus SA. This leads us to a test of the proportional odds assumption, which is also known as the *parallel regression assumption* for reasons that are now considered.

5.5. The Parallel Regression Assumption

The assumption of proportional odds in the ordered logit model corresponds more generally to the idea of *parallel regressions* in both the ordered logit and probit models. The idea of parallel regressions can be seen by rewriting the model in terms of the cumulative probability that an outcome is less than or equal to m. From Equation 5.10,

$$\Pr(y \leq m \mid \mathbf{x}) = F(\tau_m - \mathbf{x}\boldsymbol{\beta}) \qquad [5.12]$$

The cumulative probability is the cumulative distribution function F evaluated at $\tau_m - \mathbf{x}\boldsymbol{\beta}$. Since $\boldsymbol{\beta}$ is the same for all m's, Equation 5.12 defines a set of binary response models with different intercepts. To see this, note that

$$\tau_m - \mathbf{x}\boldsymbol{\beta} = (\tau_m - \beta_0) - \sum_{k=1}^{K} \beta_k x_k$$

Thus, the model for $y \leq 1$ is

$$\Pr(y \leq 1 \mid \mathbf{x}) = F\left((\tau_1 - \beta_0) - \sum_{k=1}^{K} \beta_k x_k \right)$$

with the intercept $\tau_1 - \beta_0$. The model for $y \leq 2$ is

$$\Pr(y \leq 2 \mid \mathbf{x}) = F\left((\tau_2 - \beta_0) - \sum_{k=1}^{K} \beta_k x_k \right)$$

In this model, the intercept has changed to $\tau_2 - \beta_0$, but the coefficients for the variables x_k are unchanged.

As shown in Chapter 3 (p. 63), changing the intercept shifts the probability curve to the right or to the left, but does not change the slope.

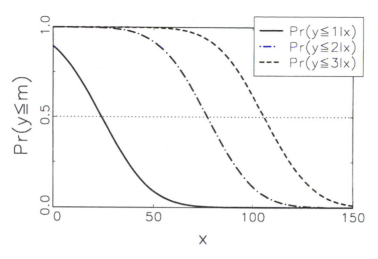

Figure 5.4. Illustration of the Parallel Regression Assumption

For example, Figure 5.4 plots the cumulative probability curves when there are four ordered categories, resulting in three curves with intercepts $\tau_1 - \beta_0$, $\tau_2 - \beta_0$, and $\tau_3 - \beta_0$. To see why these curves are parallel, pick a value of the outcome probability. For example, the probability .5 is indicated by a dotted, horizontal line. When we examine the slope of the three probability curves at this point, we find that

$$\frac{\partial \Pr(y \leq 1 \mid x)}{\partial x} = \frac{\partial \Pr(y \leq 2 \mid x)}{\partial x} = \frac{\partial \Pr(y \leq 3 \mid x)}{\partial x}$$

It is in this sense that the regression curves are parallel.

An Informal Test. We can informally assess the assumption of parallel regressions by estimating $J - 1$ binary regressions:

$$\Pr(y \leq m \mid \mathbf{x}) = F(\tau_m - \mathbf{x}\boldsymbol{\beta}_m)$$

The first binary regression is for the binary outcome defined as 1 if $y \leq 1$, else 0. The second regression is for the outcome equal to 1 if $y \leq 2$, else 0. And so on up to the outcome equal to 1 if $y \leq J - 1$. This results in $J - 1$ estimates $\widehat{\boldsymbol{\beta}}_m$. If the assumption of parallel regressions is true, then

$$\boldsymbol{\beta}_1 = \boldsymbol{\beta}_2 = \cdots = \boldsymbol{\beta}_{J-1} = \boldsymbol{\beta}$$

TABLE 5.8 Ordered Logit and Cumulative Logit Regressions

Variable		Ordered Logit	Cumulative Logits		
			$m \leq 1$	$m \leq 2$	$m \leq 3$
YR89	β	0.524	0.965	0.565	0.319
	z	6.33	6.26	6.09	2.80
MALE	β	−0.733	−0.305	−0.691	−1.084
	z	−9.23	−2.36	−7.68	−8.88
WHITE	β	−0.391	−0.553	−0.314	−0.393
	z	−3.27	−2.40	−2.24	−2.49
AGE	β	−0.022	−0.016	−0.025	−0.019
	z	−8.52	−4.06	−8.84	−4.94
ED	β	0.067	0.105	0.053	0.058
	z	4.20	4.14	2.86	2.27
PRST	β	0.006	−0.001	0.010	0.006
	z	1.84	−0.25	2.50	1.14

NOTE: β is an unstandardized coefficient; z is a z-test of β.

and each $\widehat{\boldsymbol{\beta}}_m$ is a consistent estimate of the $\boldsymbol{\beta}$ in Equation 5.12 (Clogg & Shihadeh, 1994, pp. 159–160). Examining the similarities and differences among the $\widehat{\boldsymbol{\beta}}_m$'s from the binary logits (or probits) and $\widehat{\boldsymbol{\beta}}$ from the ordered logit (or probit) provides an informal assessment of the parallel regression assumption.

For our example, the estimates from the ordered logit are given in the first column of Table 5.8. The estimates from three binary logits are given in the last three columns. While some of the estimates are similar across equations (e.g., WHITE), others are quite different (e.g., MALE). There are two formal tests of the parallel regression assumption that can be used to confirm these informal results.

A Score Test. A score test (or LM test) of the parallel regression assumption is included in SAS's LOGISTIC (SAS Institute, 1990b, p. 1090). Recall from Chapter 4 (p. 88) that a score test estimates a constrained model and assesses how the likelihood function would change if the constraints were relaxed. To understand how a score test can be used to assess the parallel regression assumption, think of the ORM as a set of $J - 1$ binary logits:

$$\Pr(y \leq m \mid \mathbf{x}) = F(\tau_m - \mathbf{x}\boldsymbol{\beta}_m)$$

where we impose the constraint that the β_m's are equal across the $J - 1$ regressions:

$$\beta_1 = \beta_2 = \cdots = \beta_{J-1} = \beta \qquad [5.13]$$

Thus, we are estimating the model:

$$\Pr(y \leq m \mid \mathbf{x}) = F(\tau_m - \mathbf{x}\beta) \qquad [5.14]$$

The score test evaluates how the log likelihood of the ORM would change if the constraint in Equation 5.13 was removed. The resulting test statistic is distributed as chi-square with $K(J - 2)$ degrees of freedom. (*Show that this is the correct number of degrees of freedom by counting the number of constraints being tested.*) For our example, the score test equals 48.4 with 12 degrees of freedom ($p \leq .001$). This provides strong evidence that the parallel regression assumption is violated.

A Wald Test. The score test is an omnibus test that does not show whether the parallel regression assumption is violated for all independent variables or only for some. A Wald test proposed by Brant (1990) allows both an overall test that all β_m's are equal and tests of the equality of coefficients for individual variables. While this test is not implemented by commercial programs, it is straightforward, albeit tedious, to compute with programs that include a matrix language (e.g., SAS, LIMDEP, GAUSS). The test is constructed as follows.

1. *Estimate β_m's and* $\mathrm{Var}(\widehat{\beta}_m)$*'s.* Run $J - 1$ binary logits on the outcomes defined by

$$z_m = \begin{cases} 1 & y > m \\ 0 & y \leq m \end{cases}$$

with estimated slopes $\widehat{\beta}_m$ and covariance matrices $\widehat{\mathrm{Var}}(\widehat{\beta}_m)$. Then the estimated probability that $z_{im} = 1$ given $\mathbf{x}_i$ is

$$\widehat{\pi}_m(\mathbf{x}_i) = F(\widehat{\tau}_m + \mathbf{x}_i\widehat{\beta}_m)$$

2. *Estimate the covariance between* $\widehat{\underline{\beta}}_m$ *and* $\widehat{\underline{\beta}}_\ell$ where the underline indicates that the constant has been removed from the vector. Define

$$w_{im\ell} = \widehat{\pi}_\ell(\mathbf{x}_i) - \widehat{\pi}_m(\mathbf{x}_i)\widehat{\pi}_\ell(\mathbf{x}_i)$$

and let $\mathbf{W}_{m\ell}$ be a $N \times N$ diagonal matrix whose ith element is $w_{im\ell}$. Let $\mathbf{X}$ be the $N \times (K + 1)$ matrix with 1's in the first column and the independent variables in the remaining columns. Brant shows that the covariances among the $\widehat{\beta}$'s from different binary equations, $\widehat{\mathrm{Var}}(\widehat{\underline{\beta}}_m, \widehat{\underline{\beta}}_\ell)$, are estimated by deleting the first row and column of

$$(\mathbf{X}'\mathbf{W}_{mm}\mathbf{X})^{-1}(\mathbf{X}'\mathbf{W}_{m\ell}\mathbf{X})(\mathbf{X}'\mathbf{W}_{\ell\ell}\mathbf{X})^{-1}$$

3. *Combine all estimates.* Define $\widehat{\boldsymbol{\beta}}^* = (\underline{\widehat{\boldsymbol{\beta}}}_1' \underline{\widehat{\boldsymbol{\beta}}}_2' \cdots \underline{\widehat{\boldsymbol{\beta}}}_{J-1}')'$ and

$$
\widehat{\text{Var}}(\widehat{\boldsymbol{\beta}}^*) = \begin{pmatrix} \widehat{\text{Var}}(\underline{\widehat{\boldsymbol{\beta}}}_1) & \cdots & \widehat{\text{Var}}(\underline{\widehat{\boldsymbol{\beta}}}_1, \underline{\widehat{\boldsymbol{\beta}}}_{J-1}) \\ \vdots & \ddots & \vdots \\ \widehat{\text{Var}}(\underline{\widehat{\boldsymbol{\beta}}}_{J-1}, \underline{\widehat{\boldsymbol{\beta}}}_1) & \cdots & \widehat{\text{Var}}(\underline{\widehat{\boldsymbol{\beta}}}_{J-1}) \end{pmatrix}
$$

The diagonal elements $\widehat{Var}(\underline{\widehat{\boldsymbol{\beta}}}_m)$ are the covariance matrices from each binary regression. The off-diagonal elements were defined in step 2.

4. *Construct the Wald test of* H_0: $\underline{\boldsymbol{\beta}}_1 = \cdots = \underline{\boldsymbol{\beta}}_{J-1}$. This hypothesis corresponds to H_0: $\mathbf{D}\boldsymbol{\beta}^* = \mathbf{0}$, where

$$
\mathbf{D} = \begin{pmatrix} \mathbf{I} & -\mathbf{I} & \mathbf{0} & \cdots & \mathbf{0} \\ \mathbf{I} & \mathbf{0} & -\mathbf{I} & \cdots & \mathbf{0} \\ \vdots & \vdots & \vdots & \ddots & \vdots \\ \mathbf{I} & \mathbf{0} & \mathbf{0} & \cdots & -\mathbf{I} \end{pmatrix}
$$

$\mathbf{I}$ is a $(K+1) \times (K+1)$ identity matrix and $\mathbf{0}$ is a $(K+1) \times (K+1)$ matrix of 0's. (*Verify that this matrix results in the appropriate linear combination for the hypothesis being tested.*) The Wald statistic takes the standard form discussed in Chapter 4:

$$
W = (\mathbf{D}\widehat{\boldsymbol{\beta}}^*)'[\mathbf{D}\widehat{\text{Var}}(\widehat{\boldsymbol{\beta}}^*)\mathbf{D}']^{-1}(\mathbf{D}\widehat{\boldsymbol{\beta}}^*)
$$

with $(J-2)K$ degrees of freedom.

5. *Construct tests for individual variables.* The hypothesis H_0: $\beta_{k1} = \cdots = \beta_{k,J-1}$ can be tested by selecting only those rows and columns of $\mathbf{D}$, $\widehat{\boldsymbol{\beta}}^*$, and $\widehat{\text{Var}}(\widehat{\boldsymbol{\beta}}^*)$ that correspond to the coefficients being tested. The resulting test statistic has $J-2$ degrees of freedom.

For our example, the results of the Wald tests are contained in Table 5.9. The omnibus Wald test is quite close to the result from the

TABLE 5.9 Wald Tests of the Parallel Regression
Assumption

Test for	X^2	df	Probability
Omnibus	49.18	12	< 0.01
YR	13.01	2	< 0.01
MALE	22.24	2	< 0.01
WHITE	1.27	2	0.53
AGE	7.38	2	0.03
ED	4.31	2	0.12
PRST	4.33	2	0.12

score test ($S = 48.4$). The tests of the equality of coefficients for each variable examined individually show, as suggested by Table 5.8, that there is strong evidence for the violation of the assumption for some variables but not for others.

My experience suggests that the parallel regression assumption is frequently violated based on either an informal test, the score test, or the Wald test. When the assumption of parallel regressions is rejected, alternative models should be considered that do not impose the constraint of parallel regressions. These models are considered in the next chapter.

5.6. Related Models for Ordinal Data

While ordered logit and ordered probit are the most frequently used models for ordinal outcomes in the social sciences (with perhaps the exception of the misuse of the LRM), there are a number of other models that are also available.

5.6.1. The Grouped Regression Model

In the ORM, the observed variable is defined by

$$y = m \quad \text{if } \tau_{m-1} \leq y^* < \tau_m \text{ for } m = 1 \text{ to } J$$

where the cutpoints are *unknown*. A similar type of variable occurs when a continuous variable is grouped at *known* values of τ. For example, income might be measured as

$$y = \begin{cases} 1 & \text{if } y^* < \$10,000 \\ 2 & \text{if } \$10,000 \leq y^* < \$20,000 \\ \vdots & \vdots \\ J & \text{if } y^* \geq \$100,000 \end{cases}$$

Such variables are often analyzed by recoding their values to the midpoint of each interval, with some reasonable value used for the highest and lowest categories. The problem is that there is only weak justification for the recoded values. Alternatively, such variables are sometimes treated as though they are ordinal and the ORM is used (e.g., Anderson, 1984). However, since the cutpoints are known, they do not need to be estimated. Further, with known cutpoints it is possible to estimate Var(ε), which must be assumed in the ORM. Stewart (1983) suggested this model as an extension of the tobit model (see Chapter 7) and developed both two-stage and ML estimators. The ML estimator is available in LIMDEP (Greene, 1995, p. 629), Stata (1997) and SAS's LIFEREG using interval censoring.

5.6.2. Other Models for Ordinal Data

The *adjacent categories model* specifies

$$\ln\left[\frac{\Pr(y = m \mid \mathbf{x})}{\Pr(y = m + 1 \mid \mathbf{x})}\right] = \tau_m - \mathbf{x}\boldsymbol{\beta}$$

where the outcome is the log of the odds of category m versus category $m + 1$. Unlike the ORM, this model is a special case of the multinomial logit model considered in the next chapter. The *continuation ratio model* was proposed by Fienberg (1980, p. 110):

$$\ln\left[\frac{\Pr(y = m \mid \mathbf{x})}{\Pr(y > m \mid \mathbf{x})}\right] = \tau_m - \mathbf{x}\boldsymbol{\beta}$$

The outcome is the log of the odds of category m versus categories greater than m. In this model, estimates will differ if adjacent categories are combined. Anderson (1984) proposed the *stereotype model*:

$$\ln\left[\frac{\Pr(y = j \mid \mathbf{x})}{\Pr(y = m \mid \mathbf{x})}\right] = \tau_j - \mathbf{x}\boldsymbol{\beta}_j$$

where constraints are imposed on the τ's to ensure ordinality and the $\boldsymbol{\beta}$'s differ by outcome category, thus avoiding the parallel regression assumption. This model is closely related to the multinomial logit model and is discussed in the next chapter.

Fienberg (1980, Chapter 6), Agresti (1990, pp. 318–336), and Clogg and Shihadeh (1994, Chapter 7) review these models with an emphasis on their relationship to log-linear models. Greenwood and Farewell (1988) compare several of these models in an analysis of medical data.

5.7. Conclusions

The linear regression model used with ordinal dependent variables can provide incorrect results. The ordered regression model is an alternative that is designed explicitly for ordinal outcomes. While it is straightforward to estimate these models, the nonlinear relationship between the independent variables and the predicted probabilities makes interpretation difficult. Further, care must be taken to ensure that the dependent variable is unidimensional and ordinal, and that the assumption of parallel regressions holds. In practice, it is often useful to analyze ordinal outcomes both with models for ordinal data and with models for nominal data, such as considered in Chapter 6.

5.8. Bibliographic Notes

The ordered probit model grew out of Aitchison and Silvey's (1957) work in bioassay where the latent continuous variable was an organism's tolerance to some exposure, such as a poison. The tolerance could not be observed, but the general state of the organism as unaffected, slightly affected, moribund, or dead could be assessed. Their model was limited to a single independent variable. The origins of the ordered logit model can be found in Snell (1964). McKelvey and Zavoina (1975), in a paper written for social scientists, extended the work of Aitchison and Silvey to the case where there are multiple independent variables and presented a computationally efficient method of estimation. Independently, the ordered logit and probit models were developed by McCullagh (1980), whose analyses were limited to a single independent variable. His focus was on the ordered logit model, which he referred to as the proportional odds model. McCullagh's work stimulated a great deal of research in biostatistics, all of which seems to be unaware of the earlier work by McKelvey and Zavoina.

Several authors provide a review of models for ordinal variables. Agresti (1990, pp. 318–336) and Clogg and Shihadeh (1994, Chapter 7) discuss models for ordinal variables with particular attention to their relationship to log-linear models. McCullagh and Nelder (1989, Chapter 5) discuss several of these models in the context of the generalized linear model. Winship and Mare (1984) reviewed models for ordinal variables with applications in sociology.

6 Nominal Outcomes: Multinomial Logit and Related Models

When a variable is nominal, the categories cannot be ordered. Nominal outcomes are found in every area of the social sciences. Schmidt and Strauss (1975) examined occupational attainment in an early application of the multinomial logit model. Meng and Miller (1995) examined sex differences in occupations in China. Arum and Shavit (1995) studied the effects of high school vocational education on occupational attainment. Examples are also found in other areas. Hoffman and Duncan (1988) compared the conditional logit and the multinomial logit models in a study of marital and welfare status. Spector and Mazzeo (1980) examined the effects of an experimental teaching program on class performance as indicated by grade. Other examples include: reasons for leaving the parents' home (Goldscheider & DaVanzo, 1989), the organizational context of scientific work (Long & McGinnis, 1981), and the choice of language in a multilingual society (Stevens, 1992).

Models for nominal outcomes are often used when the dependent variable is ordinal. Sometimes this is done to avoid the parallel regression assumption of the ordered regression model. Other times there may be uncertainty as to whether the dependent variable should be considered as ordinal. Or, a researcher may simply be more familiar with the multinomial logit model. If a dependent variable is ordinal and a model for nominal variables is used, there is a loss of efficiency since information is being ignored. On the other hand, when a method for ordinal variables is applied to a nominal dependent variable, the resulting estimates are biased or even nonsensical. If there is any question about the ordinality of the dependent variable, the potential loss of efficiency in using models for nominal outcomes is outweighed by avoiding potential bias.

This chapter focuses on two closely related models. The *multinomial logit model* is the most frequently used model for nominal outcomes. The effects of the independent variables are allowed to differ for each outcome. With the *conditional logit model*, characteristics of the outcomes are used to predict the choice that is made. While probit versions of these models are theoretically possible, computational difficulties make such models impractical.

6.1. Introduction to the Multinomial Logit Model

The multinomial logit model (MNLM) can be thought of as simultaneously estimating binary logits for all possible comparisons among the outcome categories. Indeed, estimates from binary logits provide consistent estimates of the parameters of the MNLM (Begg & Gray, 1984). In this sense, multinomial logit is a simple extension of the binary logit model. However, the extension is made difficult by the large number of comparisons that are involved. With three outcomes, multinomial logit is roughly equivalent to running three binary logits comparing outcomes 1 to 2, 1 to 3, and 2 to 3. With four outcomes, you must add three more comparisons: 1 to 4, 2 to 4, and 3 to 4. Just the notation to keep track of the comparisons can be off-putting, and the sheer number of comparisons can be overwhelming. To explain the model as clearly as possible, I begin with a simple example using three outcomes and a single independent variable. The model is presented as a set of three binary logits. Accordingly, you might want to review Section 3.4 of Chapter 3 before proceeding.

Consider a nominal outcome y with categories A, B, and C, with N_A, N_B, and N_C observations in each category. Assume that there is a single independent variable x. We could analyze the relationship between x and y by running a series of binary logits. To examine the effect of x on the odds of A versus B, we select the $N_A + N_B$ observations with outcomes A or B and estimate the binary logit:

$$\ln\left[\frac{\Pr(A\,|\,\mathbf{x})}{\Pr(B\,|\,\mathbf{x})}\right] = \beta_{0,A\,|\,B} + \beta_{1,\,A\,|\,B}x \qquad [6.1]$$

The dependent variable is the log of the odds of A versus B. The β coefficients have the added subscript $A\,|\,B$ to indicate that they are from the logit for A versus B. The coefficient $\beta_{1,A\,|\,B}$ can be interpreted using the methods introduced in Chapter 3: for a unit increase in x, the odds of A versus B change by a factor of $\exp(\beta_{1,A\,|\,B})$.

The remaining comparisons can be analyzed in the same way. For outcome B versus C, select $N_B + N_C$ observations and estimate the binary logit:

$$\ln\left[\frac{\Pr(B\,|\,\mathbf{x})}{\Pr(C\,|\,\mathbf{x})}\right] = \beta_{0,B\,|\,C} + \beta_{1,B\,|\,C}x \qquad [6.2]$$

Then select the $N_A + N_C$ observations for the logit:

$$\ln\left[\frac{\Pr(A\,|\,\mathbf{x})}{\Pr(C\,|\,\mathbf{x})}\right] = \beta_{0,A\,|\,C} + \beta_{1,A\,|\,C}x \qquad [6.3]$$

Are all three binary logits necessary? If we know how x affects the odds of A versus B, and how x affects the odds of B versus C, it seems reasonable that this information would tell us something about how x affects the odds of A versus C. Indeed, there is a necessary relationship among the three logits:

$$\ln\left[\frac{\Pr(A\,|\,\mathbf{x})}{\Pr(B\,|\,\mathbf{x})}\right] + \ln\left[\frac{\Pr(B\,|\,\mathbf{x})}{\Pr(C\,|\,\mathbf{x})}\right] = \ln\left[\frac{\Pr(A\,|\,\mathbf{x})}{\Pr(C\,|\,\mathbf{x})}\right] \qquad [6.4]$$

This equality can be proven quite simply by using the identity: $\ln(a/b) = \ln a - \ln b$. (Derive Equation 6.4.)

Since the left-hand side of Equation 6.1 plus the left-hand side of Equation 6.2 equals the left-hand side of Equation 6.3, the equality must also hold for the right-hand sides of the equations:

$$(\beta_{0,A\,|\,B} + \beta_{1,A\,|\,B}x) + (\beta_{0,B\,|\,C} + \beta_{1,B\,|\,C}x) = (\beta_{0,A\,|\,C} + \beta_{1,A\,|\,C}x)$$

Or, looking at the intercepts and slopes separately,

$$\beta_{0,A\,|\,B} + \beta_{0,B\,|\,C} = \beta_{0,A\,|\,C} \qquad [6.5]$$

$$\beta_{1,A\,|\,B} + \beta_{1,B\,|\,C} = \beta_{1,A\,|\,C}$$

Therefore, some of the comparisons are redundant: if you know the results for the binary logit of A versus B, and the results from the binary logit of B versus C, you can derive the results for the logit of A versus C.

There is, however, one complication. The equalities in Equation 6.5 describe necessary relationships among the parameters in the population. They will *not* hold with sample estimates from the three binary logits. (*Try this using your own data.*) The reason is simple: the three logits are based on different samples. The first sample has $N_A + N_B$ observations, the second has $N_B + N_C$ observations, and the third has $N_A + N_C$ observations. In the multinomial logit model, all of the logits are estimated simultaneously, which enforces the logical relationship among the parameters and uses the data more efficiently. Nonetheless, thinking of the multinomial logit model as a linked set of binary logits is essentially correct.

6.2. The Multinomial Logit Model

The formal presentation of the MNLM begins by specifying the probability of each outcome as a nonlinear function of the x's. After issues of identification are resolved, I show that the nonlinear probability model leads to a model that is linear in the log of the odds; this is the form of the model that we have just considered. Two methods of interpretation are recommended: discrete change in the probabilities and factor change in the odds. While these methods are basically the same as those used for the binary logit model, the number of probabilities and odds involved requires graphical methods to summarize the results. To make the discussion concrete, I use the example of occupational attainment.

Example of the MNLM: Occupational Attainment

The 1982 General Social Survey asked respondents to indicate their occupation. These occupations were recoded to correspond to the broad categories of occupations that were used by Schmidt and Strauss (1975) in an early application of the MNLM. In a sample of 337 currently employed men, respondents were distributed among the following groups of occupations: menial jobs (9%), blue-collar jobs (21%), craft jobs (25%), white-collar jobs (12%), and professional jobs (33%). Three independent variables are expected to affect an individual's probability of being in a given occupation: race, which is measured as a dummy variable equal to 1 if the respondent is white, else 0; years of education; and an estimate

TABLE 6.1 Descriptive Statistics for the Occupational Attainment Example

Name	Mean	Standard Deviation	Minimum	Maximum	Description
OCC	—	—	—	—	Occupation: M = menial; B = blue collar; C = craft; W = white collar; P = professional
WHITE	0.92	0.28	0.0	1.0	Race: 1 = white; 0 = nonwhites
ED	13.09	2.95	3.0	20.0	Education: number of years of formal education
EXP	20.50	13.96	2.0	66.0	Possible years of work experience: age minus years of education minus 5

NOTE: $N = 337$.

of the number of years a respondent could have been in the labor force. The descriptive statistics and abbreviations for these variables are given in Table 6.1.

6.2.1. The MNLM as a Probability Model

Let y be the dependent variable with J nominal outcomes. The categories are numbered 1 through J, but are not assumed to be ordered. Let $\Pr(y = m \mid \mathbf{x})$ be the probability of observing outcome m given $\mathbf{x}$. A probability model for y can be constructed as follows.

1. Assume that $\Pr(y = m \mid \mathbf{x})$ is a function of the linear combination $\mathbf{x}\boldsymbol{\beta}_m$. The vector $\boldsymbol{\beta}_m = (\beta_{0m} \cdots \beta_{km} \cdots \beta_{Km})'$ includes the intercept β_{0m} and coefficients β_{km} for the effect of x_k on outcome m. In contrast to the ordered logit model, $\boldsymbol{\beta}_m$ differs for each outcome. For example, the coefficient for the effect of education on the probability of being a blue-collar worker is different from the coefficient for the effect of education on the probability of being a craft worker.

2. To ensure that the probabilities are nonnegative, we take the exponential of $\mathbf{x}\boldsymbol{\beta}_m$: $\exp(\mathbf{x}\boldsymbol{\beta}_m)$. While the result is nonnegative, the sum $\sum_{j=1}^{J} \exp(\mathbf{x}\boldsymbol{\beta}_j)$ does not equal 1 which it must for probabilities.

3. In order to make the probabilities sum to 1, we divide $\exp(\mathbf{x}\boldsymbol{\beta}_m)$ by $\sum_{j=1}^{J} \exp(\mathbf{x}\boldsymbol{\beta}_j)$:

$$\Pr(y_i = m \mid \mathbf{x}_i) = \frac{\exp(\mathbf{x}_i \boldsymbol{\beta}_m)}{\sum_{j=1}^{J} \exp(\mathbf{x}_i \boldsymbol{\beta}_j)} \qquad [6.6]$$

With this normalization, it follows that $\sum_{m=1}^{J} \Pr(y = m \mid \mathbf{x}) = 1$. (*Prove that the probabilities sum to 1.*)

While the probabilities now sum to 1, they are unidentified since more than one set of parameters generates the same probabilities of the observed outcomes.[1] To see why this is the case, we can multiply Equation 6.6 by $\exp(\mathbf{x}\boldsymbol{\tau}) / \exp(\mathbf{x}\boldsymbol{\tau})$. Since this is just multiplying by 1, the value of the probability does not change:

$$\Pr(y_i = m \mid \mathbf{x}_i) = \frac{\exp(\mathbf{x}_i \boldsymbol{\beta}_m)}{\sum_{j=1}^{J} \exp(\mathbf{x}_i \boldsymbol{\beta}_j)} \times \frac{\exp(\mathbf{x}_i \boldsymbol{\tau})}{\exp(\mathbf{x}_i \boldsymbol{\tau})}$$

$$= \frac{\exp(\mathbf{x}_i \boldsymbol{\beta}_m + \mathbf{x}_i \boldsymbol{\tau})}{\sum_{j=1}^{J} \exp(\mathbf{x}_i \boldsymbol{\beta}_j + \mathbf{x}_i \boldsymbol{\tau})}$$

$$= \frac{\exp(\mathbf{x}_i[\boldsymbol{\beta}_m + \boldsymbol{\tau}])}{\sum_{j=1}^{J} \exp(\mathbf{x}_i[\boldsymbol{\beta}_j + \boldsymbol{\tau}])}$$

While the values of the probabilities are unchanged, the original parameters $\boldsymbol{\beta}_m$ have been replaced by $\boldsymbol{\beta}_m + \boldsymbol{\tau}$. Accordingly, for every nonzero $\boldsymbol{\tau}$ there is a different set of parameters that results in the same predictions. That is, the model is not identified.

To identify the model, we must impose constraints on the $\boldsymbol{\beta}$'s such that for any $\boldsymbol{\tau} \neq \mathbf{0}$ the constraints are violated. Two types of constraints are commonly used. First, we could assume that $\sum_{j=1}^{J} \boldsymbol{\beta}_j = 0$. This constraint is often used with hierarchical log-linear models (Agresti, 1990, p. 132). Second, and more commonly for the MNLM, one of the $\boldsymbol{\beta}$'s is constrained to equal 0, such as $\boldsymbol{\beta}_1 = \mathbf{0}$ or $\boldsymbol{\beta}_J = \mathbf{0}$. The choice is arbitrary, and we assume that

$$\boldsymbol{\beta}_1 = \mathbf{0}$$

Clearly, if we add a nonzero $\boldsymbol{\tau}$ to $\boldsymbol{\beta}_1$, the assumption that $\boldsymbol{\beta}_1 = \mathbf{0}$ is violated.

Adding this constraint to the model results in the probability equation:

$$\Pr(y_i = m \mid \mathbf{x}_i) = \frac{\exp(\mathbf{x}_i \boldsymbol{\beta}_m)}{\sum_{j=1}^{J} \exp(\mathbf{x}_i \boldsymbol{\beta}_j)} \quad \text{where } \boldsymbol{\beta}_1 = \mathbf{0} \qquad [6.7]$$

---

[1] In Chapter 3, the logit model was derived using a latent variable y^* and the model was not identified since the variance of y^* was unknown. While the derivation of the model in this chapter does not use a latent variable, the model is still not identified.

Since $\exp(\mathbf{x}_i\boldsymbol{\beta}_1) = \exp(\mathbf{x}_i 0) = 1$, the model is commonly written as

$$\Pr(y_i = 1 \mid \mathbf{x}_i) = \frac{1}{1 + \sum_{j=2}^{J} \exp(\mathbf{x}_i\boldsymbol{\beta}_j)}$$

$$\Pr(y_i = m \mid \mathbf{x}_i) = \frac{\exp(\mathbf{x}_i\boldsymbol{\beta}_m)}{1 + \sum_{j=2}^{J} \exp(\mathbf{x}_i\boldsymbol{\beta}_j)} \quad \text{for } m > 1$$

6.2.2. The MNLM as an Odds Model

The MNLM can also be expressed in terms of the odds, as was done in Section 6.1. The odds of outcome m versus outcome n given $\mathbf{x}$, indicated by $\Omega_{m \mid n}(\mathbf{x})$, equal

$$\Omega_{m \mid n}(\mathbf{x}_i) = \frac{\Pr(y_i = m \mid \mathbf{x}_i)}{\Pr(y_i = n \mid \mathbf{x}_i)} = \frac{\dfrac{\exp(\mathbf{x}_i\boldsymbol{\beta}_m)}{\sum_{j=1}^{J} \exp(\mathbf{x}_i\boldsymbol{\beta}_j)}}{\dfrac{\exp(\mathbf{x}_i\boldsymbol{\beta}_n)}{\sum_{j=1}^{J} \exp(\mathbf{x}_i\boldsymbol{\beta}_j)}} = \frac{\exp(\mathbf{x}_i\boldsymbol{\beta}_m)}{\exp(\mathbf{x}_i\boldsymbol{\beta}_n)}$$

Combining exponents leads to the odds equation:

$$\Omega_{m \mid n}(\mathbf{x}_i) = \exp(\mathbf{x}_i[\boldsymbol{\beta}_m - \boldsymbol{\beta}_n])$$

Taking logs shows that the MNLM is linear in the logit:

$$\ln \Omega_{m \mid n}(\mathbf{x}_i) = \mathbf{x}_i(\boldsymbol{\beta}_m - \boldsymbol{\beta}_n)$$

The difference $\boldsymbol{\beta}_m - \boldsymbol{\beta}_n$, called a *contrast*, is the effect of $\mathbf{x}$ on the logit of outcome m versus outcome n.

Since the model is linear in the logit, it is simple to compute the partial derivative:

$$\frac{\partial \ln \Omega_{m \mid n}(\mathbf{x})}{\partial x_k} = \frac{\partial \mathbf{x}(\boldsymbol{\beta}_m - \boldsymbol{\beta}_n)}{\partial x_k} = \frac{\partial \mathbf{x}\boldsymbol{\beta}_m}{\partial x_k} - \frac{\partial \mathbf{x}\boldsymbol{\beta}_n}{\partial x_k} = \beta_{km} - \beta_{kn}$$

This allows us to interpret $\beta_{km} - \beta_{kn}$ as:

- For a unit change in x_k, the logit of outcome m versus outcome n is expected to change by $\beta_{km} - \beta_{kn}$ units, holding all other variables constant.

Since $\boldsymbol{\beta}_1 = \boldsymbol{0}$, the equation for the comparison with outcome 1 simplifies to

$$\ln \Omega_{m|1}(\mathbf{x}_i) = \mathbf{x}_i(\boldsymbol{\beta}_m - \boldsymbol{\beta}_1) = \mathbf{x}_i\boldsymbol{\beta}_m$$

Therefore, given the identifying constraint that $\boldsymbol{\beta}_1 = \boldsymbol{0}$, β_{km} is the effect of x_k on the logit of outcome m relative to outcome 1:

- For a unit change in x_k, the logit of outcome m versus outcome 1 is expected to change by β_{km} units, holding all other variables constant.

This interpretation of β_{km} is simple since the effect of a unit change in x_k on the logit does not depend on the level of x_k or on the level of any other variable. Unfortunately, it is also unsatisfactory since it is hard to convey the substantive meaning of a change in the log of the odds. Alternative methods of interpretation are discussed in Section 6.6.

This is the multinomial logit model that was suggested by Theil (1969), who derived the model in much the same way that I have presented it. The model can also be derived as a discrete choice model, which is now considered.

6.2.3. The Multinomial Logit Model as a Discrete Choice Model

In an influential paper published in 1973, McFadden demonstrated that Luce's (1959) model of choice behavior can be used to derive a variety of econometric models, including the multinomial and conditional logit models. This section examines the basic ideas underlying what is known as the discrete choice model. For a more detailed discussion, see Ben-Akiva and Lerman (1985, Chapters 3–5) or Pudney (1989, Chapters 1 and 3).

The discrete choice model is based on the principle that an individual chooses the outcome that maximizes the utility gained from that choice. For simplicity, assume that there are two choices, numbered 1 and 2. The utility for choice 1 is u_1 and the utility for choice 2 is u_2. A person chooses alternative 1 when $u_1 > u_2$, and chooses alternative 2 when $u_2 > u_1$. We assume that ties do not occur. A person is rational in the sense of choosing the alternative that maximizes the utility derived from the choice.

The utility derived from choice m for individual i equals

$$u_{im} = \mu_{im} + \varepsilon_{im}$$

where μ_{im} is the average utility associated with choice m for individual i, and ε_{im} is the random error associated with that choice. The probability of choosing alternative 1 is the probability that the utility from alternative 1 exceeds the utility from alternative 2:

$$\Pr(y_i = 1) = \Pr(u_{i1} > u_{i2})$$
$$= \Pr(\mu_{i1} + \varepsilon_{i1} > \mu_{i2} + \varepsilon_{i2})$$
$$= \Pr(\varepsilon_{i1} - \varepsilon_{i2} > \mu_{i2} - \mu_{i1})$$

When there are J choices, the probability of choice m is

$$\Pr(y = m) = \Pr(u_m > u_j \text{ for all } j \neq m)$$

For example, the probability of a craft occupation equals the probability that the utility obtained from a craft occupation exceeds that of all other occupations.

The specific form of the discrete choice model is determined by the assumed distribution of ε and the specification of how μ_m, the average utility for choice m, is related to measured variables. To obtain the MNLM, let the average utility be a linear combination of the characteristics of an individual:

$$\mu_{im} = \mathbf{x}_i \boldsymbol{\beta}_m$$

McFadden (1973) proved that the MNLM results if and only if the ε's are independent and have a type I extreme-value distribution:

$$f(\varepsilon) = \exp[-\varepsilon - \exp(-\varepsilon)]$$

This distribution looks like a normal curve that is skewed to the right, with a thinner tail on the left and a thicker tail on the right. It has mode 0, mean .58, and standard deviation 1.28. The choice of the distribution is motivated by the simplicity, tractability, and usefulness of the resulting model.

6.3. ML Estimation

Regardless of which approach is used to derive the model, the equation for the probability of an outcome is the same. This equation is the basis for the ML estimator. From Equation 6.7, let

$\Pr(y_i = m \mid x_i, \beta_2, \ldots, \beta_J)$ be the probability of observing $y_i = m$ given x_i with parameters β_2 through β_J. Let p_i be the probability of observing whatever value of y was actually observed for the ith observation. If the observations are independent, the likelihood equation is

$$L(\beta_2, \ldots, \beta_J \mid y, X) = \prod_{i=1}^{N} p_i$$

The β's are introduced into the likelihood equation by substituting the right-hand side from Equation 6.7 for p_i:

$$L(\beta_2, \ldots, \beta_J \mid y, X) = \prod_{m=1}^{J} \prod_{y_i=m} \frac{\exp(x_i \beta_m)}{\sum_{j=1}^{J} \exp(x_i \beta_j)}$$

where $\prod_{y_i=m}$ is the product over all cases for which y_i is equal to m. Taking logs, we obtain the log likelihood equation which can be maximized with numerical methods to estimate the β's. In practice, convergence tends to be very quick. The resulting estimates are consistent, asymptotically normal, and asymptotically efficient. Amemiya (1985, pp. 295–296) shows that under conditions that are likely to apply in practice, the likelihood function is globally concave, ensuring the uniqueness of the ML estimates.

6.3.1. Software Issues

Different programs analyzing the same data *appear* to give quite different results. This can be understood most readily by considering the equation:

$$\ln \Omega_{m \mid n}(x_i) = x_i(\beta_m - \beta_n)$$

Different programs estimate different sets of contrasts $\beta_m - \beta_n$. The contrasts that are estimated are a minimal set in the sense that all other contrasts can be computed from them. LIMDEP and Stata estimate the $J-1$ contrasts $\beta_m - \beta_1 = \beta_m$, for $m = 2$ to J. SAS's CATMOD estimates the contrasts $\beta_m - \beta_J$ for $m = 1$ to $J - 1$. (*Show that with these contrasts you can compute any other contrast $\beta_m - \beta_n$.*) Markov optionally estimates all contrasts $\beta_m - \beta_n$.

Unfortunately, some programs do not indicate which contrasts are being estimated. If you assume that your program is estimating one set of contrasts when it is estimating another, *all of your interpretations will be incorrect*. It is prudent to compare your program's output to known results. Here is a simple benchmark. Let $\mathbf{y}' = (1\ 2\ 3\ 1\ 2\ 3)$ and $\mathbf{x}' = (1\ 2\ 3\ 4\ 5\ 7)$. (The last x is 7, not 6.) The estimates are:

		Outcome n		
$\widehat{\beta}_{xm} - \widehat{\beta}_{xn}$		*1*	*2*	*3*
Outcome	*1*	—	−0.3791	−0.8237
m	*2*	0.3791	—	−0.4445
	3	0.8237	0.4445	—

6.4. Computing and Testing Other Contrasts

Standard software estimates a minimal set of contrasts. For example, your output might only show the $J - 1$ contrasts with the reference outcome r:

$$\beta_{km} - \beta_{kr} = \beta_{k, m | r} \quad \text{for all } m \neq r \qquad [6.8]$$

where $\beta_{k, m | r}$ is new notation for the contrast $\beta_{km} - \beta_{kr}$. (Before proceeding, you should determine which contrasts are being estimated by your software.) The contrasts estimated by your software can be used to compute other contrasts that may be of substantive interest. To see how this is done, consider our model of occupational attainment.

Example of the MNLM: Occupational Attainment

The coefficients in Table 6.2 are the standard output from a program that estimates the MNLM. The minimal set of contrasts involves all possible comparisons with outcome M. These coefficients correspond to the equations:

$$\ln \Omega_{B | M}(\mathbf{x}_i) = \beta_{0, B | M} + \beta_{1, B | M} WHITE + \beta_{2, B | M} ED + \beta_{3, B | M} EXP$$

$$\ln \Omega_{C | M}(\mathbf{x}_i) = \beta_{0, C | M} + \beta_{1, C | M} WHITE + \beta_{2, C | M} ED + \beta_{3, C | M} EXP$$

$$\ln \Omega_{W | M}(\mathbf{x}_i) = \beta_{0, W | M} + \beta_{1, W | M} WHITE + \beta_{2, W | M} ED + \beta_{3, W | M} EXP$$

$$\ln \Omega_{P | M}(\mathbf{x}_i) = \beta_{0, P | M} + \beta_{1, P | M} WHITE + \beta_{2, P | M} ED + \beta_{3, P | M} EXP$$

TABLE 6.2 Logit Coefficients for a Multinomial Logit Model of Occupational Attainment

Comparison		Constant	WHITE	ED	EXP
			Logit Coefficient for		
$B\,|\,M$	β	0.741	1.237	−0.099	0.0047
	z	0.49	1.71	−0.97	0.27
$C\,|\,M$	β	−1.091	0.472	0.094	0.0277
	z	−0.75	0.78	0.96	1.66
$W\,|\,M$	β	−6.239	1.571	0.353	0.0346
	z	−3.29	1.74	3.01	1.84
$P\,|\,M$	β	−11.518	1.774	0.779	0.0357
	z	−6.23	2.35	6.79	1.98

NOTE: $N = 337$. β is a logit coefficient for the indicated comparison; z is a z-value. Job types: M = menial; B = blue collar; C = craft; W = white collar; P = professional.

If our substantive interest is in a comparison that was not computed by the program, such as the effect of race on having a craft versus a white-collar occupation (i.e., $\beta_{1,\,C\,|\,W}$), we need to compute and test the "missing" coefficients.

Computing Other Contrasts

Assume that your software estimates the contrasts for all outcomes relative to outcome r, where r stands for the reference category. For variable x_k, the program estimates the $J-1$ coefficients $\beta_{k,\,p\,|\,r}$ for $p \neq r$. In Table 6.2, r corresponds to menial occupations. The coefficients for the comparison of p versus q can be computed by taking the difference between two of the known parameters:

$$\beta_{k,\,p\,|\,q} = \beta_{k,\,p\,|\,r} - \beta_{k,\,q\,|\,r} \qquad [6.9]$$

This identity holds since

$$\beta_{k,\,p\,|\,q} = \beta_{kp} - \beta_{kq}$$
$$= (\beta_{kp} - \beta_{kr}) - (\beta_{kq} - \beta_{kr})$$
$$= \beta_{k,\,p\,|\,r} - \beta_{k,\,q\,|\,r}$$

For example, the effect of race on the logit of C versus W is

$$\widehat{\beta}_{1,\,C\,|\,W} = \widehat{\beta}_{1,\,C\,|\,M} - \widehat{\beta}_{1,\,W\,|\,M} = 0.47 - 1.57 = -1.10$$

The variance for the new estimate is

$$\widehat{\text{Var}}(\widehat{\beta}_{1,\,C|W}) = \widehat{\text{Var}}(\widehat{\beta}_{1,\,C|M} - \widehat{\beta}_{1,\,W|M})$$

$$= \widehat{\text{Var}}(\widehat{\beta}_{1,\,C|M}) + \widehat{\text{Var}}(\widehat{\beta}_{1,\,W|M}) - 2\widehat{\text{Cov}}(\widehat{\beta}_{1,\,C|M},\,\widehat{\beta}_{1,\,W|M})$$

The information needed to compute the new variance is obtained from the covariance matrix for the estimates computed by your software. Usually, you will need to explicitly request that this matrix be printed. The variances are located on the diagonal, with the covariances on the off-diagonal. In order to avoid serious rounding error, you must make the computations using as many decimal digits as are available. Once $\widehat{\text{Var}}(\widehat{\beta}_{1,\,C|W})$ is computed, the coefficient for race on the logit of C versus W can be tested with a standard z-test:

$$z = \frac{\widehat{\beta}_{1,\,C|W}}{\sqrt{\widehat{\text{Var}}(\widehat{\beta}_{1,\,C|W})}}$$

Alternatively, and in my experience more reliably, your software can be "tricked" into computing the missing coefficients. The software that I used for the example computed the contrasts for outcomes 2 through J against category 1. The dependent variable was coded: $M = 1$, $B = 2$, $C = 3$, $W = 4$, and $P = 5$. This resulted in the coefficients in Table 6.2. If occupation is recoded so that $M = 2$, $B = 3$, $C = 4$, $W = 5$, and $P = 1$, and if the model is reestimated with the recoded outcome variable, the program will estimate the coefficients and standard errors for $\beta_{M|P}$, $\beta_{B|P}$, and so on. Other contrasts can be estimated with similar recodings of the categories.

6.5. Two Useful Tests

This section presents two tests that are very useful when using the MNLM. The first is a test that the effect of a variable is 0. The second is a test of whether a pair of outcome categories can be combined. Since it is important to understand how these tests can be implemented with the output from your software, the tests are presented in terms of the contrasts with outcome r.

6.5.1. Testing That a Variable Has No Effect

With J dependent categories, there are $J - 1$ parameters $\beta_{k,m|r}$ associated with each variable x_k. The hypothesis that x_k does not affect the dependent variable can be written as

$$H_0: \beta_{k,1|r} = \cdots = \beta_{k,J|r} = 0$$

Since $\beta_{k,r|r}$ is necessarily 0, the hypothesis imposes constraints on $J - 1$ parameters. This hypothesis can be tested with either a Wald or a LR test.

A LR Test. First, estimate the full model M_F that contains all of the variables, with the resulting LR statistic G_F^2. Second, estimate the restricted model M_R formed by excluding variable x_k, with the resulting LR test statistic G_R^2. This model has $J-1$ fewer parameters. Finally, compute the difference $G_{RvsF}^2 = G_F^2 - G_R^2$ which is distributed as chi-square with $J - 1$ degrees of freedom if the hypothesis that x_k does not affect the outcome is true. The practical weakness of this test is that you must estimate the full model and then K restricted models corresponding to excluding each of the x_k's.

A Wald Test. Since the Wald test only requires estimating a single model, it is easier to apply when there are many variables to test. Consequently, it is included in the standard output of most programs for the MNLM. Let $\widehat{\boldsymbol{\beta}}_k = (\widehat{\beta}_{k,2|1} \cdots \widehat{\beta}_{k,J|1})'$ be the ML estimates for variable x_k from the full model. For simplicity, I have assumed that the software is estimating the coefficients against the reference category 1. If your software uses a different reference category, $\widehat{\boldsymbol{\beta}}_k$ would simply contain the $J - 1$ coefficients that were estimated for x_k. Let $\widehat{\mathrm{Var}}(\widehat{\boldsymbol{\beta}}_k)$ be the estimated covariance matrix. The Wald statistic for $H_0: \boldsymbol{\beta}_k = \mathbf{0}$ has the standard form:

$$W_k = \widehat{\boldsymbol{\beta}}_k' \widehat{\mathrm{Var}}(\widehat{\boldsymbol{\beta}}_k)^{-1} \widehat{\boldsymbol{\beta}}_k$$

If the null hypothesis is true, then W_k is distributed as chi-square with $J - 1$ degrees of freedom.

Example of Wald and LR Tests. Table 6.3 contains the Wald and LR tests for each variable from our example. The LR test for the variable

TABLE 6.3 LR and Wald Tests That Each Variable Has No Effect

	G^2	df	p	W	df	p
WHITE	8.10	4	0.09	8.15	4	0.09
ED	156.94	4	< 0.01	84.97	4	< 0.01
EXP	8.56	4	0.07	7.99	4	0.09

WHITE can be interpreted as follows:

- If the hypothesis that *WHITE* has no effect on occupation is true, we would observe a G^2 of 8.10 or larger 9% ($p = .09$) of the time due to sampling variation. Therefore, the hypothesis that *WHITE* does not affect occupational attainment can be rejected at the .10 level, but not at the .05 level.

Or, we could say:

- The effect of race is significant at the .09 level.

The conclusion from the Wald test is the same. While the LR and Wald tests are asymptotically equivalent, the table shows that they have different values in finite samples.

6.5.2. Testing That Two Outcomes Can Be Combined

If none of the x_k's significantly affects the odds of outcome m versus outcome n, we say that m and n are *indistinguishable* with respect to the variables in the model (Anderson, 1984). If $\beta_{1, m|n}, \ldots, \beta_{K, m|n}$ are the coefficients for x_1 through x_K from the logit of m versus n, then the hypothesis that outcomes m and n are indistinguishable corresponds to

$$H_0: \beta_{1, m|n} = \cdots = \beta_{K, m|n} = 0 \qquad [6.10]$$

or, equivalently, in terms of the coefficients estimated by your software,

$$H_0: (\beta_{1,m|r} - \beta_{1,n|r}) = \cdots = (\beta_{K, m|r} - \beta_{K, n|r}) = 0$$

In our example, the hypothesis that P and W are indistinguishable is

$$H_0: \beta_{1, P|W} = \beta_{2, P|W} = \beta_{3, P|W} = 0 \qquad [6.11]$$

or, in terms of the parameters in Table 6.2 (using the identity in Equation 6.9),

$$H_0: \beta_{1, P|M} - \beta_{1, W|M} = \beta_{2, P|M} - \beta_{2, W|M} = \beta_{3, P|M} - \beta_{3, W|M} = 0$$

A Wald Test. The hypothesis that m and n are indistinguishable can be tested with a Wald test:

$$W_{m \mid n} = [\mathbf{Q}\widehat{\boldsymbol{\beta}}^*]'[\mathbf{Q}\widehat{\text{Var}}(\widehat{\boldsymbol{\beta}}^*)\mathbf{Q}'][\mathbf{Q}\widehat{\boldsymbol{\beta}}^*]$$

where $\boldsymbol{\beta}^*$ contains estimates from all of the parameters in the model and $\mathbf{Q}$ imposes the constraints implied by Equation 6.10. (*Construct the* $\mathbf{Q}$ *to test the hypothesis in Equation 6.11.*) This test is cumbersome to apply, which makes the following test far more practical.

A LR Test.[2] A simpler but statistically less powerful LR test can also be used. First, select only those observations with outcomes equal to the two categories being considered. Second, estimate a binary logit on the new sample. Finally, compute a LR test that all of the slope coefficients (not the intercept) in the binary logit are simultaneously 0. This test is easy to apply since it is part of the standard output from most programs for binary logit.

Example of Wald and LR Tests. The hypothesis that professional and white-collar occupations can be combined can be tested as follows. First, select the 153 individuals who have professional or white-collar jobs. Second, estimate the binary logit:

$$\ln \Omega_{P \mid W}(\mathbf{x}) = \beta_0 + \beta_1 WHITE + \beta_2 ED + \beta_3 EXP$$

Third, compute the LR test of $H_0: \beta_1 = \beta_2 = \beta_3 = 0$. For our data, $G^2_{P \mid W} = 23.4$, $df = 3$, $p < .01$. The Wald test gives a similar result: $W_{P \mid W} = 22.2$. The hypothesis that professional and white-collar occupations are indistinguishable with respect to race, education, and experience is rejected at the .01 level.

6.5.3. Specification Searches

Given the difficulties of interpretation that are discussed in the next section, it is tempting to search for a more parsimonious model constructed by excluding variables or combining outcome categories. While the two tests presented in this section can be used in a specification search, great care is required. First, both of these tests involve multi-

---

[2] I thank Paul Allison for suggesting this test.

ple coefficients. While the overall test may indicate that *as a group* the parameters are not significantly different from 0, an *individual* parameter may still be substantively and statistically significant. Accordingly, you need to carefully examine the individual coefficients involved in each test before deciding to revise your model. For example, while $W_{B|M}$ may suggest that you can combine these two occupations, one of the independent variables may still have an important effect differentiating these occupations. Second, as with all searches that use repeated, sequential tests, there is a danger of overfitting the data. When models are constructed based on prior testing using the same data, the significance levels should only be used as rough guidelines.

6.6. Interpretation

In even a simple MNLM, there are a lot of parameters. With three outcomes and five independent variables, there are 12 unique parameters. With five outcomes, there are 24 parameters. With seven outcomes, there are 36 parameters. If every possible contrast is examined, the numbers are even larger. All too often in practice, the MNLM is estimated, the parameters are listed, and statistical significance is noted, while the magnitudes and even directions of the effects are ignored. In this section, I show that by extending the methods of interpretation for binary and ordered logit models and by adding graphical summaries, it is possible to readily interpret the many parameters of the MNLM.

6.6.1. Predicted Probabilities

The predicted probability that $y = m$ given $\mathbf{x}$ is

$$\Pr(y = m \mid \mathbf{x}_i) = \frac{\exp(\mathbf{x}_i \boldsymbol{\beta}_m)}{\sum_{j=1}^{J} \exp(\mathbf{x}_i \boldsymbol{\beta}_j)} \qquad [6.12]$$

where $\boldsymbol{\beta}_1 = \mathbf{0}$. Since predicted probabilities are the basis for interpretation, it is essential to understand how to compute the predicted probabilities from the estimates provided by your software. Assume that your software is estimating the contrasts: $\beta_{k,m|r} = \beta_{km} - \beta_{kr}$. Multiplying Equation 6.12 by $\exp(-\mathbf{x}\boldsymbol{\beta}_r)/\exp(-\mathbf{x}\boldsymbol{\beta}_r)$ leads to an equivalent formula for the predicted probabilities in terms of the parameters being estimated:

$$\Pr(y = m \mid \mathbf{x}_i) = \frac{\exp(\mathbf{x}_i\boldsymbol{\beta}_m)}{\sum_{j=1}^{J} \exp(\mathbf{x}_i\boldsymbol{\beta}_j)} \frac{\exp(-\mathbf{x}_i\boldsymbol{\beta}_r)}{\exp(-\mathbf{x}_i\boldsymbol{\beta}_r)}$$

$$= \frac{\exp(\mathbf{x}_i[\boldsymbol{\beta}_m - \boldsymbol{\beta}_r])}{\sum_{j=1}^{J} \exp(\mathbf{x}_i[\boldsymbol{\beta}_j - \boldsymbol{\beta}_r])}$$

$$= \frac{\exp(\mathbf{x}_i\boldsymbol{\beta}_{m \mid r})}{\sum_{j=1}^{J} \exp(\mathbf{x}_i\boldsymbol{\beta}_{j \mid r})}$$

where $\boldsymbol{\beta}_{m \mid r}$ is a vector with the coefficients $\beta_{k, m \mid r}$ for all k.

Probabilities can be computed at a variety of values and presented in various ways. For example, to determine the variation in the predicted probabilities, you can compute the mean, minimum, and maximum probabilities over the sample. To examine the effect of a single x_k, you can fix all variables except x_k at some level and plot the predicted probability as x_k changes over its range. If you want to highlight differences among important groups, you can construct a table of probabilities at key combinations of values of the independent variables. These approaches were illustrated in Chapters 3 and 5 and are not considered further here.

6.6.2. Partial Change

For continuous independent variables, the partial change in the probability is computed by taking the derivative of Equation 6.12 with respect to x_k:

$$\frac{\partial \Pr(y = m \mid \mathbf{x})}{\partial x_k} = \Pr(y = m \mid \mathbf{x}) \left[\beta_{km} - \sum_{j=1}^{J} \beta_{kj} \Pr(y = j \mid \mathbf{x}) \right] \quad [6.13]$$

The partial change, or marginal effect, is the slope of the curve relating x_k to $\Pr(y = m \mid \mathbf{x})$, holding all other variables constant. The value of the marginal effect depends on the values of all independent variables and on the coefficients for each outcome. Most frequently, the marginal is computed when variables are held at their means, possibly with dummy variables held at 0 or 1.

Since Equation 6.13 combines all of the β_{kj}'s, the marginal effect of x_k on m does not need to have the same sign as the corresponding coefficient β_{km}. Further, as x_k changes, the sign of the marginal can change. For example, at one point the marginal effect of education on having a craft occupation could be positive, while at another point the marginal could be negative. This situation is comparable to that for the ORM, which was illustrated in panel A of Figure 5.3 (p. 132). Not surprisingly, the marginal is rarely used for the MNLM.

6.6.3. Discrete Change

Measures of discrete change in probabilities are an effective method of interpretation that can be used for continuous and dummy independent variables. The change in the predicted probability when x_k changes from x_S (for the starting value) to x_E (for the ending value) is

$$\frac{\Delta \Pr(y = m \mid \mathbf{x})}{\Delta x_k} = \Pr(y = m \mid \mathbf{x}, x_k = x_E) - \Pr(y = m \mid \mathbf{x}, x_k = x_S)$$

where $\Pr(y = m \mid \mathbf{x}, x_k)$ is the probability that $y = m$ given $\mathbf{x}$, noting the specific value of x_k. The discrete change can be interpreted as:

- For a change in variable x_k from x_S to x_E, the predicted probability of outcome m changes by $\Delta \Pr(y = m \mid \mathbf{x})/\Delta x_k$, holding all other variables constant.

Because of the nonlinearity of the model, the amount of change in the probability depends on: (1) the amount of change in x_k; (2) the starting value of x_k; and (3) the values of all other variables. Most often, other variables are held at their means, with dummy variables possibly held at 0 or 1. It is essential to keep in mind that the amount and even the direction of the discrete change depends on the values at which the independent variables are being held constant.

Your choice of the amount of change in the variable being assessed depends on the purpose of the analysis and the type of variable. Dummy variables should be changed from 0 to 1. The effects of other variables can be computed by allowing the variable to change by 1 or by a standard deviation. It is often useful to center these changes around the variable's mean (see Chapter 3, p. 77, for details). The total possible effect of a variable is computed by changing a variable from its minimum to its maximum. For further details, see Sections 3.7.5 and 5.4.4.

After a decision is made on how to compute the discrete change, there will be J values of change, one for each of the outcomes. These changes can be summarized by computing the *average absolute discrete change*:

$$\bar{\Delta} = \frac{1}{J} \sum_{j=1}^{J} \left| \frac{\Delta \Pr(y = j \mid \mathbf{x})}{\Delta x_k} \right|$$

The absolute value is taken before adding since the sum of the changes would otherwise necessarily equal 0.

Example of Discrete Change: Occupational Attainment

Table 6.4 contains estimates of discrete change from our model of occupational attainment. First, consider the dummy variable *WHITE*. Holding all other variables at their means, being white decreases the probability of having a menial job by .13 and increases the probability of a professional job by .16. By comparison, the average absolute change for a standard deviation change in education is .16, and is .03 for experience. The effect of education is largest on the probability of having a professional job, where the expected change for a standard deviation change in education is 0.38.

While it is possible to examine these changes by scanning the table, a *discrete change plot* quickly summarizes the information. Figure 6.1 shows the change in the probability along the horizontal axis, with each variable listed on the vertical axis. The letters corresponding to the occupations show the magnitude of the discrete change in the probability of an outcome for a given change in the independent variable, with the other variables held at their means. (Remember that different results would be obtained if the variables were held at other values.) It is easy to see that the effects of a standard deviation change in education are largest, with an increase of over .35 for professional occupations. The effects

TABLE 6.4 Discrete Change in Probability for a Multinomial Logit Model of Occupations. Jobs Are Classified as: M = Menial; C = Craft; B = Blue Collar; W = White Collar; and P = Professional

Variable	Change	$\bar{\Delta}$	M	B	C	W	P
WHITE	$0 \rightarrow 1$	0.12	−0.13	0.05	−0.16	0.08	0.16
ED	$\Delta 1$	0.06	−0.03	−0.07	−0.05	0.01	0.13
	$\Delta \sigma$	0.16	−0.07	−0.19	−0.15	0.03	0.38
	ΔRange	0.39	−0.13	−0.70	−0.15	0.02	0.96
EXP	$\Delta 1$	0.00	−0.00	−0.00	0.00	0.00	0.00
	$\Delta \sigma$	0.03	−0.03	−0.05	0.01	0.02	0.04
	ΔRange	0.12	−0.12	−0.19	0.03	0.09	0.18
Probability at Mean			0.09	0.18	0.29	0.16	0.27

NOTE: $0 \rightarrow 1$ is discrete change from 0 to 1; $\Delta 1$ is the centered change of one unit around the mean; $\Delta \sigma$ is the centered change of one standard deviation around the mean; ΔRange is the change from the minimum to its maximum. All other variables are held at their means. $\bar{\Delta}$ is the average absolute change.

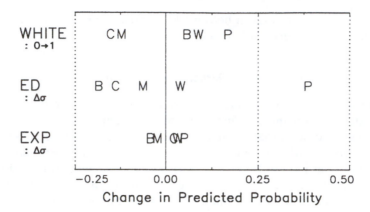

Figure 6.1. Discrete Change Plot for the Multinomial Logit Model of Occupations. Control Variables Are Held at Their Means. Jobs Are Classified as: M = Menial; C = Craft; B = Blue Collar; W = White Collar; and P = Professional

of race are also substantial, with average blacks being less likely to enter blue-collar, white-collar, or professional jobs. The expected changes due to a standard deviation change in experience are much smaller and show that experience increases the probabilities of more highly skilled occupations.

6.6.4. Interpreting Odds Ratios

While computing the change in the probability is a useful way to assess the magnitudes of effects in the MNLM, it is limited in two ways. First, discrete change indicates the change for a particular set of values of the independent variables. At different levels of the variables, the changes will be different. Second, measures of discrete change do not indicate the dynamics among the dependent outcomes. For example, a decrease in education increases the probability of both blue-collar and craft jobs. But how does it affect the odds of a person choosing a craft job relative to a blue-collar job? To answer this type of question, we need to consider the odds formulation of the model.

Earlier, I showed that the MNLM can be written as

$$\Omega_{m \mid n}(\mathbf{x}) = \exp(\mathbf{x}\boldsymbol{\beta}_{m \mid n})$$

Where $\Omega_{m|n}(\mathbf{x})$ is the odds of outcome m versus outcome n given $\mathbf{x}$. Expanding $\mathbf{x}\boldsymbol{\beta}_{m|n}$ leads to

$$\Omega_{m|n}(\mathbf{x}, x_k) = e^{\beta_{0,m|n}} e^{\beta_{1,m|n} x_1} \ldots e^{\beta_{k,m|n} x_k} \ldots e^{\beta_{K,m|n} x_K}$$

If x_k is changed by δ, then

$$\Omega_{m|n}(\mathbf{x}, x_k + \delta) = e^{\beta_{0,m|n}} e^{\beta_{1,m|n} x_1} \ldots e^{\beta_{k,m|n} x_k + \delta} \ldots e^{\beta_{K,m|n} x_K}$$

$$= e^{\beta_{0,m|n}} e^{\beta_{1,m|n} x_1} \ldots e^{\beta_{k,m|n} x_k} e^{\beta_{k,m|n} \delta} \ldots e^{\beta_{K,m|n} x_K}$$

The effect of x_k can be measured by the ratio of the odds before and after the change in x_k:

$$\frac{\Omega_{m|n}(\mathbf{x}, x_k + \delta)}{\Omega_{m|n}(\mathbf{x}, x_k)}$$

$$= \frac{e^{\beta_{0,m|n}} e^{\beta_{1,m|n} x_1} \ldots e^{\beta_{k,m|n} x_k} e^{\beta_{k,m|n} \delta} \ldots e^{\beta_{K,m|n} x_K}}{e^{\beta_{0,m|n}} e^{\beta_{1,m|n} x_1} \ldots e^{\beta_{k,m|n} x_k} \ldots e^{\beta_{K,m|n} x_K}}$$

$$= e^{\beta_{k,m|n} \delta}$$

All terms cancel except for $\exp(\beta_{k,m|n} \times \delta)$, which equals the odds ratio. The odds ratio can be interpreted as:

- For a change of δ in x_k, the odds of outcome m versus outcome n are expected to change by a factor of $\exp(\beta_{k,m|n} \times \delta)$, holding all other variables constant.

When $\delta = 1$, the *unstandardized odds ratio* can be interpreted as:

- For a unit change in x_k, the odds are expected to change by a factor of $\exp(\beta_{k,m|n})$, holding all other variables constant.

When δ is the standard deviation of x_k, the *x-standardized odds ratio* can be interpreted as:

- For a standard deviation change in x_k, the odds are expected to change by a factor of $\exp(\beta_{k,m|n} \times s_k)$, holding all other variables constant.

Very importantly, the factor change in the odds for a change in x_k does not depend on the level of x_k or on the level of any other variable.

While the interpretation of each odds ratio is simple, the number of comparisons makes the task difficult. To appreciate the problem, con-

TABLE 6.5 Factor Change in the Odds for Being White

				Outcome n			
Factor Change in the Odds of m vs. n			M	B	C	W	P
Outcome m	M	Menial	—	0.29	0.62	0.21	0.17
	B	Blue Collar	3.44	—	2.15	0.72	0.58
	C	Craft	1.60	0.47	—	0.33	0.27
	W	White collar	4.81	1.40	3.00	—	0.82
	P	Professional	5.90	1.71	3.68	1.22	—

NOTE: The coefficients in the table are $\exp(\hat{\beta}_{1,\,m\,|\,n})$. Jobs are classified as: M = menial; C = craft; B = blue collar; W = white collar; and P = professional.

sider the coefficients for the effect of race on occupational attainment in Table 6.5. (The coefficients in the first column are the exponential of coefficients in Table 6.2.) For example:

- The odds of having a professional occupation relative to a menial occupation are 5.9 times greater for whites than for blacks, holding education and experience constant.

If interest is in other comparisons, say craft compared to blue-collar occupations, these coefficients are computed by using Equation 6.8 and then taking the exponential. (*Use the methods from Section 6.4 and the estimates in Table 6.2 to verify the values in Table 6.5.*)

Even though coefficients for comparisons among all pairs of outcomes provide a great deal of redundant information, such comparisons may be substantively useful. However, even for a single variable with only five dependent outcomes, there is a lot of information to evaluate. (*Spend some time describing the relationship between race and occupation. Even if you do not arrive at a satisfactory description, the attempt will make what follows clearer.*)

6.6.5. Plotting the Coefficients

While examining all possible comparisons is useful for understanding the factors affecting nominal outcomes, the large number of coefficients makes it difficult to see patterns in the results. If you also keep track of which coefficients are statistically significant, the difficulty increases. An *odds ratio plot* makes it simple to find patterns among the coefficients (Long, 1987).

To explain how to graph the coefficients, I begin with a binary logit. Assume that there are outcomes A and B with four independent variables x_1 through x_4. The hypothetical coefficients for the model are shown in Table 6.6, where p is the significance level for a two-tailed test. The column $\exp(\beta_{B|A})$ shows that for a unit increase in x_1 the odds of B relative to A are cut in half; x_2 has no effect on the odds; x_3 increases the odds by a factor of $\sqrt{2}$ ($= 1.414$); and x_4 doubles the odds. The strength of the effects of x_1 and x_4 are equal, but in opposite directions (i.e., $2 = 1/.5$). The effect of x_3 is half as strong as that of x_4 in the sense that a two-unit increase in x_3 has the same effect on the odds as a one unit increase in x_4 (i.e., $\sqrt{2} \times \sqrt{2} = 2$).

To plot these coefficients, think of the magnitude of the odds ratio $\exp(\beta_{B|A})$ as the distance between A and B. The larger the odds ratio, the greater the distance. If an increase in x_k increases the odds of A over B, then A would be plotted to the right of B and vice versa. Figure 6.2 plots the coefficients from Table 6.6. At the bottom is a scale in the units of the original β's. The β's are plotted relative to category A. Consider x_1. Category A is located at 0 on the bottom scale to indicate that a change in x_1 does not change the logit of A relative to A (obviously). Category B is located at $-.69$, indicating that a unit increase in x_1 decreases the logit of B versus A by .69. While the coefficients are plotted relative to outcome A, they could have been plotted relative to outcome B.

Since our interest is in the factor change in the odds, a factor change scale is printed at the top of the figure. This is a logarithmic scale with each value equal to the exponential of the value on the bottom scale. For example, the B for x_1 is located at $.5 = \exp(-.69)$, indicating that a unit change in x_1 decreases the odds by a factor of .5. The remaining coefficients are plotted in the same way.

TABLE 6.6 Logit Coefficients From a
Hypothetical Binary Logit Model

x	$\beta_{B|A}$	$\exp(\beta_{B|A})$	p
x_1	-0.693	0.500	0.02
x_2	0.000	1.000	0.99
x_3	0.347	1.414	0.11
x_4	0.693	2.000	0.04

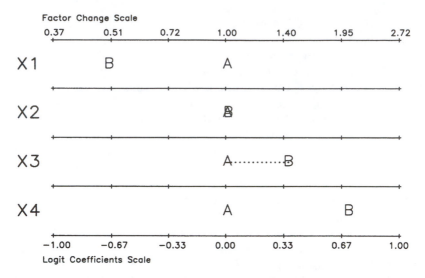

Figure 6.2. Odds Ratio Plot for a Hypothetical Binary Logit Model

The relative magnitudes of the effects for each variable are shown by the distance between A and B. The effects of x_1 and x_4 are of equal but opposite magnitude, which is indicated by the distance from A to B being the same for both variables. The magnitude of the effect of x_4 is twice that of x_3, which is indicated by the distance being half as large for x_3. The effect of x_2 is 0, which is indicated by A being placed on top of B.

The *lack* of statistical significance is shown by a connecting line. The intuition is that if a coefficient is not statistically significant, then the variable does not differentiate the two outcomes, and so those outcomes are linked. This is indicated on the graph by "$A \cdots B$" for x_3.

There is little gain from plotting coefficients for two outcomes. However, with three or more outcomes, plotting is useful for grasping the overall pattern of relationships between an independent variable and the odds among all pairs of outcomes. Consider a hypothetical model with three outcomes: A, B, and C. The logit coefficients are given in Table 6.7. The variables x_1 and x_2 have equal but opposite effects on the odds of outcome B versus A, with the effect of x_3 being half as large. That is, a two-unit increase in x_3 has the same effect on the odds of B versus A as a one-unit change in x_2. x_1 and x_2 also have equal and opposite effects on C versus A, with magnitudes that are half as large as those for the odds of B versus A. The effects on outcome C versus

TABLE 6.7 Logit Coefficients for a Hypothetical Multinomial Logit Model

Comparison		*Logit Coefficient for*		
		x_1	x_2	x_3
$B \mid A$	$\beta_{B \mid A}$	−0.693	0.693	0.347
	$\exp(\beta_{B \mid A})$	0.500	2.000	1.414
	p	0.04	0.01	0.42
$C \mid A$	$\beta_{C \mid A}$	0.347	−0.347	0.693
	$\exp(\beta_{C \mid A})$	1.414	0.707	2.000
	p	0.21	0.04	0.37
$C \mid B$	$\beta_{C \mid B}$	1.040	−1.040	0.346
	$\exp(\beta_{C \mid B})$	2.828	0.354	1.414
	p	0.02	0.03	0.21

NOTE: β is a logit coefficient; $\exp(\beta)$ is a factor change; p is a significance level.

B can be examined in a similar way. Even with this simple example, it is difficult to keep track of all of the comparisons.

Figure 6.3 plots these coefficients relative to category A, which is located on the factor change scale at 1. The plot makes it immediately clear that x_1 and x_2 have equal but opposite effects: increasing x_1 by 1 has the same effect as decreasing x_2 by 1. We also see that x_3 has a larger effect on A versus C, but smaller effects on A versus B and B versus C. To add links among outcomes that are not significantly affected by a variable, I have expanded the vertical spacing for the letters. This spacing is needed so that connecting lines can be seen and has no substantive meaning. Adding significance levels shows, for example, that x_3 does not significantly differentiate among any of the outcomes. You should take some time to study this figure to make sure that you see how it represents all of the information in Table 6.7.

Figure 6.3 shows the coefficients relative to category A, which is why the A's are located at 0 on the logit scale and 1 on the factor scale. The information could also be plotted relative to either category B or C. Plotting the information relative to outcome B would shift the plots for each variable so that they are located with B at 0 on the bottom scale. For x_1, this would require moving all letters to the right by .69 units. The relative positions would remain the same. (*Plot the coefficients relative to category C. Convince yourself that the information is unchanged.*)

To more fully appreciate how plotting the factor change coefficients can help you interpret the results, I use these plots with our model of

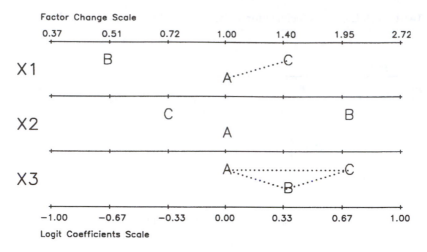

Figure 6.3. Odds Ratio Plot of Coefficients for a Hypothetical Multinomial Logit Model With Three Outcomes

occupational attainment and the model of attitudes toward working mothers from Chapter 5.

Example of the Odds Ratio Plot: Occupational Attainment

The coefficients for the MNLM for occupational attainment were given in Table 6.2 and are plotted in Figure 6.4. Race orders the occupations from menial to craft to blue collar to white collar to professional. The dotted lines show that none of the adjacent categories is significantly differentiated by race. For example, being white increases the odds of being a craft worker relative to having a menial job, but the effect is not significant. Occupations that are farther apart are significantly affected by race. Being white significantly increases the odds of being a blue-collar worker, a white-collar worker, or a professional relative to having a menial job.

x-standardized coefficients have been plotted for education and experience. Overall, the effect of a standard deviation change in education is larger than the effect of race, as indicated by the greater spread in the plot. While white-collar versus professional jobs are not differentiated by race, there is a strong and significant effect of education, as would be expected given the educational requirements of professional jobs. Education also significantly differentiates white-collar jobs from menial, craft, and blue-collar jobs. Craft, menial, and blue-collar jobs themselves are

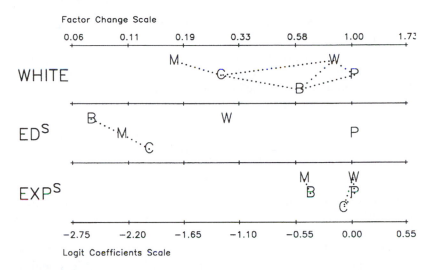

Figure 6.4. Odds Ratio Plot for a Multinomial Logit Model of Occupational Attainment. Jobs Are Classified as: M = Menial; C = Craft; B = Blue Collar; W = White Collar; and P = Professional

not strongly differentiated by education. The effects of experience are much weaker than those of either race or education. Experience splits jobs into two groups. Increasing experience increases the odds of white-collar, craft, and professional jobs relative to menial and blue-collar jobs.

In comparing the effects of the variables on the various outcomes, it is important to note the different ordering of categories for the different variables. If an ordered logit model had been used, this change in ordering would have been lost.

The Importance of the Predicted Probability

When using an odds ratio plot, it is essential to understand that the substantive meaning of a factor change of a given magnitude is dependent on the predicted probability or odds. See Chapter 3 (p. 82) for a detailed discussion of this point. For example, if the odds increase by a factor of 10 but the current odds are 1 in 10,000, then the substantive impact is small. Consequently, the odds ratio plot must be interpreted while keeping in mind the base probabilities and the discrete changes in the probabilities. The plot can be modified to incorporate this information by making the height of the letters in the odds ratio plot proportional to the square root of the discrete change in the odds. The square root is used since letters are approximately square, and thus the area of the letters is proportional to the magnitude of the discrete change. While I think that adding information on the discrete change in probabilities is valuable for understanding the complex results of a MNLM, you must keep in mind that the information indicated by the size of the letters is contingent upon the values at which the discrete change is assessed. *While the factor change in the odds is constant across the levels of all variables, the discrete change becomes larger or smaller at different values of the variables.*

An example of an *enhanced odds ratio plot* is shown in Figure 6.5, which should be compared to Figures 6.1 and 6.4. Consider the results for education. The odds ratio for *M* versus *W* is about the same as the odds ratio for *W* versus *P*. This is shown by the letters being approximately the same distance apart. However, as education increases, with all variables held at their means, the probability of being a professional increases much more than the probability of either white-collar or menial professions.

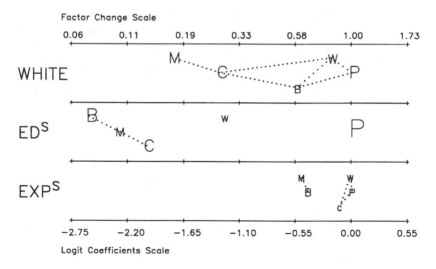

Figure 6.5. Enhanced Odds Ratio Plot With the Size of Letters Corresponding to Magnitude of the Discrete Change in the Probability. Discrete Changes Are Computed With All Variables Held at Their Means. Jobs Are Classified as: *M* = Menial; *C* = Craft; *B* = Blue Collar; *W* = White Collar; and *P* = Professional

Example of the Odds Ratio Plot: Attitudes Toward Working Mothers

In Chapter 5, we examined responses to the question of whether a working mother could have as warm a relationship with her child as a mother who does not work. The ordered response categories were: 1 = strongly disagree; 2 = disagree; 3 = agree; and 4 = strongly agree, where the larger values reflect stronger agreement. Here, the question is reanalyzed with the MNLM. While the respondent's race and prestige were included in the model, their effects are weaker than those of the other variables and are not discussed.

Figure 6.6 shows the odds ratios with the size of the numbers within the plot corresponding to the size of the discrete change in probabilities when variables are held at their means. In 1989 relative to 1977, the odds of all outcomes were significantly more likely relative to strongly disagreeing. The effects of the year of the survey on the odds among all categories arrange the outcomes as would be expected with an ordinal variable. Being a woman has the strongest effect on differentiating between strongly agreeing and all other categories, and has a significant effect on differentiating the positive categories from disagreeing. Age divides attitudes into those that are positive and those that are negative, with no significant effects within the two groups. Education has a weaker effect, although it significantly increases the odds of any category relative to strongly disagreeing.

In this example, the ordinal rankings have been maintained for all variables, except where there are no significant differences between adjacent categories. This does not mean that the results are equivalent to those for the ordered regression model. By using the MNLM, we have eliminated the parallel regression restriction that forced the effect of each independent variable to be the same regardless of the outcome category.

Conclusions on Interpreting the Multinomial Logit Model

While the interpretation of the multinomial logit model is complicated when there are more than a few outcome categories, the graphical methods presented in this section can be used to uncover the complex patterns of effects. In some applications, these plots reveal patterns that can be described easily in a few sentences, and there is little need to present the graphs. In other cases, the patterns are complex, and the plots themselves need to be included as part of your description of the results.

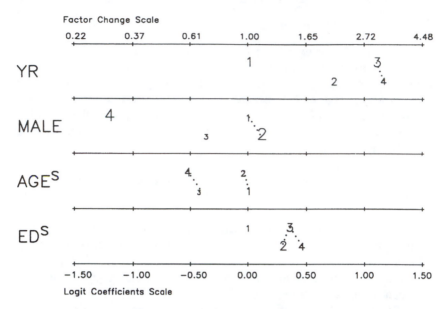

Figure 6.6. Enhanced Odds Ratio Plot for the Multinomial Logit Model of Attitudes Toward Working Mothers. Discrete Changes Were Computed With All Variables Held at Their Means. Categories Are: 1 = Strongly Disagree; 2 = Disagree; 3 = Agree; and 4 = Strongly Agree

6.7. The Conditional Logit Model

In the MNLM, each explanatory variable has a different effect on each outcome. For example, the effect of x_k on outcome m is β_{km}, while the effect on outcome n is β_{kn}. The conditional logit model (CLM), sometimes referred to as the Luce model or (confusingly) the multinomial logit model, is a closely related model in which the *coefficients* for a variable are the same for each outcome, but the *values of the variables* differ for each outcome. For example, if we are trying to explain a commuter's choice of transportation among the options of train, bus, and private automobile, we might consider the amount of time or the cost per trip for each option. The *effect* of time would be the same for each mode of travel, but the *amount* of time would differ by the mode of transportation.

The CLM was developed by McFadden and others, largely within the context of research on travel demand. McFadden (1968) used the model to study criteria used by a state highway department to select urban freeway routes. Boskin (1974) examined occupational choice using characteristics of the occupations. A consumer's choice of transportation for a shopping trip was studied by Domencich and McFadden (1975). Hausman and McFadden (1984) analyzed the choice between an electric dryer, gas dryer, and no dryer. Hoffman and Duncan (1988) compared the MNLM and the CLM with specific attention to applications in demography.

In the CLM, the predicted probability is

$$\Pr(y_i = m \mid z_i) = \frac{\exp(z_{im}\gamma)}{\sum_{j=1}^{J} \exp(z_{ij}\gamma)} \qquad [6.14]$$

which should be compared to the MNLM:

$$\Pr(y_i = m \mid x_i) = \frac{\exp(x_i\beta_m)}{\sum_{j=1}^{J} \exp(x_i\beta_j)} \quad \text{where } \beta_1 = 0 \qquad [6.15]$$

In Equation 6.15, there are $J-1$ parameters β_{km} for each x_k, but only a single value of x_k for each individual. In Equation 6.14, there is a single γ_k for each variable z_k, but there are J values of the variable for each individual.

An example of how the data are constructed for the CLM is useful for understanding the model. Assume there is a single independent variable z and three outcomes. For four individuals, the data might look as follows:

i	Outcome m	Outcome Chosen	Variable z_{im}
1	1	0	$z_{11} = 1$
1	2	1	$z_{12} = 7$
1	3	0	$z_{13} = 3$
2	1	1	$z_{21} = 5$
2	2	0	$z_{22} = 1$
2	3	0	$z_{23} = 2$
3	1	1	$z_{31} = 3$
3	2	0	$z_{32} = 0$
3	3	0	$z_{33} = 1$
4	1	0	$z_{41} = 3$
4	2	0	$z_{42} = 2$
4	3	1	$z_{43} = 7$

For each individual, there are three observations corresponding to the three possible outcomes. The differences in the values of z for the different outcomes determine the probabilities of various choices. To reflect this, I have listed specific values of z such that the largest value of z is associated with the outcome that is chosen by the individual.

The models can also be compared in terms of the odds form of the model. In the CLM, the odds change according to the difference in the values of the z's associated with the two outcomes:

$$\Omega_{m|n}(\mathbf{z}_i) = \exp([\mathbf{z}_{im} - \mathbf{z}_{in}]\boldsymbol{\gamma})$$

In the MNLM, the odds change according to the difference in the coefficients for the two outcomes:

$$\Omega_{m|n}(\mathbf{x}_i) = \exp(\mathbf{x}_i[\boldsymbol{\beta}_m - \boldsymbol{\beta}_n])$$

Boskin's (1974) application of the CLM to occupational attainment provides a useful comparison to our application using the MNLM. In the MNLM we examined how race, education, and experience affected the odds of different occupations. For a given individual, the values of the regressors were the same for all outcomes. For example, a person's race did not change with the choice of an occupation. In Boskin's CLM, the independent variables were the expected costs and benefits for each occupation. For example, for each person he computed the present value of full-time employment (i.e., the expected wages in that occupation times the expected number of hours the person will work in the future) for each occupation. The effect of the present value is the same for each occupation, but the present value itself differs by occupation. For a given individual, the present value of a professional occupation will exceed the present value of a menial occupation, thus making a professional occupation more likely, all else being equal.

The conditional and multinomial logit models reflect different aspects of the processes by which individuals attain occupations. I suspect that at some point the most useful models for the analysis of nominal outcomes will combine characteristics of the multinomial and conditional logit models. To see how these models can be combined, we can take advantage of the algebraic equivalence of the CLM and the MNLM (Maddala, 1983, p. 42). To illustrate this equivalence, consider a MNLM with a single independent variable and three dependent categories. Then

$$\Pr(y_i = 1 \mid \mathbf{x}_i) = \frac{1}{1 + \exp(\beta_{20} + \beta_{21}x_{i1}) + \exp(\beta_{30} + \beta_{31}x_{i1})}$$

$$\Pr(y_i = 2 \mid \mathbf{x}_i) = \frac{\exp(\beta_{20} + \beta_{21}x_{i1})}{1 + \exp(\beta_{20} + \beta_{21}x_{i1}) + \exp(\beta_{30} + \beta_{31}x_{i1})}$$

$$\Pr(y_i = 3 \mid \mathbf{x}_i) = \frac{\exp(\beta_{30} + \beta_{31}x_{i1})}{1 + \exp(\beta_{20} + \beta_{21}x_{i1}) + \exp(\beta_{30} + \beta_{31}x_{i1})}$$

To transform this into the CLM, we construct $\mathbf{z}$ vectors with four elements:

$$\mathbf{z}_{i1} = (z_{i11}\ z_{i12}\ z_{i13}\ z_{i14}) = (0\ 0\ 0\ 0)$$

$$\mathbf{z}_{i2} = (z_{i21}\ z_{i22}\ z_{i23}\ z_{i24}) = (1\ x_{i1}\ 0\ 0)$$

$$\mathbf{z}_{i3} = (z_{i31}\ z_{i32}\ z_{i33}\ z_{i34}) = (0\ 0\ 1\ x_{i1})$$

The first subscript for z is the observation number; the second is the outcome (either 1, 2, or 3), and the third is the variable number 1 through 4. $\mathbf{z}_{i1}$ is a vector of 0's for all observations, which corresponds to the constraint that $\boldsymbol{\beta}_1 = \mathbf{0}$. Within $\mathbf{z}_2$, the first elements is always 1, the second is x_i, and the last two elements are always 0. Within $\mathbf{z}_3$, the first two elements are always 0, the third is always 1, and the last is x. To see how this construction of the $\mathbf{z}$'s leads to the MNLM, define $\boldsymbol{\gamma} = (\beta_{20}\ \beta_{21}\ \beta_{30}\ \beta_{31})'$. Then

$$\mathbf{z}_{i1}\boldsymbol{\gamma} = (0 \times \beta_{20}) + (0 \times \beta_{21}) + (0 \times \beta_{30}) + (0 \times \beta_{31}) = 0$$

$$\mathbf{z}_{i2}\boldsymbol{\gamma} = (1 \times \beta_{20}) + (x_{i1} \times \beta_{21}) + (0 \times \beta_{30}) + (0 \times \beta_{31})$$

$$= \beta_{20} + \beta_{21}x_{i1}$$

$$\mathbf{z}_{i3}\boldsymbol{\gamma} = (0 \times \beta_{20}) + (0 \times \beta_{21}) + (1 \times \beta_{30}) + (x_{i1} \times \beta_{31})$$

$$= \beta_{30} + \beta_{31}x_{i1}$$

Substituting into the equations for the CLM,

$$\Pr(y_i = 1 \mid \mathbf{z}_i) = \frac{\exp(\mathbf{z}_{i1}\boldsymbol{\gamma})}{\sum_{j=1}^{J} \exp(\mathbf{z}_{ij}\boldsymbol{\gamma})}$$

$$= \frac{1}{1 + \exp(\beta_{20} + \beta_{21}x_{i1}) + \exp(\beta_{30} + \beta_{31}x_{i1})}$$

$$\Pr(y_i = 2 \mid \mathbf{z}_i) = \frac{\exp(\mathbf{z}_{i2}\boldsymbol{\gamma})}{\sum_{j=1}^{J} \exp(\mathbf{z}_{ij}\boldsymbol{\gamma})}$$

$$= \frac{\exp(\beta_{20} + \beta_{21}x_{i1})}{1 + \exp(\beta_{20} + \beta_{21}x_{i1}) + \exp(\beta_{30} + \beta_{31}x_{i1})}$$

$$\Pr(y_i = 3 \mid \mathbf{z}_i) = \frac{\exp(\mathbf{z}_{i3}\boldsymbol{\gamma})}{\sum_{j=1}^{J} \exp(\mathbf{z}_{ij}\boldsymbol{\gamma})}$$

$$= \frac{\exp(\beta_{30} + \beta_{31}x_{i1})}{1 + \exp(\beta_{20} + \beta_{21}x_{i1}) + \exp(\beta_{30} + \beta_{31}x_{i1})}$$

which is the MNLM.

This approach can be used to expand the $\mathbf{z}$ and $\boldsymbol{\gamma}$ matrices to include variables from a standard CLM. The resulting joint model has characteristics of both the multinomial and conditional logit models. See Cramer (1991, p. 70) for further details

While the conditional logit model is substantively quite appealing, its application has been limited outside of economics by a lack of familiarity and a failure to collect the type of data necessary for the conditional logit model. As researchers become more familiar with this model, its use should increase.

6.7.1. Software Issues

Stata and LIMDEP are the only commercially available software that I know of that estimates the CLM.

6.8. Independence of Irrelevant Alternatives

In the multinomial logit model, the equation for the odds of m versus n is

$$\frac{Pr(y = m \mid \mathbf{x})}{Pr(y = n \mid \mathbf{x})} = \exp(\mathbf{x}[\boldsymbol{\beta}_m - \boldsymbol{\beta}_n])$$

while in the conditional logit model, the odds equation is

$$\frac{Pr(y = m \mid \mathbf{z})}{Pr(y = n \mid \mathbf{z})} = \exp([\mathbf{z}_m - \mathbf{z}_n]\boldsymbol{\gamma})$$

In both equations, the odds are determined without reference to the other outcomes that might be available. This is known as the *independence of irrelevant alternatives* property or simply IIA. While this may appear to be an obscure mathematical detail, it has important practical implications which can be illustrated with the famous red bus/blue bus example that has been attributed to McFadden.

A person has two choices for commuting to work: a private car that is chosen with $Pr(car) = 1/2$ and a *red* bus with $Pr(red\ bus) = 1/2$. The implied odds of taking the car versus the red bus are $1 = (1/2)/(1/2)$. Suppose that a new bus company is started that is identical to the current service except that the buses are blue. IIA requires that the new probabilities are: Pr(car) = 1/3; Pr(red bus) = 1/3; and Pr(blue bus) = 1/3. This is necessary so that the odds of a car versus a red bus remain at $1 = (1/3)/(1/3)$. However, if the only thing to distinguish the new bus service from the old is the color of the bus, we would not expect car travelers to start taking the bus. Instead, the share of red bus riders would be split, resulting in: Pr(car) = 1/2; Pr(red bus) = 1/4; and Pr(blue bus) = 1/4. The new, implied odds for car versus red bus are $2 = (1/2)/(1/4)$, which violates the IIA assumption. The IIA assumption requires that if a new alternative becomes available, then all probabilities for the prior choices must adjust in *precisely* the amount necessary to retain the original odds among all pairs of outcomes. Thus, the probability of driving a car can be made arbitrarily small by adding enough different colors of buses!

The independence of irrelevant alternatives is an important and restrictive assumption. McFadden (1973) suggested that IIA implies that the multinomial and conditional logit models should only be used in cases where the outcome categories "can plausibly be assumed to be distinct and weighed independently in the eyes of each decision maker." Similarly, Amemiya (1981, p. 1517) suggests that the MNLM works well when the alternatives are dissimilar. Care in specifying the model to involve distinct outcomes that are not substitutes for one another seems to be reasonable, albeit unfortunately ambiguous, advice. A formal test provides evidence of whether IIA is violated.

6.8.1. Testing IIA

Hausman and McFadden (1984) proposed a Hausman-type test of the IIA property. A Hausman test is based on the comparison of two estimators of the same parameters. One estimator is consistent and efficient if the null hypothesis is true, while the second estimator is consistent but inefficient. For both the MNLM and the CLM, the ML estimator is consistent and efficient if the model is correctly specified. A consistent but inefficient estimator is obtained by estimating the model on a restricted set of outcomes (Ben-Akiva & Lerman, 1985, p. 184). If other alternatives are irrelevant in computing the odds for two outcomes, then omitting those alternatives should not affect the estimates of the parameters that affect the two outcomes. For example, you could estimate the coefficients in a three-category MNLM with categories A, B, and C by estimating the two binary logits comparing A to C and B to C. Since these estimators do not use all of the data simultaneously, they would not be efficient.

While the Hausman test of IIA is not included in existing software, it can be computed in programs that have a matrix language. The following steps are necessary:

1. Estimate the full model with all J outcomes included. Stack the estimates $\widehat{\beta}_{jF}$ in the vector $\widehat{\beta}_F = (\widehat{\beta}'_{2F} \cdots \widehat{\beta}'_{JF})'$ with covariance matrix $\widehat{\text{Var}}(\widehat{\beta}_F)$.
2. Estimate a restricted model by eliminating one or more outcome categories. In the MNLM, this requires deleting sample members who selected the deleted categories. For simplicity, assume that category J is deleted. Stack the resulting estimates $\widehat{\beta}_{jR}$ in the vector $\widehat{\beta}_R = (\widehat{\beta}'_{2R} \cdots \widehat{\beta}'_{J-1,R})'$ with covariance matrix $\widehat{\text{Var}}(\widehat{\beta}_R)$.
3. In the CLM, $\widehat{\beta}_F$ and $\widehat{\beta}_R$ have the same dimension, while in the MNLM $\widehat{\beta}_F$ is larger due to the inclusion of $\widehat{\beta}_{JF}$. If $\widehat{\beta}_F$ and $\widehat{\beta}_R$ have different dimensions, create a new vector by eliminating $\widehat{\beta}_{JF}$: $\widehat{\beta}_F^* = (\widehat{\beta}'_{2F} \cdots \widehat{\beta}'_{J-1,F})'$ with covariance matrix $\widehat{\text{Var}}(\widehat{\beta}_F^*)$. Otherwise, $\widehat{\beta}_F^* = \widehat{\beta}_F$.
4. The Hausman test of IIA is defined as:

$$H_{\text{IIA}} = (\widehat{\beta}_R - \widehat{\beta}_F^*)'[\widehat{\text{Var}}(\widehat{\beta}_R) - \widehat{\text{Var}}(\widehat{\beta}_F^*)]^{-1}(\widehat{\beta}_R - \widehat{\beta}_F^*)$$

which is asymptotically distributed as chi-square with degrees of freedom equal to the rows in $\widehat{\beta}_R$ if IIA is true. Significant values of H_{IIA} indicate that the IIA assumption has been violated.

Hausman and McFadden (1984, p. 1226) note that H_{IIA} can be negative when $\widehat{\text{Var}}(\widehat{\beta}_R) - \widehat{\text{Var}}(\widehat{\beta}_F^*)$ is not positive semidefinite. They examine an alternative estimator of $\widehat{\text{Var}}(\widehat{\beta}_R)$ to ensure that the difference is positive definite, and conclude that a negative H_{IIA} is evidence that IIA holds.

McFadden, et. al. (1977) proposed an approximate likelihood ratio test of IIA that was improved by Small and Hsiao (1985). Zhang and Hoffman (1993) present details on applying the test with current software.

6.9. Related Models

There are several related models that should be mentioned.

The Multinomial Probit Model. The *multinomial probit model* can be derived by assuming that the errors in the discrete choice model are normally distributed. This model was proposed by Aitchison and Bennett (1970) and has been applied with three outcome categories by Hausman and Wise (1978). A significant advantage of the multinomial probit model is that the errors can be correlated across choices, which eliminates the IIA restriction. This is possible since it is simple to incorporate correlations among errors in a multivariate normal distribution. Unfortunately, the computational burden of computing multidimensional normal integrals makes the model impractical. McFadden (1989) has made progress in solving the computational problems.

The Stereotype Model. The *stereotype model* was proposed by Anderson (1984) in response to the restrictive assumption of parallel regressions in the ordered regression model. The stereotype model begins with the MNLM and adds the constraint that $\boldsymbol{\beta}_m = \phi_m \boldsymbol{\beta}$. This results in the model $\Pr(y = m \mid \mathbf{x}) = \exp(\mathbf{x}\boldsymbol{\beta}\phi_m)/\sum_{j=1}^{J} \exp(\mathbf{x}\boldsymbol{\beta}\phi_j)$. The ordinality of the outcomes is ensured by the added constraints that $\phi_1 = 1 > \phi_2 > \cdots > \phi_{J-1} > \phi_J = 0$. There is no software specifically to estimate the stereotype model. DiPrete (1990) used a general ML program in GAUSS. The model can be informally assessed by examining the parameters from the MNLM to see if the structure of the stereotype model is approximated. This approach was taken by Greenwood and Farewell (1988).

The Nested Logit Model. The *nested logit model* divides the choices into a hierarchy of levels and thus avoids the IIA property. References are: Amemiya (1981, 1985, pp. 300–307), Cramer (1991, pp. 79–82), Greene (1995, Chapters 24 and 25), Maddala (1983, pp. 67–76), and McFadden (1981, p. 238).

Models for Ranked Data. Models for ranked data are also similar to the MNLM. Rank data occurs when an individual ranks preferences from a set of choices. For example, a person might indicate the rank order of preference for three candidates running for office. References include: Allison and Christakis (1994), Beggs, et al. (1981), and Hausman and Ruud (1987).

6.10. Conclusions

The multinomial logit model is extremely useful for the analysis of nominal and ordinal variables. While the model is simple to estimate, interpretation is complicated by the large number of parameters involved. However, the graphical methods of interpretation presented in this chapter can be applied effectively even with a large number of independent variables and dependent categories.

6.11. Bibliographic Notes

A special case of the MNLM was presented by Gurland et al. (1960). The multinomial logit model in the form commonly used in the social sciences was introduced by Theil (1969, 1970). The more general conditional logit model was developed by McFadden (1973), whose derivation was related to work by experimental psychologists such as Luce (1959). Aitchison and Silvey (1957) and Aitchison and Bennett (1970) were the first to present the multinomial probit model, whose origin can be traced to the work of Thurstone (1927). The model was derived from the assumptions of rational choice theory by McFadden (1973). Nerlove and Press (1973) published a short monograph that made an important contribution by including Fortran programs for estimating the multinomial logit model.

7

Limited Outcomes: The Tobit Model

In the linear regression model, the values of all variables are known for the entire sample. This chapter considers the situation in which the sample is limited by censoring or truncation. *Censoring* occurs when we observe the independent variables for the entire sample, but for some observations we have only limited information about the dependent variable. For example, we might know that the dependent variable is less than 100, but not know how much less. *Truncation* limits the data more severely by excluding observations based on characteristics of the dependent variable. For example, in a truncated sample all *cases* where the dependent variable is less than 100 would be deleted. While truncation changes the sample, censoring does not.

The classic example of censoring is Tobin's (1958) study of household expenditures. A consumer maximizes utility by purchasing durable goods under the constraint that total expenditures do not exceed income. Expenditures for durable goods must at least equal the cost of the least expensive item. If a consumer has only $50 left after other expenses and the least expensive item costs $100, the consumer can spend nothing on durable goods. The outcome is censored since we do not know how much a household would have spent if a durable good could be purchased for less than $100. Many other examples of censored outcomes

187

can be found: hours worked by wives (Quester & Greene, 1982), scientific publications (Stephan & Levin, 1992), extramarital affairs (Fair, 1978), foreign trade and investment (Eaton & Tamura, 1994), austerity protests in Third World countries (Walton & Ragin, 1990), damage caused by a hurricane (Fronstin & Holtmann, 1994), and IRA contributions (LeClere, 1994). Amemiya (1985, p. 365) lists many additional examples.

Hausman and Wise's (1977) analysis of the New Jersey Negative Income Tax Experiment is an early application of models for truncated data. In this study, families with incomes more than 1.5 times the poverty level were excluded from the sample. Thus, the sample itself is affected and is no longer representative of the population.

Many models have been developed for censoring and truncation. This chapter focuses on the most frequently used model for censoring, the tobit model. Section 7.6 briefly reviews related models for truncation, multiple censoring, and sample selection.

7.1. The Problem of Censoring

Let y^* be a dependent variable that is *not* censored. Panel A of Figure 7.1 shows the distribution of y^*, where the height of the curve indicates the relative frequency of a given value of y^*. If we do not know the value of y^* when $y^* \leq 1$, corresponding to the shaded region, then y^* is a *latent* variable that cannot be observed over its entire range. The *censored* variable y is defined as

$$y_i = \begin{cases} y_i^* & \text{if } y_i^* > 1 \\ 0 & \text{if } y^* \leq 1 \end{cases}$$

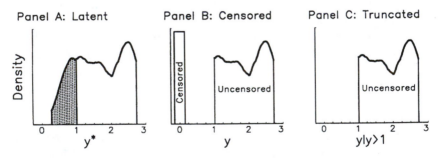

Figure 7.1. Latent, Censored, and Truncated Variables

Panel B plots the censored variable y with censored cases stacked at 0. The bar contains cases from the shaded region in panel A. Panel C plots the truncated variable $y \mid y > 1$ (i.e., y given that $y > 1$), which simply deletes the shaded region from panel A.

To see how censoring and truncation affect the LRM, consider the model $y^* = 1.2 + .08x + \varepsilon$, where all of the assumptions of the LRM apply, including the normality of the errors. Panel A of Figure 7.2 shows a sample of 200 with *no* censoring. The solid line is the OLS estimate $\widehat{y}^* = 1.18 + .08x$. If y^* were censored below at 1, we would know x for all observations, but observe y^* only for $y^* > 1$. In panel B, values of y^* at or below 1 are censored with $y = 0$ for censored cases. These are plotted with triangles. The three thick lines are the results of three approaches to estimation.

One way to estimate the parameters is with an OLS regression of y on x for all observations, with the censored data included as 0's. The resulting estimate $\widehat{y} = .95 + .11x$ is the long dashed line in panel B. The censored observations on the left pull down that end of the line, resulting in underestimates of the intercept and overestimates of the slope. This approach to censoring produces inconsistent estimates.

Since including censored observations causes problems, we might use OLS to estimate the regression after truncating the sample to exclude cases with a censored dependent variable. This changes the problem of censoring into the problem of a truncated sample. After deleting the cases at $y = 0$, the OLS estimate $\widehat{y} = 1.41 + .61x$ overestimates the intercept and underestimates the slope, as shown by the short dashed line. The uncensored observations at the left have pulled the line up, since those observations with large negative errors have been deleted. Truncation causes a correlation between x and ε which produces inconsistent estimates.

A third approach is to estimate the *tobit model*, sometimes referred to as the *censored regression model*. The tobit model uses all of the information, including information about the censoring, and provides consistent estimates of the parameters. ML estimates for the tobit model are shown by the solid line, which is indistinguishable from the estimates in panel A where there is no censoring.

Example of Censoring and Truncation: Prestige of the First Job

Chapter 2 used as an example the regression of the prestige of a scientist's first academic job. (See Table 2.1, p. 19, for a description of the

Panel A: Regression without Censoring

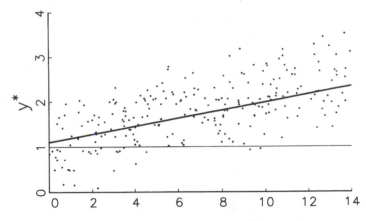

Panel B: Regression with Censoring and Truncation

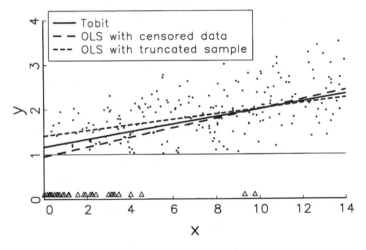

Figure 7.2. Linear Regression Model With and Without Censoring and Truncation

variables used.) The prestige of the job was unavailable for graduate programs rated below 1.0 and for departments without graduate programs. These cases were recoded to 1.0 and OLS was used to estimate the model. The estimates from Chapter 2 are reproduced in the column "OLS with Censored Data" in Table 7.1. Alternatively, we could trun-

TABLE 7.1 Censoring and Truncation in the Analysis of the Prestige of the First Academic Job

Variable		OLS with Censored Data	OLS with a Truncated Sample	Tobit Analysis
Constant	β	1.067	1.413	0.685
	t/z	6.42	8.71	3.15
FEM	β	−0.139	0.101	−0.237
	β^{S_y}	−0.143	0.130	−0.194
	t/z	−1.54	1.19	−2.05
PHD	β	0.273	0.297	0.323
	β^S	0.267	0.354	0.252
	t/z	5.53	6.36	5.08
MENT	β	0.001	0.001	0.001
	β^S	0.080	0.069	0.072
	t/z	1.69	1.27	1.52
FEL	β	0.234	0.141	0.325
	β^{S_y}	0.240	0.180	0.267
	t/z	2.47	1.57	2.68
ART	β	0.023	0.006	0.034
	β^S	0.053	0.018	0.028
	t/z	0.79	0.24	0.93
CIT	β	0.004	0.002	0.005
	β^S	0.152	0.098	0.138
	t/z	2.28	1.27	2.06
	N	408	309	408
	R^2	0.210	0.201	

NOTE: β is an unstandardized coefficient; β^S is a fully standardized coefficient; β^{S_y} is a y-standardized coefficient; t/z is a t- or z-test of β.

cate the sample by deleting the censored cases. The OLS estimates from the truncated sample are in the column "OLS with a Truncated Sample." Finally, tobit estimates are listed in the column "Tobit Analysis."

The most important difference between the results of the tobit analysis and the two OLS regressions concerns the effect of gender. In the tobit analysis, the effect of being a woman is significant and negative. In the regression with censored data, the effect is substantially smaller and not significant. In the truncated regression, the effect is positive, although not significant. Thus, a key substantive result is dependent on the method of analysis. Other differences in relative magnitude and level of significance are also found.

7.2. Truncated and Censored Distributions

Before formally considering the tobit model, we need some results about truncated and censored normal distributions. These distributions are at the foundation of most models for truncation and censoring. Results are given for censoring and truncation on the left, which translates into censoring from below in the tobit model. Corresponding formulas for censoring and truncation on the right, and both on the left and on the right are available. For more details, see Johnson et al. (1994, pp. 156–162) or Maddala (1983, pp. 365–368).

7.2.1. The Normal Distribution

To indicate that y^* is distributed normally with mean μ and variance σ^2, we write $y^* \sim \mathcal{N}(\mu, \sigma^2)$. y^* has the pdf:

$$f(y^* \mid \mu, \sigma) = \frac{1}{\sigma\sqrt{2\pi}} \exp\left[-\frac{1}{2}\left(\frac{y^* - \mu}{\sigma} \right)^2 \right]$$

which is plotted in panel A of Figure 7.3. The cdf is

$$F(y^* \mid \mu, \sigma) = \int_{-\infty}^{y^*} f(z \mid \mu, \sigma)dz = \Pr(Y^* \leq y^*)$$

so that

$$\Pr(Y^* > y^*) = 1 - F(y^* \mid \mu, \sigma)$$

$F(\tau \mid \mu, \sigma)$ is the shaded region in panel A and $1 - F(\tau \mid \mu, \sigma)$ is the region to the right of τ.

Panel A: Normal   Panel B: Truncated   Panel C: Censored

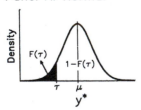  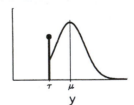

Figure 7.3. Normal Distribution With Truncation and Censoring

When $\mu = 0$ and $\sigma = 1$, the *standard normal distribution* is written in the simplified notation:

$$\phi(y^*) = f(y^* \mid \mu = 0, \sigma = 1)$$
$$\Phi(y^*) = F(y^* \mid \mu = 0, \sigma = 1)$$

Any normal distribution, regardless of its mean μ and variance σ^2, can be written as a function of the standard normal distribution. The pdf can be written as

$$f(y^* \mid \mu, \sigma) = \frac{1}{\sigma\sqrt{2\pi}} \exp\left[-\frac{1}{2}\left(\frac{y^* - \mu}{\sigma}\right)^2\right] = \frac{1}{\sigma} \phi\left(\frac{y^* - \mu}{\sigma}\right) \qquad [7.1]$$

and the cdf of y^* can be written as

$$\Pr(Y^* \leq y^*) = \Phi\left(\frac{y^* - \mu}{\sigma}\right) \qquad [7.2]$$

So that,

$$\Pr(Y^* > y^*) = 1 - \Phi\left(\frac{y^* - \mu}{\sigma}\right)$$

Since the standard normal distribution is symmetric with a mean of 0, two identities follow that are frequently used to simplify other formulas:

$$\phi(\delta) = \phi(-\delta)$$
$$\Phi(\delta) = 1 - \Phi(-\delta)$$

These results are often used to simplify the equations in this chapter. For example, Equations 7.1 and 7.2 can be written as

$$f(y^* \mid \mu, \sigma) = \frac{1}{\sigma} \phi\left(\frac{\mu - y^*}{\sigma}\right)$$

$$\Pr(Y^* > y^*) = \Phi\left(\frac{\mu - y^*}{\sigma}\right)$$

7.2.2. The Truncated Normal Distribution

When values below τ are deleted, the variable $y \mid y > \tau$ has a truncated normal distribution. In terms of panel A of Figure 7.3, we want to consider the distribution of y^* in the unshaded region, while ignoring all cases in the shaded region. The truncated pdf is created by dividing the pdf of the original distribution by the region to the right of τ. This forces the resulting distribution to have an area of 1:

$$f(y \mid y > \tau, \mu, \sigma) = \frac{f(y^* \mid \mu, \sigma)}{\Pr(Y^* > \tau)}$$

The truncated distribution is shown in panel B by the solid line. The mass of the shaded region has been distributed over the region to the right of τ, making the curve slightly higher over this region. This is seen by comparing the solid curve for the truncated distribution to the dotted line for the normal distribution without truncation. Using the results from Equations 7.1 and 7.2, we can write the truncated distribution as

$$f(y \mid y > \tau, \mu, \sigma) = \frac{\dfrac{1}{\sigma} \phi\left(\dfrac{y^* - \mu}{\sigma}\right)}{1 - \Phi\left(\dfrac{\tau - \mu}{\sigma}\right)} = \frac{\dfrac{1}{\sigma} \phi\left(\dfrac{\mu - y^*}{\sigma}\right)}{\Phi\left(\dfrac{\mu - \tau}{\sigma}\right)}$$

Given that the left-hand side of the distribution has been truncated, $E(y \mid y > \tau)$ must be larger than $E(y^*) = \mu$. Specifically, if y^* is normal (Johnson et al., 1994, p. 156),

$$E(y \mid y > \tau) = \mu + \sigma \frac{\phi\left(\dfrac{\mu - \tau}{\sigma}\right)}{\Phi\left(\dfrac{\mu - \tau}{\sigma}\right)} = \mu + \sigma \lambda\left(\dfrac{\mu - \tau}{\sigma}\right) \qquad [7.3]$$

where $\lambda(\cdot) = \phi(\cdot)/\Phi(\cdot)$ is the *inverse Mills ratio*.

The inverse Mills ratio is used so frequently in this chapter that it deserves a careful examination. Figure 7.4 plots λ and its components ϕ and Φ as a function of $(\mu - \tau)/\sigma$. The quantity $(\mu - \tau)/\sigma$ is the number of standard deviations that the mean μ is above or below the truncation point. For example, $(\mu - \tau)/\sigma = 2$ means that μ is 2 standard deviations larger than τ. In Figure 7.4, assume that the mean μ is fixed, and consider the effects of changing τ. At the left of the figure, τ exceeds μ and truncation is more extreme. ϕ is larger than Φ, generating values of λ greater than 1. Moving to the right, τ decreases, the amount of truncation decreases, and $(\mu - \tau)/\sigma$ increases. With this change, Φ increases and is eventually larger than ϕ, resulting in smaller values of λ that eventually approach 0. Equation 7.3 shows that as λ approaches 0, the expected value of the truncated variable approaches μ. That is, as

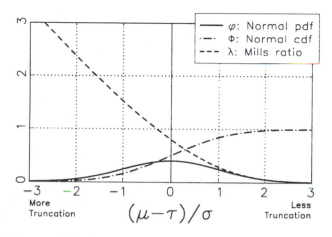

Figure 7.4. Inverse Mills Ratio

the area of truncation decreases, the effect of truncation on the mean approaches 0.

7.2.3. The Censored Normal Distribution

When a distribution is censored on the left, observations with values at or below τ are set to τ_y:

$$y = \begin{cases} y^* & \text{if } y^* > \tau \\ \tau_y & \text{if } y^* \leq \tau \end{cases}$$

Most often, $\tau_y = \tau$, but other values such as zero are also useful. Panel C of Figure 7.3 plots a censored normal variable, where the censored observations are indicated by the spike at $y = \tau$. From Equation 7.2, we know that if y^* is normal, then the probability of an observation being censored is

$$\Pr(\text{Censored}) = \Pr(y^* \leq \tau) = \Phi\left(\frac{\tau - \mu}{\sigma}\right)$$

and the probability of a case not being censored is

$$\Pr(\text{Uncensored}) = 1 - \Phi\left(\frac{\tau - \mu}{\sigma}\right) = \Phi\left(\frac{\mu - \tau}{\sigma}\right)$$

Thus, the expected value of a censored variable equals

$$E(y) = [\Pr(\text{Uncensored}) \times E(y \mid y > \tau)] \qquad [7.4]$$
$$+ [\Pr(\text{Censored}) \times E(y \mid y = \tau_y)]$$
$$= \left\{ \Phi\left(\frac{\mu - \tau}{\sigma}\right) \left[\mu + \sigma\lambda\left(\frac{\mu - \tau}{\sigma}\right) \right] \right\} + \Phi\left(\frac{\tau - \mu}{\sigma}\right) \tau_y$$

where the last equality uses Equation 7.3. Consider how the expected value of the censored value depends on τ. As τ approaches ∞, the probability of being censored approaches 1 and $E(y)$ approaches the censoring value τ_y. As τ approaches $-\infty$, the probability of being censored approaches 0 and $E(y)$ approaches the uncensored mean μ.

These results are now used to present the tobit model.

7.3. The Tobit Model for Censored Outcomes

For the tobit model, the structural equation is

$$y_i^* = \mathbf{x}_i\boldsymbol{\beta} + \varepsilon_i \qquad [7.5]$$

where $\varepsilon_i \sim \mathcal{N}(0, \sigma^2)$. The x's are observed for all cases. y^* is a latent variable that is observed for values greater than τ and is censored for values less than or equal to τ. The observed y is defined by the measurement equation:

$$y_i = \begin{cases} y_i^* & \text{if } y_i^* > \tau \\ \tau_y & \text{if } y^* \leq \tau \end{cases} \qquad [7.6]$$

Combining Equations 7.5 and 7.6,

$$y_i = \begin{cases} y_i^* = \mathbf{x}_i\boldsymbol{\beta} + \varepsilon_i & \text{if } y_i^* > \tau \\ \tau_y & \text{if } y_i^* \leq \tau \end{cases} \qquad [7.7]$$

The tobit model can also be used in situations where there is censoring from above. For example, if incomes over \$100,000 were combined into the category "over \$100,000," income would be censored from above and the tobit model would be

$$y_i = \begin{cases} y_i^* = \mathbf{x}_i\boldsymbol{\beta} + \varepsilon_i & \text{if } y_i^* < \tau \\ \tau_y & \text{if } y_i^* \geq \tau \end{cases}$$

Results for censoring from above are given in Section 7.6.1.

In this section, I present the implications of censoring in several steps. First, I show the effects of independent variables on the probability of censoring. Next, I demonstrate the problems associated with using OLS with censored data or a truncated sample. These problems lead to the ML estimator for the tobit model. Finally, I consider several methods for interpreting the parameters in the tobit model. Before proceeding, I want to consider a potential source of confusion.

7.3.1. The Distinction Between τ and τ_y

Many authors assume that $\tau = \tau_y = 0$ or that $\tau = \tau_y$. This results in formulas that are simpler than mine. Unfortunately, this simplification can lead to confusion and incorrect results since in applications it is often the case that $\tau \neq \tau_y \neq 0$. Consequently, I make the distinction between τ and τ_y explicit. *The threshold τ determines whether y^* is censored. τ_y is the value assigned to y if y^* is censored.* While τ_y is often equal to τ, this is not always appropriate. Consider Tobin's original application. The cost of the cheapest durable good (i.e., τ) is not \$0, but for censored cases it is most reasonable to code $y = \tau_y = 0$ since these people did not purchase any goods. In my formulas, you can substitute $\tau = \tau_y = 0$ or $\tau = \tau_y$ to obtain formulas that match those in other sources. However, if you use formulas that equate these quantities, it is *essential* that these restrictions apply to your data.

7.3.2. The Distribution of Censoring

The probability of being censored depends on the proportion of the distribution of y^*, or, equivalently, ε, that falls below τ. The distribution of y given x is shown in panel A of Figure 7.5. $E(y^* \mid x)$ is the solid line with the distribution of y^* shown at three values of x. For example, at x_1 a vertical line is drawn with a normal curve coming out of the page. Censoring occurs when observations fall at or below the line $y^* = \tau$, which is indicated by the shaded region of the distribution. As the value of x increases, $E(y^* \mid x)$ increases, causing the proportion of the distribution that is censored to decrease. Thus, the region labeled A is larger than B, which is larger than C.

The probability of a case being censored for a given $\mathbf{x}$ is the region of the normal curve less than or equal to τ:

$$\Pr(\text{Censored} \mid \mathbf{x}_i) = \Pr(y_i^* \leq \tau \mid \mathbf{x}_i) = \Pr(\varepsilon_i \leq \tau - \mathbf{x}_i\boldsymbol{\beta} \mid \mathbf{x}_i)$$

Panel A: Distribution of y* given x

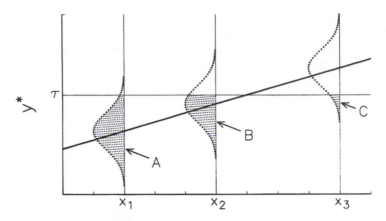

Panel B: Probability of Censoring

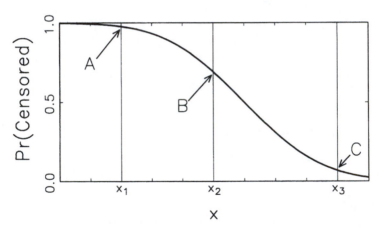

Figure 7.5. Probability of Being Censored in the Tobit Model

Since ε is distributed $\mathcal{N}(0, \sigma^2)$, ε/σ is distributed $\mathcal{N}(0, 1)$. Therefore,

$$\Pr(\text{Censored} \mid \mathbf{x}_i) = \Pr\left(\frac{\varepsilon_i}{\sigma} \leq \frac{\tau - \mathbf{x}_i\boldsymbol{\beta}}{\sigma} \,\middle|\, \mathbf{x}_i \right) = \Phi\left(\frac{\tau - \mathbf{x}_i\boldsymbol{\beta}}{\sigma} \right)$$

and

$$\Pr(\text{Uncensored} \mid \mathbf{x}_i) = 1 - \Phi\left(\frac{\tau - \mathbf{x}_i\boldsymbol{\beta}}{\sigma} \right) = \Phi\left(\frac{\mathbf{x}_i\boldsymbol{\beta} - \tau}{\sigma} \right)$$

To simplify the formulas that follow, let

$$\delta_i = \frac{\mathbf{x}_i\boldsymbol{\beta} - \tau}{\sigma}$$

δ is the number of standard deviations that $\mathbf{x}\boldsymbol{\beta}$ is above τ. (*How are $\phi(\delta)$ and $\phi(-\delta)$ related? $\Phi(\delta)$ and $\Phi(-\delta)$?*) Using this definition,

$$\Pr(\text{Censored} \,|\, \mathbf{x}_i) = \Phi(-\delta_i) \qquad [7.8]$$

$$\Pr(\text{Uncensored} \,|\, \mathbf{x}_i) = \Phi(\delta_i) \qquad [7.9]$$

Equation 7.8 is plotted in panel B of Figure 7.5. The points on the curve labeled *A*, *B*, and *C* correspond to the shaded regions in panel A. At the left, the change in $\Pr(\text{Censored} \,|\, x)$ is gradual as the thin tail moves over the threshold. The probability then decreases rapidly as the fat center of the curve passes over the threshold, and then changes slowly as the bottom tail passes over the threshold.

The Link Between Tobit and Probit

Deriving the probability of a case being censored is very similar to the derivation of the probability of an event in the probit model of Chapter 3. The structural models for probit and tobit are the same, but the measurement models differ. In the tobit model, we know the *value* of y^* when $y^* > \tau$, while in the probit model we only know *if* $y^* > \tau$. Since more information is available in tobit (i.e., we know y^* for same cases), estimates of the β's from tobit are more efficient than the estimates that would be obtained from a probit model. Further, since all cases are censored in probit, we have no way to estimate the variance of y^* and must assume that $\text{Var}(\varepsilon \,|\, \mathbf{x}) = 1$, while $\text{Var}(\varepsilon \,|\, \mathbf{x})$ can be estimated in the tobit model.

Example of the Probability of Censoring: Prestige of the First Job

The effects of doctoral prestige, gender, and having a postdoctoral fellowship on the probability that the prestige of the first job is censored are illustrated in Figure 7.6. The solid line with open squares shows the probability of censoring for women who were not fellows. Female fellows are less likely to have the prestige of their first job censored (i.e., to have a first job with prestige below 1), as shown by the solid line with

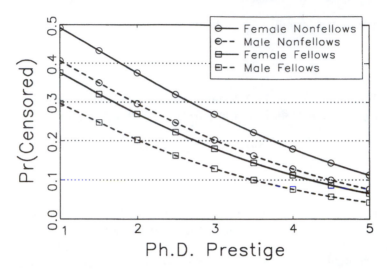

Figure 7.6. Probability of Being Censored by Gender, Fellowship Status, and Prestige of Doctoral Department

solid squares. When doctoral prestige is 1, female fellows have a probability of being censored of .38, which is .11 less than female nonfellows. When doctoral prestige is 5, female fellows have a probability of being censored of .07, which is .04 less than female nonfellows. Notice that the effect of being a fellow depends on doctoral prestige. The dashed lines show similar results for men. For male nonfellows, the probability decreases from .41 to .08, while for male fellows the probability decreases from .30 to .04. Being a female scientist increases the probability of being censored by .08 when doctoral prestige is 1 and .03 when doctoral prestige is 5.

These results suggest why our OLS results are biased in Table 7.1. Being a woman increases the probability of being censored, or, equivalently, of having a lower prestige job. When censored jobs were excluded from the analysis, the negative effect of being a woman on having a ranked job is not reflected in the sample. Consequently, the estimated effect of being a woman is positive, as shown in the column "OLS with a Truncated Sample" in Table 7.1. When unranked jobs are coded 1 and left in the sample, results are biased since these jobs are assigned a higher score than they would have had if the variable were not censored. That is, most of these cases would have had prestige scores lower than 1 if the data had been available. Consequently, the negative effect of being a woman is underestimated, as shown in the column "OLS with Censored Data" in Table 7.1.

A more formal demonstration of the consequences of censoring for OLS estimation is now given.

7.3.3. Problems Introduced by Censoring

Being unable to observe y^* over its entire range causes problems for the LRM. Most immediately, a decision must be made on how to handle the censored observations. There are two approaches that were used frequently prior to the acceptance of the tobit model:

1. A truncated sample is created by deleting cases where the dependent variable is censored. The model is estimated with OLS using the truncated sample.
2. A censored dependent variable is created in which all censored observations are assigned the value τ_y. The model is estimated with OLS using the censored dependent variable.

Berndt (1991, pp. 614–617) provides an interesting analysis of the consequences of using these approaches in research on the labor supply. Here, I demonstrate the problems with these approaches, and in the process present results that are useful for interpreting the tobit model.

Analyzing a Truncated Sample

The structural model for the latent variable is $y^* = \mathbf{x}\boldsymbol{\beta} + \varepsilon$. Since $E(\varepsilon \mid \mathbf{x}) = 0$, $E(y^* \mid \mathbf{x}) = \mathbf{x}\boldsymbol{\beta}$. With truncation, our model is

$$y_i = \mathbf{x}_i\boldsymbol{\beta} + \varepsilon_i \quad \text{for all } i \text{ such that } y_i > \tau$$

The dependent variable is the truncated variable $y \mid y > \tau$. Taking expectations,

$$E(y_i \mid y_i > \tau, \mathbf{x}_i) = E(\mathbf{x}_i\boldsymbol{\beta} + \varepsilon_i \mid y_i > \tau, \mathbf{x}_i)$$
$$= \mathbf{x}_i\boldsymbol{\beta} + E(\varepsilon_i \mid y_i > \tau, \mathbf{x}_i)$$

If $E(\varepsilon \mid y > \tau, \mathbf{x}) = 0$, then $E(y \mid y > \tau, \mathbf{x}) = \mathbf{x}\boldsymbol{\beta}$ and the model remains linear, which would justify OLS estimation. However, $E(\varepsilon \mid y > \tau, \mathbf{x})$ is not zero. From Equation 7.3, it follows that

$$E(y_i \mid y_i > \tau, \mathbf{x}_i) = \mathbf{x}_i\boldsymbol{\beta} + \sigma\,\lambda(\delta_i) \qquad [7.10]$$

where σ is the standard deviation of ε, $\delta = (\mathbf{x}\boldsymbol{\beta} - \tau)/\sigma$, and λ is the inverse Mills ratio.

Figure 7.7 illustrates the effects of truncation. If there were no truncation or censoring, the sample would correspond to the dots, both above and below the truncation point at $y^* = \tau$, with the OLS estimate of $E(y^* \mid x)$ shown by the solid line. Truncation occurs at $\tau = 2$, which is indicated by a horizontal line. With truncation, all observations at or below τ are dropped from the analysis. The relationship between x and the truncated expectation $E(y \mid y > \tau, x)$ is shown by the long dashed curve. This is the top curve. At the right, $E(y \mid y > \tau, x)$ is indistinguishable from $E(y^* \mid x)$ since so few cases are truncated. As we move to the left, $E(y \mid y > \tau, x)$ moves above $E(y^* \mid x)$ since smaller values of y^* have been excluded from the sample. As x continues to move to the left, $E(y \mid y > \tau, x)$ becomes closer and closer to τ. Given the difference between $E(y^* \mid x)$ and $E(y \mid y > \tau, x)$, it is clear why OLS produces inconsistent estimates when the sample is truncated.

Another way of thinking about the problems introduced by truncation is to consider the regression model implied by Equation 7.10:

$$y_i = \mathbf{x}_i\boldsymbol{\beta} + \sigma\lambda_i + e_i \qquad\qquad [7.11]$$

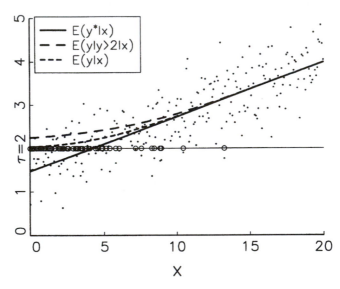

Figure 7.7. Expected Values of y^*, $y \mid y > \tau$, and y in the Tobit Model

where λ_i is used for $\lambda(\delta_i)$ to emphasize that λ_i may be thought of as another variable in the equation and σ can be thought of as the slope coefficient for the variable λ. If we estimate β using $y = \mathbf{x}\beta + \varepsilon$, we have a misspecified model that excludes λ. The OLS estimates will be inconsistent.

Analyzing Censored Data

A second approach is to analyze the entire sample after assigning $y = \tau_y$ to censored cases. In Figure 7.7, the censored observations are indicated by the circles located on the line $\tau = 2$. Since values of y^* below 2 have been set equal to 2, $E(y|x)$ is above $E(y^*|x)$ as shown by the short dashed line. This line is below $E(y|y > \tau, x)$ since the censored cases have not been eliminated, but only given an unrealistically large value. If we use OLS to estimate a regression using the entire sample after assigning τ_y to censored observations, the estimates are inconsistent.

More formally, with censoring our model becomes

$$y_i = \begin{cases} y_i^* = \mathbf{x}_i\beta + \varepsilon_i & \text{if } y_i^* > \tau \\ \tau_y & \text{if } y_i^* \leq \tau \end{cases} \qquad [7.12]$$

Applying Equation 7.4, the expected value of y given $\mathbf{x}$ is the sum of components for uncensored and censored cases:

$$E(y_i \mid \mathbf{x}_i) = [\Pr(\text{Uncensored} \mid \mathbf{x}_i) \times E(y_i \mid y_i > \tau, \mathbf{x}_i)] \qquad [7.13]$$

$$+ [\Pr(\text{Censored} \mid \mathbf{x}_i) \times \tau_y]$$

Using Equations 7.8 and 7.9 with $\delta = (\mathbf{x}\beta - \tau)/\sigma$,

$$E(y_i \mid \mathbf{x}_i) = [\Phi(\delta_i) \times E(y_i \mid y_i > \tau, \mathbf{x}_i)] + [\Phi(-\delta_i) \times \tau_y] \qquad [7.14]$$

Substituting results from Equations 7.10 and 7.12, and simplifying,

$$E(y_i \mid \mathbf{x}_i) = \Phi(\delta_i)\mathbf{x}_i\beta + \sigma\phi(\delta_i) + \Phi(-\delta_i)\tau_y \qquad [7.15]$$

$E(y|x)$ is nonlinear in $\mathbf{x}$, so that estimating the regression of y on $\mathbf{x}$ results in inconsistent estimates of the parameters for the regression of y^* on $\mathbf{x}$. (*What happens to Equation 7.15 if $\Phi(\delta) = 1$? If $\Phi(\delta) = 0$?*)

7.4. Estimation

In the presence of censoring, OLS is inconsistent. One approach to estimating the tobit model is based on Equation 7.11: $y = \mathbf{x}\boldsymbol{\beta} + \sigma\lambda + e$. Heckman (1976) proposed a two-stage estimator in which λ is estimated by probit in the first stage, and $y = \mathbf{x}\boldsymbol{\beta} + \sigma\widehat{\lambda} + e$ is estimated by OLS in the second stage. Since this estimator is less efficient and no easier to compute than the ML estimator, I do not consider it further.

ML estimation for the tobit model involves dividing the observations into two sets. The first set contains uncensored observations, which ML treats in the same way as the LRM. The second set contains censored observations. For these observations, we do not know the specific value of y^*, but can proceed by computing the probability of being censored and using this quantity in the likelihood equation. Figure 7.8 illustrates the approach used for three observations represented by solid circles. At each value of x, there is a normal curve showing the distribution of y^* given x. For uncensored observations, the distance from the observation to the normal curve is the likelihood of that observation for a given $\boldsymbol{\beta}$ and σ. The line at $y^* = \tau$ indicates where censoring occurs. For the censored observations, such as (x_1, y_1^*), we do not know the value of y^* and hence cannot use the height of the normal curve at that point for the likelihood. Since all we know for censored cases is that $y^* \leq \tau$, we

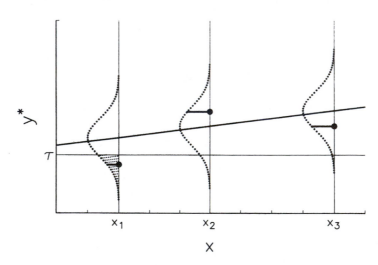

Figure 7.8. Maximum Likelihood Estimation for the Tobit Model

use the probability of being censored as the likelihood. This is indicated by the shaded region.

Formally, for uncensored observations,

$$y_i = \mathbf{x}_i\boldsymbol{\beta} + \varepsilon_i \quad \text{for } y^* > \tau$$

where $\varepsilon_i \sim \mathcal{N}(0, \sigma^2)$. As in Equation 2.8, the log likelihood equation for uncensored observations is

$$\ln L_U(\boldsymbol{\beta}, \sigma^2) = \sum_{\text{Uncensored}} \ln \frac{1}{\sigma} \phi\left(\frac{y_i - \mathbf{x}_i\boldsymbol{\beta}}{\sigma}\right)$$

In Figure 7.8, $\ln L_U$ is the sum of the logs of the spikes at (x_2, y_2^*) and (x_3, y_3^*).

For censored observations, we know $\mathbf{x}$ and that $y^* \leq \tau$, so we can compute

$$\Pr(y_i^* \leq \tau \mid \mathbf{x}_i) = \Phi\left(\frac{\tau - \mathbf{x}_i\boldsymbol{\beta}}{\sigma}\right) \tag{7.16}$$

Thus, for the first observation in Figure 7.8, we are computing the area of the shaded region at or below $y = \tau$ rather than the height of the pdf at y^*. Using Equation 7.16, we can write that part of the likelihood function that applies to censored observations as

$$L_C(\boldsymbol{\beta}, \sigma^2) = \prod_{\text{Censored}} \Phi\left(\frac{\tau - \mathbf{x}_i\boldsymbol{\beta}}{\sigma}\right)$$

Taking logs,

$$\ln L_C(\boldsymbol{\beta}, \sigma^2) = \sum_{\text{Censored}} \ln \Phi\left(\frac{\tau - \mathbf{x}_i\boldsymbol{\beta}}{\sigma}\right)$$

Combining the results for censored and uncensored observations,

$$\ln L(\boldsymbol{\beta}, \sigma^2 \mid \mathbf{y}, \mathbf{X})$$
$$= \sum_{\text{Uncensored}} \ln \frac{1}{\sigma} \phi\left(\frac{y_i - \mathbf{x}_i\boldsymbol{\beta}}{\sigma}\right) + \sum_{\text{Censored}} \ln \Phi\left(\frac{\tau - \mathbf{x}_i\boldsymbol{\beta}}{\sigma}\right)$$

While this likelihood equation is unusual with its combination of the pdf for uncensored observations and the cdf for censored observations,

Amemiya (1973) shows that if the assumptions of the tobit model hold, the usual properties of ML will apply.

Many programs estimate the tobit model by ML, including LIMDEP, Markov, Stata, and SAS's LIFEREG. Each program requires a method for specifying which observations are censored. Most commonly, you specify the value of τ and the program assumes that each observation with the dependent variable less than or equal to τ is censored.

7.4.1. Violations of Assumptions

The ML estimator for the tobit model assumes that the errors are normal and homoscedastic. In the LRM, if these assumptions are violated the estimates remain consistent, but not efficient. This is not the case in the tobit model.

Heteroscedasticity. Maddala and Nelson (1975) show that the ML estimator for the tobit model is inconsistent if there is heteroscedasticity. Maddala (1983, pp. 179–182) illustrates the effects of heteroscedasticity in estimates for several models, and Arabmazar and Schmidt (1981) provide further analysis of the robustness of the ML estimator to heteroscedasticity. The log likelihood equation can be modified to account for heteroscedasticity by replacing σ by σ_i. LIMDEP provides ML estimates when heteroscedasticity is of the form: $\sigma_i = \sigma \exp(\mathbf{z}_i \boldsymbol{\gamma})$. See Greene (1993, pp. 698–700) for further discussion.

Nonnormal Errors. The ML estimator is inconsistent when the errors are nonnormal (Arabmazar & Schmidt, 1982). Estimation of the tobit model with nonnormal errors is possible using programs for event history analysis such as SAS's LIFEREG or LIMDEP. The link between tobit analysis and event history analysis is considered further in Chapter 9.

7.5. Interpretation

There are three outcomes that can be of interest in the tobit model: (1) the latent variable y^*; (2) the truncated variable $y \mid y > \tau$; and (3) the censored variable y. This section presents methods for interpreting changes in the expected values of each of these outcomes using partial and discrete change. Since $y \mid y > \tau$ and y are rarely used except in economics, they are discussed only briefly.

7.5.1. Change in the Latent Outcome

In many applications, changes in the latent y^* are of primary interest. Tobit analysis provides consistent estimates of the effects of the independent variables on the latent y^*. The expected value of y^* is

$$E(y^* \mid \mathbf{x}) = \mathbf{x}\boldsymbol{\beta}$$

and the partial derivative with respect to x_k is

$$\frac{\partial E(y^* \mid \mathbf{x})}{\partial x_k} = \beta_k$$

For a continuous independent variable x_k, we can state:

- For a unit increase in x_k, there is an expected change of β_k units in y^*, holding all other variables constant.

For a dichotomous variable,

- Having characteristic x_k (as opposed to not having the characteristic) increases the expected value of y^* by β_k units, holding all other variables constant.

Since the model is linear in y^*, the effect of x_k does not depend on the value of x_k or the values of the other x's.

Standardized Coefficients

Following the arguments presented in Section 2.2.1 (p. 15) for the LRM, fully standardized and semi-standardized coefficients can be computed as

$$\beta_k^{S_x} = \sigma_k \beta_k, \qquad \beta_k^{S_{y^*}} = \frac{\beta_k}{\sigma_{y^*}} \qquad \beta_k^{S} = \frac{\sigma_k \beta_k}{\sigma_{y^*}}$$

where σ_{y^*} is the *unconditional* standard deviation of y^* and σ_k is the standard deviation of x_k. Since y^* is a latent variable, σ_{y^*} cannot be computed directly from the observed data. To deal with this problem, Roncek (1992) suggested an "analogue to a standardized coefficient" that uses the standard deviation of y^* *conditional* on $\mathbf{x}$: $\beta_k^{S^*} = \beta_k \sigma_k / \sigma_{y^* \mid \mathbf{x}}$. Since $\sigma_{y^* \mid \mathbf{x}}$ and σ_{y^*} can be quite different (*Why?*), Roncek's approximation should not be used. Instead, the unconditional variance of y^* should be computed with the quadratic form:

$$\widehat{\sigma}_{y^*}^2 = \widehat{\boldsymbol{\beta}}' \widehat{\text{Var}}(\mathbf{x}) \widehat{\boldsymbol{\beta}} + \widehat{\sigma}_\varepsilon^2$$

where $\widehat{\text{Var}}(\mathbf{x})$ is the estimated covariance matrix among the x's and $\widehat{\sigma}_\varepsilon^2$ is the ML estimate of the variance of ε.

Example of Partial Change in y^*: Prestige of the First Job

The *tobit* coefficients in Table 7.1 can be interpreted in the same way as the results of the LRM in Chapter 2. To illustrate this, consider the effects of *FEM* and *PHD*.

- Being a female scientist decreases the expected prestige of the first job by .24 points on a five-point scale, holding all other variables constant. Further, being a female scientist decreases the expected prestige of the first job by .19 standard deviations, holding all other variables constant.

- For a unit increase in the prestige of the doctoral department, the prestige of the first job is expected to increase by .32 units, holding all other variables constant. For a standard deviation increase in the prestige of the doctoral department, the prestige of the first job is expected to increase by .25 standard deviations, holding all other variables constant.

The effects of being female and doctoral prestige are significant at the .01 level for one-tailed tests.

7.5.2. Change in the Truncated Outcome

The truncated variable $y \mid y > \tau$ is defined only for those observations that are not truncated. If the dependent variable is expenditures on durable goods, the truncated outcome is how much was spent by people who purchased durable goods. Those who did not purchase goods are excluded from the sample. In economics, this outcome may be of considerable interest. For example, manufacturers of durable goods might want to know how much money consumers will spend and may be uninterested in how much consumers would have spent if durable goods could have been purchased for less than the threshold τ. Whether the truncated outcome is of interest depends on the substantive focus of the research.

Earlier, we showed that the expected value of the truncated outcome is

$$E(y \mid y > \tau, \mathbf{x}) = \mathbf{x}\boldsymbol{\beta} + \sigma \lambda(\delta) \qquad [7.17]$$

where $\lambda(\cdot) = \phi(\cdot)/\Phi(\cdot)$ and $\delta = (\mathbf{x}\boldsymbol{\beta} - \tau)/\sigma$. The expected value is nonlinear in the x's, and, consequently, β_k cannot be interpreted as the effect of a unit increase in x_k on the expected value of the truncated outcome. The partial derivative of $E(y | y > \tau, \mathbf{x})$ with respect to x_k is

$$\frac{\partial E(y | y > \tau)}{\partial x_k} = \beta_k [1 - \delta \lambda(\delta) - \lambda(\delta)^2] \qquad [7.18]$$

Greene (1993, p. 688) shows that the quantity in square brackets must fall between 0 and 1, approaching 1 as $\mathbf{x}\boldsymbol{\beta}$ increases. Thus, $\partial E(y | y > \tau, \mathbf{x}) / \partial x_k$ approaches $\partial E(y^* | \mathbf{x}) / \partial x_k$ as $\mathbf{x}\boldsymbol{\beta}$ increases. This is seen by comparing the solid and long dashed lines in Figure 7.7. For a dichotomous variable, the discrete change as the variable moves from 0 to 1 should be used instead of the partial derivative:

$$\frac{\Delta E(y | y > \tau, \mathbf{x})}{\Delta x_k} = E(y | y > \tau, \mathbf{x}, x_k = 1) - E(y | y > \tau, \mathbf{x}, x_k = 0)$$

For both the partial and the discrete change, the change depends on the level of all of the x's in the model. As a summary measure, the partial or discrete change for each x_k with all other variables held at their means is often used.

7.5.3. Change in the Censored Outcome

The censored outcome y equals the latent y^* when the dependent variable is observed, and equals τ_y (usually τ or 0) when the dependent variable is censored. If the dependent variable is expenditures on durable goods, it is useful to let $\tau_y = 0$. Then $E(y | \mathbf{x})$ is the expected actual expenditures of those with a given $\mathbf{x}$. Those who are censored on y^* are included as 0's, which is how much they actually spent.

From Equation 7.15,

$$E(y | \mathbf{x}) = \Phi(\delta)\mathbf{x}\boldsymbol{\beta} + \sigma \phi(\delta) + \Phi(-\delta)\tau_y$$

where $\delta = (\mathbf{x}\boldsymbol{\beta} - \tau)/\sigma$. The partial derivative with respect to x_k is

$$\frac{\partial E(y | \mathbf{x})}{\partial x_k} = \Phi(\delta)\beta_k + (\tau - \tau_y) \, \phi(\delta) \frac{\beta_k}{\sigma}$$

If $\tau_y = \tau$, then we obtain the simpler result:

$$\frac{\partial E(y | \mathbf{x})}{\partial x_k} = \Phi(\delta)\beta_k = \Pr(\text{Uncensored} | \mathbf{x})\beta_k \qquad [7.19]$$

Regardless of the value of τ_y, as the probability of a case being censored approaches 0, the partial derivative of y approaches the partial for y^*. This is illustrated by comparing the solid and short dashed lines in Figure 7.7. For a dichotomous variable, the discrete change as the variable moves from 0 to 1 should be used instead of the partial derivative:

$$\frac{\Delta E(y\,|\,\mathbf{x})}{\Delta x_k} = E(y\,|\,\mathbf{x}, x_k = 1) - E(y\,|\,\mathbf{x}, x_k = 0)$$

For both the partial and the discrete change, the change depends on the level of all of the x's in the model. As a summary measure, the partial or discrete change for each x_k with all other variables held at their means is often used.

7.5.4. McDonald and Moffitt's Decomposition

McDonald and Moffitt (1980) suggest a decomposition of $\partial E(y)/\partial x_k$ that highlights two sources of change in the censored outcome. The simplest way to derive their decomposition is to differentiate Equation 7.13 by parts and apply the product rule. After a great deal of algebra,

$$\frac{\partial E(y\,|\,\mathbf{x})}{\partial x_k} = \Pr(U\,|\,\mathbf{x})\frac{\partial E(y\,|\,y > \tau, \mathbf{x})}{\partial x_k} + [E(y\,|\,y > \tau, \mathbf{x}) - \tau_y]\frac{\partial \Pr(U\,|\,\mathbf{x})}{\partial x_k}$$

where $\Pr(U\,|\,\mathbf{x})$ is the probability of an observation being uncensored given $\mathbf{x}$. When $\tau_y = 0$, this results in the more commonly found version of this decomposition. It is important to realize that if τ_y is not 0, the simpler formula is not appropriate.[1]

The decomposition shows that when x_k changes, it affects the expectation of y^* for uncensored cases weighted by the probability of being uncensored, and it affects the probability of being uncensored weighted by the expected value for uncensored cases minus the censoring value τ_y. While this decomposition is useful for understanding how changes in the observed cases occur, its application depends on one's interest in y as opposed to y^*.

---

[1] Roncek (1992) provides a detailed discussion of the McDonald–Moffitt decomposition. While his formulas assume $\tau = \tau_y = 0$, his example has $\tau = \tau_y \neq 0$.

7.6. Extensions

The tobit model has been extended in many ways. Amemiya (1985, pp. 360–411), Berndt (1991, pp. 716–649), Breen (1996), and Maddala (1983, pp. 149–290) discuss many of these extensions, most of which can be estimated with LIMDEP (Greene, 1995, Chapter 27). In this section, I consider several basic extensions. The discussion is by no means comprehensive.

7.6.1. Upper Censoring

The simplest extension of the tobit model with censoring from below is the tobit model with censoring from above:

$$y = \begin{cases} \mathbf{x}\boldsymbol{\beta} + \varepsilon & \text{if } y^* < \tau \\ \tau_y & \text{if } y^* \geq \tau \end{cases}$$

This model can be obtained from the model with lower censoring simply by changing the sign of y. Censoring y from above at τ is identical to censoring $-y$ from below at $-\tau$. Since this simple change has subtle effects on the signs in many formulas, I present key results here. The probability of censoring is

$$\Pr(\text{Censored} \,|\, \mathbf{x}) = \Phi(\delta)$$

where $\delta = (\mathbf{x}\boldsymbol{\beta} - \tau)/\sigma$. Expected values are

$$E(y^* \,|\, \mathbf{x}) = \mathbf{x}\boldsymbol{\beta}$$
$$E(y \,|\, y < \tau, \mathbf{x}) = \mathbf{x}\boldsymbol{\beta} - \sigma\,\lambda(-\delta)$$
$$E(y \,|\, \mathbf{x}) = \Phi(-\delta)\mathbf{x}\boldsymbol{\beta} - \sigma\,\phi(\delta) + \Phi(\delta)\tau_y$$

The partial derivatives with respect to x_k are

$$\frac{\partial E(y^*)}{\partial x_k} = \beta_k$$
$$\frac{\partial E(y \,|\, y < \tau)}{\partial x_k} = \beta_k[\,1 + \delta\lambda(-\delta) - \lambda(-\delta)^2\,]$$
$$\frac{\partial E(y \,|\, \mathbf{x})}{\partial x_k} = \Phi(-\delta)\beta_k + (\tau_y - \tau)\phi(\delta)\frac{\beta_k}{\sigma}$$

7.6.2. Upper and Lower Censoring

Rosett and Nelson (1975) developed the *two-limit tobit model* to allow both upper and lower censoring. With upper and lower censoring,

$$y = \begin{cases} \tau_L & \text{if } y^* \leq \tau_L \\ y^* = \mathbf{x\beta} + \varepsilon_i & \text{if } \tau_L < y^* < \tau_U \\ \tau_U & \text{if } y^* \geq \tau_U \end{cases}$$

A common application of this model is when the outcome is a probability or a percentage. For example, Saltzman (1987) examines the effects of political action committee contributions on the voting of members of the House of Representatives on labor issues. The dependent variable is the percentage of times that a member of the House voted for issues benefiting labor. Saltzman argues that the dependent variable is truncated at 100 since some representatives that voted pro-labor 100% of the time would probably have voted for strongly pro-labor bills that were never introduced for a vote. Thus, they were more positive than indicated by the 100% vote. The same logic would apply to those who never voted pro-labor. Similar reasoning was used by Fronstin and Holtmann (1994) in studying the percentage of houses in a development that were damaged by Hurricane Andrew, and by Sullivan and Worden (1990) in their study of the probability that an individual will file for bankruptcy.

With two limits, the likelihood function includes components for upper censoring, lower censoring, and no censoring. Defining $\delta_L = (\tau_L - \mathbf{x\beta})/\sigma$ and $\delta_U = (\tau_U - \mathbf{x\beta})/\sigma$, it can be shown that

$$\Pr(y = \tau_L \mid \mathbf{x}_i) = \Phi(\delta_L)$$
$$\Pr(y = \tau_U \mid \mathbf{x}_i) = 1 - \Phi(\delta_U) = \Phi(-\delta_U)$$

Then

$$\ln L = \sum_{\text{Lower}} \ln \Phi\left(\frac{\tau_L - \mathbf{x\beta}}{\sigma}\right) + \sum_{\text{Uncensored}} \ln \frac{1}{\sigma}\phi\left(\frac{y - \mathbf{x}_i\mathbf{\beta}}{\sigma}\right)$$
$$+ \sum_{\text{Upper}} \ln \Phi\left(\frac{\mathbf{x\beta} - \tau_U}{\sigma}\right)$$

Interpretation proceeds along the lines used for the single-limit tobit model. For the latent outcome,

$$E(y^* \mid \mathbf{x}) = \mathbf{x\beta}$$

such that

$$\frac{\partial E(y^* \mid \mathbf{x})}{\partial x_k} = \frac{\Delta E(y^* \mid \mathbf{x})}{\Delta x_k} = \beta_k$$

The formulas for truncated and censored outcomes are generalizations of those discussed above. The expected value for the truncated outcome is (Maddala, 1983, pp. 160–162)

$$E(y \mid \tau_U > y > \tau_L, \mathbf{x}) = \mathbf{x}\boldsymbol{\beta} + \sigma \frac{\phi(\delta_L) - \phi(\delta_U)}{\Phi(\delta_U) - \Phi(\delta_L)}$$

The partial with respect to x_k is

$$\frac{\partial E(y \mid \tau_U > y > \tau_L, \mathbf{x})}{\partial x_k}$$

$$= \beta_k \left(1 + \frac{\delta_L \phi(\delta_L) - \delta_U \phi(\delta_U)}{\Phi(\delta_U) - \Phi(\delta_L)} - \left[\frac{\phi(\delta_L) - \phi(\delta_U)}{\Phi(\delta_U) - \Phi(\delta_L)} \right]^2 \right)$$

If x_k is dichotomous,

$$\frac{\Delta E(y \mid \tau_U > y > \tau_L, \mathbf{x})}{\Delta x_k} = E(y \mid \tau_U > y > \tau_L, \mathbf{x}, x_k = 1)$$

$$- E(y \mid \tau_U > y > \tau_L, \mathbf{x}, x_k = 0)$$

For the observed outcome:

$$E(y \mid \mathbf{x}) = [\tau_L \times \Pr(y = \tau_L \mid \mathbf{x}_i)] + [\tau_U \times \Pr(y_i = \tau_U \mid \mathbf{x}_i)]$$

$$+ [E(y \mid \tau_L < y^* < \tau_U, \mathbf{x}) \times \Pr(\tau_L < y^* < \tau_U \mid \mathbf{x}_i)]$$

$$= \tau_L \Phi(\delta_L) + \tau_U \Phi(-\delta_U)$$

$$+ [\Phi(\delta_U) - \Phi(\delta_L)] \left[\mathbf{x}\boldsymbol{\beta} + \sigma \frac{\phi(\delta_L) - \phi(\delta_U)}{\Phi(\delta_U) - \Phi(\delta_L)} \right]$$

Differentiating results in the simple expression:

$$\frac{\partial E(y \mid \mathbf{x})}{\partial x_k} = [\Phi(\delta_U) - \Phi(\delta_L)]\beta_k = \Pr(\text{Uncensored} \mid \mathbf{x})\beta_k$$

If x_k is a dichotomous variable,

$$\frac{\Delta E(y \mid \mathbf{x})}{\Delta x_k} = E(y \mid \mathbf{x}, x_k = 1) - E(y \mid \mathbf{x}, x_k = 0)$$

7.6.3. The Truncated Regression Model

Truncation occurs when no information for the dependent or independent variables is available for cases where the dependent variable is above or below a given level. For example, if you sample only individuals with incomes above $100,000, you have a sample that is truncated from below. The *truncated regression model* is used to analyze these types of data. The structural model is

$$y_i = \mathbf{x}_i\boldsymbol{\beta} + \varepsilon_i \quad \text{for all } i \text{ such that } y_i < \tau$$

This corresponds to the first part of the structural equation for the tobit model with censoring from above. The likelihood of each observation is the same as for uncensored observations in the tobit model, except that the likelihood must be adjusted by the area of the normal distribution that has been truncated:

$$f(y_i) = \frac{\dfrac{1}{\sigma}\phi\left(\dfrac{y_i - \mathbf{x}_i\boldsymbol{\beta}}{\sigma}\right)}{\Phi\left(\dfrac{\tau - \mathbf{x}_i\boldsymbol{\beta}}{\sigma}\right)}$$

The log likelihood function becomes $\ln L = \sum_i \ln f(y_i)$. The expected value $E(y \mid y < \tau, \mathbf{x})$ and the partial derivatives are the same as for the tobit model.

The importance of taking truncation into account is illustrated with results from Hausman and Wise's (1977) analysis of the New Jersey Negative Income Tax Experiment. In this study, the sample was truncated to exclude families with incomes more than 1.5 times the poverty level. Table 7.2 presents OLS estimates that ignore truncation and ML estimates of the truncated regression model. The ML estimates are as much as 5.4 times larger, with coefficients often having larger z-values. These results clearly illustrate how large the bias introduced by OLS estimation can be.

7.6.4. Individually Varying Limits

The tobit model can be generalized to allow censoring limits that differ from individual to individual. This extension is closely related to event history analysis and is discussed in Section 9.4.

TABLE 7.2 Hausman and Wise's OLS and ML Estimates From a Sample With Truncation

Variable		OLS Estimates	ML Estimates	Ratio ML/OLS
Constant	β	8.203	9.102	1.11
	t/z	90.14	356.95	3.96
Education	β	0.010	0.015	1.54
	t/z	1.67	2.09	1.25
IQ	β	0.002	0.006	3.81
	t/z	1.00	1.27	1.27
Training	β	0.002	0.007	2.95
	t/z	1.38	2.10	1.52
Union	β	0.090	0.246	2.74
	t/z	2.95	2.78	0.94
Illness	β	−0.076	−0.226	2.97
	t/z	−2.01	−2.11	1.05
Age	β	−0.003	−0.016	5.40
	t/z	−1.67	−3.06	1.83

NOTE: $N = 684$. β is an unstandardized coefficient. t/z is a z-test of β for ML and a t-test of β for OLS.

7.6.5. Models for Sample Selection

Sample selection models generalize the tobit and truncated regression models by explicitly modeling the mechanism that selects observations as being censored or uncensored. There is a vast and growing literature on sample selection models (see Amemiya, 1985, Chapter 10; Maddala, 1983, Chapters 7–8; Manski, 1995, for further details). Here, I consider only the simplest model for sample selection, sometimes known as the Heckman model (1976).

In the tobit and truncated regression models, the structural model, is

$$y_i^* = \mathbf{x}_i \boldsymbol{\beta} + \varepsilon_i$$

Instead of y^* being observed when $y^* > \tau$, assume that y^* is observed based on the value of a second latent variable z^*, where

$$z_i^* = \mathbf{w}_i \boldsymbol{\alpha} + \nu_i \qquad [7.20]$$

$\mathbf{x}$ and $\mathbf{w}$ can have variables in common. y^* is observed only when $z^* > 0$. To estimate the model, we assume that the errors are normally distributed such that

$$\begin{pmatrix} \varepsilon_i \\ \nu_i \end{pmatrix} \sim \mathcal{N}\left[\begin{pmatrix} 0 \\ 0 \end{pmatrix}, \begin{pmatrix} \sigma_\varepsilon^2 & \rho\sigma_\varepsilon \\ \rho\sigma_\varepsilon & 1 \end{pmatrix} \right]$$

where ρ is the correlation between ε and ν, and Var(ν) is assumed to be 1 to identify the model. Since ν is distributed normally, Equation 7.20 specifies a probit model where $z = 1$ (and y^* is observed) if $z^* > 0$.

Using derivations similar to those for the tobit model (Greene, 1993, pp. 709–711) results in the expected value of the observed y:

$$E(y_i \mid z_i = 1) = \mathbf{x}_i\boldsymbol{\beta} + \gamma\frac{\phi(-\mathbf{w}_i\boldsymbol{\alpha})}{\Phi(-\mathbf{w}_i\boldsymbol{\alpha})} = \mathbf{x}_i\boldsymbol{\beta} + \gamma\lambda_i$$

which is very similar to Equation 7.10. Regressing y on $\mathbf{x}$ for observations where $z = 1$ would produce inconsistent estimates since λ has been excluded. Heckman's two-step estimation involves first estimating the probit model in Equation 7.20 and computing

$$\widehat{\lambda}_i = \frac{\phi(-\mathbf{w}_i\widehat{\boldsymbol{\alpha}})}{\Phi(-\mathbf{w}_i\widehat{\boldsymbol{\alpha}})}$$

and then estimating the regression of y on $\mathbf{x}$ and $\widehat{\lambda}$.

7.7. Conclusions

This chapter has only touched on the rich set of models that deal with censoring, truncation, and sample selection. In all of these models, the basic problem is the same. Due to some data collection mechanism, data are missing on some of the observations in a systematic way. As a consequence, the LRM provides biased and inconsistent estimates.

7.8. Bibliographic Notes

While censored and truncated distributions have a long history in biometrics, engineering, and statistics, within the social sciences structural models for censoring and truncation originated with Tobin's (1958) article on household expenditures for durable goods. Indeed, this entire class of models is sometimes referred to as *tobit* models, a term coined by Goldberger (1964) to stand for "Tobin's probit." In the 1970s, a series of extensions of Tobin's original model appeared that stimulated a great deal of empirical and theoretical work. These include Grounau (1973), Heckman (1974, 1976), and Hausman and Wise (1977). See Amemiya (1985, Chapter 10) for an extensive review of this literature, and Breen (1996) for a good introduction.

8   Count Outcomes: Regression Models for Counts

Variables that count the number of times that something has happened are common in the social sciences. Hausman et al. (1984) examined the effect of R&D expenditures on the number of patents received by U.S. companies; Cameron and Trivedi (1986) analyzed factors affecting how frequently a person visited the doctor; Grogger (1990) studied the deterrent effects of capital punishment on daily homicides; and King (1989b) examined the effects of alliances on the number of nations at war. Other count outcomes include derogatory reports in an individual's credit history (Greene, 1994); consumption of beverages (Mullahy, 1986); illnesses caused by pollution (Portney & Mullahy, 1986); party switching by members of the House of Representatives (King, 1988); industrial injuries (Ruser, 1991); the emergence of new companies (Hannan & Freeman, 1989, p. 230); and police arrests (Land, 1992).

Count variables are often treated as though they are continuous and the linear regression model is applied. The use of the LRM for count outcomes can result in inefficient, inconsistent, and biased estimates. Fortunately, there are a variety of models that deal explicitly with characteristics of count outcomes. The Poisson regression model is the most basic model. With this model the probability of a count is determined by a Poisson distribution, where the mean of the distribution is a function

217

of the independent variables. This model has the defining characteristic that the conditional mean of the outcome is equal to the conditional variance. In practice, the conditional variance often exceeds the conditional mean. Dealing with this problem leads to the negative binomial regression model, which allows the variance to exceed the mean. A second problem is that the number of 0's in a sample often exceeds the number predicted by either the Poisson or the negative binomial regression model. Zero modified count models explicitly model the number of predicted 0's, and also allow the variance to differ from the mean. A third problem is that many count variables are only observed after the first count occurs. This requires a truncated count model, corresponding to the truncated regression model of Chapter 7. Each of these models for counts is based on the Poisson distribution, which is now considered.

8.1. The Poisson Distribution

Let y be a random variable indicating the number of times that an event has occurred during an interval of time. y has a Poisson distribution with parameter $\mu > 0$ if

$$\Pr(y \mid \mu) = \frac{\exp(-\mu)\mu^y}{y!} \quad \text{for } y = 0, 1, 2, \ldots \quad [8.1]$$

For example, if $y = 0$, then $\Pr(y = 0 \mid \mu) = \exp(-\mu)\mu^0/0! = \exp(-\mu)$; for $y = 1$, $\Pr(y = 1 \mid \mu) = \exp(-\mu)\mu^1/1! = \exp(-\mu)\mu$; and for $y = 3$, $\Pr(y = 3 \mid \mu) = \exp(-\mu)\mu^3/3! = \exp(-\mu)\mu^3/6$. Figure 8.1 plots the Poisson distribution for μ equal to .8, 1.5, 2.9, and 10.5, and illustrates several important properties of the Poisson distribution (see Taylor & Karlin, 1994, pp. 241–242, for proofs):

1. As μ increases, the mass of the distribution shifts to the right. Specifically,

$$E(y) = \mu$$

   The parameter μ is known as the *rate* since it is the expected number of times that an event has occurred per unit of time. μ can also be thought of as the mean or expected count.

2. The variance equals the mean:

$$\text{Var}(y) = E(y) = \mu$$

   The equality of the mean and the variance is known as *equidispersion*. In practice, count variables often have a variance greater than the mean, which

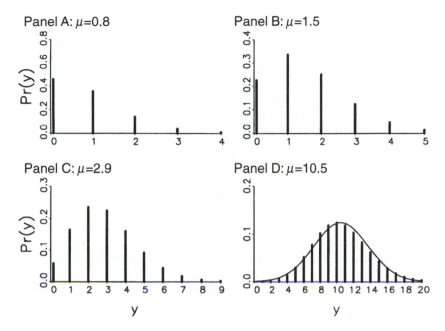

Figure 8.1. Poisson Probability Distribution

is called *overdispersion*. The development of many models for count data is an attempt to account for overdispersion.

3. As μ increases, the probability of 0's decreases. For $\mu = .8$, the probability of a 0 is .45; for $\mu = 1.5$, it is .22; for $\mu = 2.9$, it is .05; and for $\mu = 10.5$, the probability is .00002. For many count variables, there are more observed 0's than predicted by the Poisson distribution.

4. As μ increases, the Poisson distribution approximates a normal distribution. This is shown in panel D where a normal distribution with a mean and variance of 10.5 has been superimposed on the Poisson distribution.

The Poisson distribution can be derived from a simple stochastic process, known as a Poisson process, where the outcome is the number of times that something has happened (see Taylor & Karlin, 1994, pp. 252–258, for a formal derivation of the Poisson distribution). A critical assumption of a Poisson process is that events are *independent*. This means that when an event occurs it does not affect the probability of the event occurring in the future. For example, consider the publication of articles by scientists. The assumption of independence implies that when a scientist publishes a paper, her rate of publication does not change. Past success in publishing does not affect future success.

Example of Fitting the Poisson Distribution: Article Counts

In a study of scientific productivity, Long (1990) considered factors affecting the number of papers published during graduate school by a sample of 915 biochemists. The average number of articles was 1.7 with a variance of 3.7, which indicates that there is overdispersion in the distribution of articles. The form of this overdispersion is shown in Figure 8.2. The observed proportions for each count are indicated by diamonds that are connected by a solid line. The circles show the predicted probabilities from a Poisson distribution with $\mu = 1.7$. Compared to the Poisson distribution, the observed distribution has substantially more 0's, fewer cases in the center of the distribution, and more observations in the upper tail. Overall, the sample variance is larger than would be expected if the publication of articles was governed by a Poisson process in which all scientists had the same rate of productivity. Of course, the idea that all scientists have the same rate of productivity is unrealistic, which leads us to the idea of heterogeneity.

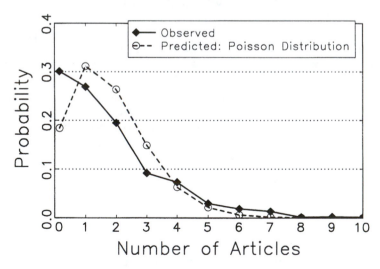

Figure 8.2. Distribution of Observed and Predicted Counts of Articles

8.1.1. The Idea of Heterogeneity

One explanation for the failure of the Poisson distribution to fit the observed data is that the rate of productivity μ differs across individuals. This is known as *heterogeneity*. Failure to account for heterogeneity in the rate results in overdispersion in the marginal distribution of the count. For example, suppose that the mean productivity for men is $\mu + \delta$, with a corresponding variance of $\mu + \delta$, while the mean and variance for women is $\mu - \delta$. Publications are assumed to be generated by a Poisson process in which the rate of publication differs for men and women. What will the marginal distribution look like? Assume there are equal numbers of men and women. Then the mean rate of productivity for the combined sample is the average of the rates for men and women, $\mu = [(\mu + \delta) + (\mu - \delta)]/2$, but the variance will exceed μ. (*Draw the two conditional distributions and show that the marginal distribution would have a larger variance.*) In general, *failure to account for heterogeneity among individuals in the rate of a count variable leads to overdispersion in the marginal distribution.* This result leads to the Poisson regression model which introduces heterogeneity based on observed characteristics.

8.2. The Poisson Regression Model

In the Poisson regression model, hereafter the PRM, the number of events y has a Poisson distribution with a *conditional* mean that depends on an individual's characteristics according to the structural model:

$$\mu_i = E(y_i \mid \mathbf{x}_i) = \exp(\mathbf{x}_i\boldsymbol{\beta}) \tag{8.2}$$

Taking the exponential of $\mathbf{x}\boldsymbol{\beta}$ forces the expected count μ to be positive, which is required for the Poisson distribution. While other relationships between μ and the x's are possible, such as $E(y \mid \mathbf{x}) = \mathbf{x}\boldsymbol{\beta}$, they are rarely used.

Panel A of Figure 8.3 illustrates the PRM for a single independent variable x. The relationship $\mu = \exp(-.25 + .13x)$ is shown by a solid line. Since y is a count, it can only have nonnegative integer values. These values are represented by dotted lines which should be thought of as coming out of the page. The height of the line indicates the probability of a count given x. Specifically,

$$\Pr(y_i \mid \mathbf{x}_i) = \frac{\exp(-\mu_i)\mu_i^{y_i}}{y_i!}$$

Panel A: E(ylx) for x=0 to 25

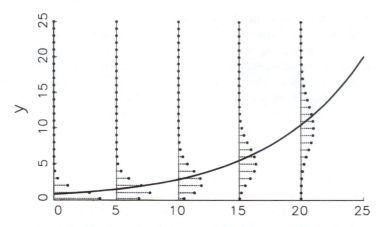

Panel B: E(ylx) for x=15 to 20

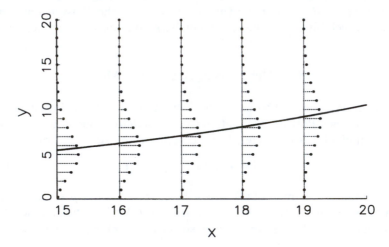

Figure 8.3. Distribution of Counts for the Poisson Regression Model

For example, at $x = 0$, $\mu = \exp(-.25) = .78$. Using this value of μ, the probabilities for various counts are (*Verify these values.*)

$$
\begin{aligned}
\Pr(y = 0 \mid \mu) &= .46 & \Pr(y = 1 \mid \mu) &= .36 \\
\Pr(y = 2 \mid \mu) &= .14 & \Pr(y = 3 \mid \mu) &= .04
\end{aligned}
$$

Other probabilities can be computed similarly.

The distribution of counts around the conditional mean of y in panel A of Figure 8.3 reflects the characteristics of the Poisson distribution that were discussed using Figure 8.1. Indeed, I constructed Figure 8.3 so that the means at x equal to 0, 5, 10, and 20 correspond to the means in the earlier figure. You can see that as μ increases: (1) the conditional variance of y increases; (2) the proportion of predicted 0's decreases; and (3) the distribution around the expected value becomes approximately normal.

The figure also shows why the PRM can be thought of as a non-linear regression model with errors equal to $\varepsilon = y - E(y|x)$. While the conditional mean of ε is 0, the errors are heteroscedastic since $\text{Var}(\varepsilon|x) = E(y|x) = \exp(x\beta)$. Note, however, that if your data are limited to a range of x where the relationship is approximately linear, the LRM is a reasonable approximation to the PRM. This is shown in panel B which expands that portion of the figure in panel A between $x = 15$ and $x = 20$. The relationship between μ and x is nearly linear, the errors are approximately normal, and there is only slight heteroscedasticity.

8.2.1. Estimation

The likelihood function for the PRM is

$$L(\beta\,|\,y, X) = \prod_{i=1}^{N} \Pr(y_i\,|\,\mu_i) = \prod_{i=1}^{N} \frac{\exp(-\mu_i)\mu_i^{y_i}}{y_i!} \qquad [8.3]$$

where $\mu = \exp(x\beta)$. After taking the log, numerical maximization can be used. The gradients and Hessian of the log likelihood are given by Maddala (1983, p. 52). Since the likelihood function is globally concave, if a maximum is found it will be unique.

8.2.2. Interpretation

The way in which you interpret a count model depends on whether you are interested in the expected value of the count variable or in the distribution of counts. If interest is in the expected count, several methods can be used to compute the change in the expectation for a change in an independent variable. If interest is in the distribution of counts or perhaps just the probability of a specific count, the probability of a count for a given level of the independent variables can be computed. Each of these methods is now considered.

Changes in the Conditional Mean

For the PRM, the expected value of y for a given $\mathbf{x}$ is

$$\mu = E(y \mid \mathbf{x}) = \exp(\mathbf{x}\boldsymbol{\beta}) \qquad\qquad [8.4]$$

The change in $E(y \mid \mathbf{x})$ can be assessed in several ways.

Partial Change in $E(y \mid \mathbf{x})$. The partial derivative of $E(y \mid \mathbf{x})$ with respect to x_k, sometimes called the marginal effect, can be computed using the chain rule:

$$\frac{\partial E(y \mid \mathbf{x})}{\partial x_k} = \frac{\partial \exp(\mathbf{x}\boldsymbol{\beta})}{\partial \mathbf{x}\boldsymbol{\beta}} \frac{\partial \mathbf{x}\boldsymbol{\beta}}{\partial x_k} = \exp(\mathbf{x}\boldsymbol{\beta})\beta_k = E(y \mid \mathbf{x})\beta_k$$

Since the model is nonlinear, the value of the marginal effect depends on both the coefficient for x_k and the expected value of y given $\mathbf{x}$. The larger the value of $E(y \mid \mathbf{x})$, the larger the rate of change in $E(y \mid \mathbf{x})$. Further, since $E(y \mid \mathbf{x})$ depends on the values of all independent variables, the value of the marginal depends on the levels of all variables. Often, the marginal effect is computed with all variables held at their means.

Since the PRM and the other count models in this chapter are nonlinear, the partial derivative cannot be interpreted as the change in the expected count for a unit change in x_k. Further, the partial with respect to a dummy variables does not make sense. For these reasons, this measure of change is less informative than the factor change or discrete change.

Factor and Percentage Change in $E(y \mid \mathbf{x})$. The factor or percentage change in the expected count can be computed simply from the parameters of the model. To see this (Section 3.8, p. 79, provides a more detailed derivation), Equation 8.4 can be rewritten as

$$E(y \mid \mathbf{x}, x_k) = \exp(\beta_0)\exp(\beta_1 x_1)\cdots\exp(\beta_k x_k)\cdots\exp(\beta_K x_K)$$

where $E(y \mid \mathbf{x}, x_k)$ makes explicit the value of x_k. If x_k changes by δ,

$$E(y \mid \mathbf{x}, x_k + \delta)$$
$$= \exp(\beta_0)\exp(\beta_1 x_1)\cdots\exp(\beta_k x_k)\exp(\beta_k \delta)\cdots\exp(\beta_K x_K)$$

The factor change in the expected count for a change of δ in x_k equals

$$\frac{E(y \mid \mathbf{x}, x_k + \delta)}{E(y \mid \mathbf{x}, x_k)}$$

$$= \frac{\exp(\beta_0) \exp(\beta_1 x_1) \cdots \exp(\beta_k x_k) \exp(\beta_k \delta) \cdots \exp(\beta_K x_K)}{\exp(\beta_0) \exp(\beta_1 x_1) \cdots \exp(\beta_k x_k) \cdots \exp(\beta_K x_K)}$$

$$= \exp(\beta_k \delta)$$

Therefore, the parameters can be interpreted as follows:

- For a change of δ in x_k, the expected count increases by a factor of $\exp(\beta_k \times \delta)$, holding all other variables constant.

For specific values of δ:

- *Factor change.* For a unit change in x_k, the expected count changes by a factor of $\exp(\beta_k)$, holding all other variables constant.

- *Standardized factor change.* For a standard deviation change in x_k, the expected count changes by a factor of $\exp(\beta_k \times s_k)$, holding all other variables constant.

Alternatively, the percentage change in the expected count for a δ unit change in x_k, holding other variables constant, can be computed as

$$100 \times \frac{E(y \mid \mathbf{x}, x_k + \delta) - E(y \mid \mathbf{x}, x_k)}{E(y \mid \mathbf{x}, x_k)} = 100 \times [\exp(\beta_k \times \delta) - 1]$$

Notice that the effect of a change in x_k does not depend on the level of x_k or on the level of any other variable.

Discrete Change in $E(y \mid \mathbf{x})$. The effect of a variable can also be assessed by computing the discrete change in the expected value of y for a change in x_k starting at x_S and ending at x_E:

$$\frac{\Delta E(y \mid \mathbf{x})}{\Delta x_k} = E(y \mid \mathbf{x}, x_k = x_E) - E(y \mid \mathbf{x}, x_k = x_S) \qquad [8.5]$$

This can be interpreted as:

- For a change in x_k from x_S to x_E, the expected count changes by $\Delta E(y \mid \mathbf{x})/\Delta x_k$, holding all other variables constant.

As was the case in earlier chapters, the discrete change can be computed in a variety of ways, depending on your purpose:

1. The total possible effect of x_k is found by letting x_k change from its minimum to its maximum.
2. The effect of a binary variable is obtained by letting x_k change from 0 to 1.
3. The effect of a unit change in x_k is computed by changing from $\bar{x}_k$ to $\bar{x}_k + 1$, while the centered discrete change can be computed by changing from $(\bar{x}_k - 1/2)$ to $(\bar{x}_k + 1/2)$.
4. The effect of a standard deviation change in x_k is computed by changing from $\bar{x}_k$ to $\bar{x}_k + s_k$, while centered change is computed by changing from $(\bar{x}_k - s_k/2)$ to $(\bar{x}_k + s_k/2)$.

Unlike the factor or percentage change, the magnitude of the discrete change depends on the levels of all variables in the model.

Predicted Probabilities

The parameters can also be used to compute the probability distribution of counts for a given level of the independent variables. For a given **x**, the probability that $y = m$ is

$$\widehat{Pr}(y = m \mid \mathbf{x}) = \frac{\exp(-\widehat{\mu})\,\widehat{\mu}^m}{m!} \qquad [8.6]$$

where $\widehat{\mu} = \exp(\mathbf{x}\boldsymbol{\beta})$. The predicted probabilities can be computed for each observation for each count m that is of interest. Then the *mean predicted probability* for each count m can be used to summarize the predictions of the model:

$$\overline{Pr}(y = m) = \frac{1}{N}\sum_{i=1}^{N}\widehat{Pr}(y_i = m \mid \mathbf{x}_i) = \frac{1}{N}\sum_{i=1}^{N}\frac{\exp(-\widehat{\mu}_i)\,\widehat{\mu}_i^m}{m!} \qquad [8.7]$$

The mean probabilities, which are computed after controlling for independent variables, can be compared to the observed proportions of the sample at each count. This is now illustrated with the data on scientific productivity.

TABLE 8.1 Descriptive Statistics for the Doctoral Publications Example

Name	Mean	Standard Deviation	Minimum	Maximum	Description
ART	1.69	1.93	0.00	19.00	Articles during last 3 years of Ph.D.
LnART	0.44	0.86	−0.69	2.97	Log of (ART + .5)
FEM	0.46	0.50	0.00	1.00	1 if female scientist; else 0
MAR	0.66	0.47	0.00	1.00	1 if married; else 0
KID5	0.50	0.76	0.00	3.00	Number of children 5 or younger
PHD	3.10	0.98	0.76	4.62	Prestige of Ph.D. department
MENT	8.77	9.48	0.00	77.00	Articles by mentor during last 3 years

NOTE: $N = 915$.

Example of the Poisson Regression Model: Article Counts

The failure of the univariate Poisson distribution to account for the distribution of article counts could be due to heterogeneity in the characteristics of the scientists. If scientists who differ in their rate of productivity are combined, the univariate distribution of articles will be overdispersed. Research by Long (1990) suggests that gender, marital status, number of young children, prestige of the graduate program, and the number of articles written by a scientist's mentor could affect a scientist's level of publication. Table 8.1 contains descriptive statistics for these variables. Table 8.2 presents estimates from the PRM and the negative binomial regression model (NBRM) that is considered in Section 8.3.

For purposes of comparison, I have also included results from the LRM. By taking the log of Equation 8.2, the PRM can be written as the log-linear model:

$$\ln \mu_i = \mathbf{x}_i \boldsymbol{\beta}$$

This suggests that the PRM can be approximated by the LRM:

$$\ln y_i = \mathbf{x}_i \boldsymbol{\beta} + \varepsilon_i$$

However, since $\ln(0)$ is undefined, it is necessary to add a positive constant c to y before taking the log. Values of c equal to .5 or .01 are frequently used. This suggests the regression model:

$$\ln(y_i + c) = \mathbf{x}_i \boldsymbol{\beta} + \varepsilon_i$$

King (1988) demonstrates that estimating this model results in biased estimates of the parameters of the corresponding PRM. However, as

TABLE 8.2 Linear Regression, Poisson Regression, and Negative Binomial
Regression of Doctoral Publications

Variable		LRM of LnART	PRM of ART	NBRM of ART
Constant	β	0.178	0.305	0.256
	t/z	1.65	2.96	1.82
FEM	β	−0.135	−0.225	−0.216
	t/z	−2.35	−4.11	−2.82
MAR	β	0.133	0.155	0.150
	t/z	2.04	2.53	1.79
KID5	β	−0.133	−0.185	−0.176
	β^{S_x}	−0.102	−0.141	−0.135
	t/z	−3.28	−4.61	−3.28
PHD	β	0.026	0.013	0.015
	β^{S_x}	0.025	0.013	0.015
	t/z	0.90	0.49	0.42
MENT	β	0.025	0.026	0.029
	β^{S_x}	0.241	0.242	0.276
	t/z	8.61	12.73	9.10
Dispersion	α	—	—	0.442
	z	—	—	8.45
	$\Pr(y = 0)$	—	0.21	0.34
	$-2 \ln L$	2215.32	3302.11	3121.92

NOTE: $N = 915$. β is an unstandardized coefficient; β^{S_x} is an x-standardized coefficient; t/z is a t-test of β for LRM and a z-test of β for the PRM and NBRM.

illustrated in Table 8.2, the estimates from the LRM can be of roughly the same size and significance as the coefficients from the PRM. This is more likely to be true when large counts are frequent.

The simplest way to interpret the results of the PRM is by using the factor changes in the expected count. For example, the coefficient for *FEM* can be interpreted as:

- Being a female scientist decreases the expected number of articles by a factor of .80 (= exp[−.225]), holding all other variables constant.

Or, equivalently,

- Being a female scientist decreases the expected number of articles by 20% (= 100[exp(−.225) − 1]), holding all other variables constant.

Similarly, the effect of the mentor's productivity can be interpreted as:

- For every additional article by the mentor, a scientist's mean productivity increases by 2.6%, holding all other variables constant.

The standardized coefficient can be interpreted as:

- For a standard deviation increase in the mentor's productivity, a scientist's mean productivity increases by 27%, holding all other variables constant.

(*Verify these numbers.*)

The results just given refer to the multiplicative factor change in the expected count. It can also be informative to examine the additive change in the expected count. For example, the change in the expected count for a change in *FEM* from 0 to 1 can be computed using Equation 8.5. First, hold all variables at their means except for *FEM*. If *FEM* is 1, indicating a female scientist, the expected productivity is 1.43; if *FEM* is 0, indicating a male scientist, the expected productivity is 1.79. Therefore, we conclude:

- Being a female scientist decreases the expected productivity by .36 articles, holding all other variables at their means.

Notice that the change of .36 articles from 1.79 to 1.43 corresponds to the 20% decrease that was computed using the measure of percentage change. (*Verify these values using Table 8.1.*)

The results of the PRM can also be interpreted in terms of predicted probabilities using Equation 8.7. In Figure 8.4, the observed proportions are shown by solid diamonds connected by solid lines. The mean pre-

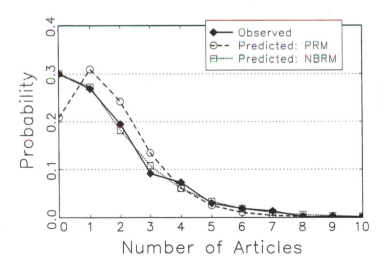

Figure 8.4. Comparisons of the Mean Predicted Probabilities From the Poisson and Negative Binomial Regression Models

dicted probabilities for the PRM are shown with open circles connected by dashed lines. (The predictions from the negative binomial regression, shown with squares, are discussed in the next section.) While the predictions from the PRM are somewhat better than those from the univariate Poisson distribution in Figure 8.2, the PRM still underpredicts 0's, overpredicts counts from 1 to 3, and slightly underpredicts counts in the upper tail. Large differences between the mean probabilities and the observed proportions suggest that a model is inappropriate. However, since an incorrect model can provide predictions that are close to the observed data, a close match is *not* clear evidence that a model is appropriate.

8.3. The Negative Binomial Regression Model

The Poisson regression model rarely fits in practice since in most applications the conditional variance is greater than the conditional mean. If the mean structure is correct, but there is overdispersion, the estimates from the PRM are consistent, but inefficient (Gourieroux et al., 1984). Further, the standard errors from the PRM will be biased downward, resulting in spuriously large z-values (Cameron & Trivedi, 1986, p. 31). For example, if there is overdispersion in the data analyzed in Table 8.2 (which later is shown to be the case), the z-tests may over estimate the significance of the variables.

A useful way to understand the limitation imposed by constraining the conditional variance to equal the conditional mean is to compare the PRM to the LRM. In the LRM, y given $\mathbf{x}$ is conditionally distributed with variance σ^2, where σ^2 is estimated along with the β's. Even though σ^2 is not of substantive interest, it allows the variance of the errors to be determined independently of the β's. In the PRM, y has a conditional Poisson distribution with a variance that is a function of the x's and the β's: $\text{Var}(y \mid \mathbf{x}) = \exp(\mathbf{x}\boldsymbol{\beta})$. Our first extension of the PRM adds a parameter that allows the conditional variance of y to exceed the conditional mean. This is the negative binomial regression model, hereafter the NBRM. While the NBRM can be derived in several ways, I consider the most common motivation of the model in terms of unobserved heterogeneity.

In the PRM, the conditional mean of y given $\mathbf{x}$ is known: $\mu = \exp(\mathbf{x}\boldsymbol{\beta})$. In the NBRM, the mean μ is replaced with the random variable $\tilde{\mu}$:

$$\tilde{\mu}_i = \exp(\mathbf{x}_i\boldsymbol{\beta} + \varepsilon_i) \qquad [8.8]$$

ε is a random error that is assumed to be uncorrelated with **x**. You can think of ε either as the combined effects of unobserved variables that have been omitted from the model (Gourieroux et al., 1984) or as another source of pure randomness (Hausman et al., 1984). In the PRM, variation in μ is introduced through *observed heterogeneity*. Different values of **x** result in different values of μ, but all individuals with the same **x** have the same μ. In the NBRM, variation in $\widetilde{\mu}$ is due both to variation in **x** among individuals but also to *unobserved heterogeneity* introduced by ε. For a given combination of values for the independent variables, there is a distribution of $\widetilde{\mu}$'s rather than a single μ.

The relationship between $\widetilde{\mu}$ and our original μ follows readily:

$$\widetilde{\mu}_i = \exp(\mathbf{x}_i\boldsymbol{\beta})\exp(\varepsilon_i) = \mu_i\exp(\varepsilon_i) = \mu_i\delta_i$$

where δ_i is defined to equal $\exp(\varepsilon_i)$. Recall that the LRM was not identified until an assumption was made about the mean of the error (see Section 2.5.1). For similar reasons, the NBRM is not identified without an assumption about the mean of the error term. The most convenient assumption is that

$$E(\delta_i) = 1 \qquad [8.9]$$

This assumption implies that the expected count after adding the new source of variation is the same as it was for the PRM:

$$E(\widetilde{\mu}_i) = E(\mu_i\delta_i) = \mu_iE(\delta_i) = \mu_i$$

The distribution of observations given **x** *and* δ is still Poisson:

$$\Pr(y_i \mid \mathbf{x}_i, \delta_i) = \frac{\exp(-\widetilde{\mu}_i)\,\widetilde{\mu}_i^{y_i}}{y_i!} = \frac{\exp(-\mu_i\delta_i)\,(\mu_i\delta_i)^{y_i}}{y_i!} \qquad [8.10]$$

However, since δ is unknown we cannot compute $\Pr(y \mid \mathbf{x}, \delta)$ and instead need to compute the distribution of y given only **x**. To compute $\Pr(y \mid \mathbf{x})$ without conditioning on δ, we average $\Pr(y \mid \mathbf{x}, \delta)$ by the probability of each value of δ. If g is the pdf for δ, then

$$\Pr(y_i \mid \mathbf{x}_i) = \int_0^\infty [\Pr(y_i \mid \mathbf{x}_i, \delta_i) \times g(\delta_i)]\, d\delta_i \qquad [8.11]$$

To clarify what this important equation is doing, assume that δ has only two values, d_1 and d_2. The counterpart to Equation 8.11 is

$$\Pr(y_i \mid \mathbf{x}_i) = [\Pr(y_i \mid \mathbf{x}_i, \delta_i = d_1) \times \Pr(\delta_i = d_1)] \qquad [8.12]$$
$$+ [\Pr(y_i \mid \mathbf{x}_i, \delta_i = d_2) \times \Pr(\delta_i = d_2)]$$

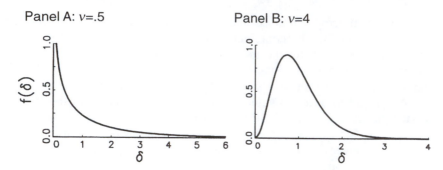

Figure 8.5. Probability Density Function for the Gamma Distribution

This equation weights $\Pr(y\,|\,\mathbf{x}, \delta)$ by $\Pr(\delta)$, and adds over all values of δ. Thus, Equation 8.12 computes the probability of y as a mixture of two probability distributions.

To solve Equation 8.11, we must specify the form of the pdf for δ. While several distributions have been considered, the most common assumption is that δ_i has a gamma distribution with parameter ν_i:

$$g(\delta_i) = \frac{\nu_i^{\nu_i}}{\Gamma(\nu_i)}\, \delta_i^{\nu_i-1} \exp(-\delta_i \nu_i) \quad \text{for } \nu_i > 0 \qquad [8.13]$$

where the gamma function is defined as $\Gamma(\nu) = \int_0^\infty t^{\nu-1}e^{-t}\,dt$. It can be shown (Johnson et al., 1994, pp. 337–342) that if δ_i has a gamma distribution, then $E(\delta_i) = 1$, as required by Equation 8.9, and $\mathrm{Var}(\delta_i) = 1/\nu_i$. The parameter ν also affects the shape of the distribution, as shown in Figure 8.5. As ν increases, the distribution becomes increasingly bell shaped and centered around 1.

The negative binomial, hereafter NB, probability distribution is obtained by solving Equation 8.11 using Equation 8.10 for $\Pr(y\,|\,\mathbf{x}, \delta)$ and Equation 8.13 for $g(\delta)$ (see Cameron & Trivedi, 1996, for details):

$$\Pr(y_i\,|\,\mathbf{x}_i) = \frac{\Gamma(y_i + \nu_i)}{y_i!\,\Gamma(\nu_i)}\left(\frac{\nu_i}{\nu_i + \mu_i}\right)^{\nu_i}\left(\frac{\mu_i}{\nu_i + \mu_i}\right)^{y_i}$$

The expected value of y for the NB distribution is the same as for the Poisson distribution:

$$E(y_i\,|\,\mathbf{x}_i) = \exp(\mathbf{x}_i\mathbf{x}\boldsymbol{\beta}) = \mu_i \qquad [8.14]$$

but the conditional variance differs:

$$\text{Var}(y_i \mid \mathbf{x}) = \mu_i\left(1 + \frac{\mu_i}{\nu_i}\right) = \exp(\mathbf{x}_i\boldsymbol{\beta})\left(1 + \frac{\exp(\mathbf{x}_i\boldsymbol{\beta})}{\nu_i}\right) \qquad [8.15]$$

Since μ and ν are positive, the conditional variance of y in the NBRM must exceed the conditional mean $\exp(\mathbf{x}\boldsymbol{\beta})$. (*What must happen to ν to reduce the variance to that of the PRM?*)

The larger conditional variance in y increases the relative frequency of low and high counts. This is seen in Figure 8.6 where the Poisson and NB distributions are compared for means of 1 and 10. The NB distribution corrects a number of sources of poor fit that are often found when the Poisson distribution is used. First, the variance of the NB distribution exceeds the variance of the Poisson distribution for a given mean. Second, the increased variance in the NBRM results in substantially larger probabilities for small counts. In panel A, the probability of a zero count increases from .37 for the Poisson distribution to .50, .77, and .85 as the variance of the NB distribution increases. Finally, there are slightly larger probabilities for larger counts in the NB distribution.

While the mean structure is fully specified by Equation 8.14, the variance is unidentified in Equation 8.15. The problem is that if ν varies by individual, then there are more parameters than observations. The most common identifying assumption is that ν is the same for all individuals:

$$\nu_i = \alpha^{-1} \quad \text{for } \alpha > 0$$

This assumption simply states that the variance of δ is constant. (We set the variance to α^{-1} rather than α to simplify the formulas that follow.) α is known as the *dispersion parameter* since increasing α increases the conditional variance of y. This is seen by substituting $\nu = \alpha^{-1}$ into Equation 8.15:

$$\text{Var}(y_i \mid \mathbf{x}) = \mu_i\left(1 + \frac{\mu_i}{\alpha^{-1}}\right) = \mu_i(1 + \alpha\mu_i) = \mu_i + \alpha\mu_i^2 \qquad [8.16]$$

(*What happens if $\alpha = 0$?*) Under this specification of ν, the conditional variance is quadratic in the mean, which has led Cameron and Trivedi (1986) to call this the Negbin 2 model.

Figure 8.7 shows the effect of the added variation in the NBRM. While the mean structure is identical to that used to illustrate the PRM, namely $E(y \mid x) = \exp(-.25 + .13x)$, the distribution around the mean differs. In panel A, $\alpha = .5$ and the difference from the PRM is subtle. Compared

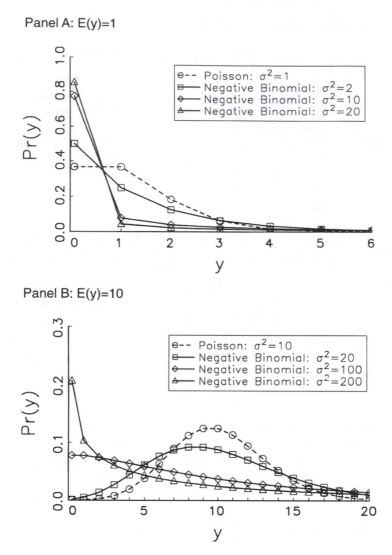

Figure 8.6. Comparisons of the Negative Binomial and Poisson Distributions

to Figure 8.3, the differences are barely noticeable at $x = 0$, but can be clearly seen for larger values of x. When α is increased to 1 in panel B, the effects are more pronounced. Note, for example, that the conditional mode for all values of x is now 0 and that the errors no longer appear normal as μ increases.

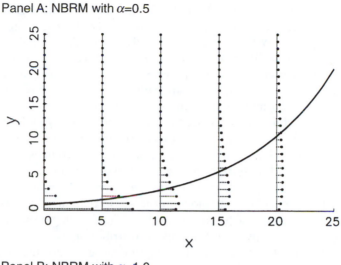

Panel A: NBRM with α=0.5

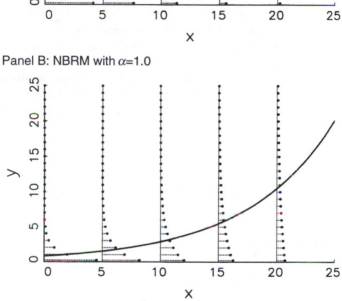

Panel B: NBRM with α=1.0

Figure 8.7. Distribution of Counts for the Negative Binomial Regression Model

8.3.1. Heterogeneity and Contagion

The NB distribution can be derived in a variety of ways as shown by Feller (1971, pp. 57–58) and Johnson et al. (1992, pp. 203–207). The derivation used above is based on unobserved heterogeneity, which is represented by the error ε in Equation 8.8. This derivation dates to work by Greenwood and Yule in 1920. Alternatively, the NB distribution can be derived from a process known as *contagion*, using an approach suggested by Eggenberger and Pólya in 1923. Contagion occurs when individuals with a given set of x's initially have the same probability of an event occurring, but this probability changes as events occur. For example, assume that there are two scientists who have identical characteristics and initially have the same rate of productivity μ. If the first scientist publishes an article, her rate of productivity increases by a fixed amount τ to $\mu + \tau$ as a result of contagion from the initial publication. For example, she might receive additional resources as a result of her success, and these resources may increase her rate of publication. The second scientist's rate would stay the same as long as he did not publish. The process is contagious in the sense that success in publishing increases the rate of future publishing. Thus, contagion violates the independence assumption of the Poisson distribution.

Unobserved heterogeneity and contagion can generate the same NB distribution of observed counts. Consequently, heterogeneity is sometimes referred to as "spurious" or "apparent" contagion, as opposed to "true" contagion. With cross-sectional data, it is impossible to determine whether the observed distribution of counts arose from true or spurious contagion.

8.3.2. Estimation

The NBRM model can be estimated by ML. The likelihood equation is

$$L(\beta \mid \mathbf{y}, \mathbf{X}) = \prod_{i=1}^{N} \Pr(y_i \mid \mathbf{x}_i)$$

$$= \prod_{i=1}^{N} \frac{\Gamma(y_i + \alpha^{-1})}{y_i!\Gamma(\alpha^{-1})} \left(\frac{\alpha^{-1}}{\alpha^{-1} + \mu_i} \right)^{\alpha^{-1}} \left(\frac{\mu_i}{\alpha^{-1} + \mu_i} \right)^{y_i}$$

where $\mu = \exp(\mathbf{x}\beta)$. After taking logs, the log likelihood equation can be maximized with numerical methods. Lawless (1987) provides gradients and Hessians.

8.3.3. Testing for Overdispersion

It is important to test for overdispersion if you use the PRM. Even with the correct specification of the mean structure, estimates from the

PRM when there is overdispersion are inefficient with standard errors that are biased downward (Cameron & Trivedi, 1986). If software is available to estimate the NBRM, a one-tailed z-test of $H_0: \alpha = 0$ can be used to test for overdispersion, since when α is zero the NBRM reduces to the PRM. Or, a LR test can be computed. If $\ln L_{\text{PRM}}$ is the log likelihood from the PRM and $\ln L_{\text{NBRM}}$ is the log likelihood from the NBRM, then $G^2 = 2(\ln L_{\text{NBRM}} - \ln L_{\text{PRM}})$ is a test of $H_0: \alpha = 0$. To test at the p level of significance, a critical value of X^2_{2p} should be used since α must be positive. Cameron and Trivedi (1990) present several tests based on the residuals from the PRM that do not require estimation of the NBRM.

8.3.4. Interpretation

Methods of interpretation based on the expected count $E(y \mid x)$ are identical to those for the PRM, since the mean structures are the same. Computations of predicted probabilities are based on the formula:

$$\widehat{\Pr}(y \mid \mathbf{x}) = \frac{\Gamma(y + \widehat{\alpha}^{-1})}{y! \, \Gamma(\widehat{\alpha}^{-1})} \left(\frac{\widehat{\alpha}^{-1}}{\widehat{\alpha}^{-1} + \widehat{\mu}} \right)^{\widehat{\alpha}^{-1}} \left(\frac{\widehat{\mu}}{\widehat{\alpha}^{-1} + \widehat{\mu}} \right)^y \qquad [8.17]$$

where $\widehat{\mu} = \exp(\mathbf{x}\widehat{\boldsymbol{\beta}})$.

Example of the NBRM: Article Counts

Estimates of the NBRM for published articles are given in Table 8.2. The β's can be interpreted in the same way as the β's from the PRM considered above. There is strong evidence that there is overdispersion. The dispersion parameter α is positive with $z_\alpha = 8.45$, which is significant at the .01 level. Alternatively, a LR test can be computed: $G^2 = 2(\ln L_{\text{NBRM}} - \ln L_{\text{PRM}}) = 180.2$, which is even more highly significant. Notice that the z-values for the NBRM are smaller than those for the PRM, which would be expected with overdispersion.

Figure 8.4 shows that the NBRM does a much better job than the PRM in predicting the counts from 0 to 3. Another way to see the differences between the two models is to compare their predictions for the probability of not publishing as the level of other variables change. In Figure 8.8, the probability of having zero publications is computed when each variable except the mentor's number of articles is held at its mean. For both models, the probability of a 0 decreases as the mentor's articles increase, but the proportion of predicted 0's is significantly higher for the NBRM. Since both models have the same expected number of

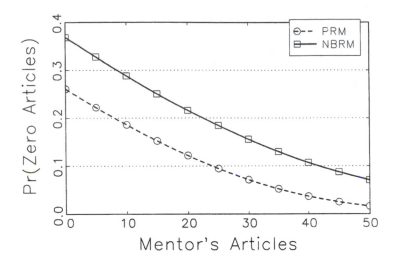

Figure 8.8. Probability of 0's From the Poisson and Negative Binomial Regression Models

publications, the higher proportion of predicted zeros for the NBRM is offset by the higher proportion of larger counts that are also predicted by this model.

8.3.5. Related Models

The NBRM is one of a class of models constructed by mixing the Poisson distribution with a second distribution using Equation 8.11. The mixture of the Poisson and gamma distributions is particularly convenient given the closed form of the resulting negative binomial distribution. In addition to the Negbin 2 models considered above, Cameron and Trivedi (1986) suggest a Negbin k model in which $\text{Var}(y \mid \mathbf{x}) = \mu + \alpha\mu^{2-k}$. If $k = 1$, then $\text{Var}(y \mid \mathbf{x}) = \mu + \alpha\mu$ which corresponds to replacing the assumption $\nu = \alpha^{-1}$ of the Negbin 2 model with $\nu = \mu/\alpha$. This is known as the Negbin 1 model. Other distributions and mixtures can also be used. Hinde (1982) considered a Poisson and normal mixture; Dean et al. (1989) used a Poisson and inverse Gaussian mixture. King (1989a) proposed a generalized event count (GEC) model that allows for either overdispersion or underdispersion. See Winkelmann (1994, pp. 112–120) for further details.

8.4. Models for Truncated Counts

Zero truncated samples occur when observations enter the sample only after the first count occurs. For example, consider the problem of explaining the number of times a person seeks medical treatment. If your sample is based on the records of those who visited a hospital, a person must visit the hospital at least once before entering the sample. If a sample of scientists is drawn from the authors of papers published in some journal, those without publications are excluded. A study of the number of TVs in a household might be based on a sample of those who returned their warranty card after purchasing a TV; those who do not own TVs are necessarily excluded from the sample. Gurmu (1991) and Grogger and Carson (1991) extended the PRM and NBRM to deal with truncated counts. While truncation can occur at any value, I focus on truncation at 0, which occurs most frequently in practice.

Let y be a Poisson random variable:

$$\Pr(y_i \mid \mathbf{x}) = \frac{\exp(-\mu_i)\mu_i^{y_i}}{y_i!} \qquad [8.18]$$

where $\mu = \exp(\mathbf{x}\boldsymbol{\beta})$. The probabilities of zero and positive counts are

$$\Pr(y_i = 0 \mid \mathbf{x}_i) = \exp(-\mu_i)$$
$$\Pr(y_i > 0 \mid \mathbf{x}_i) = 1 - \exp(-\mu_i) \qquad [8.19]$$

The conditional probability of observing y events given that $y > 0$ is computed with the law of conditional probability: $\Pr(A \mid B) = \Pr(A \text{ and } B)/\Pr(B)$. From Equations 8.18 and 8.19,

$$\Pr(y_i \mid y_i > 0, \mathbf{x}_i) = \frac{\Pr(y_i \mid \mathbf{x}_i)}{\Pr(y_i > 0 \mid \mathbf{x}_i)} = \frac{\exp(-\mu_i)\mu_i^{y_i}}{y_i![1 - \exp(-\mu_i)]} \qquad [8.20]$$

Each probability is increased by the factor $[1 - \exp(-\mu)]^{-1}$, which distributes the probability of a zero count across all positive counts in the truncated sample. This forces the truncated pdf to sum to 1.

Grogger and Carson (1991) provide the mean and variance of the truncated variable $y \mid y > 0$, which can be derived using methods similar to those used in Chapter 7 for the tobit model (see Johnson et al., 1992, pp. 181–184, 225). Since zero counts are excluded, the expected value is increased by the inverse of the probability of a positive count:

$$E(y_i \mid y_i > 0, \mathbf{x}_i) = \frac{\mu_i}{\Pr(y_i > 0 \mid \mathbf{x}_i)} = \frac{\mu_i}{1 - \exp(-\mu_i)} \qquad [8.21]$$

The expected value for the zero truncated count converges to the expected value of y without truncation as the probability of a zero count approaches 0. With zero counts excluded, the variance is less than that of the untruncated Poisson distribution and equals

$$\text{Var}(y_i \mid y_i > 0, \mathbf{x}_i) = E(y \mid y_i > 0, \mathbf{x}_i)[1 - \Pr(y_i = 0 \mid \mathbf{x}_i)E(y \mid y_i > 0, \mathbf{x}_i)]$$

$$= \frac{\mu_i}{1 - \exp(-\mu_i)}\left[1 - \frac{\mu_i}{\exp(\mu_i) - 1}\right]$$

The same ideas can be applied to the NBRM where

$$\Pr(y_i \mid \mathbf{x}_i) = \frac{\Gamma(y_i + \alpha^{-1})}{y_i!\Gamma(\alpha^{-1})}\left(\frac{\alpha^{-1}}{\alpha^{-1} + \mu_i}\right)^{\alpha^{-1}}\left(\frac{\mu_i}{\alpha^{-1} + \mu_i}\right)^{y_i}$$

so that

$$\Pr(y_i = 0 \mid \mathbf{x}_i) = (1 + \alpha\mu_i)^{-\alpha^{-1}}$$

$$\Pr(y_i > 0 \mid \mathbf{x}_i) = 1 - (1 + \alpha\mu_i)^{-\alpha^{-1}}$$

Combining these equations,

$$\Pr(y_i \mid y_i > 0, \mathbf{x}_i) = \frac{\dfrac{\Gamma(y_i + \alpha^{-1})}{y_i!\Gamma(\alpha^{-1})}\left(\dfrac{\alpha^{-1}}{\alpha^{-1} + \mu_i}\right)^{\alpha^{-1}}\left(\dfrac{\mu_i}{\alpha^{-1} + \mu_i}\right)^{y_i}}{1 - (1 + \alpha\mu)^{-\alpha^{-1}}} \qquad [8.22]$$

The conditional mean and variance are (Grogger & Carson, 1991)

$$E(y \mid y_i > 0, \mathbf{x}_i) = \frac{\mu_i}{\Pr(y_i > 0 \mid \mathbf{x}_i)} \qquad [8.23]$$

$$\text{Var}(y_i \mid y_i > 0, \mathbf{x}_i) = \frac{E(y \mid y_i > 0, \mathbf{x}_i)}{\Pr(y_i = 0 \mid \mathbf{x}_i)^{\alpha}}$$

$$\times \left[1 - \Pr(y_i = 0 \mid \mathbf{x}_i)^{1+\alpha}E(y \mid y_i > 0, \mathbf{x}_i)\right]$$

8.4.1. Estimation

Estimation of the truncated Poisson model involves a simple modification to the likelihood equation for the PRM (Equation 8.3):

$$L(\boldsymbol{\beta} \mid \mathbf{y}, \mathbf{X}) = \prod_{i=1}^{N} \Pr(y_i \mid y_i > 0, \mathbf{x}_i) = \prod_{i=1}^{N} \frac{\exp(-\mu_i)\mu_i^{y_i}}{y_i![1 - \exp(-\mu_i)]} \qquad [8.24]$$

Similarly, for the truncated negative binomial model,

$$L(\boldsymbol{\beta}, \alpha \mid \mathbf{y}, \mathbf{X}) = \prod_{i=1}^{N} \Pr(y_i \mid y_i > 0, \mathbf{x}_i)$$

where the conditional probability is obtained from Equation 8.22. The log likelihoods can be maximized with numerical methods. Grogger and Carson (1991, p. 228) provide the gradients and Hessians.

8.4.2. Interpretation

As with the truncated regression model of Chapter 7, interpretation can be in terms of either the untruncated or the truncated count. For both the truncated PRM and the truncated NBRM, the expected value of y without truncation is

$$E(y \mid \mathbf{x}) = \exp(\mathbf{x}\boldsymbol{\beta})$$

Interpretation in terms of partial derivatives, factor change, and discrete change can proceed as discussed in Section 8.2.2. The expected values for the truncated count $y \mid y > 0$ can be estimated using Equations 8.21 and 8.23.

Estimates of predicted probabilities for y are computed using the estimated β's from the truncated models and Equations 8.6 and 8.17 for untruncated distributions. Predicted probabilities for the truncated distribution are computed using Equations 8.20 and 8.22.

8.4.3. Overdispersion in Truncated Count Models

Grogger and Carson (1991, p. 229) make the important point that in the presence of truncation, overdispersion results in biased and inconsistent estimates of the β's and, consequently, the estimated probabilities. The reason for this is similar to the reason for inconsistency of the tobit estimator in the presence of heteroscedasticity. Without truncation, the mean structure of the PRM is correct even if there is overdispersion. Thus, the estimates are consistent even though the standard errors are biased downward. In the presence of truncation, the mean structure changes with overdispersion, resulting in inconsistent estimates of β. Gurmu and Trivedi (1992) present tests for overdispersion in the truncated count model.

8.5. Zero Modified Count Models

The NBRM responds to the underprediction of 0's in the PRM by increasing the conditional variance without changing the conditional mean. Zero modified count models change the mean structure to explicitly model the production of zero counts. This is done by assuming that 0's can be generated by a different process than positive counts. For example, the PRM and NBRM assume that each scientist has a positive probability of publishing any given number of papers. The probability differs across individuals according to their characteristics, but *all* scientists are at risk of not publishing and *all* scientists might publish. This is unrealistic since some scientists have jobs in which publishing is not possible (i.e., their probability of a 0 is 1). Zero modified models allow for this possibility, and in the process increase the conditional variance and the probability of zero counts.

8.5.1. The With Zeros Model

The *with zeros model* proposed by Mullahy (1986) assumes that the population consists of two groups. A person is in group 1 with probability ψ and is in group 2 with probability $1 - \psi$. Here, ψ is an unknown parameter that is to be estimated. The first group consists of people who always have zero counts. For example, a scientist who will never publish, perhaps because of the nature of her job, would be in this group. On the other hand, a scientist who does not publish but tries to (e.g., his papers were rejected) would not be in this group. We do not know whether a scientist with zero publications is in the first or the second group. If we did, this could be entered explicitly in the regression as an independent variable. Thus, the distinction between the two groups is a form of discrete, unobserved heterogeneity.

In the second group, counts are governed by a PRM or a NBRM. For the Poisson case,

$$\Pr(y_i \mid \mathbf{x}_i) = \frac{\exp(-\mu_i)\mu_i^{y_i}}{y_i!} \qquad [8.25]$$

where $\mu = \exp(\mathbf{x}\boldsymbol{\beta})$. In this group, zero counts occur by chance with probability $\Pr(y = 0 \mid \mathbf{x}) = \exp(-\mu)$. This corresponds to the scientist who tries but fails to publish.

Zero counts are generated by two different processes, depending on the group. The overall probability of 0's is a combination of the probabilities of 0's from each group, weighted by the probability of an individual being in that group. Following Equation 8.12,

$$\Pr(y_i = 0 \mid \mathbf{x}_i) = [\psi \times 1] + [(1 - \psi) \times \exp(-\mu_i)] = \psi + (1 - \psi)\exp(-\mu_i)$$

Since the Poisson process only applies to $1 - \psi$ of the sample, the probability of positive counts must be adjusted:

$$\Pr(y_i \mid \mathbf{x}_i) = (1 - \psi)\frac{\exp(-\mu_i)\mu_i^{y_i}}{y_i!} \quad \text{for } y > 0$$

(*Prove that* $\sum \Pr(y \mid \mathbf{x}) = 1$.)

Since the with zeros model is superseded by the zero inflated models that follow, I do not consider estimation or interpretation of the with zeros model. However, it is important to understand the logic of the with zeros model since it is the basis for the zero inflated models.

8.5.2. Zero Inflated Models

Lambert (1992) and Greene (1994) extend the with zeros model to allow ψ to be determined by characteristics of the individual. As in the with zeros model, counts are generated by two processes, which I illustrate with the Poisson version of the model. First, both zero and positive counts can be generated by a Poisson process:

$$\Pr(y_i \mid \mathbf{x}_i) = \frac{\exp(-\mu_i)\mu_i^{y_i}}{y_i!} \qquad [8.26]$$

where $\mu = \exp(\mathbf{x}\boldsymbol{\beta})$. In addition, 0's arise with probability ψ from a second process. In this process, ψ is a function of characteristics of the individual. In the *zero inflated Poisson* (ZIP) *model*, ψ is determined by either a logit or a probit model:

$$\psi_i = F(\mathbf{z}_i \boldsymbol{\gamma}) \qquad [8.27]$$

where F is either the normal or the logistic cdf. See Chapter 3 for details. The z's can be the same as the x's.

In the ZIP(τ) model, the z's are the same as the x's, and the parameters in the binary model are assumed to be a scalar multiple of the parameters in the count model. Specifically,

$$\psi_i = F(\mathbf{x}_i[\tau\boldsymbol{\beta}])$$

While the ZIP(τ) model reduces the number of parameters, it is difficult to imagine a social science application in which one would expect the parameters in the binary process to be a simple multiple of the parameters in the Poisson process. Indeed, the differences between the β and γ parameters may be of substantive interest. Accordingly, I do not consider the τ versions of the zero inflated models any further.

Combining the Poisson count model and the binary process for the ZIP model,

$$\Pr(y_i = 0 \mid x_i) = \psi_i + (1 - \psi_i) \exp(-\mu_i) \qquad [8.28]$$

$$\Pr(y_i \mid x_i) = (1 - \psi_i) \frac{\exp(-\mu_i)\mu_i^{y_i}}{y_i!} \quad \text{for } y_i > 0$$

The *zero inflated negative binomial* (ZINB) *model* is created by replacing Equation 8.26 with the NBRM, with corresponding adjustments to Equation 8.28.

For both the ZIP and the ZINB models, Greene (1994) shows that

$$E(y_i \mid x_i, z_i) = [0 \times \psi_i] + [\mu_i \times (1 - \psi_i)] = \mu_i - \mu_i\psi_i$$

The conditional mean of the model has been changed by lowering the expected count by $\mu\,\psi$. The conditional variance is also changed. For the ZIP model,

$$\mathrm{Var}(y_i \mid x_i, z_i) = \mu_i(1 - \psi_i)(1 + \mu_i\psi_i)$$

If ψ is 0, we have the standard PRM. Otherwise, the variance exceeds the mean. For the ZINB model,

$$\mathrm{Var}(y_i \mid x_i, z_i) = \mu_i(1 - \psi_i)[1 + \mu_i(\psi_i + \alpha)]$$

If ψ is 0, we have the standard NBRM, but for ψ greater than 0 the dispersion is greater than that of the NBRM.

Estimation

While Lambert (1992) proposed using the EM algorithm, Greene (1994) provides the gradients that allow ML estimation using the BHHH method. LIMDEP (Greene, 1995) implements this method of estimation. For the ZIP model,

$$L(\beta, \gamma \mid y, X, Z) = \prod_{i=1}^{N} \Pr(y_i \mid x_i, z_i)$$

Using Equations 8.27 and 8.28, $\Pr(y \mid \mathbf{x}, \mathbf{z})$ is defined as

$$\Pr(y_i = 0 \mid \mathbf{x}_i, \mathbf{z}_i) = F(\mathbf{z}_i \boldsymbol{\gamma}) + [1 - F(\mathbf{z}_i \boldsymbol{\gamma})] \exp(-\exp[\mathbf{x}_i \boldsymbol{\beta}])$$

$$\Pr(y_i \mid \mathbf{x}_i, \mathbf{z}_i) = [1 - F(\mathbf{z}_i \boldsymbol{\gamma})] \frac{\exp(-\exp[\mathbf{x}_i \boldsymbol{\beta}]) \exp(\mathbf{x}_i \boldsymbol{\beta})^{y_i}}{y_i!} \quad \text{for } y_i > 0$$

Comparable formulas are available for the other zero inflated models.

Interpretation

For the ZIP model, predicted probabilities of a zero count are based on Equation 8.28:

$$\widehat{\Pr}(y = 0 \mid \mathbf{x}) = \widehat{\psi} + (1 - \widehat{\psi}) e^{-\widehat{\mu}}$$

where $\widehat{\mu} = \exp(\mathbf{x}\boldsymbol{\beta})$ and $\widehat{\psi} = F(\mathbf{z}\widehat{\boldsymbol{\gamma}})$. The predicted probability of a positive count applies to the $1 - \widehat{\psi}$ at risk of the event:

$$\widehat{\Pr}(y \mid \mathbf{x}) = (1 - \widehat{\psi}) \frac{\exp(-\widehat{\mu}_i) \widehat{\mu}^y}{y!}$$

Similarly, for the ZINB model, the predicted probability of a zero count is

$$\widehat{\Pr}(y = 0 \mid \mathbf{x}) = \widehat{\psi} + (1 - \widehat{\psi}) \left(\frac{\widehat{\alpha}^{-1}}{\widehat{\alpha}^{-1} + \widehat{\mu}_i} \right)^{\widehat{\alpha}^{-1}}$$

and the predicted probability for a positive count is

$$\widehat{\Pr}(y \mid \mathbf{x}) = (1 - \widehat{\psi}) \frac{\Gamma(y + \widehat{\alpha}^{-1})}{y! \, \Gamma(\widehat{\alpha}^{-1})} \left(\frac{\widehat{\alpha}^{-1}}{\widehat{\alpha}^{-1} + \widehat{\mu}} \right)^{\widehat{\alpha}^{-1}} \left(\frac{\widehat{\mu}}{\widehat{\alpha}^{-1} + \widehat{\mu}} \right)^y$$

The definitions of $\widehat{\mu}$ and $\widehat{\psi}$ are unchanged.

The β parameters are interpreted in the same way as the parameters from the PRM or the NBRM. Furthermore, the γ parameters are interpreted in the same way as the parameters for the binary logit or probit models of Chapter 3, where the outcome event is having a zero count. Thus, a positive coefficient in the binary process increases the probability of being in the group where the probability of a zero count is 1.

Example of Zero Inflated Models: Article Counts

Estimates from the ZIP and ZINB models with a binary logit model
are given in Table 8.3. While I will not discuss the interpretation of individual parameters, which can be interpreted with methods already introduced, there are several things to note. First, the estimates from the
two models are generally similar, although the parameters from the ZIP
model are somewhat larger and more significant. Second, the signs of the
γ's in the binary process are the opposite of the β's for the count process. The binary process is predicting membership in the group that must
have a zero count. A positive γ is associated with lower expected productivity. If variables that positively affect the expected count (i.e., those
with positive β's) also positively affect the chances of being in the group
where positive counts are possible, then the β's and γ's would have opposite signs. For most substantive situations, this would seem reasonable.

TABLE 8.3 Zero Inflated Poisson and Zero Inflated Negative Binomial
Regression Models for Doctoral Publications

Variable		ZIP Logit	ZIP Poisson	ZINB Logit	ZINB NB
Constant	γ/β	−0.577	0.641	−0.193	0.417
	z	−1.15	6.83	−0.16	2.82
FEM	γ/β	0.110	−0.209	0.637	−0.195
	z	0.40	−3.93	0.85	−2.48
MAR	γ/β	−0.354	0.104	−1.499	0.098
	z	−1.14	1.81	−1.82	1.14
KID5	γ/β	0.217	−0.143	0.628	−0.152
	γ^{S_x}/β^{S_x}	0.166	−0.110	0.481	−0.116
	z	1.15	−3.96	1.37	−2.81
PHD	γ/β	0.001	−0.006	−0.038	−0.001
	γ^{S_x}/β^{S_x}	0.001	−0.006	−0.037	−0.001
	z	0.01	−0.27	−0.12	−0.02
MENT	γ/β	−0.134	0.018	−0.882	0.025
	γ^{S_x}/β^{S_x}	−1.272	0.172	−8.367	0.235
	z	−4.29	12.70	−2.33	7.97
	α	—	—	—	0.377
	z	—	—	—	7.46
Pr$(y=0)$		0.300		0.312	
$-2\ln L$		3209.55		3099.98	

NOTE: $N = 915$. β and γ are unstandardized coefficients; β^{S_x} and γ^{S_x} are x-standardized coefficients;
z is a z-test of β or γ.

Third, the magnitudes (ignoring signs) and significance levels of the parameters for the binary process are quite different from the parameters from the count process. The level of productivity of the mentor has the strongest effect in the binary process differentiating potential publishers from nonpublishers. None of the other variables is significant in the logit portion of the ZIP model, although being married makes it more likely that a scientist has the potential to publish in the ZINB model.

8.6. Comparisons Among Count Models

We have considered four models explaining doctoral publications: the Poisson regression model, the negative binomial regression model, the zero inflated Poisson model, and the zero inflated negative binomial model. One way to compare these models is with the mean probabilities computed using Equation 8.7:

$$\overline{\Pr}(y = m) = \frac{1}{N} \sum_{i=1}^{N} \widehat{\Pr}(y_i = m \mid \mathbf{x}_i)$$

Figure 8.9 plots the difference between the observed proportions for each count and the mean probability from the four models. We see immediately that the major failure of the PRM is in predicting the number of zeros, with an underprediction of about .1. The ZIP does much better at predicting zeros, but has poor predictions for counts one through three. The NBRM predicts the zeros very well and also has much better predictions for the counts from one to three. The ZINB slightly over predicts zeros and under predicts ones, with similar predictions to the NBRM for other counts. Overall, the NBRM model provides the most accurate predictions, which are slightly better than those for the ZINB.

We can also test differences between pairs of models. Section 8.3.3 showed that the PRM and the NBRM can be compared by testing the dispersion parameter α. Since the NBRM reduces to the PRM when $\alpha = 0$, the models are nested. For our example, we found that α was significant, with a Wald test of $z_\alpha = 8.45$ and a LR test of $G^2 = 180.2$. There is clear evidence supporting the NBRM over the PRM. The ZIP and ZINB models are also nested, and we can test H_0: $\alpha = 0$ with either the z-statistic for $\widehat{\alpha}$ in the ZINB ($z = 7.46$) or a LR test: $G^2 = 2(\ln L_{\text{ZINB}} - \ln L_{\text{ZIP}}) = 109.6$. There is evidence that the ZINB improves the fit over the ZIP model.

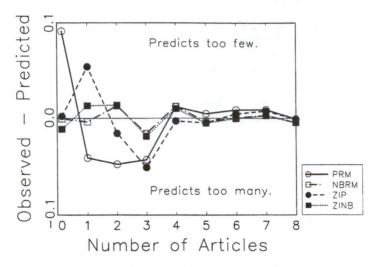

Figure 8.9. Comparison of the Predictions From Four Count Models

Greene (1994) points out that PRM and ZIP are not nested (and similarly for the NBRM and the ZINB). For the ZIP model to reduce to the PRM, it is necessary for ψ to equal 0. This does not occur when $\gamma = \mathbf{0}$. To see this, consider Equation 8.27: $\psi = F(\mathbf{z0}) = .5$. This implies that half of the sample will always have zero counts with certainty. Consequently, Greene proposes using a test by Vuong (1989, p. 319) for nonnested models. To define this test, consider two models where $\widehat{\Pr}_1(y_i \mid x_i)$ is the predicted probability of observing y_i based on the first model; $\widehat{\Pr}_2(y_i \mid x_i)$ is the predicted probability for the second model. Let

$$m_i = \ln \left[\frac{\widehat{\Pr}_1(y_i \mid x_i)}{\widehat{\Pr}_2(y_i \mid x_i)} \right]$$

and let $\overline{m}$ be the mean and let s_m be the standard deviation of m_i. Then the Vuong statistic

$$V = \frac{\sqrt{N}\,\overline{m}}{s_m}$$

can be used to test the hypothesis that $E(m) = 0$. V is asymptotically distributed as normal. If V is greater than the critical value, say 1.96, the first model is favored; if V is less than -1.96, the second model is favored; and otherwise neither model is preferred. For our example, $V(\text{ZIP}|\text{PRM}) = 5.98$ which favors the ZIP model, and $V(\text{ZINB}|\text{NBRM}) = 2.32$ which favors the ZINB model.

Overall, these tests provide evidence that the ZINB models fits the data best. However, when fitting a series of models without any theoretical rationale, it is easy to overfit the data. In our example, the most compelling evidence for the ZINB is that it makes substantive sense. Within science, there are scientists who for structural reasons will not publish. Other scientist do not publish only by chance in a given period. This is the basis of the zero inflated models. The NB version of the model seems preferable since it is likely that there are unobserved sources of heterogeneity that differentiate the scientists. Overall, the ZINB makes substantive sense and fits the data well. However, the NBRM also fits extremely well.

8.7. Conclusions

While the Poisson regression model is central to the development of models for counts, it rarely fits. A variety of additional models have been developed that modify the conditional variance, the conditional mean, or both. The motivation is to construct models that correct the various ways in which the PRM fails to fit. The PRM and the NBRM have the same mean structure, but the NBRM introduces unobserved heterogeneity which allows the conditional variance to exceed the conditional mean. The modified count models mix two processes that generate the counts. The first process generates only zero counts, while the second process affects both zero and positive counts. As a consequence of mixing these two processes, the conditional means for the with zeros and zero inflated models differ from those of the PRM and NBRM. However, they each relax the restrictive assumption of the Poisson model that the mean equals the variance. Many additional models for counts are available, including models for time series and panel data. In addition, specification tests and robust methods of estimation are rapidly being developed. Cameron and Trivedi (1986, 1996), Gurmu and Trivedi (1995), and Winkelmann (1994) provide detailed reviews of this literature.

8.8. Bibliographic Notes

Count models have a long history in the social sciences. Indeed, Poisson's introduction of what came to be known as the Poisson distribution was within the context of a study of criminal behavior. Coleman (1964,

Chapter 11) considered a variety of applications of the Poisson distribution and suggested what is now known as the Poisson regression model. Further applications of count models in the social sciences were relatively rare until the 1980s when Hausman et al. (1984) presented the Poisson regression model, the negative binomial model, and models for panel data, and Gourieroux, et al. (1984) considered a variety of pseudo maximum likelihood methods of estimation which were illustrated with the Poisson regression model. Cameron and Trivedi (1986) presented a large number of models, estimators, and tests for count models. King (1988, 1989a, 1989b) introduced the count model to political science and extended the Poisson regression and negative binomial regression models in several ways. Zero modified count models grew out of work on univariate distributions (reviewed in Johnson et al., 1992, Chapter 4). Mullahy (1986) proposed a with zeros model to deal with the frequency of zero counts in the data. Gurmu (1991) and Grogger and Carson (1991) considered modifications of the Poisson model to deal with truncated outcomes. Independently, Lambert (1992) developed an extension of the with zeros model that she referred to as the zero inflated Poisson model. Greene (1994) extended Lambert's idea to the negative binomial model and added these models to LIMDEP Version 7. Taylor and Karlin (1994) and Ross (1972) are good and relatively nontechnical introductions to stochastic processes related to the Poisson distribution. Lancaster (1990) provides similar information and also considers related models for duration data.

9 Conclusions

We have considered many models in the last 250 pages. If you are encountering these models for the first time, it may be hard to keep track of the differences and similarities. Still, there are many important models that have not been considered, some of which are very closely related to the models in this book. In this brief concluding chapter, I try to address both issues. First, I summarize the connections among the models from the prior chapters in several ways using three distinct but complementary approaches: latent variables, the generalized linear model, and probability models. Hopefully, this will serve to review what has been covered and will provide new insights into the models. Second, I show the connections between the models we have studied and two important classes of models, log-linear models and models for survival analysis. This brief discussion will be most useful for those who are already familiar with log-linear and survival models and who are interested in their connections to the models in this book. Additional links between the models in this book and models for ordinal variables are found in Clogg and Shihadeh (1994, Chapter 7). Heinen's (1996) book on latent class and discrete latent trait models also illustrates many links between these models and the models we have discussed.

9.1. Links Using Latent Variable Models

Many of the models in earlier chapters were based on a structural model in which the dependent variable y^* is latent:

$$y^* = \mathbf{x}\boldsymbol{\beta} + \varepsilon \qquad [9.1]$$

$\mathbf{x}$ contains independent variables, $\boldsymbol{\beta}$ is a vector of structural coefficients, and ε is a random error. For now, assume that ε has a normal distribution. To estimate a model with latent variables, there must be a link between the latent y^* and the observed y. The nature of this link defines the specific model. To show this, I begin with the linear regression model and then consider how different measurement models lead to other models.

The Linear Regression Model. Most simply, we can assume that the latent variable equals the observed variable:

$$y = y^* \quad \text{for all } y^*$$

This leads to the linear regression model:

$$y = \mathbf{x}\boldsymbol{\beta} + \varepsilon$$

OLS or ML can be used to estimate the β's and σ_ε^2. Since y^* is observed, we can estimate the variance of $\sigma_{y^*}^2$. Accordingly, the unstandardized β_k's can be interpreted as the expected change in y^* for a unit change in x_k, holding all other variables constant.

The Tobit Model. The tobit model is formed by assuming that when y^* is below some value τ we do not know its value, but only that y^* is at or below τ. Thus, our measurement model is

$$y = \begin{cases} y^* & \text{if } y^* > \tau \\ 0 & \text{if } y^* \leq \tau \end{cases} \qquad [9.2]$$

This model is illustrated in Figure 9.1. Consider the distribution of y^* at x_2. In the region of the distribution labeled A, y is equal to the latent y^*. In the region B, y^* is censored and all we know is that $y^* \leq \tau$. Since some of the y^*'s are observed, it is possible to estimate both $\sigma_{y^*}^2$ and σ_ε^2. Consequently, the estimated β's can be interpreted in terms of the units of y^*, just as for the LRM.

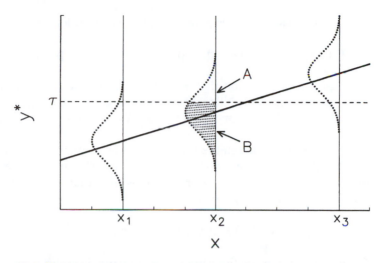

Figure 9.1. Similarities Between the Tobit and Probit Models

We can also compute the probability of a case being censored, which corresponds to area *B* in Figure 9.1. For a given *x*, the probability that y^* is at or below τ is

$$\Pr(\text{Censored} \mid \mathbf{x}) = \Pr(y^* \leq \tau \mid \mathbf{x}) = \Pr(\varepsilon \leq \tau - \mathbf{x}\boldsymbol{\beta} \mid \mathbf{x}) \qquad [9.3]$$

The Binary Probit Model. The binary probit model can be thought of as a tobit model in which values both above *and* below τ are censored. The measurement model is

$$y = \begin{cases} 1 & \text{if } y^* > \tau = 0 \\ 0 & \text{if } y^* \leq \tau = 0 \end{cases}$$

Therefore, y^* is not observed for any observations, and we assume that $\tau = 0$.

Interpretation of the probit model often focuses on the probability that a 1 was observed (i.e., y^* is above the censoring point) or that a 0 was observed (i.e., y^* is at or below the censoring point). The equation for the probability of a 0 illustrates the close relationship between the probit and tobit models. From Chapter 3,

$$\Pr(y = 0 \mid \mathbf{x}) = \Pr(\varepsilon \geq \mathbf{x}\boldsymbol{\beta} \mid \mathbf{x})$$

Since the normal distribution is symmetric, this is equivalent to

$$\Pr(y = 0 \,|\, \mathbf{x}) = \Pr(\varepsilon \le 0 - \mathbf{x}\boldsymbol{\beta} \,|\, \mathbf{x}) = \Pr(\varepsilon \le \tau - \mathbf{x}\boldsymbol{\beta} \,|\, \mathbf{x}) \qquad [9.4]$$

where we use the assumption that $\tau = 0$. Equation 9.4 is identical to Equation 9.3 for the probability that a case is censored in the tobit model. This is why the tobit model is sometimes referred to as "Tobin's probit."

A major difference between the probit model and either the LRM or the tobit model is that in the probit model it is impossible to estimate the variance of ε or y^*. Recall that in probit we assume that $\mathrm{Var}(\varepsilon \,|\, \mathbf{x}) = 1$, which determines the variance of y^*:

$$\widehat{\mathrm{Var}}(y^*) = \widehat{\boldsymbol{\beta}}' \widehat{\mathrm{Var}}(\mathbf{x}) \widehat{\boldsymbol{\beta}} + \mathrm{Var}(\varepsilon)$$

A different assumption for the variance of ε results in a different variance of y^*. Consequently, since the β's in the probit model are affected by the assumed variance of ε (which is why the β's in the logit and probit models are so different in magnitude), the β's in the probit model are not estimating the same thing as the β's in the tobit model. However, fully standardized and y^*-standardized coefficients, which standardize the variance of y^* to 1, will be similar in the tobit and probit models.

To explore the relationships among the LRM, the tobit model, and the probit model, try the following experiment with some real data. Using a large sample will make the results clearer. Pick a variable as y^* and another as x. Estimate the linear regression of y^* on x, and compute the y^*-standardized coefficients. Next, create y_T by censoring values of y^* below some τ. Estimate the tobit regression of y_T on x, and compute the y^*-standardized coefficients. The unstandardized and y^*-standardized coefficients from the LRM and tobit models should be similar. Now, create y_P where values of y^* above τ are coded as 1 and values at or below τ are coded as 0. Estimate the probit of y_P on x, and estimate the y^*-standardized coefficients. While the β's from the probit will be very different from the β's from the tobit or LRM (unless you pick an unusual example in which the variance of y^* happens to be close to the variance implied by the probit model), the fully standardized and y^*-standardized coefficients should be similar. Another difference is that the z-tests from the LRM should be more significant than those from the tobit model which should be more significant than those from the probit model. This is because increasingly less information is available for estimation.

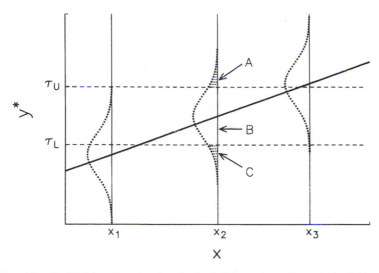

Figure 9.2. Similarities Among the Ordinal Regression, Two-Limit Tobit, and Grouped Regression Models

The Two-Limit Tobit Model. The two-limit tobit model is in between the tobit and probit models. Consider Figure 9.2 for the observation x_2. In the two-limit model, y^* is observed in the region B, but is censored above in region A and below in region C. Thus, the measurement model is

$$y = \begin{cases} \tau_L & \text{if } y^* \leq \tau_L \\ y^* & \text{if } \tau_L < y^* < \tau_U \\ \tau_U & \text{if } y^* \geq \tau_U \end{cases}$$

Since y^* is observed for some cases, the variance of y^* can be estimated, and consequently, the β's reflect the scale of y^*.

The links to other models can be seen by changing the τ's. If $\tau_L = \tau_U$, then the model reduces to the probit model. As τ_U goes to ∞, we have the tobit model with censoring from below. As τ_L goes to $-\infty$, we have the tobit model with censoring from above.

The Grouped Regression Model. In the grouped regression model, all cases are censored with known thresholds. Assuming there are three categories, the measurement model is

$$y = \begin{cases} 1 & \text{if } y^* \leq \tau_L \\ 2 & \text{if } \tau_L < y^* < \tau_U \\ 3 & \text{if } y^* \geq \tau_U \end{cases}$$

where, importantly, the τ's are known. In terms of Figure 9.2, the middle region B for the grouped regression model is also censored; all that we know is that these cases are between τ_L and τ_U. While we do not have much information about the scale of y^*, we do know the values of τ_L and τ_U which are measured in the same metric as the latent y^*. This allows us to estimate the variance of y^* and the unstandardized β's in the structural model.

The Ordered Probit Model. The ordered probit model is identical to the grouped regression model, except that the values of the thresholds are unknown. Since the τ's are unknown, we have no way to link our observed data to any values of y^*, and, consequently, there is no way to estimate the variance of y^*. This requires us to assume the variance of the error. Accordingly, we can only interpret fully standardized and y^*-standardized β's, but not the unstandardized β's.

Links to Logit Models. Each of these models has a logit counterpart that is obtained by assuming that the errors are distributed as logistic rather than as normal.

Multiple Equation Systems. One of the advantages of the latent variable formulation of models for categorical and limited dependent variables is that it is possible to use the single equation models in a multiple equation system. To see this, consider the extension of the LRM to the simultaneous equation model (see Greene, 1993, Chapter 20):

$$y_1 = \gamma_{12}y_2 + \gamma_{13}y_3 + \beta_{11}x_1 + \beta_{12}x_2 + \beta_{13}x_3 + \varepsilon_1 \qquad [9.5]$$

$$y_2 = \gamma_{21}y_1 + \gamma_{23}y_3 + \beta_{21}x_1 + \beta_{22}x_2 + \beta_{23}x_3 + \varepsilon_2$$

$$y_3 = \gamma_{31}y_1 + \gamma_{32}y_2 + \beta_{31}x_1 + \beta_{32}x_2 + \beta_{33}x_3 + \varepsilon_3$$

where various coefficients can be constrained to 0. If we replace the y's in Equation 9.5 with y^*'s, the equations can represent any of the latent variable models considered above: linear regression, tobit, probit, two-limit tobit, ordered probit, and grouped regression. Browne and Arminger

(1995, pp. 220–226) review these models which are known as mean and covariance structures with nonmetric dependent variables. Versions for the logit model are not available since there is no counterpart to the multivariate normal distribution of ε which is used to allow correlations across equations.

9.2. The Generalized Linear Model

Another way to see links among many of the models that we have studied is in terms of the generalized linear model, hereafter GLM (McCullagh & Nelder, 1989). The observed y is assumed to have a random distribution with mean:

$$E(y) = \mu$$

For example, in the LRM, y is assumed to be distributed conditionally normally with mean μ. The systematic part of the GLM assumes that

$$\eta = \mathbf{x}\boldsymbol{\beta}$$

where η is called the *linear predictor*. The expected value μ is linked to the linear predictor through the *link function g*:

$$\eta = g(\mu)$$

The specification of the random error and the link function defines the model. For example, if the link is the identity function $\eta = \mu$ and the errors are normal, we have the LRM:

$$\mu = \eta = \mathbf{x}\boldsymbol{\beta}$$

If y has a binomial distribution with the logit link:

$$\ln\left(\frac{\mu}{1-\mu}\right) = \eta = \mathbf{x}\boldsymbol{\beta}$$

the logit model is obtained. Or, with the inverse normal link:

$$\Phi^{-1}(\mu) = \eta = \mathbf{x}\boldsymbol{\beta}$$

the probit model is obtained. When y has a Poisson distribution, with the log link, the Poisson model results:

$$\ln \mu = \eta = \mathbf{x}\boldsymbol{\beta}$$

The first program to estimate the generalized linear model was GLIM (Payne, 1986). More recently, SAS's GENMOD and Stata's GLM can estimate the generalized linear model.

9.3. Similarities Among Probability Models

Without appealing to latent variables or the generalized linear model, it is possible to see links among the models when they are viewed as nonlinear probability models. Most obviously, the multinomial logit model and the ordinal logit model reduce to the binary logit model when there are two outcome categories. There are also other, more subtle links among the models. For example, consider the truncated Poisson regression model where counts at 2 or above are truncated (Winkelmann, 1994, p. 132). If we define $\mu = \exp(\mathbf{x}\boldsymbol{\beta})$, then

$$\Pr(y \mid y < 2, \mathbf{x}) = \frac{\Pr(y \mid \mathbf{x})}{\Pr(y < 2 \mid \mathbf{x})} = \frac{\exp(-\mu)\mu^y}{y![\exp(-\mu) + \mu \exp(-\mu)]}$$

Since only 0's and 1's are observed, there are only two probabilities:

$$\Pr(y = 0 \mid y < 2, \mathbf{x}) = \frac{\exp(-\mu)}{\exp(-\mu) + \mu \exp(-\mu)} = \frac{1}{1 + \mu}$$

$$\Pr(y = 1 \mid y < 2, \mathbf{x}) = \frac{\mu \exp(-\mu)}{\exp(-\mu) + \mu \exp(-\mu)} = \frac{\mu}{1 + \mu}$$

Substituting $\mu = \exp(\mathbf{x}\boldsymbol{\beta})$,

$$\Pr(y = 0 \mid y < 2, \mathbf{x}) = \frac{1}{1 + \exp(\mathbf{x}\boldsymbol{\beta})}$$

$$\Pr(y = 0 \mid y < 2, \mathbf{x}) = \frac{\exp(\mathbf{x}\boldsymbol{\beta})}{1 + \exp(\mathbf{x}\boldsymbol{\beta})}$$

which is just the binary logit model.

9.4. Event History Analysis

Event history analysis, also known as survival analysis, deals with longitudinal data on the occurrence of events. The dependent variable is how long it takes until something has happened. While there are many methods of survival analysis (see Allison, 1984, 1995; Kalbfleisch & Prentice, 1980; Lancaster, 1990, for detailed discussions), one method of analyzing duration data is very closely related to the tobit model. These are called accelerated failure time (AFT) models (Allison, 1995, Chapter 4). For example, Daula et al. (1990) examined the effects of race on times to promotion in the military. The dependent variable, mean months in the service at time of promotion, was censored since some soldiers left the service before promotion. This problem differs from the standard tobit model since the time until censoring differs for each individual. Since soldiers entered at different times and left the service at different times without promotion, the value of τ differs among the soldiers. The model becomes

$$y_i = \begin{cases} y_i^* = \mathbf{x}_i\boldsymbol{\beta} + \varepsilon_i & \text{if } y_i^* < \tau_i \\ \tau_i & \text{if } y_i^* \geq \tau_i \end{cases}$$

where the censoring points differ by individual and τ is uncorrelated with the x's. Another difference between the tobit model of Chapter 7 and AFT models is that in the tobit model ε is typically assumed to be normal. In AFT models, many other distributions are considered, such as the one- or two-parameter extreme value distribution, the log-gamma distribution, or the logistic distribution. A practical illustration of the link between tobit analysis with individually varying limits and the AFT model is that programs for the AFT model (e.g., SAS's LIFEREG) can be used for tobit analysis if normal errors are specified. Or, if the normality of the error term in tobit is inappropriate, these programs can be used to estimate a tobit model with other error distributions.

9.5. Log-Linear Models

Log-linear models are a large and important class of models for the analysis of contingency tables (Agresti, 1990). The objective of log-linear analysis is to determine if the distribution of counts among the cells of a table can be explained be some simpler, underlying structure. By comparing models that specify different structures, the researcher can test hypotheses about the interrelationships among the variables representing the rows, columns, and layers of the table.

To illustrate the links between log-linear models and the models in this book, consider Table 9.1, which was originally analyzed by Radelet (1981) and later examined by Agresti (1990, pp. 135–138, 171–174). This three-way table is based on 326 murder cases. The variables are the defendant's race (D), the victim's race (V), and whether the sentence was the death penalty. The number of observations for cell $D = i$, $V = j$, and $P = k$ is y_{ijk}.

The number of observations y_{ijk} is assumed to have a Poisson distribution with mean μ_{ijk}. In a simple model of independence, μ is determined

TABLE 9.1 Death Penalty Verdict by Race of Defendant and Victim

		Death Penalty (P)	
Defendant's Race (D)	Victim's Race (V)	Yes = 1	No = 2
White = 1	White = 1	19	132
	Black = 2	0	9
Black = 2	White = 1	11	52
	Black = 2	6	97

SOURCE: Radelet (1981).

by the log-linear equation:

$$\ln \mu_{ijk}^{DVP} = \lambda + \lambda_i^D + \lambda_j^V + \lambda_k^P$$

Notice that the means for all cells where $D = 1$ include the parameter λ_1^D; all cells where $V = 2$ include the parameter λ_2^V; and so on. For example, for cell $(1, 1, 1)$,

$$\ln \mu_{111}^{DVP} = \lambda + \lambda_1^D + \lambda_1^V + \lambda_1^P$$

while for cell $(2, 2, 2)$,

$$\ln \mu_{222}^{DVP} = \lambda + \lambda_2^D + \lambda_2^V + \lambda_2^P$$

To identify the model, constraints are imposed on the parameters. Identification in this model is similar to the situation with dummy variables in the LRM. For example, you cannot have one parameter for being a female (e.g., λ_1^S) and another for being a male (e.g., λ_2^S). As with dummy variables in the LRM, we identify the model by assuming that the first level of each group of parameters is fixed at 0:

$$\lambda_1^D = 0; \qquad \lambda_1^V = 0 \qquad \lambda_1^P = 0$$

With these constraints,

$$\ln \mu_{111}^{DVP} = \lambda \qquad\qquad\qquad\qquad\qquad [9.6]$$
$$\ln \mu_{211}^{DVP} = \lambda + \lambda_2^D$$
$$\ln \mu_{222}^{DVP} = \lambda + \lambda_2^D + \lambda_2^V + \lambda_2^P$$

and so on.

To see the link between log-linear models and Poisson regression, define three dummy variables that equal 1 to indicate that observation is in level 2 of a given variable:

$$x_{ijk}^D = \begin{cases} 0 & \text{if } D = 1 \\ 1 & \text{if } D = 2 \end{cases}$$

$$x_{ijk}^V = \begin{cases} 0 & \text{if } V = 1 \\ 1 & \text{if } V = 2 \end{cases}$$

$$x_{ijk}^P = \begin{cases} 0 & \text{if } P = 1 \\ 1 & \text{if } P = 2 \end{cases}$$

Thus, whenever you are in a cell where $D = i = 2$, then x^D equals 1. For example, $x_{111}^D = 0$, $x_{211}^D = 1$, and $x_{121}^D = 0$. Then

$$\ln \mu_{ijk}^{DVP} = \beta_0 + \beta_D x_{ijk}^D + \beta_V x_{ijk}^V + \beta_P x_{ijk}^P$$

specifies a Poisson regression model. Consider several cells of the table, corresponding to Equation 9.6,

$$\ln \mu_{111}^{DVP} = \beta_0$$

$$\ln \mu_{211}^{DVP} = \beta_0 + \beta_D$$

$$\ln \mu_{222}^{DVP} = \beta_0 + \beta_D + \beta_V + \beta_P$$

The estimates from this model are identical to those from a log-linear model, where

$$\beta_0 = \lambda \qquad \beta_D = \lambda_2^D \qquad \beta_V = \lambda_2^V \qquad \beta_P = \lambda_2^P$$

These parameters can be interpreted in the same way as the parameters for the Poisson regression model.

Interactions are added to the model to allow the frequencies in some combinations of cells to be more likely than would be expected if the variables were independent of one another. For example,

$$\ln \mu_{ijk}^{DVP} = \lambda + \lambda_i^D + \lambda_j^V + \lambda_k^P + \lambda_{ij}^{DV} + \lambda_{ik}^{DP} + \lambda_{jk}^{VP} \qquad [9.7]$$

To identify the model, we assume that $\lambda_{ij}^{DV} = \lambda_{ik}^{DP} = \lambda_{jk}^{VP} = 0$ for all i, j, and k equal to 1. Equation 9.7 translates into a Poisson regression model with the interaction variables:

$$x_{ijk}^{DV} = x_{ijk}^D x_{ijk}^V \qquad x_{ijk}^{DP} = x_{ijk}^D x_{ijk}^P \qquad x_{ijk}^{VP} = x_{ijk}^V x_{ijk}^P$$

Then

$$\ln \mu_{ijk}^{DVP} = \beta_0 + \beta_D x_{ijk}^D + \beta_V x_{ijk}^V + \beta_P x_{ijk}^P + \beta_{DV} x_{ijk}^{DV} + \beta_{DP} x_{ijk}^{DP} + \beta_{VP} x_{ijk}^{VP}$$

where

$$\beta_{DV} = \lambda_{22}^{DV} \qquad \beta_{DP} = \lambda_{22}^{DP} \qquad \beta_{VP} = \lambda_{22}^{VP}$$

Notice that the dependent variable has been the number of observations in each cell. Yet, our substantive focus is likely to be on the effects of the defendant's and the victim's race on the sentence received. The effects of race can be analyzed by taking the difference between the log of two expected counts when $P = 2$ and $P = 1$:

$$\ln \mu_{ij2}^{DVP} - \ln \mu_{ij1}^{DVP} = \ln \left(\frac{\mu_{ij2}^{DVP}}{\mu_{ij1}^{DVP}} \right)$$

This is the log of the odds, or logit, of not giving the death penalty given the races of the defendant and victim. Taking the difference of Equation 9.7 for a given combination of D and V for two levels of P,

$$\ln \mu_{ij2}^{DVP} - \ln \mu_{ij1}^{DVP} = (\lambda + \lambda_i^D + \lambda_j^V + \lambda_2^P + \lambda_{ij}^{DV} + \lambda_{i2}^{DP} + \lambda_{j2}^{VP})$$
$$- (\lambda + \lambda_i^D + \lambda_j^V + \lambda_1^P + \lambda_{ij}^{DV} + \lambda_{i1}^{DP} + \lambda_{j1}^{VP})$$
$$= (\lambda_2^P - \lambda_1^P) + (\lambda_{i2}^{DP} - \lambda_{i1}^{DP}) + (\lambda_{j2}^{VP} - \lambda_{j1}^{VP})$$

Since any λ with a subscript equal to 1 is constrained to equal 0 to identify the model, the model becomes

$$\ln \mu_{ij2}^{DVP} - \ln \mu_{ij1}^{DVP} = \lambda_2^P + \lambda_{i2}^{DP} + \lambda_{j2}^{VP} \qquad [9.8]$$

To show the link to the logit model, define some new dummy variables:

$$x_{ij}^D = \begin{cases} 0 & \text{if } D = 1 \\ 1 & \text{if } D = 2 \end{cases}$$

$$x_{ij}^V = \begin{cases} 0 & \text{if } V = 1 \\ 1 & \text{if } V = 2 \end{cases}$$

Then Equation 9.8 can be written as

$$\ln \left(\frac{\mu_{ij2}^{DVP}}{\mu_{ij1}^{DVP}} \right) = \beta_0 + \beta_D x_{ij}^D + \beta_V x_{ij}^V$$

where

$$\beta_0 = \lambda_2^P \qquad \beta_D = \lambda_{i2}^{DP} \qquad \beta_V = \lambda_{22}^{VP}$$

This is simply the logit model of Chapter 3, and it can interpreted using predicted probabilities and factor changes in the odds in the same way.

While my discussion of log-linear models oversimplifies a number of important issues, the basic ideas should be clear. See Agresti (1990) for a comprehensive discussion of log-linear models, or Agresti (1996) for an excellent introduction.

A Answers to Exercises

The appendix contains brief answers to the exercises contained in italics within the text.

Chapter 1: Introduction

Page 6: If

$$y = \frac{\exp(\alpha^* + \beta^* x + \delta^* d)}{1 + \exp(\alpha^* + \beta^* x + \delta^* d)}$$

then

$$1 - y = \frac{1}{1 + \exp(\alpha^* + \beta^* x + \delta^* d)}$$

Taking the ratio and canceling denominators,

$$\frac{y}{1 - y} = \exp(\alpha^* + \beta^* x + \delta^* d)$$

Taking the log,

$$\ln\left(\frac{y}{1 - y}\right) = \alpha^* + \beta^* x + \delta^* d.$$

Chapter 2: Continuous Outcomes

Page 23:

$$E(\varepsilon^* \mid \mathbf{x}) = E(\varepsilon - \delta \mid \mathbf{x}) = E(\varepsilon \mid \mathbf{x}) - E(\delta \mid \mathbf{x}) = \delta - \delta = 0.$$

Page 25: $Cor(x_1, \nu) = Cor(x_1, \beta_2 x_2 + \varepsilon)$. Since x_1 and x_2 are assumed to be correlated, x_1 and ν ($= \beta_2 x_2 + \varepsilon$) must be correlated.

Chapter 3: Binary Outcomes

Page 38: Let y be a dummy variable with $E(y) = \mu$. By definition, $Var(y) = E[(y - \mu)^2] = E(y^2 - 2y\mu + \mu^2) = E(y^2) - 2\mu E(y) + \mu^2$. Since y equals 1 or 0, $E(y^2) = E(y)$. Therefore, $Var(y) = E(y) - 2\mu E(y) + \mu^2$. Substituting $E(y) = \mu$, $Var(y) = \mu - \mu^2 = \mu(1 - \mu)$.

Page 38: The dashed ellipse shows $E(y \mid x) \pm \sqrt{Var(y \mid x)}$. The dotted lines are located at $\mathbf{x\beta} = 0$ and 1:

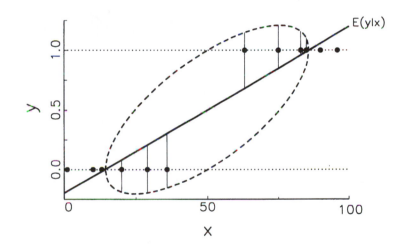

Page 39: From Tables 3.1 and 3.2, $Pr(y = 1) = 1.144 + (-.295 \times 4) + (-.011 \times 1.35) + (-.013 \times 35) + (.164 \times 0) + (.019 \times 0) + (.123 \times 1.10) + (-.007 \times 20.13) = -.51$ based on rounding to three decimal digits. Using the full precision stored by the computer, the probability is $-.48$. Note that you should use full precision in making these computations.

Page 42: The point is located at $(0.0, 0.50)$.

Page 45: At x_1, $\widehat{y}_1^* = \alpha + \beta x_1$; at x_2, $\widehat{y}_2^* = \alpha + \beta x_2$. The change in the expected value of y^* is $\widehat{y}_2^* - \widehat{y}_1^* = (\alpha + \beta x_2) - (\alpha + \beta x_1) = \beta(x_2 - x_1)$. At x_1,

$\Pr(y = 1 \mid x_1) = F(\alpha + \beta x_1)$; at x_2, $\Pr(y = 1 \mid x_2) = F(\alpha + \beta x_2)$. The probability changes by $F(\alpha + \beta x_2) - F(\alpha + \beta x_1)$.

Page 48: By assumption, $\mathrm{Var}(\varepsilon_L) = \pi^2/3$ and $\mathrm{Var}(\varepsilon_P) = 1$. It follows that

$$\frac{\pi^2}{3}\,\mathrm{Var}(\varepsilon_P) = \frac{\pi^2}{3} = \mathrm{Var}(\varepsilon_L)$$

Page 49: Recall that $\exp(-a) \times \exp(a) = 1$. Then

$$\frac{\exp(\mathbf{x}\boldsymbol{\beta})}{1 + \exp(\mathbf{x}\boldsymbol{\beta})} = \frac{\exp(-\mathbf{x}\boldsymbol{\beta})}{\exp(-\mathbf{x}\boldsymbol{\beta})}\frac{\exp(\mathbf{x}\boldsymbol{\beta})}{1 + \exp(\mathbf{x}\boldsymbol{\beta})} = \frac{1}{\exp(-\mathbf{x}\boldsymbol{\beta}) + 1}$$

Page 51: It is easiest to work backwards:

$$\frac{\Pr(y = 1 \mid \mathbf{x})}{1 - \Pr(y = 1 \mid \mathbf{x})} = \frac{\exp(\mathbf{x}\boldsymbol{\beta})/[1 + \exp(\mathbf{x}\boldsymbol{\beta})]}{1 - [\exp(\mathbf{x}\boldsymbol{\beta})/1 + \exp(\mathbf{x}\boldsymbol{\beta})]}$$

$$= \frac{\exp(\mathbf{x}\boldsymbol{\beta})/[1 + \exp(\mathbf{x}\boldsymbol{\beta})]}{[1 + \exp(\mathbf{x}\boldsymbol{\beta}) - \exp(\mathbf{x}\boldsymbol{\beta})]/[1 + \exp(\mathbf{x}\boldsymbol{\beta})]}$$

$$= \exp(\mathbf{x}\boldsymbol{\beta})$$

Take the log of both sides and you are done.

Page 55: The solid curve is changing more rapidly, so it would have a larger Hessian than the dashed curve. Consequently, in trying to find the maximum, you would move more slowly with the solid curve.

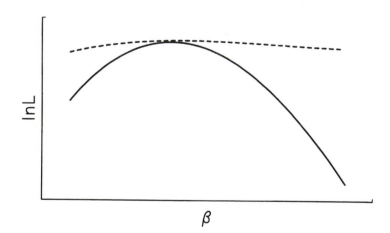

Page 56: The larger the Hessian, call it **H**, the faster the change in ln L is occurring and the slower we want to adjust our guess. The larger **H**, the smaller **H**$^{-1}$, and hence the smaller the change.

Page 62: Consider Figure 3.6. If α increases in panel A, for a given x more of the distribution is above τ, resulting in a larger value of $\Pr(y = 1 \mid \mathbf{x})$. That is, the curve in Panel B will shift to the left.

Page 69: The following figure shows the probabilities for those attending and not attending college for values of $K5$ ranging from -4 to 4. The vertical dashed lines mark off the range of data shown in Table 3.5. The circles mark the predicted probabilities for those who attended college; the squares are for those who did not attend college. At 0, the probability curves are almost parallel, but diverge slightly around 1. They then begin to converge.

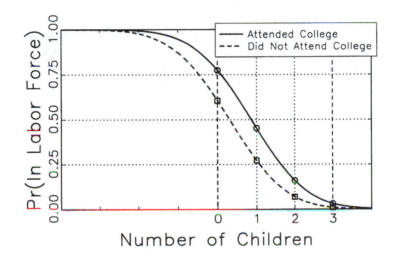

Page 70: In the LRM, the dependent variable is observed and, consequently, its scale will not change as variables are added to the model.

Page 72: From Equation 3.7,

$$P = \frac{\exp(\mathbf{x}\boldsymbol{\beta})}{1 + \exp(\mathbf{x}\boldsymbol{\beta})} \quad \text{and} \quad 1 - P = \frac{1}{1 + \exp(\mathbf{x}\boldsymbol{\beta})}$$

Therefore,

$$P(1 - P) = \frac{\exp(\mathbf{x}\boldsymbol{\beta})}{[1 + \exp(\mathbf{x}\boldsymbol{\beta})]^2}$$

which is the result we need.

Page 76: This follows immediately from the symmetry of the probability curve around $\Pr(y = 1 | \mathbf{x}) = .5$.

Chapter 4: Hypothesis Testing and Goodness of Fit

Page 87: The slope of $\ln L$ is not changing.

Page 88: Increasing N makes $\ln L$ more curved, thereby increasing the absolute value of the second derivative.

Page 91: If the variance is larger, we are less confident in the estimate and, consequently, would want to give it less weight in making a decision.

Page 92: Let $\mathbf{0}$ be a 7×1 vector of 0's; let $\mathbf{I}$ be a 7×7 identity matrix. Then let $\mathbf{Q} = [\mathbf{0} \ \ \mathbf{I}]$ and $\mathbf{r} = \mathbf{0}$.

Page 93: M_1, M_2, and M_3 are nested in M_4.

Page 104: $\sum (y_i - \bar{y})^2 = \sum y_i^2 - 2\bar{y} \sum y_i + \sum \bar{y}^2$. Summing just the cases where $y = 0$, $\sum_{y=0}(y_i - \bar{y})^2 = 0 - 0 + n_0 \bar{y}^2$. Summing the cases where $y = 1$, $\sum_{y=1}(y_i - \bar{y})^2 = n_1 - 2\bar{y}n_1 + n_1\bar{y}^2$. Combining the two sums, $\sum (y_i - \bar{y})^2 = n_1 - 2\bar{y}n_1 + N\bar{y}^2$. Since $\bar{y} = n_1/N$, $\sum (y_i - \bar{y})^2 = n_1 - 2n_1^2/N + n_1^2 N/N^2 = [n_1 N - n_1^2]/N = n_1(N - n_1)/N = n_1 n_0 / N$.

Page 111: This follows since $D(M_S) = 0$ and $df_S = 0$.

Chapter 5: Ordinal Outcomes

Page 121: For $x = 15$,

$$\Pr(y_i = 1 | x = 15) = \Phi[.75 - (-.5) - .052(15)] = 0.68$$

$$\Pr(y_i = 2 | x = 15) = \Phi[3.5 - (-.5) - .052(15)]$$

$$- \Phi[.75 - (-.5) - .052(15)] = 0.32$$

$$\Pr(y_i = 3 | x = 15) = \Phi[5.0 - (-.5) - .052(15)]$$

$$- \Phi[3.5 - (-.5) - .052(15)] = 0.00$$

$$\Pr(y_i = 4 | x = 15) = 1 - \Phi[5.0 - (-.5) - .052(15)] = 0.00$$

Page 123: Fix any one threshold to any value; or fix the intercept to any value. For example, $\tau_3 = -13.9$ or $\alpha = 33.3$.

Page 129: When both the logistic and normal distributions are standardized to have the same variance, they are similar in shape but not exactly the same.

Page 133: Consider $m = 3$. Then

$$\Pr(y \le 3 \,|\, \mathbf{x}) = \Pr(y = 1 \,|\, \mathbf{x}) + \Pr(y = 2 \,|\, \mathbf{x}) + \Pr(y = 3 \,|\, \mathbf{x})$$

From Equation 5.6, $\Pr(y = m \,|\, \mathbf{x}) = F(\tau_m - \mathbf{x}\boldsymbol{\beta}) - F(\tau_{m-1} - \mathbf{x}\boldsymbol{\beta})$. Substituting and noting that $F(\tau_0 - \mathbf{x}\boldsymbol{\beta}) = 0$,

$$\begin{aligned}
\Pr(y \le 3 \,|\, \mathbf{x}) &= F(\tau_1 \mathbf{x}\boldsymbol{\beta}) - F(\tau_0 - \mathbf{x}\boldsymbol{\beta}) + F(\tau_2 - \mathbf{x}\boldsymbol{\beta}) \\
&\quad - F(\tau_1 - \mathbf{x}\boldsymbol{\beta}) + F(\tau_3 - \mathbf{x}\boldsymbol{\beta}) - F(\tau_2 \mathbf{x}\boldsymbol{\beta}) \\
&= F(\tau_3 - \mathbf{x}\boldsymbol{\beta}) - F(\tau_0 - \mathbf{x}\boldsymbol{\beta}) = F(\tau_3 - \mathbf{x}\boldsymbol{\beta})
\end{aligned}$$

Page 138: Combining Equations 5.2 and 5.10,

$$\Pr(y \le m \,|\, \mathbf{x}) = \frac{\exp(\tau_m - \mathbf{x}\boldsymbol{\beta})}{1 + \exp(\tau_m - \mathbf{x}\boldsymbol{\beta})}$$

Then

$$\Pr(y > m \,|\, \mathbf{x}) = 1 - \frac{\exp(\tau_m - \mathbf{x}\boldsymbol{\beta})}{1 + \exp(\tau_m - \mathbf{x}\boldsymbol{\beta})} = \frac{1}{1 + \exp(\tau_m - \mathbf{x}\boldsymbol{\beta})}$$

Dividing,

$$\frac{\Pr(y \le m \,|\, \mathbf{x})}{\Pr(y > m \,|\, \mathbf{x})} = \frac{\exp(\tau_m - \mathbf{x}\boldsymbol{\beta})/[1 + \exp(\tau_m - \mathbf{x}\boldsymbol{\beta})]}{1/[1 + \exp(\tau_m - \mathbf{x}\boldsymbol{\beta})]} = \exp(\tau_m - \mathbf{x}\boldsymbol{\beta})$$

Page 143: Excluding the intercept, $\boldsymbol{\beta}_m$ has K coefficients for each of the $J - 1$ binary logits, for a total of $(J - 1)K$ coefficients; $\boldsymbol{\beta}$ has K coefficients excluding the intercept. Therefore, we are imposing $(J - 1)K - K = K(J - 2)$ constraints.

Page 144:

$$\mathbf{D}\boldsymbol{\beta}^* = \begin{pmatrix} \mathbf{I} & -\mathbf{I} & \mathbf{0} & \cdots & \mathbf{0} \\ \mathbf{I} & \mathbf{0} & -\mathbf{I} & \cdots & \mathbf{0} \\ \vdots & \vdots & \vdots & \ddots & \vdots \\ \mathbf{I} & \mathbf{0} & \mathbf{0} & \cdots & -\mathbf{I} \end{pmatrix} \begin{pmatrix} \boldsymbol{\beta}_1 \\ \boldsymbol{\beta}_2 \\ \vdots \\ \boldsymbol{\beta}_{J-1} \end{pmatrix} = \begin{pmatrix} \boldsymbol{\beta}_1 - \boldsymbol{\beta}_2 \\ \boldsymbol{\beta}_1 - \boldsymbol{\beta}_3 \\ \vdots \\ \boldsymbol{\beta}_1 - \boldsymbol{\beta}_{J-1} \end{pmatrix}$$

Chapter 6: Nominal Outcomes

Page 150:

$$\ln\left[\frac{\Pr(A \,|\, \mathbf{x})}{\Pr(B \,|\, \mathbf{x})}\right] + \ln\left[\frac{\Pr(B \,|\, \mathbf{x})}{\Pr(C \,|\, \mathbf{x})}\right] = [\ln \Pr(A \,|\, \mathbf{x}) - \ln \Pr(B \,|\, \mathbf{x})]$$
$$+ [\ln \Pr(B \,|\, \mathbf{x}) - \ln \Pr(C \,|\, \mathbf{x})]$$

After canceling the $\ln \Pr(B \mid \mathbf{x})$'s, we have:

$$\ln \Pr(A \mid \mathbf{x}) - \ln \Pr(C \mid \mathbf{x}) = \ln\left[\frac{\Pr(A \mid \mathbf{x})}{\Pr(C \mid \mathbf{x})}\right]$$

Page 151: Using the data from the example later in the chapter, consider three occupations: P = professional; C = craft, and M = menial. The MNLM is estimated with a single independent variable, ED (education). Then the parameters are estimated with two binary logits, the first comparing outcomes P and M, and the second comparing outcomes P and C. Notice that the estimates from the binary and multinomial logits differ.

Comparison		ED
$P \mid M$	β_{MNL}	0.725
	β_{BRM}	0.607
$P \mid C$	β_{MNL}	0.690
	β_{BRM}	0.664

NOTE: β_{MNL} is the MNLM estimate; β_{BRM} is the binary logit estimate.

Page 153:

$$\sum_{m=1}^{J} \Pr(y_i = m \mid \mathbf{x}_i) = \sum_{m=1}^{J} \frac{\exp(\mathbf{x}_i \boldsymbol{\beta}_m)}{\sum_{j=1}^{J} \exp(\mathbf{x}_i \boldsymbol{\beta}_j)} = \frac{\sum_{m=1}^{J} \exp(\mathbf{x}_i \boldsymbol{\beta}_m)}{\sum_{j=1}^{J} \exp(\mathbf{x}_i \boldsymbol{\beta}_j)} = 1$$

Page 157: Let $\beta_{k,m \mid J} = \beta_{km} - \beta_{kJ}$. Then $\beta_{k,\,p \mid q}$ can be computed as

$$\begin{aligned}
\beta_{k,p \mid q} &= \beta_{k,p \mid J} - \beta_{k,q \mid J} \\
&= (\beta_{kp} - \beta_{kJ}) - (\beta_{kq} - \beta_{kJ}) \\
&= \beta_{kp} - \beta_{kq}
\end{aligned}$$

Page 163: Let $\boldsymbol{\beta}_{x_k} = (\beta_{k,B \mid M}\ \beta_{k,C \mid M}\ \beta_{k,W \mid M}\ \beta_{k,P \mid M})'$. Then stack all parameters into a single vector: $\boldsymbol{\beta}^* = (\boldsymbol{\beta}_0'\ \boldsymbol{\beta}_{x_1}'\ \boldsymbol{\beta}_{x_2}'\ \boldsymbol{\beta}_{x_3}')'$. Let

$$\mathbf{Q} = \begin{pmatrix}
0\ 0\ 0\ 0 & 0\ 0\ {-1}\ 1 & 0\ 0\ \ \ 0\ 0 & 0\ 0\ \ \ 0\ 0 \\
0\ 0\ 0\ 0 & 0\ 0\ \ \ 0\ 0 & 0\ 0\ {-1}\ 1 & 0\ 0\ \ \ 0\ 0 \\
0\ 0\ 0\ 0 & 0\ 0\ \ \ 0\ 0 & 0\ 0\ \ \ 0\ 0 & 0\ 0\ {-1}\ 1
\end{pmatrix}$$

The first four columns of $\mathbf{Q}$ correspond to the four intercepts, the next four to the coefficients for *WHITE*, and so on.

Page 170: For example, the factor change in the odds of being craft versus blue collar equals $\exp(.472 - 1.237) = .466$.

Page 173: Notice that the *C*'s are lined up. The relative location of the other categories is unchanged.

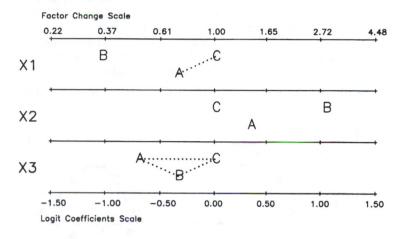

Chapter 7: Limited Outcomes

Page 199: Since the normal distribution is symmetric, $\phi(\delta) = \phi(-\delta)$. Again, due to symmetry, $\Phi(-\delta) = 1 - \Phi(\delta)$.

Page 203: If $\Phi(\delta) = 1$, then $\phi(\delta) = 0$ and $\Phi(-\delta) = 0$, so $E(y \mid \mathbf{x}) = \mathbf{x}\boldsymbol{\beta}$. That is, there is no censoring. If $\Phi(\delta) = 0$, then all cases are censored and $E(y \mid \mathbf{x}) = \tau_y$.

Page 207: Consider a regression with two values of x, with the conditional distributions A and B. The marginal distribution of y^* would combine A and B to form a single marginal distribution indicated by the two peaks a and b. The marginal distribution has a much larger variance.

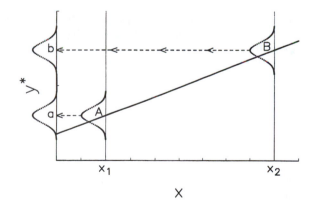

Chapter 8: Count Outcomes

Page 221: Panel A plots two Poisson distributions. The solid line is for $\mu - \delta = 1.5$ for women; the dashed line is for $\mu + \delta = 4.5$ for men. Panel B plots two possible distributions that are not conditional on gender. The solid line is a Poisson distribution with $\mu = 3.0$; the dashed line averages the two distributions in panel A. Notice that the averaged distribution has greater dispersion than the Poisson distribution.

Panel A: Conditional Distribution   Panel B: Marginal Distribution

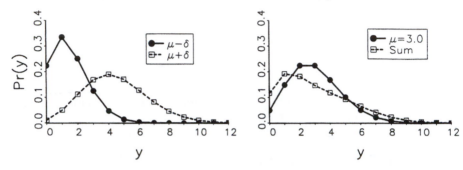

Page 222: For example, at $x = 0$, $\mu = \exp(-.25) = .779$. Using this value, we can compute the probabilities for various counts:

$$\Pr(y = 0 \mid \mu) = \frac{\exp(-\mu)\mu^0}{0!} = \exp(-\mu) = .46$$

$$\Pr(y = 1 \mid \mu) = \frac{\exp(-\mu)\mu^1}{1!} = \mu \exp(-\mu) = .36$$

$$\Pr(y = 2 \mid \mu) = \frac{\exp(-\mu)\mu^2}{2!} = .14 \quad \Pr(y = 3 \mid \mu) = \frac{\exp(-\mu)\mu^3}{3!} = .04$$

Page 229: From Table 8.2, the unstandardized coefficient for *MENT* is 0.026, so the percentage change is $100 \times [\exp(0.026) - 1] = 2.6$; the x-standardized coefficient is 0.242, so the percentage change is $100 \times [\exp(0.242) - 1] = 27.3$.

Page 229: Let $\mathbf{x} = (1\ 1\ 66\ 50\ 3.10\ 8.77)$ contain the means of all variables except for *FEM* $= 1$. Then

$$\begin{aligned}
\mathbf{x}\boldsymbol{\beta} &= (1 \times 0.305) + (1 \times -0.225) + (.66 \times .155) + (.50 \times -.185) \\
&\quad + (3.10 \times .013) + (8.77 \times .026) \\
&= 0.358
\end{aligned}$$

Therefore, $E(y \mid \mathbf{x}) = \exp(\mathbf{x}\boldsymbol{\beta}) = \exp(.36) = 1.43$. And similarly for *FEM* $= 0$.

Page 233: As $\nu \to \infty$, $\mathrm{Var}(y \,|\, \mathbf{x}) = \mu(1 + \mu/\nu) \to \mu$ since $\mu/\nu \to 0$.

Page 233: If $\alpha = 0$, there will be equidispersion: $\mathrm{Var}(y \,|\, \mathbf{x}) = \mu + \alpha\mu^2 = \mu$.

Page 243:

$$\sum_{m=0}^{\infty} \Pr(y \,|\, \mathbf{x}) = [\psi + (1 - \psi)\exp(-\mu)] + \sum_{m=1}^{\infty}(1 - \psi)\frac{\exp(-\mu)\mu^y}{y!}$$

$$= \psi + (1 - \psi)\sum_{m=0}^{\infty}\frac{\exp(-\mu)\mu^y}{y!} = \psi + (1 - \psi) = 1$$

References

Agresti, A. (1990). *Categorical data analysis*. New York: John Wiley.

Agresti, A. (1996). *An introduction to categorical data analysis*. New York: John Wiley.

Aitchison, J., & Bennett, J. (1970). Polychotomous quantal response by maximum indicant. *Biometrika, 57*, 253–262.

Aitchison, J., & Silvey, S. D. (1957). The generalization of probit analysis to the case of multiple responses. *Biometrika, 44*, 131–140.

Akaike, H. (1973). Information theory and an extension of the maximum likelihood principle. In B. N. Petrov & F. Csaki (Eds.), *Second international symposium on information theory* (pp. 267–281). Budapest: Akademiai Kiado.

Aldrich, J., & Cnudde, C. F. (1975). Probing the bounds of conventional wisdom: A comparison of regression, probit, and discriminant analysis. *American Journal of Political Science, 19*, 571–608.

Aldrich, J. H., & Nelson, F. D. (1984). *Linear probability, logit, and probit models*. Beverly Hills, CA: Sage.

Allen, M. P. (1991). Capitalist response to state intervention: Theories of the state and political finance in the New Deal. *American Sociological Review, 56*, 679–689.

Allison, P. D. (1984). *Event history analysis*. Beverly Hills, CA: Sage.

Allison, P. D. (1995). *Survival analysis using the SAS system*. Cary, NC: SAS Institute, Inc.

Allison, P. D., & Christakis, N. A. (1994). Logit models for sets of ranked items. In P. V. Marsden (Ed.), *Sociological methodology* (Vol. 24, pp. 199–228). Oxford: Basil Blackwell.

Amemiya, T. (1973). Regression analysis when the dependent variables are truncated normal. *Econometrica, 41*, 997–1016.

Amemiya, T. (1981). Qualitative response models: A survey. *Journal of Economic Literature, 19*, 1483–1536.

Amemiya, T. (1985). *Advanced Econometrics*. Cambridge, MA: Harvard University Press.

Anderson, J. A. (1984). Regression and ordered categorical variables (with discussion). *Journal of the Royal Statistical Society Series B, 46*, 1–30.

Aptech Systems, Inc. (1996). *GAUSS 3.2*. Maple Valley, WA: Aptech Systems, Inc.

Arabmazar, A., & Schmidt, P. (1981). Further evidence on the robustness of the tobit estimator to heteroscedasticity. *Journal of Econometrics, 17*, 253–258.

Arabmazar, A., & Schmidt, P. (1982). An investigation of the robustness of the tobit estimator to non-normality. *Econometrica, 50*, 1055–1063.

Arminger, G. (1995). Specification and estimation of mean structures: Regression models. In G. Arminger, C. C. Clogg, & M. E. Sobel (Eds.), *Handbook of statistical modeling for the social and behavioral sciences* (pp. 77–183). New York: Plenum.

Arum, R., & Shavit, Y. (1995). Secondary vocational education and the transition from school to work. *Sociology of Education, 68*, 187–204.

Begg, C. B., & Gray, R. (1984). Calculation of polychotomous logistic regression parameters using individualized regressions. *Biometrika, 71*, 11–18.

Beggs, S., Cardell, S., & Hausman, J. (1981). Assessing the potential demand for electric cars. *Journal of Econometrics, 17*, 1–19.

Ben-Akiva, M., & Lerman, S. R. (1985). *Discrete choice analysis: Theory and application to travel demand*. Cambridge, MA: MIT Press.

Berkson, J. (1944). Application of the logistic function to bioassay. *Journal of the American Statistical Association, 39*, 357–365.

Berkson, J. (1951). Why I prefer logits to probits. *Biometrics, 7*, 327–339.

Berndt, E. R. (1991). *The practice of econometrics: Classic and contemporary*. Reading, MA: Addison-Wesley.

Berndt, E. R., Hall, B. H., Hall, R. E., & Hausman, J. A. (1974). Estimation and inference in non-linear structural models. *Annals of Economic and Social Measurement, 3*, 653–665.

Bishop, Y. V. V., Fienberg, S. E., & Holland, P. W. (1975). *Discrete multivariate analysis: Theory and practice*. Cambridge, MA: MIT Press.

Bliss, C. I. (1934). The method of probits. *Science, 79*, 409–410.

Bollen, K. A. (1989). *Structural equations with latent variables*. New York, NY: John Wiley.

Boskin, M. J. (1974). A conditional logit model of occupational choice. *Journal of Political Economy, 62*, 389–398.

Brant, R. (1990). Assessing proportionality in the proportional odds model for ordinal logistic regression. *Biometrics, 46*, 1171–1178.

Breen, R. (1996). *Regression models: Censored, sample selected, or truncated data*. Thousand Oaks, CA: Sage.

Browne, M. W., & Arminger, G. (1995). Specification and estimation of mean- and covariance-structures models. In G. Arminger, C. C. Clogg, & M. E. Sobel (Eds.), *Handbook of statistical modeling for the social and behavioral sciences* (pp. 185–249). New York: Plenum.

Buse, A. (1982). The likelihood ratio, Wald, and Lagrange multiplier tests: An expository note. *American Statistician, 36*, 153–157.

Cameron, A. C., & Trivedi, P. K. (1986). Econometric models based on count data: Comparisons and applications of some estimators and tests. *Journal of Applied Econometrics, 1*, 29–53.

Cameron, A. C., & Trivedi, P. K. (1990). Regression-based tests for overdispersion in the Poisson model. *Journal of Econometrics, 46*, 347–364.

Cameron, A. C., & Trivedi, P. K. (1996). *Analysis of count data*. Unpublished manuscript.

Carter, L. F. (1971). Inadvertent sociological theory. *Social Forces, 50,* 12–25.

Chambers, E. A., & Cox, D. R. (1967). Discrimination between alternative binary response models. *Biometrika, 54,* 573–578.

Clogg, C. C., & Shihadeh, E. S. (1994). *Statistical models for ordinal variables.* Thousand Oaks, CA: Sage.

Coleman, J. S. (1964). *Introduction to mathematical sociology.* New York: Free Press.

Cox, D. R. (1970). *The analysis of binary data.* London: Methuen & Co.

Cragg, J. G., & Uhler, R. (1970). The demand for automobiles. *Canadian Journal of Economics, 3,* 386–406.

Cramer, J. S. (1986). *Econometric applications of maximum likelihood methods.* Cambridge: Cambridge University Press.

Cramer, J. S. (1991). *The logit model.* New York: E. Arnold.

Daula, T., Smith, D. A., & Nord, R. (1990). Inequality in the military: Fact or fiction? *American Sociological Review, 55,* 714–718.

Davidson, R., & MacKinnon, J. G. (1993). *Estimation and inference in econometrics.* New York: Oxford University Press.

Dean, C., Lawless, J. F., & Willmot, G. E. (1989). A mixed Poisson-inverse Gaussian regression model. *Canadian Journal of Statistics, 17,* 171–181.

DiPrete, T. A. (1990). Adding covariates to loglinear models for the study of social mobility. *American Sociological Review, 55,* 757–773.

Domencich, T. A., & McFadden, D. (1975). *Urban travel demand: A behavioral analysis.* Amsterdam: North-Holland.

Eaton, J., & Tamura, A. (1994). Bilateralism and regionalism in Japanese and U.S. trade and direct foreign investment patterns. *Journal of the Japanese and International Economies, 8,* 478–510.

Efron, B. (1978). Regression and ANOVA with zero-one data: Measures of residual variation. *Journal of the American Statistical Association, 73,* 113–121.

Eliason, S. R. (1993). *Maximum likelihood estimation: Logic and practice.* Newbury Park, CA: Sage.

Fair, R. C. (1978). A theory of extramarital affairs. *Journal of Political Economy, 86,* 45–61.

Feller, W. (1971). *An introduction to probability theory and its applications, vol. 2* (2nd ed.). New York: John Wiley.

Fienberg, S. E. (1980). *The analysis of cross-classified categorical data* (2nd ed.). Cambridge, MA: MIT Press.

Finney, D. J. (1971). *Probit analysis* (3rd ed.). Cambridge: Cambridge University Press.

Fox, J. (1991). *Regression diagnostics: An introduction.* Newbury Park, CA: Sage.

Fronstin, P., & Holtmann, A. G. (1994). The determinants of residential property damage caused by Hurricane Andrew. *Southern Economic Journal, 61,* 387–397.

Gaddum, J. H. (1933). *Methods of biological assay depending on a quantal response.* Reports on Biological Standard III. Special Report Series, 183. London: Medical Research Council.

Godfrey, L. G. (1988). *Misspecification tests in econometrics.* Cambridge: Cambridge University Press.

Goldberger, A. S. (1964). *Econometric theory.* New York: John Wiley.

Goldberger, A. S. (1991). *A course in econometrics.* Cambridge, MA: Harvard University Press.

Goldscheider, F. K., & DaVanzo, J. (1989). Pathways to independent living in early adulthood: Marriage, semiautonomy, and premarital residential independence. *Demography, 26,* 597–614.

Gourieroux, C., Monfort, A., & Trognon, A. (1984). Pseudo maximum likelihood methods: Applications to Poisson models. *Econometrica, 52,* 701–720.

Greene, W. H. (1993). *Econometric analysis* (2nd ed.). New York: Macmillan.

Greene, W. H. (1994). Accounting for excess zeros and sample selection in Poisson and negative binomial regression models. Working Paper No. 94–10. New York: Stern School of Business, New York University, Department of Economics.

Greene, W. H. (1995). *LIMDEP Version 7.0.* Bellport, NY: Econometric Software.

Greenwood, C., & Farewell, V. (1988). A comparison of regression models for ordinal data in an analysis of transplanted-kidney function. *Canadian Journal of Statistics, 16,* 325–335.

Griffiths, W. E., Hill, R. C., & Judge, G. G. (1993). *Learning and practicing econometrics.* New York: John Wiley.

Grogger, J. (1990). The deterrent effect of capital punishment: An analysis of daily homicide counts. *Journal of the American Statistical Association, 85,* 295–303.

Grogger, J. T., & Carson, R. T. (1991). Models for truncated counts. *Journal of Applied Econometrics, 6,* 225–238.

Grounau, R. (1973). The effect of children on the housewife's value of time. *Journal of Political Economy, 81,* s168–s199.

Gunderson, M. (1974). Probit and logit estimates of labor force participation. *Industrial Relations, 19,* 216–220.

Gurland, J., Lee, I., & Dahm, P. A. (1960). Polychotomous quantal response in biological assay. *Biometrics, 16,* 382–398.

Gurmu, S. (1991). Tests for detecting overdispersion in the positive poisson regression model. *Journal of Business and Economic Statistics, 9,* 215–222.

Gurmu, S., & Trivedi, P. K. (1992). Overdispersion tests for truncated Poisson regression models. *Journal of Econometrics, 54,* 347–370.

Gurmu, S., & Trivedi, P. K. (1995). Recent developments in models of event counts. Paper No. 261. Charlottesville, VA: University of Virginia, Jefferson Center for Political Economy.

Hagle, T. M., & Mitchell II, G. E. (1992). Goodness-of-fit measures for probit and logit. *American Journal of Political Science, 36,* 762–784.

Hannan, M. T., & Freeman, J. (1989). *Organizational ecology.* Cambridge, MA: Harvard University Press.

Hanushek, E. A., & Jackson, J. E. (1977). *Statistical methods for social scientists.* New York: Academic Press.

Hartog, J., Ridder, G., & Visser, M. (1994). Allocation of individuals to job levels under rationing. *Journal of applied econometrics, 9,* 437–451.

Hauck, W. W., & Donner, A. (1977). Wald's tests as applied to hypotheses in logit analysis. *Journal of the American Statistical Association, 72,* 851–853.

Hausman, J. A., Hall, B. H., & Griliches, Z. (1984). Econometric models for count data with an application to the patents-R&D relationship. *Econometrica, 52,* 909–938.

Hausman, J. A., & McFadden, D. (1984). Specification tests for the multinomial logit model. *Econometrica, 52,* 1219–1240.

Hausman, J. A., & Ruud, P. A. (1987). Specifying and testing econometric models for rank-ordered data. *Journal of Econometrics, 34,* 83–104.

Hausman, J. A., & Wise, D. A. (1977). Social experimentation, truncated distributions and efficient estimation. *Econometrica, 45,* 919–939.

Hausman, J. A., & Wise, D. A. (1978). A conditional probit model for qualitative choice: Discrete decisions recognizing interdependence and heterogeneous preferences. *Econometrica, 46,* 403–426.

Heckman, J. J. (1974) Shadow prices, Market wages, and labor supply. *Econometrica, 42*, 679–693.

Heckman, J. J. (1976) The common structure of statistical models of truncation, sample selection and limited dependent variables and a simple estimator for such models. *Annals of Economic and Social Measurement, 5*, 475–492.

Hedström, P. (1994). Local employment contexts and job attainment in Swedish manufacturing industry. *Work and Occupations, 21*, 355–368.

Heinen, T. (1996). *Latent class and discrete latent trait models: Similarities and differences.* Thousand Oaks, CA: Sage.

Hinde, J. (1982). Compound Poisson regression models. In R. Gilchrist (Ed.), *GLIM 1982: Proceedings of the International Conference on Generalized Linear Models* (pp. 109–121). Berlin: Springer-Verlag.

Hoffman, S. D., & Duncan, G. J. (1988). Multinomial and conditional logit discrete-choice models in demography. *Demography, 25*, 415–427.

Hosmer, D. W., & Lemeshow, S. (1989). *Applied logistic regression.* New York: John Wiley.

Jeffreys, H. (1961). *Theory of probability* (2nd ed.). New York: Oxford University Press.

Johnson, N. L., Kotz, S., & Balakrishnan, N. (1994). *Continuous univariate distributions, vol. 1.* (2nd ed.). New York: John Wiley.

Johnson, N. L., Kotz, S., & Kemp, A. W. (1992). *Univariate discrete distributions.* New York: John Wiley.

Judge, G. G., Griffiths, W. E., Hill, R. C., & Lee, T.-C. (1985). *The theory and practice of econometrics* (2nd ed.). New York: John Wiley.

Kalbfleisch, J. D., & Prentice, R. L. (1980). *The statistical analysis of failure time data.* New York: John Wiley.

Kaufman, R. L. (1996). Comparing effects in dichotomous logistic regression: A variety of standardized coefficients. *Social Science Quarterly, 77*, 90–109.

King, G. (1988). Statistical models for political science event counts: Bias in conventional procedures and evidence for the exponential Poisson regression model. *American Journal of Political Science, 32*, 838–863.

King, G. (1989a). *Unifying political methodology: The likelihood theory of statistical inference.* Cambridge: Cambridge University Press.

King, G. (1989b). Event count models for international relations: generalizations and applications. *International Studies Quarterly, 33*, 123–147.

Kmenta, J. (1986). *Elements of econometrics* (2nd ed.). New York: Macmillan.

Laitila, T. (1993). A pseudo-R^2 measure for limited and qualitative dependent variable models. *Journal of Econometrics, 56*, 341–356.

Lambert, D. (1992). Zero-inflated poisson regression with an application to defects in manufacturing. *Technometrics, 34*, 1–14.

Lancaster, T. (1990). *The econometric analysis of transition data.* New York: Cambridge University Press.

Land, K. C. (1992). Models of criminal careers: Some suggestions for moving beyond the current debate. *Criminology, 30*, 149–155.

Landwehr, J. M., Pregibon, D., & Shoemaker, A. C. (1984). Graphical methods for assessing logistic regression models. *Journal of the American Statistical Association, 79*, 61–71.

Lawless, J. F. (1987). Negative binomial and mixed Poisson regression. *Canadian Journal of Statistics, 15*, 171–181.

LeClere, M. J. (1994). The decomposition of coefficients in censored regression models: Understanding the effect of independent variables on taxpayer behavior. *National Tax Journal, 47*, 837–845.

Lesaffre, E., & Albert, A. (1989). Multiple-group logistic regression diagnostics. *Applied Statistics, 38*, 425–440.

Liao, T. F. (1994). *Interpreting probability models: Logit, probit and other generalized linear models*. Thousand Oaks, CA: Sage.

Little, R. J. A., & Rubin, D. B. (1987). *Statistical analysis with missing data*. New York: John Wiley.

Long, J. S. (1983). *Confirmatory factor analysis*. Newbury Park, CA: Sage.

Long, J. S. (1987). A graphical method for the interpretation of multinomial logit analysis. *Sociological Methods and Research, 15*, 420–446.

Long, J. S. (1990). The origins of sex differences in science. *Social Forces, 68*, 1297–1315.

Long, J. S. (1993). *MARKOV: A statistical environment for GAUSS. Version 2*. Maple Valley, WA: Aptech Systems, Inc.

Long, J. S., Allison, P. D., & McGinnis, R. (1980). Entrance into the academic career. *American Sociological Review, 44*, 816–830.

Long, J. S., & McGinnis, R. (1981). Organizational context and scientific Productivity. *American Sociological Review, 46*, 422–442.

Longford, N. T. (1995). Random coefficient models. In G. Arminger, C. C. Clogg, & M. E. Sobel (Eds.), *Handbook of statistical modeling for the social and behavioral sciences* (pp. 519–578). New York: Plenum.

Luce, R. D. (1959). *Individual choice behavior*. New York: John Wiley.

Maddala, G. S. (1983). *Limited-dependent and qualitative variables in econometrics*. Cambridge: Cambridge University Press.

Maddala, G. S. (1992). *Introduction to econometrics* (2nd ed.). New York: Macmillan.

Maddala, G. S., & Nelson, F. D. (1975). Switching regression models with exogenous and endogenous switching. *Proceedings of the American Statistical Association (Business and Economics Section)*, 423–426.

Maddala, G. S., & Trost, R. P. (1982). On measuring discrimination in loan markets. *Housing Finance Review, 1*, 245–268.

Magee, L. (1990). R^2 Measures based on Wald and likelihood ratio joint significance tests. *American Statistician, 44*, 250–253.

Manski, C. F. (1995). *Identification problems in the social sciences*. Cambridge, MA: Harvard University Press.

Marcus, A., & Greene, W. H. (1985). *The determinants of rating assignment and performance*, Working Paper, No. CRC528. Alexandria, VA, Center for Naval Analyses.

McCullagh, P. (1980). Regression models for ordinal data (with discussion). *Journal of Royal Statistical Society, 42*, 109–142.

McCullagh, P. (1986). The conditional distribution of goodness-of-fit statistics for discrete data. *Journal of the American Statistical Association, 81*, 104–107.

McCullagh, P., & Nelder, J. A. (1989). *Generalized linear models* (2nd ed.). New York: Chapman and Hall.

McDonald, J. F., & Moffitt, R. A. (1980). The uses of tobit analysis. *Review of Economics and Statistics, 62*, 318–321.

McFadden, D. (1968). *The revealed preferences of a government bureaucracy*. Working Paper. Berkeley, CA: University of California, Department of Economics.

McFadden, D. (1973). Conditional logit analysis of qualitative choice behavior. In P. Zarembka (Ed.), *Frontiers of econometrics* (pp. 105–142). New York: Academic Press.

McFadden, D. (1981). Econometric models of probabilistic choice. In C. F. Manski & D. McFadden (Eds.), *Structural analysis of discrete data* (pp. 198–272). Cambridge, MA: MIT Press.

McFadden, D. (1989). A method of simulated moments for estimation of discrete response models without numerical integration. *Econometrica*, *57*, 995–1026.

McFadden, D., Tye, W., & Train, K. (1976). An application of diagnostic tests for the independence from irrelevant alternatives property of the multinomial logit model. *Transportation Research Board Record*, *637*, 39–45.

McKelvey, R. D., & Zavoina, W. (1975). A statistical model for the analysis of ordinal level dependent variables. *Journal of Mathematical Sociology*, *4*, 103–120.

Menard, S. (1995). *Applied logistic regression analysis*. Thousand Oaks, CA: Sage.

Meng, X., & Miller, P. (1995). Occupational segregation and its impact on gender wage discrimination in China's rural industrial sector. *Oxford Economic Papers*, *47*, 136–155.

Miller, P. W., & Volker, P. A. (1985). On the determination of occupational attainment and mobility. *Journal of Human Resources*, *20*, 197–213.

Mroz, T. A. (1987). The sensitivity of an empirical model of married women's hours of work to economic and statistical assumptions. *Econometrica*, *55*, 765–799.

Mullahy, J. (1986). Specification and testing of some modified count data models. *Journal of Econometrics*, *33*, 341–365.

Nakamura, A., & Nakamura, M. (1981). A comparison of the labor force behavior of married women in the United States and Canada, with special attention to the impact of income taxes. *Econometrica*, *49*, 451–489.

Nerlove, M., & Press, S. J. (1973). *Univariate and multivariate log-linear and logistic models*. Santa Monica, CA: Rand.

Payne, C. D. (Ed.) (1986). *The GLIM Manual, Release 3.77*. Oxford: NAG.

Petersen, T. (1985). A comment on presenting results from logit and probit models. *American Sociological Review*, *50*, 130–131.

Petersen, T. (1995). Analysis of event histories. In G. Arminger, C. C. Clogg, & M. E. Sobel (Eds.), *Handbook of statistical modeling for the social and behavioral sciences* (pp. 453–518). New York: Plenum.

Pindyck, R. S., & Rubinfeld, D. L. (1991). *Econometric models and economic forecasts* (3rd ed.). New York: McGraw-Hill.

Portney, P. R., & Mullahy, J. (1986). Urban air quality and acute respiratory illness. *Journal of Urban Economics*, *20*, 21–38.

Pratt, J. W. (1981). Concavity of the log-likelihood. *Journal of the American Statistical Association*, *76*, 137–159.

Pregibon, D. (1981). Logistic regression diagnostics. *Annals of Statistics*, *9*, 705–724.

Pudney, S. (1989). *Modelling individual choice: The econometrics of corners, kinks and holes*. Oxford: Basil Blackwell.

Quester, A. O., & Greene, W. H. (1982). Divorce risk and wives' labor supply behavior. *Social Science Quarterly*, *63*, 17–27.

Radelet, M. (1981). Racial characteristics and the imposition of the death penalty. *American Sociological Review*, *46*, 918–927.

Raftery, A. E. (1996). Bayesian model selection in social research. In P. V. Marsden (Ed.), *Sociological methodology*, (Vol. 25, pp. 111–163). Oxford: Basil Blackwell.

Ragsdale, L. (1984). The politics of presidential speechmaking, 1949–1980. *American Political Science Review*, *78*, 971–984.

Roncek, D. W. (1992). Learning more from tobit coefficients: Extending a comparative analysis of political protest. *American Sociological Review*, *57*, 503–507.

Rosett, R. N., & Nelson, F. D. (1975). Estimation of the two-limit probit regression model. *Econometrica*, *43*, 141–146.

Ross, S. M. (1972). *Introduction to probability models.* New York: Academic Press.

Rothenberg, T. J. (1984). Hypothesis testing in linear models when the error covariance matrix is nonscalar. *Econometrica, 52,* 827–842.

Ruser, J. W. (1991). Workers' compensation and occupational injuries and illnesses. *Journal of Labor Economics, 9,* 325–350.

Saltzman, G. M. (1987). Congressional voting on labor issues: The role of PACs. *Industrial and Labor Relations Review, 40,* 163–179.

SAS Institute, Inc. (1990a). *SAS user's guide. Version 6* (3rd ed.). Cary, NC: SAS Institute, Inc.

SAS Institute, Inc. (1990b). *SAS/STAT user's guide. Version 6.* (4th ed.). Cary, NC: SAS Institute, Inc.

Schmidt, P., & Strauss, R. P. (1975). The prediction of occupation using multiple logit models. *International Economic Review, 16,* 471–486.

Schwarz, G. (1978). Estimating the dimension of a model. *Annals of statistics, 6,* 461–464.

Searle, S. R. (1971). *Linear models.* New York: John Wiley.

Small, K. A., & Hsiao, C. (1985). Multinomial logit specification tests. *International Economic Review, 26,* 619–627.

Snell, E. J. (1964). A scaling procedure for ordered categorical data. *Biometrics, 20,* 592–607.

Sobel, M. E. (1995). Causal inference in the social and behavioral sciences. In G. Arminger, C. C. Clogg, & M. E. Sobel (Eds.), *Handbook of statistical modeling for the social and behavioral sciences* (pp. 1–38). New York: Plenum.

Spector, L., & Mazzeo, M. (1980). Probit analysis and economic education. *Journal of Economic Education, 11,* 37–44.

Stata Corporation. (1997). *Stata Statistical Software: Release 5.0.* College Station, TX: Stata Corporation.

Stephan, P. E., & Levin, S. G. (1992). *Striking the mother lode in science: The importance of age, place, and time.* New York: Oxford University Press.

Stevens, G. (1992). The social and demographic context of language use in the United States. *American Sociological Review, 57,* 171–185.

Stewart, M. B. (1983). On least squares estimation when the dependent variable is grouped. *Review of Economic Studies, L,* 737–753.

Stokes, M. E., Davis, C. S., & Koch, G. G. (1995). *Categorical data analysis using the SAS system.* Cary, NC: SAS Institute, Inc.

Sullivan, A. C., & Worden, D. D. (1990). Rehabilitation or liquidation: Consumers' choices in bankruptcy. *Journal of Consumer Affairs, 24,* 69–88.

Taylor, H. M., & Karlin, S. (1994). *An introduction to stochastic modeling.* San Diego, CA: Academic Press.

Theil, H. (1969). A multinomial extension of the linear logit model. *International Economic Review, 10,* 251–259.

Theil, H. (1970). On the estimation of relationships involving qualitative variables. *American Journal of Sociology, 76,* 103–154.

Theil, H. (1971). *Principles of econometrics.* New York: John Wiley.

Thurstone, L. (1927). A law of comparative judgment. *Psychological Review, 34,* 273–286.

Tillman, R., & Pantell, H. (1995). Organizations and fraud in the savings and loan industry. *Social Forces, 73,* 1439–1463.

Tobin, J. (1958). Estimation of relationships for limited dependent variables. *Econometrica, 26,* 24–36.

Vuong, Q. H.. (1989). Likelihood ratio tests for model selection and non-nested hypotheses. *Econometrica, 57,* 307–333.

Walton, J., & Ragin, C. (1990). Global and national sources of political protest: Third World responses to the debt crisis. *American Sociological Review, 55,* 876–890.

Weisberg, S. (1980). *Applied linear regression.* New York: John Wiley.

Windmeijer, F. A. G. (1995). Goodness-of-fit measures in binary choice models. *Econometric Reviews, 14,* 101–116.

Winkelmann, R. (1994). *Count data models: Econometric theory and an application to labor mobility.* New York: Springer-Verlag.

Winship, C., & Mare, R. D. (1984). Regression models with ordinal variables. *American Sociological Review, 49,* 512–525.

Zhang, J., & Hoffman, S. D. (1993). Discrete-choice logit models: Testing the IIA property. *Sociological Methods and Research, 22,* 193–213.

Author Index

Subject Index

About the Author

J. SCOTT LONG is Professor of Sociology and Chair at Indiana University. He was editor of *Sociological Methods and Research* from 1987 to 1994. Prior books in statistics include *Confirmatory Factor Analysis*, *Covariance Structure Analysis*, and the edited books *Common Problems/Proper Solutions*, *Modern Methods of Data Analysis* (with John Fox), and *Testing Structural Equation Models* (with Ken Bollen). His substantive research is in the sociology of science, where he has contributed articles to the *American Sociological Review*, *Social Forces*, and other journals. He is current chairing a panel at the National Academy of Sciences that is studying gender differences in the careers of scientists and engineers.